THE
STRUCTURE
OF CUBAN
HISTORY

THE STRUCTURE OF
CUBAN
HISTORY

Meanings and Purpose of the Past   Louis A. Pérez Jr.

THE UNIVERSITY OF NORTH CAROLINA PRESS

Chapel Hill

This book was published with the assistance of the Eugene and Lillian
Youngs Lehman Fund of the University of North Carolina Press. A complete
list of books published in the Lehman Series appears at the end of the book.

Designed by Richard Hendel
Set in Quadraat, Block, and Scala Sans types
by Tseng Information Systems, Inc.
Manufactured in the United States of America

The paper in this book meets the guidelines for permanence
and durability of the Committee on Production Guidelines for
Book Longevity of the Council on Library Resources.

The University of North Carolina Press has been a member
of the Green Press Initiative since 2003.

Library of Congress Cataloging-in-Publication Data
Pérez, Louis A., 1943–
The structure of Cuban history : meanings and purpose
of the past / Louis A. Pérez Jr.
    pages cm.
Includes bibliographical references and index.
ISBN 978-1-4696-0692-7 (cloth : alk. paper)
ISBN 978-1-4696-2659-8 (pbk.: alk. paper)
ISBN 978-1-4696-0886-0 (ebook)
1. Cuba—History. 2. National characteristics, Cuban.
3. Cuba—History—Revolution, 1895–1898—Influence.
4. Collective memory—Cuba. 5. Memory—Political
aspects—Cuba. I. Title.
F1760.P473 2013
972.91—dc23   2013008288

THIS BOOK WAS PRINTED DIGITALLY

For GLADYS MAREL GARCÍA-PÉREZ

For all the many years of collaboration and friendship

How does one tell the story of a country

whose history is far larger than its size?

— *Los cubanos: Bretón es un bebé* (2008)

CONTENTS

ILLUSTRATIONS

ACKNOWLEDGMENTS

Debts of gratitude—personal and professional—have accumulated over the many years this book has been in preparation: first and foremost with the staffs of libraries and archives—the librarians, the bibliographers, the archivists, the curators—without whose assistance the completion of this book would have been impossible. The reference staff of Davis Library at the University of North Carolina at Chapel Hill generously contributed time and expertise to the completion of this book, especially Tommy Nixon and Beth Rowe. Geneva Holliday and the staff in the Interlibrary Loan office have been nothing short of spectacular in their ability to locate and obtain materials published over the last 150 years. Teresa Chapa and her staff—most notably Rebecca Huckaby—have provided sustained support all through the multiple phases of research and writing. I have also received invaluable assistance from the staffs at the Library of Congress, particularly in the Hispanic Division and the Manuscript Division, as well as the staffs of the National Archives in Washington, D.C., the National Archives in London, the Robert W. Woodruff Library at Emory University, the Rare Book and Manuscript Library at Columbia University, Special Collections at the University of Florida Library, the New-York Historical Society, and the New York Public Library.

Nor would the research necessary to complete this book have advanced very far without the support—often under difficult circumstances—of the staffs and directors of archives and libraries in Cuba. A special debt of gratitude is acknowledged here to the Archivo Nacional de Cuba, particularly to Julio López Valdés and director Martha Ferriol Marchena. The hospitality of Nuria Gregori Torada, director of the Instituto de Literatura y Lingüística, and her staff facilitated consultation of important serial collections. I received the utmost professional courtesy from Eugenio Suárez Pérez and Elsa Montero and access to important research materials in the office of Asuntos Históricos del Consejo de Estado. At the Biblioteca Nacional 'José Martí,' I received the unfailing assistance of director Eduardo Torres-Cuevas. I am deeply indebted to Miguel Barnet and Nancy Morejón of the Unión de Escritores y Artistas de Cuba for the generosity of support during the final years in which the research for this book was completed.

This book would not have taken the form it has without the collaboration of friends and colleagues who, in the course of the last ten years, in different settings and on different occasions, offered thoughtful counsel and insightful comments, often in the form of hours of conversations and at other times by way of written communications—exchanges that provided an opportunity to develop many of the arguments advanced in this book. In this regard, I owe much to María del Carmen Barcia, María Cecilia Bermúdez García, Soraya Castro Mariño, Ambrosio Fornet, Orlando García, Rafael Hernández, Jorge Ibarra, Félix Masud-Piloto, José Vega Suñol, José Viera Linares, Oscar Zanetti, and the late Francisco Pérez Guzmán. They shared knowledge and experience, offered insights, and brought relevant research materials to my attention. The manuscript benefited from the comments and suggestions made by Susan Fernández, Cornelia Waterfall, Allen Welles, and James Woodard, for which I am enormously appreciative. A special thanks to Eduardo Roca Salazar (Choco), who graciously provided permission to use his painting *Gente y bandera* for the dustjacket of the book. The Research and Study Leave program of the College of Arts and Sciences and the Department of History at the University of North Carolina at Chapel Hill allowed me to complete the writing of the manuscript in a timely fashion. I am, lastly, most appreciative of the attention given to the manuscript by Dorothea Anderson, whose splendid copyediting contributed to improving the book.

Elaine Maisner, senior executive editor at the University of North Carolina Press, provided sustained support for the idea of this project. She engaged the premise of the book and offered encouragement through the years of its writing.

Deborah M. Weissman listened critically and read assiduously the formulations of many of the ideas that sustain the narrative on the pages that follow. The process allowed for the refinement of some arguments and the abandonment of others. This too was vital to the way the ideas ebbed and flowed and the form in which the arguments eventually converged into the final draft of the manuscript.

It is almost impossible to imagine how this book would have been completed without the many years of collaboration provided by Fidel J. Requeijo, who gave of his time, technical knowledge, and street smarts—in so many different ways and on so many different occasions—to enable the research to come to a successful conclusion.

Finally, to Gladys Marel García-Pérez, to whom this book is dedicated, a heartfelt acknowledgment of a debt of gratitude that can never be repaid. She is of the history that this book seeks to engage. This project could not have been brought to a successful conclusion—perhaps not even started—without the more than thirty years of collaboration. She made so much possible.

Chapel Hill, North Carolina
September 2012

INTRODUCTION

This book is less a history of Cuba than about the history of Cuba, its course and its contours—and its consequences: about the capacity of the past to shape the character of a people, about the very logic with which historical knowledge insinuated itself into the popular imagination and thereupon acted to induce collective conduct and influence individual behavior. It seeks to understand the relationship between the use of history as a means of national formation, on one hand, and national formation as an outcome of history, on the other. The book examines the ways that knowledge of the past—as a matter of memory and oral tradition, in the form of lived experience and written record—acted to confirm the propriety of purpose with which successive generations of Cubans engaged the circumstances of the times in which they lived.

To contemplate structure in the history of Cuba is to understand the intended purpose to which knowledge of the past was put—that is, the past as a presence in the life of a people, possessed of discernible patterns, as legacy to uphold and patrimony to pass on. It is to take note of the meaning ascribed to the past, as a moral imperative to live by and didactic narrative to live up to, and specifically to appreciate the ways in which the experience of the past contributed to shaping the normative determinants of nationality.

The influence of the present as a factor in the production of historical knowledge is a commonly understood phenomenon. There is indeed much truth to Benedetto Croce's dictum that all history is contemporary history, that the experience of the present acts—often decisively—to inform the purpose and shape the perspective with which historians interrogate the past.

Not as often appreciated, however, is the degree to which knowledge of the past acts as a determinant of the present, particularly the ways a people use knowledge of their history to address the needs of their times. That knowledge of the past is itself selective and subjective, susceptible to the bias of memory and belief in myth, serves to underscore the instrumental purport to which meanings of the past readily lend themselves. This implies the need to approach the historical narrative as a record of the past, to be sure. But it is also necessary to contemplate the record of the past as an artifact of its time, to understand how the past conceived of the past: knowledge of the past as product of context and circumstance, in part cultural production, in part ideological construct, always historically conditioned, and which when turned in on itself can be made to yield insight into the assumptions that informed the purpose to which the past was put. The historical narrative was shaped by the history from which it emerged, and inevitably the text reveals its relationship to the history it purports to chronicle. To understand the reach of the Cuban past implies the need to understand how Cubans have understood their history; for embedded in the structure of historical knowledge—prepared as text, preserved as memory, and passed on as received wisdom—resides the national narrative upon which the plausibility of historical outcomes was validated.

■ ■ ■

Cubans considered the possibility of a history of their own at about the time they contemplated the plausibility of a nation of their own. The relationship of the past to the future was recognized early, for the premise of nation could not be sustained without the presumption of a past. The conceptual affinities of each were entwined together at the time of the inception of both. That the proposition of nation was itself a work in progress, divided from within and contested from without, suggested the need to deploy history as a means of national formation: a past summoned by the very circumstances it produced. Cubans derived a sense of bearing from their history, from which they assembled much of what came to constitute the meaning of nationality, specifically, what it meant to be Cuban—those ideals and values that have made Cubans the people they have become.

Norms of nationality were forged under actual historical circumstances as lived, thereupon transmuted into legacy to which Cubans were inextricably bound as means of collective fulfillment—simply put, cognizance of the past as source of consciousness of Cuban. There was a dialectics at work here, of course, knowledge of the past acting on perception of the present, loaded with normative precepts and prescriptive purpose through which to enact meanings ascribed to nationality. Knowledge of the past served to inspire devotion and induce duty, a way to heighten appreciation of a common experience and to unite a people with their past as a means of unity with each other.

Cubans lived continuously with and within the conventions of their past, for better and for worse. That it was often both for better and for worse also meant that Cubans were in a constant state of deliberative engagement with the received dictums of their history, seeking to make them respond to changing needs during times of change, and especially during times that did not change. The ways that Cubans came to an understanding of the times in which they lived often had very much to do with the ways they understood the meaning of the times in which Cubans had previously lived, specifically the past structured into an accessible narrative order as a morality tale. This was history possessed of prescriptive purport, a source of useful precedents and usable models, but most of all the past as repository of values that served continuously to inform collective purpose deep into the twentieth century.

The meaning of Cuban—what constituted lo cubano—drew upon ideals forged during the nineteenth century under circumstances of adversity, on profoundly impressive human energies, over the course of years of struggle and sacrifice, decade after decade, the way a people learn to cope and make do during long times of misfortune, undaunted and undeterred, resolved to persist and determined to prevail—or perish in the process. This involved years of adaptation and accommodation as a requirement of short-term survival and long-run success, not always a matter of choice, to be sure, but most assuredly always as a matter of need: a process produced by the history that forged the cultural determinants by which Cubans arrived at a sense of themselves and by which successive generations of Cubans were socialized into the meaning of nationality.

■ ■ ■

The Cuban struggle for independence from Spain spanned the entire second half of the nineteenth century, a pursuit of change by which Cubans were themselves changed. Between the expeditions of Narciso López, the uprisings of Joaquín de Agüero in Puerto Príncipe and José Isidoro de Armenteros in Trinidad in the early 1850s, and the siege of Santiago de Cuba in 1898, Cubans mounted three wars and launched a score of armed uprisings—nearly fifty years of intermittent warfare during which, the Cuban National Congress of History estimated in 1943, occurred "10,000 military actions and the total devastation of national wealth."[1]

No Latin American country in the nineteenth century experienced wars of independence of longer duration or greater destruction than Cuba. Three successive generations of Cubans endured recurring cycles of privation and impoverishment; incalculable material losses were surpassed only by incomprehensible personal ones. Hundreds of thousands of men, women, and children perished. Tens of thousands of households plunged permanently into conditions of disarray and destitution. Cubans committed themselves singlemindedly to the defeat of Spain: nothing was spared, nothing was saved. Victory over Spain had left Cubans exhausted—and vulnerable. Cubans disposed to sacrifice everything for the nation—todo por la patria—suffered the consequences of their disposition, only in the end to lose control of the nation for which they had struggled so long and sacrificed so much to create.

Cuban aspirations to independence were articulated principally as claims to national sovereignty. And in this regard, the Cuban purpose was not dissimilar to the early nineteenth-century independence movements in Latin America. The Constitution of Jimaguayú (1895) proclaimed the Cuban purpose as the "separation of the island of Cuba from the monarchy of Spain and the establishment of a Free and Independent State, with its own government, and possessed of supreme authority under the name of the Republic of Cuba."[2]

But there was also something distinctly "modern" about the Cuban liberation project. The Cuban pursuit of independence was as much about means as it was about ends, informed as it was by the conviction that national sovereignty contained within its premise the promise of self-determination and that through the exercise of self-determination Cubans collectively could do something about the forces that governed their lives. This was to invest in the proposition of the sovereign nation the means of well-being, endowed with the capacity to ameliorate inequity, remedy the sources of Cuban discontent, and redress the causes of Cuban grievances: the purpose to which the nation would be devoted as the reason for its existence in the first place. Nation implied overturning old forms of oppression and creating new ways of expression, apprehended as a means to accommodate demands for wider political participation and the desire for expanded social inclusion.

Much had to do with the egalitarian vision contained within the nineteenth-century project of nation, from the populist impulses that evoked social justice, racial equality, gender equity, and economic opportunity: the purposes to which the sovereign nation was to be dedicated. The proposition of national sovereignty drew into its possibilities the hopes of vast numbers of men and women for whom the commitment to independence was predicated on the promise of a nation given to the defense of Cuban interests as the object of national sovereignty. Cubans gave themselves unconditionally to the proposition of nation, for, as historian Antoni Kapcia has argued persuasively, "one needed a notion of 'nation,' rather than that of 'state,' for a concept of 'national independence' to exist."[3]

Nation promised agency and autonomy—for Cubans to be responsible only to themselves, the means by which to address the needs of the multiple constituencies that had coalesced around the cause of Cuba. This was the proposition of nation, rational in structure and functional in purpose, of Cuba for Cubans, possessed of the promise of uplift and the prospect of upward mobility in a nation of their own. The idea of sovereign nationhood was conceived as a means of self-fulfillment and source of self-esteem, always with the promise of a better life as reason to struggle and sacrifice. That was the point: the creation of a nation entrusted with the defense of Cuban interests as the reason for being.

Nationality developed as a sentiment and sensibility, into which was inscribed a value system by which the meaning of Cuban was configured. But it was more complex still, for the claim to nationality also developed as a deepening recognition of the need to relocate power within Cuba and reorder the purpose of power in behalf of things Cuban, and especially as affirmation of the prerogative of Cuban in Cuba. It was out of the premise of the primacy of Cuban interests, derived from the proposition of sovereign nationhood, that the dominant formulations of nationality entered the discursive realms of Cuban self-awareness: the sovereign nation as motive for mobilization and means of mobility, but most of all the sovereign nation as the minimum condition of Cuban fulfillment.

■■■

The *independentista* polity began as an unlikely combination of social constituencies, at times representing interests often as incompatible as they were incongruent. But it is also true that the experience of national formation in the nineteenth century was itself the means by which tensions in the separatist polity were reconciled within an all-encompassing paradigm of sovereign nationhood. The determination to develop unity of purpose out of the contradictions of diverse interests was surpassed only by the resolve to defeat Spain, and indeed must be understood as the process by which Cubans fashioned the consensual framework from which the normative basis of nationality developed.

The result was a running narrative of nation as a project in progress, possessed of discursive malleability as it evolved in response to the experience of liberation as lived, at times as a matter of improvisation, at other times as a function of necessity. That this implied instrumental purport can hardly be gainsaid, of course. The Cuban purpose could succeed only by way of a moral system in which the virtue of duty and the value of dedication were celebrated as dispositions intrinsic to the very meaning of Cuban. The process served to consecrate an ensemble of values with which to sustain collective resolve over the course of decades of struggle and sacrifice, from one generation to another and another. These attributes fused together into the larger metaphysics through which Cubans arrived at an understanding of who they were as a people: a process of self-definition in pursuit of self-determination, at once binding and integrative, the means by which the multiple and often mutually exclusive elements of Cuban discontent were accommodated within an expanding voluntary association as the basis of an emerging consensus of nationality.

That these were the circumstances under which the terms of national identity were assembled is commonly recognized. But the discussion of national identity often fails to probe deeper into domains of explanation, as if the matter of identity has to do only with the multiple ways and the diverse means by which a people arrive at a collective sense of themselves. The study of national identity must expand beyond analysis of the value systems and moral order by which a people—sometimes more, sometimes less—choose purposefully to bind themselves into a national community. Attention must also be directed to the ways that the shared normative systems with which a people come together as a nation offer insight into the workings of those socially constructed dispositions that influence conduct and inform behavior. Simply put, how is it that the ways that one people act are often discernibly different from the ways another people act, that the way one society responds to one set of historical circumstances often differs from the way another society responds, that one people are more disposed to some things and to some forms of understanding than others.

Insight into the workings of trait systems can often be best obtained through understanding the cultural transformations attending the process of national formation. This implies the need to understand the experience of the past as a source of the normative determinants from which nationality developed, to discern the presence of historical circumstances in the forces that shaped the determinants of the character of a people, those elements that made Cubans susceptible to one set of moral exhortations and not another, disposed to choose one course of action and not another. Inscribed into the experience of the history of Cuba is the development of the very value system by which a people assembled the meaning of nationality, and more: the experience of the past as source of the moral framework in which a people defined themselves—and others.

The proposition of national character—as compared to national identity—or perhaps, more precisely, the values that serve to exemplify the ideal of national character, suggest a far more compelling analytical framework with which to understand the Cuban past and present. This involves an examination of the formation of those attitudes and attributes by which a people arrive at a consensus of nationality, always—of course—as an ongoing process of formation of affinities by which national solidarities take form.

The generations of men and women who committed themselves to the realization of sovereign nationhood assembled a complex moral system, as both a concept of nationality and a condition of nation, an ensemble of shared values that served to inscribe the fulfillment of Cuban into the project of national sovereignty. The moral attributes necessary to sustain the collective purpose during the second half of the nineteenth century expanded fully into an all-encompassing value system from which norms of nationality developed, as a code of ethics and a mode of behavior that men and women could demand of themselves and of each other, and which subsequently insinuated itself deeply into the sensibility of a people. The circumstances under which Cubans arrived at national identity were matters of a lived experience—and memory of that experience—precisely the conditions that served to shape national character: consciousness of Cuban implied at one and the same time conduct as Cuban.

■ ■ ■

Cubans have long contemplated the meaning of national character, often with exaggerated pretensions to exceptionalism. The forms through which Cubans developed the terms of collective self-awareness must themselves be understood as facets of the character of Cuban: a people confident of a special destiny foretold in their history. At some point in the nineteenth century, Cubans developed the capacity to adopt an external vision as a perspective on themselves, to see themselves from the outside as a way to both contemplate the world at large and take measure of their place in that world. That they belonged they never doubted. They would be marked permanently by the experience: a people imbued with a sense of rightful claim for inclusion among the modern nations of the world at large, a persuasion that as much as anything else acted to drive the course of Cuban history.

Successive generations of historians, sociologists, literary critics, novelists, and poets have represented the proposition of Cuban—lo cubano—in multiple forms, formulated variously as cubanidad, cubanía, cubaneo, and cubanismo. Cubanness has been a Cuban preoccupation. Salvador Massip attributed "geographic factors" to cubanidad (factores geográficos de la cubanidad), while Fernando Ortiz wrote of the "human factors" of cubanidad (los factores humanos de la cubanidad), a condition he described as "the quality of Cuban, their way of being, their character, their nature, their distinctive condition, [and] a condition of the soul, a complex of sentiments, ideas, and attitudes." Ortiz wrote of the

"Cuban soul" (el alma cubana), "the psychology of our people" (la psicología de nuestro pueblo), and "the national psychology" (la psicología nacional).[4] Elías Entralgo wrote of "cubanidad in function of cubanía" (cubanidad en función de cubanía). Entralgo explained the meaning of the verb cubanear as the very "definition of national conduct" and at another point wrote of a "Cuban personality" and a "national ethology" consisting of "the psychic and ethical values of a nationality."[5] Mario Guiral Moreno and Ramiro Guerra y Sánchez each insisted on the existence of a discernible "Cuban character."[6] Jorge Mañach similarly alluded to the "peculiarities of the Cuban character"; María de la Cinta Ramblado Minero made a case for the "singularity of the Cuban character"; and Salvador Bueno alluded to "our temperament . . . and our special collective psychology."[7] Calixto Masó y Vázquez wrote of "Cuban character," as demonstrated "by the warriors of 1868 and 1895, [to be] possessed of the capacity to conceive of an ideal and fully dedicate themselves to its realization."[8] Manuel Márquez Sterling propounded the existence of "our psychology" and "our national personality," while Raimundo Menocal alluded to the existence of a "Cuban mentality" (la mentalidad cubana) and Mariano Aramburo y Machado called attention to "the Cuban imagination."[9] Fe Iglesias García wrote of a "Cuban psyche"; Ricardo Pau-Llosa alluded to a "Cuban national psyche"; and Mercedes Cros Sandoval posited the existence of a "Cuban personality."[10] Florinda Alzaga could imagine a "historical essence of the Cuban"; and Ana María Alvarado advanced the proposition of a "Cuban idiosyncracy."[11] José Antonio Ramos insisted that the "most solid bases of our nationality" were derived from the "Cuban character and a series of incontrovertible psychological characteristics."[12] Cintio Vitier discerned "a way of being Cuban" (un 'modo de ser' cubano) based on "distinctive traits of our peculiar sensibility and attitude vis-à-vis the island and the world," thereupon to evolve into "character, soul, and spirit."[13] Leví Marrero argued that Cuban nationality—"integral and real," he offered—emerged as a process of "consciousness of cubanía" (conciencia de la cubanía). In the course of the nineteenth-century liberation project, Marrero observed, "Cubans acquired consciousness of their specific personality, of their cubanía."[14]

One is not obliged to accept Cubans' assessments of their own character uncritically, of course. But it is important to pay attention to what Cubans say about themselves, for the presence of a widely shared consensus on the nature of national character is itself an important source of consciousness of character, which when ordered into coherent narrative form often serves to extol ideals to aspire to and indeed—if necessary—furnishes an intrinsically coercive means by which to exact compliance with the ideals of nationality.

To propound a set of values as facets central to nationality serves as powerful incentive to live up to the ideal. The plausibility of national character was most vividly revealed in its capacity to command conformity to dispositions and demeanors that almost everyone agreed—at least in principle—was conduct becoming Cuban.

This is not to suggest, of course, that all Cubans uniformly subscribed to the same set of values as a source of conduct. Many did not. Rather, it is to argue that a paradigm of nationality early on insinuated itself into the consciousness of a people: a moral order with which Cubans came to a sense of collective continuity, received as historically determined values into which successive generations of Cubans were implicated and to which they were eminently susceptible as a matter of a shared memory of the circumstances of national formation. The dominant representation of Cuban was forged within the experience of liberation, and that vast numbers of men and women lived through the nineteenth century outside that experience matters less than the fact that the experience served to fix the standard by which nationality was subsequently measured.

■■■

The process of national formation was a profoundly transformative experience, the source of many of the cultural cues and moral codes from which the normative foundations of nationality developed. The cultural transformations transacted in the course of the nineteenth-century *independentista* experience were as decisive to the formation of the ideal of nationality as the political objectives were to the goal of national sovereignty. As this book will argue, the latter could not have been sustained without the support of the former. Historian Juan Remos properly called attention to a nineteenth-century "cultural process" from which developed "national consciousness formed by virtue of the ideals of independence and liberty" (*los ideales de independencia y libertad*) and from which emerged "a defined aesthetic, moral, and political sensibility."[15]

The defining circumstances of national formation developed over the course of the second half of the nineteenth century, during which men and women were inducted into a value system organized principally around the needs of a people at war: precisely the circumstances by which culturally defined attributes of nationality assumed form and with which the multiple constituencies of national sovereignty were integrated into a nationality. Cultural adaptations were driven by the imperative of liberation, those normative systems best suited to the development of values with which to sustain the cause of *Cuba Libre* over the course of nearly half a century of continual warfare.

This involved specifically the development of a moral order relevant to the requirements of liberation, a way to define boundaries and condition behaviors, inform belief systems and shape identities: in brief, culture as the means through which the propriety of collective purpose was validated. The value system formed under these circumstance could not but act to arrange the moral determinants with which norms of nationality assumed form, all as a matter of an evolving national consciousness, thereupon to serve as a means of integration and source of unity.

Nationality in this instance was an outcome, not fixed and immutable, of course, always historically contingent and culturally conditioned, bearing discernible traces of the circumstances under which it emerged. The ideals for which Cubans had joined together also developed into the values by which they were formed. Consciousness of Cuban was consummated as a cultural condition, which meant too that nationality had expanded as a normative system from which modes of disposition and models of deportment were consecrated as a matter of character of Cuban.

Cubans were formed by the experience of their past as lived, an experience that served to inscribe a coherent if not always consistent moral purpose into the premise of the sovereign nation and from which developed a particular version of Cuban. "The Cuban character," historian Ramiro Guerra y Sánchez observed early in the twentieth century, "is a product of historic evolution, but to the extent that it has constituted itself, it has at the same time become an important factor in that very evolution." Guerra y Sánchez was indeed correct to note that "the suffering endured during the wars for Independence . . . [and] the tenacity and valor with which the Cuban people defended their ideals during the last century, with indomitable perseverance and for the fundamental purpose of independence and liberty, strengthened and unified their character."[16] These attributes were assembled into a master narrative of what the character of Cuban implied, derived from speeches heard and read, by way of manifestos, pronouncements, and proclamations, through accounts of heroic deeds and meanings assigned to heroic deaths, by way of memory and memoirs, through plans and programs, disseminated by word of mouth, sometimes transmitted through patriotic poems and song, as legend and lore, all directed to one overriding collective purpose: sovereign nationhood.

What from a distance of 150 years appears as largely a movement of wideranging political change is, in fact, upon closer examination, also a process of far-reaching cultural change, discerned as such by the people who lived within the transformations occasioned by their acts. This was a national culture in formation through continual dialectical engagement, between principle and practice, as a matter of context and condition, as a process of synthesis by which a people proceeded to make sense of their experience and expand the scope of their expectations. A people formed under conditions of adversity could not do other than fashion a value system to meet the needs of their circumstances. It could not have been otherwise.

Viewed in this light, Cuban history assumes a compelling clarity of purpose. It is informed by consciousness of continuity, successive generations spanning two centuries, a people eminently susceptible to the appeal of the values by which they were formed, under the historic circumstances of their times and as legacy of later times, all very much having to do with the proposition of the sovereign nation. The power of the cultural transformation attending national formation lay in its capacity to forge a shared moral system by which the men and women engaged in the project of nation defined the character of Cuban.

The premise of national sovereignty contained within its configuration the promise of national fulfillment, principally as a set of ideals by which Cubans arrived at an understanding of what they could advance as reasonable expectations and plausible aspirations. This was nationality as a cultural system, the means by which to integrate Cubans into a national community around a stock of values, subject always to circumstances of change, to be sure, but possessed of sufficient internal coherence to sustain commitment to a particular version of Cuban—what Fernando Ortiz identified as *cubanidad*, "the peculiar quality of a culture: that of Cuba."[17] To understand the emergence of a national culture as an outcome of the independence experience is to take stock of the values with which Cubans proceeded to assemble the meanings ascribed to nation, that is, the very moral system by which the norms of nationality shaped national consciousness.

■ ■ ■

It is possible to problematize much of the history of national formation from the vantage point of the year 1898, on the occasion of the U.S. intervention in the Cuban war for independence and the subsequent U.S. military occupation of the island (1899–1902). Almost all of the politics in Cuba for the next fifty years was marked by this event and the Cuban response to it.

It seemed as if Cuba had been overtaken by another country's history. In a sense it had. All through the nineteenth century, the status of Cuba had loomed uneasily over American meditations on national security: "Indispensable to the continuance and integrity of the Union itself," John Quincy Adams had worried.[18] The proposition of sovereign nationhood—deemed central to Cuban national fulfillment—was received in the United States as an anathema—indeed, as a menace to American national fulfillment. The Americans determined early on that an island considered vital to the national interest could not be permitted to come under the control of anyone other than themselves, including and especially not under the control of the Cubans. Senator Roger Mills gave voice to the inherited wisdom of the nineteenth century: "To protect our lives, our liberty, our institutions, our homes and families, we have the right to control the destiny of the Island of Cuba [and] in the exercise of these rights we have fixed the destiny of the people of Cuba."[19] And indeed the republic the United States established in 1902 was designed exactly "to control the destiny of the Island of Cuba" and specifically to deny Cubans the purpose to which three generations of men and women had dedicated their adult lives: national sovereignty and self-determination. So much of what Cubans had set out to change in the colony survived unchanged in the republic. The nineteenth-century struggle and sacrifice for independence, it seemed, had come to nothing.

What was not readily apparent at the time, however, was that Cubans had an interior history, one that had shaped the people they had become and which could not be readily accommodated within the purpose for which the Americans had organized the republic. Much of the internal logic from which the history of Cuba subsequently developed had to do with efforts to work through the contradictions between the nineteenth-century ideal of nation and the twentieth-century reality of the republic. It was impossible to reconcile the lofty aspirations of the late nineteenth century with the meager achievements of the early twentieth century. The expectations upon which the ideal of nation had been formulated could not be realized within the purpose for which the republic was founded.

The "problem" of Cuban history after 1902 was very much about reconciling the moral content of nationality with the political character of the republic. Essayist José Sixto de Sola correctly characterized Cubans as a people "united in nationality, in possession of a shared past . . . well-filled with noble and exalted deeds, of difficult and sad periods and other times of joy and splendor; of torment, suffering, and sacrifice, [all] fundamental to the unification of the Cuban nation."[20] It is in this sense that the proposition of national formation as a process of cultural transformation assumes salience, for it serves to set in dramatic relief the anomaly of a people formed within a value system incompatible with the moral order of the republic. It would be to remedy the latter as fulfillment of the former that Cuban efforts would subsequently be given.

The liberation project had been about pretensions to sovereign nationhood, which implied, above all, Cubans endowed with the capacity to act out and act on their will. That Cubans had not actualized the ideal of nation as a historical outcome, however, should not obscure the fact that they had been shaped by the ideal of sovereign nationhood as a condition of nationality. A powerful sense of collective selfhood had formed around the conviction that Cubans had a destiny to pursue, that they too had a right to national sovereignty and a claim to self-determination. It was at the very source of consciousness of Cuban. "The year 1895," Angel Rosende y de Zayas, an officer of the Liberation Army, recalled years later, "inaugurated a glorious stage in which the Cuban people demonstrated again before the world that they had a right to a free and sovereign nation" (tenían derecho a una patria libre y soberana).[21]

Cubans would cling tenaciously to their past, as source of salvation and means of redemption, as model of moral conduct and standard of national purpose. This was a history that could be believed in, unconditionally. It served to inspire reverence of martyrs, admiration of heroic deeds, and pride in the spirit of an indomitable effort, all assembled into a coherent narrative order as a compelling founding myth: a people acting together in behalf of shared aspirations, in a common pursuit of a nation of their own as a means to a better future for themselves and their children — the musings that Fernando Méndez Miranda confided to his wartime diary on May 29, 1897: "God is great. He alone knows that I go to war in order to leave my poor children a proper patria and freedom. I want nothing for myself. Just for them. If I die, I will die contented, because I have done everything I can do to realize my ideal, and my only wish is that my children be always disposed to shed their blood for the freedom of the patria."[22]

That the historiography of nineteenth-century Cuba has been given principally to the project of nation and the process of national liberation — "the favorite [themes] of Cuban historians," Robert Freeman Smith correctly noted[23] — must itself be understood as contributing to, and a consequence of, the formation of national consciousness. Cubans came together to make history around the proposition of the sovereign nation as an ideal into which they fully invested themselves and from which they fashioned the binding affinities of nationality. On the matter of the master narrative of the nineteenth-century liberation project, the consensus is striking — there is in fact little dispute in Cuban historiography.

But consensus did not always provide consolation. On the contrary, the historical memory also contained within its discursive boundaries a moral of another kind. For embedded in the narrative of nation was a larger truth of an anomaly: a heroic history that had indeed acquitted itself honorably but without having accomplished the purpose for which it was made. The past retained enduring relevance precisely because the aspirations around which consciousness of Cuban had formed remained unrealized. Nationality had developed within a historically conditioned value system, the product of experience and expectation, an outcome shaped within the process of national formation and from which Cubans assigned meaning to nation.

But it is also true that circumstances no less historically determined denied Cubans the opportunity to actualize the ideals around which the normative basis of nationality had formed. The goal of the sovereign nation had eluded Cubans. Novelist Antonio Benítez Rojo was prescient to evoke Cuba as the island that repeats itself—"*la isla que se repite.*" For what the practice of repetition implied was the reenactment of the past again and again, and again—which also implied a capacity of Cubans to relive their history continually as a means of self-actualization. The past could not be disengaged from the present. It suggested endlessly a purpose to pursue, principally because the ideals to which Cubans had committed themselves and from which norms of nationality had developed remained unfulfilled. The past was indeed difficult to escape because it was the point of reference from which the meaning of Cuban originated. The recurring pastness of the Cuban condition was a determinant of so much of what was to come. The past was portentous with intimations of consequences, at once prescriptive and prophetic, and seeming always to possess a timeless relevance.

■■■

Vast numbers of Cubans experienced the republic with a mixture of disillusionment and disappointment, a brooding angst that insinuated itself uneasily into the collective sensibility of a people. A malaise settled over the public culture of the republic, a sense of something gone awry, of a people dislodged from the history they had sacrificed to make and—more important—the history they were convinced they had a right to make. This was history as destiny denied. What Cubans subsequently dwelled upon was the past—obsessively—to ponder those times in their history in which lofty purpose had lifted the prospects of Cuban achievements to a higher moral commitment and inspired honorable comportment. It was a past that Cubans could be proud of—"to live in a country with a sense of historical dignity," comments the narrator in Lorenzo García Vega's novel *Rostros del reverso* (1977).[24] The past was discerned always as site of moral validation, in part because it was the source of consciousness of Cuban, but in larger part because it preserved untarnished and uncompromised those ideals that served as the moral determinants by which

Cubans sought to make themselves into what they would have themselves be. The national gaze fixed upon the past with a mixture of pride and purpose, of course, but also with a sense of nostalgia and melancholia. These sentiments came together in a remarkable national consensus, which meant too that a people so profoundly formed by their history were especially susceptible to the past as a source of moral imperatives in fulfillment of the conventions of nationality, that is, susceptible to the moral of the past as a politics. "History is a way to know ourselves as a people," as Minister of Education Ramón Vasconcelos addressed the First National Congress of History in 1943. "It is the mirror of the national consciousness."[25]

Cubans existed within a history that seemed to have led nowhere, certainly nowhere it was expected to go. Past and present locked into an inexorable dialectical relationship bound together by way of invidious comparisons, of what the nation was meant to be and what it should have been—and what it was. The past developed into the adversary of the present. The discrepancy between ideal of the nation and reality of the republic endured as a source of deepening disquiet, always with the understanding that something needed to be done. This was history as an unrelenting reminder of unfulfilled aspirations, memory as remorse, of things unsettled and issues unfinished: the past seemed to become the purpose for a people who were in a state of continual becoming.

Memory of unrealized hopes acted as a source of disquiet, a people ever ready to make good on a past by which they were formed. Simply put, social memory inscribed into a political culture. Cubans lived close to their history, for remembrance of the past implied always revival of memories of displacement, disappointment as source of anticipation, from one generation to the next. Memory of the past implied a purpose to pursue, beckoning Cubans to finish the task begun by their parents and grandparents, historical knowledge transmitted as first-person memory and deployed as second-person morality tales. What happened and what did not happen were as important as what should have happened and—more important—what needed to happen, always with the implied mandate of the need to make it happen. This was a history of heroic struggle against overwhelming odds, against seemingly insuperable adversaries and insurmountable adversities, where energies expended were far out of proportion to achievements attained.

Embedded within the structure of historical narratives was the summons to confront the past, certainly as a matter of intellectual engagement, and indeed often too as discharge of moral obligation, but especially as an act of political commitment. There was an imperative inscribed within the moral determinants of nationality, consecrated within the very logic of Cuban history, one that implied a duty to discharge as a mandate of Cuban, to make good on the ideals upon which the nation was conceived and upon which fulfillment of nationality depended. Something remained pending: an obligation to honor, a moral to heed, a task to complete. This is to suggest a structure to Cuban history invested in purpose associated with *patria irredenta*, which takes the existence of the nation not as a given but as a problem. History was always more than about the past: it was also about politics, and inevitably about the purpose of politics. Historian Fe Iglesias García was indeed correct to note that "the writing of history served a vital political function."[26]

What happened in the nineteenth century mattered because Cubans had expected to make history—and failed to meet their expectations. But they remembered their expectations, for these were the aspirations that had shaped the character of Cuban. Memory passed into history, and history insinuated itself into domains of popular awareness and eventually entered realms of public discourse, that is, as the subject of political debate: the burden of an unfinished history enacted as the moral currency of politics. The history of Cuba is very much a history of a people coming to terms with the experience of their history as a determinant of their history, that is, a people defined by their history. Memory of history developed as a means of history. The discursive framework of political opposition in the republic was derived principally from the stock of *independentista* narratives—history, in a word: the pursuit of sovereign nationhood endowed with properties of self-determination as values around which consciousness of Cuban had formed.

The expectations that had failed to become real endured as aspirations to realize, possessed of an enduring appeal precisely because they had been inscribed into the moral sources of nationality. What survived intact of the liberation project were precisely the aspirations, and the aspirations developed into legacy, and legacy assumed fully the form of a purpose: a purpose to remember and redeem. To contemplate the past implied the need to confront the mandate of legacy implicit in a history understood as unfinished and awaiting completion, an obligation as an act of conscience, to act upon the premise of national identity as a matter of national character. The past survived as legacy to live up to and task to live for. "The legacy of liberation [*el legado mambí*]," essayist Fernando Martínez Heredia observed, "retained an enormous force in the realms of the patriotic [and] the moral: it was a national gesture and a liberation project that was necessary to complete."[27]

There was a history embedded in these circumstances, of course. But history in this instance was more than a record of the past. It was a presence, an awareness of something pending, in the form of remembrance of an unfinished task, thereupon to insinuate itself deeply into multiple realms of popular culture and political discourse, within those narratives by which a people come to an understanding of the bonds that unite them as a national community. And always the past as something to reclaim and recover, the point at which Cubans committed themselves to a purpose larger than themselves, to claim affiliation with antecedents and discharge duty to descendants. There has been something of an inexorable logic in the course of Cuban history, where the past produced a future anticipated one hundred years earlier. "Our people nurtured themselves on the past," historian Enrique Gay-Calbó observed insightfully. "They have found in the past the vigor to persevere and continue through overwhelming difficulties. The sense of Cuban history [el sentido de la historia cubana] will always be the best protector of our country."[28]

Successive generations of men and women gave themselves to the task of fulfillment of the purpose of the nineteenth century, which, because of the power of its appeal, could be neither rejected nor repudiated. Cubans whose family antecedents reached deep into the liberation experience as well as Cubans without direct personal association with the independence movement—immigrants and the children of immigrants—identified deeply with the legacy associated with aspirations of Cuba Libre. José Martí was the son of peninsular parents. Fidel Castro was the son of a peninsular father and criolla mother. What made the politics of history so compelling had to do with the degree to which Cubans were persuaded of the relevance of their past as the embodiment of the purpose for which they had contemplated sovereign nationhood in the first place. This is to understand Cubans as a people who took their history seriously. "Our history [is] very rich and very dynamic," Carlos Fundora explained to Lynn Geldof in 1991. "I believe there are few like it. . . . Cubans love their own history. It forms them."[29] The history of Cuba, historian Herminio Portell Vilá insisted in 1941, was "dignified and hopeful, filled with exemplary lessons sufficient with which to construct a future for a country admirably endowed with the means to be happy, rich, free, and respected."[30] Historian Oscar Loyola Vega offered still one more attribute of national character by suggesting that the Cuban "taste for history was a salient component of the Cuban psychology."[31] Cubans were susceptible to the political meaning and the moral content of their history as values to live up to, as goals to aspire to, as ideals to make good on. "Our lives," Enrique Gay-Calbó wrote in 1934, "require that we recuperate the meaning of our history."[32]

This was a history into which Cubans deeply invested themselves, not simply as a matter of intellectual purpose or political engagement but as an emotional commitment. It was the way Cubans came to their past, whether as a lived experience—and especially as a lived experience—or as learned knowledge. Emotion was indeed central to historical pedagogy, a way to foster sentimental attachments to the past as a means of devotion to the nation. The need to develop emotional associations with the past, insisted Ramiro Guerra y Sánchez in 1911, was vital so as "to encourage [children] to love with all their hearts the patriots of the past and to follow the admirable example they bequeathed to us as an invaluable and precious legacy."[33] Almost seventy years later, in 1978, the Ministry of Education emphasized the importance of developing "among the students a sentiment shaped by the emotional influence of history as a means for them to assimilate historical knowledge." Emotions were to be stimulated by historical accounts: "Students should be made happy with accounts of the victories and saddened by the misfortunes of their heroes."[34]

■ ■ ■

The narrative arc of Cuban history follows unerringly an internal logic. Cubans inscribed themselves self-consciously into a continuum of the past, from which they assembled the value system that gave moral meaning to nationality, one profoundly imbued with a deepening sense of the propriety of agency as prerogative of nationality. They entered the twentieth century invested in their past, in part because the history they set out to make—the history they felt entitled to make—was not supposed to end the way it did, in part because the past as learned left so much more to do. History was everywhere: in the form of memoirs by the mambises—the officers and soldiers of the Liberation Army; as topics of classroom instruction and the subject of scholarship; on patriotic holidays and national commemorations; in the verse of poets, the lyrics of music, and the plots of novels; in film and as folklore; as national myth: all in all, a constant reminder of selfless sacrifice and self-abnegation, about heroes and heroic deeds, about a virtuous cause borne by a righteous people. The power of the historical narrative had to do with the normative systems around which it was configured and the historical context from which its relevance was inferred. Meanings shifted, of course, as the context changed, but they endured as usable hortatory devices for more than one hundred years, which suggests too the degree to which consciousness of Cuban could be at once changeable and changeless.

There has been something of a remorselessness to Cuban history. It has been insistent. The past has held Cubans in its thrall, uncompromisingly, what Alma Guillermoprieto appropriately characterized as "Cuba's romance with its own history."[35] Knowledge of the past shaped the history that it produced, which implied an endlessness to the reach of the past. It has been in continual flux, always on a fixed course but rarely reaching the destination—or the destiny—that Cubans set for themselves. This too was a facet of *cubanidad*, historian Eduardo Torres-Cuevas suggested in 1997: "*Cubanidad* has been, until now, a rehearsal of hope and the reality of the incomplete."[36]

Cubans lived in their own times, of course, but they also lived in the past as a condition of their times, sometimes as a burden to bear, sometimes as an ideal to celebrate, but always as a presence to confront. They contemplated the future as continuity with the past, which implied too a future understood as contingent on completing an unfinished past. History provided a means of orientation: expectations to realize and aspirations to fulfill. The past as the place where the attributes that Cubans most liked about themselves stood in uncontested clarity, and where—everyone agreed—they seemed to be moving history in the desired direction. This was the past as the origins of enduring national purpose, where Cubans drew closer to the people whom they wished to become, to contemplate the sublimity of the past as confirmation of the capacity to act with collective purpose as protagonists in a history of their own making. The past was where Cubans could find themselves as honorable agents of their destiny, and always the point of departure from which to begin anew. They referred to the past as a way to become themselves again, to be the people they were when they moved history through acts of will and deeds of determination. This was a complex process, having very much to do with the ways that Cubans strove to become the people they remembered themselves to be.

The nineteenth-century *independentista* experience served to provide the moral logic from which Cubans subsequently proceeded to make history. The men and women engaged in the liberation project produced a powerful national narrative, one that was appropriated as a discursive framework of opposition by successive political groups and which over time evolved into the idealized incarnation of Cuban.

The past had never really passed because it had never really ended. Cubans could not put their history behind them as something completed, as a course of events possessed of the outcome it was meant to have. On the contrary, the past weighed heavily on successive generations of men and women, as something to attend to: more than to comprehend, it was something to untangle, to sort out, something that seemed to have slipped out of their control, and about which they were obliged to do something. This was duty to be borne as a condition of Cuban, all through the twentieth century and into the twenty-first. To engage the past was to confront unrealized aspirations, to ponder the circumstances under which the sovereign nation had eluded the best efforts of three generations of Cubans—the many hundreds of thousands of men and women who had sacrificed mightily in behalf of a future that had never arrived.

1

ALL THIS WE PREFER

We prefer to see our Cuba converted into a mound of ashes, and the cadavers of its sons reduced to charred remains, before consenting to the continued rule over this unhappy land by Spanish domination.
— Salvador Cisneros Betancourt to Antonio Aguilera
(December 31, 1896)

[After 1868] everything was rubble, smoke, pain; and at every step a tomb was erected. In that revolution . . . [we] learned to die and kill; patriotism and self-esteem were defined along precise lines. And a sentiment of dignity took hold within the heart of the country.
— Manuel Márquez Sterling, *Alrededor de nuestra psicología*
(1906)

On January 1, 1899, the true Cuban people [*el verdadero pueblo cubano*] had no worries. . . . Everything was joy and brotherhood. If it had been possible for human beings to show their heart it would have revealed a people who yearned to see their idolized Cuba free and independent.
— Ricardo Batrell Oviedo, *Para la historia: Apuntes autobiográficos de la vida de Ricardo Batrell Oviedo* (1912)

The war ended in the summer of 1898. Only then was it possible to begin to take in the magnitude of the devastation wrought by Cuban determination to achieve independence: the culmination of nearly fifty years of protracted warfare and intermittent insurrection, marked by recurring cycles of destruction and disruption, decades of political repression alternating with economic depression interspersed with years of destitution and dispersal.

Peace found a people prostrate. The war had been especially cruel in its conduct and frightful in its consequences. Spaniards were ruthless in their defense of colonial rule, and Cubans were relentless in their demand for national sovereignty. Contending forces laid siege to the largesse of the land, preying upon the bounty of its resources, consuming cultivation and confiscating livestock as a matter of need and destroying the rest as a method of war. The wartime abundance of displacement and destruction found its inevitable consequences in the peacetime prevalence of impoverishment and indigence.

It had been total war, a campaign in which the practice of pillage and plunder was adopted as a cost-effective method of warfare, in which the systematic destruction of property and production became an acceptable if not the preferable means each side used in the effort to defeat the other. What the Cubans spared, the Spanish destroyed—and vice versa. Total, too, in that the war produced havoc in almost all the 1,000 towns and villages across the island, where the distinction between civilians and combatants lost any useful meaning, where neutrality was suspect and security was often obtained only behind one or the other battle line, rarely ever outside them, and never between them.

The losses were incalculable, the suffering was unimaginable. Powerfully destructive forces were let loose upon the land, sometimes as a matter of policy, planned and deliberate; at other times as a matter of happenstance, improvised and random. These were perhaps differences without distinction, for the results were almost always the same: chaos in the lives of the affected men, women, and children, lives shattered and forever changed.

Few Cubans in 1898 found home as they remembered it—if they found home at all. Many of the things that they had previously used as reference points in their lives had disappeared, or no longer worked. Objects of memories no longer existed, familiar landmarks had vanished, old boundaries had disappeared: not dissimilar to the experience of Iznaga in Luis Felipe Rodríguez's short story "El despojo" (1928), who returns home after the war to discover that he was "a stranger in his own land."[1]

The cause of *Cuba Libre* had been sustained with the support of Cubans of all classes, men and women, black and white. Many had abandoned their businesses, shops, and farms; others had discontinued their educations and disrupted their careers. Vast numbers of Cubans lost their principal sources of income and their only means of livelihood. Many succumbed to indebtedness from which they never recovered. They willingly had sacrificed personal assets and family fortunes, great and small, in pursuit of sovereign nationhood. Thousands of families lost the savings of a lifetime and property accumulated over several lifetimes: businesses, professional offices, retail shops, farms, and homes—almost everything of worth and anything of value—possessions and property lost to tax collectors or creditors, or to punitive confiscations or the ravages of war. They were without homes, without money, without jobs, without influence.[2]

Cubans of means plunged into vertiginous downward mobility afterward. Pawnshops flourished as families liquidated what remained of their personal property and household possessions in one last desperate effort to stave off indigence. "There are many families in Santiago who 18 months ago were in comfortable circumstances," the U.S. consul wrote from Santiago de Cuba in 1897, "and who to-day are paupers, selling the remaining pieces of furniture in their homes in order to buy bread, with no future before them but starvation, or a bare subsistence on charity."[3] Horacio Ferrer returned home to Unión de Reyes after the war to find his family in conditions of utter destitution. "Some members of the family had died," he recalled years later; "others had sought refuges abroad. My aging mother and invalid sister had suffered the vicissitudes of nearly four years of war. In the process of diminishing resources, they had to sell what little they had. First, living room and dining room furniture; later jewelry, lamps, bedroom furniture, clothing, and all kinds of utensils."[4]

Want and need extended fully across the island, with neither relief nor remedy in sight. Life assumed a nightmarish quality as a war-weary people went about the task of reconstituting their households and resuming their lives in the midst of desolation and disarray. Cubans contemplated the landscape of postwar Cuba with numb incredulity, unable to perceive order in the world. Everything seemed to have disintegrated into unrecognizable fragments. They returned to ruin, to incalculable material losses and irreplaceable human ones. Hundreds of thousands of men and women faced the prospect of permanent displacement and destitution, with no place to return to and nowhere to depart for. "Entire towns and villages remain destroyed," Avelino Sanjenís wrote at the time, "and vast numbers of families have disappeared."[5]

Some of the most prominent military and political leaders of the insurrection had come from families of means, often with property and professions, with plans and prospects. After the war, they had nothing. Captain Carlos Muecke despaired over the condition of his comrades, whose "property whether in town or in the country has been destroyed and they must begin anew. . . . [They] have sacrificed all—[their] houses, even their clothes are gone. . . . Without money they cannot rebuild their houses, restock their farms, refit their offices, or go to work."[6] Many officers and soldiers of the Liberation Army found themselves in various conditions of indigence, without resources, without representation, often far from home, and no way to get back and often nothing to go back to. "I left the army like everyone else," recalled José Isabel Herrera. "We were mustered out of service with $75 to return to our homes, most of which had disappeared. We were not even given passage back home from one part of the island to the other, for there were men from Oriente in Pinar del Río, and vice versa. Many men, upon returning to their towns, found that their families had disappeared."[7]

It was not at all clear how things would get right again, or how Cubans would find the ways and means to reclaim what had been formerly theirs and make a place for themselves in the nation for which they had sacrificed so much to claim as their own. The war had shattered life as it was previously known, and never again would conditions return to the way they used to be. No one was quite certain how, or where, or with what, to begin anew. Few could see a way ahead, and those who did look ahead did so with fear and foreboding. In *Sombras eternas* (1919), novelist Raimundo Cabrera portrayed the conditions of his protagonist in poignant terms: "Without the old home in which he had established his household and managed to put aside modest savings after twenty years of work, his farm destroyed and in debt, he was now obliged at forty-five years of age to start all over again with the difficult task of making a living, and feeling very old."[8]

Households had been shattered and families scattered, communities had dispersed and towns had disappeared. Where towns and villages once stood, there remained only scattered piles of rubble stone and charred wood. The countryside remained all but totally despoiled of its productive capabilities. What previously had been vistas of lush farming zones were now scenes of scorched earth and singed brush. The farms were untended, the fields unworked, the villages uninhabited. The pastures were vacant and the orchards barren. Abandoned houses in the interior were roofless and in ruins. "Our countryside had been transformed into sites of melancholia and sadness," recalled Santiago Rey. "The fields of cultivation were devastated; homes were reduced to charred remains. . . . Where once existed tranquil hamlets and peaceful households only desolation and ruin remained."[9] Farmers had few incentives to return to the land. For many, it was easier to move on than it was to go back. Many had no choice. Across the island, men, women, and children, the uprooted and downtrodden, often as entire households and extended families, foraged for a living, picking through rubble in the countryside and begging for alms in the cities. Novelist Pedro Pablo Martín gave first-person narration to the circumstances of his times: "The destruction of the sugar industry ruined the principal means of subsistence of many families and hunger reared its ugly face in our fertile fields. . . . We saw entire towns and villages, once filled with life and commerce, succumb to the ferocity of the war. Those towns and villages that in other times were the well-spring of wealth were reduced to mounds of rubble. . . . What horrible scenes! What a painful scene the countryside of Cuba presented."[10]

Travelers to the island that first autumn of peace were uniformly appalled by the magnitude of devastation. "I saw neither a house, nor a cow, calf, sheep or goat, and only two chickens," one journalist reported from Camagüey. "The country is wilderness," a "desert," wrote another traveler from Las Villas.[11] One rail passenger in 1897 reported frightful scenes en route to Matanzas from Havana: "The country outside the military posts was practically depopulated. Every house had been burned, banana trees cut down, cane fields swept with fire, and everything in the shape of food destroyed. It was as fair a landscape as mortal eyes ever looked upon, but I did not see a sign of life, except an occasional vulture or buzzard sailing through the air. The country was wrapped in the stillness of death and the silence of desolation."[12]

Conditions were desperate at both ends of the island. In Pinar del Río, General Fitzhugh Lee described conditions in late 1898 in the western province in bleak terms:

Business of all sorts was suspended. Agricultural operations had ceased; large sugar estates with their enormous and expensive machinery were destroyed; houses burned; stock driven off for consumption by the Spanish troops, or killed. There was scarcely an ox left to pull a plow, had there been a plow left. Not a pig had been left in the pen, or a hen to lay an egg for the poor destitute people who still held on to life, most of them sick, weary, and weak. Miles and miles of country uninhabited by either the human race or domestic animals were visible to the eye on every side. The great fertile island of Cuba in some places resembled an ash pile, in others the dreary desert.[13]

Inspector General James McLeary toured the eastern province at about the same time and reported equally desperate conditions in Oriente:

Many of the people appear to be almost destitute of clothing. . . . Taken as a whole, the people who came under my observation cannot be regarded as prosperous; commerce in the towns being entirely dead, and agriculture in the country being in a state of suspended animation. There does not appear ever to have been any such thing as manufacturers. . . . There are scarcely any work animals to be found along the route, a very few horses and still fewer mules and oxen, none of which can be obtained at any price. . . . Houses and fences are burned, fields abandoned and suffered to grow up in guinea grass, and the orchards which formerly covered it, are entirely gone. All the fruit tress in this section have been destroyed.[14]

"There does not exist a single place on the island of Cuba," Fermín Valdés-Domínguez recorded in his field diary, "not even in the most remote recesses of its forests, that does not possess a holy memory [un recuerdo sagrado] of the long and cruel struggle for independence."[15]

∎∎∎

Property damage could be assessed and in many instances verified and validated. But material losses were only part of the havoc wrought by the war. What could never be fully ascertained, and certainly never fully comprehended, was the suffering, the despair, the heartache. "Anyone who lived in those times," historian Ramiro Guerra y Sánchez wrote years later—and he did indeed live through those times—"lived through a period of chaos and tragedy." He remembered vividly: "We were a people in ruin; a little country, in misery, starving. Our only source of strength was our hope, combined with a firm and energetic determination to endure and live on."[16] Traveler Robert Porter described a people "left enfeebled by deprivation and too weak to take up their occupations," inhabitants "huddled half starved in miserable huts near the towns and cities," a "hungry and discouraged native population [standing] listlessly on the streets and in the public places," where at "each station the railroad trains were boarded by half-starving women or children begging for bread or coppers."[17]

That many survived in sound body did not always mean they were of sound mind. Vast numbers bore their pain in their memories, in sadness and sorrow, haunted by the loss of persons and places that had once given meaning to their lives, learning to reconcile themselves to the persistence of life with the permanence of loss. They carried on with broken hearts and inconsolable grief: the many tens of thousands of widows and orphans, parents who lost children, children who lost parents, the countless numbers who lost entire families, the maimed, the infirmed, the aged, penniless, homeless, and jobless—all who could not even remotely begin to imagine how to put their lives together again. "Starving children are on the streets and how it made my heart ache," wrote Mrs. W. A. Candler from Havana in December 1898. "There are thousands left wandering about the streets begging for bread. They are [so] emaciated that their hands as they stretch them out to you look like bird claws and their nakedness is embarrassing. There are tiny little ones whose parents are all dead and they are left to fight life's battle alone and unprotected."[18] Julián Sánchez remembered his hometown of San José de los Ramos at war's end, where "there was not one household that did not mourn the loss of a loved one."[19] Clara Barton wrote of early relief efforts: "The crowds of gaunt hunger that clustered about the door—the streets far back filled with half-clad, eager masses of humanity, waiting, watching, for the little packages, for the morsels of food that was to interpose between them and the death that threatened them. The gatherings were orderly, patient, respectful, but pitiful beyond description."[20] Few indeed were the numbers of Cubans who had not suffered in direct and very personal ways.

■ ■ ■

Only when the war ended, in the summer of 1898, could survivors begin to comprehend that they had lived through a population disaster of frightful proportions. The total number of Cubans to have perished in the course of the nineteenth-century wars for independence is largely a matter of estimates, but the estimates are staggering. Some 200,000 men, women, and children are believed to have perished during the Ten Years War (1868–78). Perhaps as many as 400,000 Cubans lost their lives during the War for Independence (1895–98). Tens of thousands of combatants died in the course of the campaigns: instant death in battle, the slow death of injuries and illness. Hundreds of thousands of noncombatants perished as a result of the conditions of war, especially in the Spanish reconcentration camps of 1896–97; men, women, and children died of disease, illness, and malnutrition. Soldiers and civilians, as active participants or suspected sympathizers, were killed in action or executed by firing squads; they perished in prisons on the island and in penal colonies in Africa. A population of nearly 1.8 million before 1895 was reduced to less than 1.5 million by 1899, a net loss of nearly 20 percent of the population.[21]

The postwar demographics confirmed the population calamity in other ways. An estimated 150,000 orphans remained to be cared for. Female heads of households were the salient demographic condition of the postwar years. Cuba had the highest proportion of widowed-to-married persons in the Western Hemisphere: 34.6 per 100. There was one widow or widower for every three married persons. The proportion of widowed women was higher: 51.2 per 100: one widow for every two wives.

It was not only that hundreds of thousands died. Tens of thousands of babies were never born. Fertility rates plunged during the war years by nearly 50 percent. The combined wartime effects of high infant mortality rates and low fertility levels resulted in an appalling disruption of the population structure of postwar Cuba. The census of 1899 revealed that children under five years of age made up only 8 percent of the total population. In no other country in the world for which data existed in 1899 was the proportion of children under the age of five as low as in Cuba.

■ ■ ■

Vast numbers of Cubans had sacrificed family and fortune in the pursuit of a nation of their own. The experience shaped the people they became. Much of the destruction—not all, to be sure—was purposeful, self-inflicted, the method Cubans chose to wage war to secure their independence. The liberation project produced in its own time the legend and logic with which intransigence was sustained. Too many had sacrificed too much for too long to fail. The only acceptable alternative to independence was death, and indeed *independencia o muerte* served as a commandment of the Cuban cause. "They want independence even though the land is left razed and sterile," Spanish captain general Arsenio Martínez Campos reported tersely to authorities in Madrid.[22] Cubans burned their own cities and destroyed their own properties. "The *patria* before everything," exhorted Antonio Maceo; "forward, for the homeland and the glory of sacrificing everything!"[23] These were the sentiments of Fermín Valdés-Domínguez. "Everything, absolutely everything, has to be offered to the *Patria*," he insisted. And at another point: "I should offer everything to the *patria*, and I offered everything to the *Patria* with the valor of a Cuban."[24]

The logic of sacrifice was carried to its inexorable conclusion. The moral of the "everything-for-Cuba" exhortation extended to and included Cuba itself: Cuba would be free or it would perish. "We are committed to the ruin of this beautiful country before humbling ourselves to the despotic Spanish government," proclaimed Agustín Ruiz in 1870, adding: "*Cuba Libre* even if it is in ashes is the ideal of all Cubans."[25] Provisional President Salvador Cisneros Betancourt reiterated the Cuban intent to "purify the atmosphere with fire and leave nothing left standing from San Antonio to Maisí [that is, from one end of the island to the other]. All this we prefer rather than to be ruled by Spain."[26] Cubans demanded independence, Manuel Sanguily proclaimed, and were prepared "to see our land transformed into an immense tomb, covered in ashes, bespattered with stains of blood." He continued:

> We have one unshakeable purpose: to fight [for independence], to fight without rest, to fight without pause, . . . to fight until there are no more Cubans capable of clutching a rifle or until the last Cuban is buried under the rubble of the fires set by our indignation and ire. [To fight against] the adventurers who have the temerity to cross the ocean to oppose the indomitable will of a people whose martyrs and heroes have risen unanimously to cry: no more, Spain! No more pillage! No more outrages! . . . We accept everything, we have accepted everything, we will [continue] to accept everything—death in battle, death on the gallows, death due to hunger and disease, exile, prison, assassination, ruin of our wealth, the devastation of our land—all the misery, all the torment: but all those calamities heaped on us are nothing in comparison with the affliction, the atrocity, and the shame of remaining a wretched vassal of the Spanish crown.[27]

"In the end," predicted Fermín Valdés-Domínguez, "[Spain] will not be able to defeat us—even if in the hour of our victory there is nothing left but a pile of rubble upon which to raise our avenging combat flag."[28]

The cause of *Cuba Libre* was borne over the course of five decades, over the life span of three generations of men and women, with the expectation of a better life for all Cubans, to bring into existence a sovereign nation entrusted with the defense of Cuban well-being as the principal reason for its creation. The Cuban goal was to constitute a sovereign nation united in a republic exercising authority over an independent island. Successive generations of Cubans through the course of the nineteenth century had sacrificed much to make Cuba free, to make Cuba for Cubans. They had paid dearly for the promise of a new nation that was to have fulfilled their aspirations and realized their expectations. They accepted the necessity of self-abnegation as the means of self-government with equanimity, and with equal serenity they contemplated the prospects of self-immolation as the necessary price of self-determination. Cuba for Cubans was the expectation that lifted Cuban spirits amid the ruin and desolation when the war ended in the summer of 1898.

2 INTIMATIONS OF NATIONALITY

What we are is the guarantee of what we will become.
— Domingo Méndez Capote, "Manifesto de la revolución
rechazando la autonomía" (1897)

A people define themselves by what they propose to
become.
— Jorge Mañach, *Pasado vigente* (1939)

It was not until the nineteenth century that we knew what
we wished to become.
— Fernando G. Campoamor, "Ser cubano" (1964)

Cuba's past is the best guarantee of its future.
— Cuban general Federico Cavada to Fernando Escobar
(July 22, 1870)

It cannot be said of the Cubans that they lack a history.
That is why, some say, we are unhappy.
— Manuel de la Cruz to Manuel Sanguily (May 1893)

t is not clear precisely when or exactly how the possibility of a separate nationality insinuated itself into domains of popular awareness. Until late in the eighteenth century, vernacular convention favored the use of *criollo* as the designation of choice to describe native-born residents of the island, as distinct from *peninsular*, used to denote Spanish-born inhabitants. At some point early into the nineteenth century, usage changed, and the proposition of *cubano* acquired currency among the native-born residents, that is, at about the same time that the idea of nation seized hold of the *criollo* imagination, a time too when the difference between the needs of the island and the interests of the peninsula settled into ever-sharper contrast— or perhaps it was the other way around.

But it was true too that the claim to nation (*patria*) drew into its premise a complex epistemology, principally as a perspective from which to assemble categories of usable knowledge, at once inspirational and instrumental, as a source of self-definition and means of self-determination. To contemplate the possibility of nation necessarily implied the need to develop a deeper knowledge of the collective modes through which to articulate aspirations to nationality.

The plausibility of claim to nation could not be sustained without the presence of a past: a people possessed of a history of their own as a necessary condition for a nation of their own. Historical knowledge provided the means with which to join past and present in a dialectical relationship, a way through which a people could presume to establish the basis of a separate nationality. The enduring subjectivity of the history of Cuba was thus fixed at its inception. To confer on the proposition of *patria* the premise of a proper history was to historicize pretensions to a separate nation and inscribe a record of chronology into the claim of a separate nationality, that is, to fashion something of a legitimacy to the proposition of sovereign nationhood. History offered a way with which to differentiate Cuba from Spain, to fashion the past as source of nationality and at the same time promote affection for and appreciation of the reciprocities through which to foster awareness of a shared identity.

Almost from the moment of its inception, the historical narrative was structured around and informed by oppositional intent, for to suggest the possibility of a separate Cuban past could not but challenge the premise upon which the colonial moral order depended. The very paradigm of a past implied the use of history as a means to differentiate Cubans from Spaniards and offered a discursive device of subversive purport. The claim to a proper past served to decrease or otherwise diminish the relevance of the Spanish presence from the Cuban past as a means to eliminate the Spanish presence from the Cuban future. Historical knowledge served at once as a source of national formation, for which it was summoned, and product of national consciousness, to which it contributed. The subjectivity of historical knowledge emerged out of a deepening national self-awareness, a process in which Cubans made an immense leap of faith as a means to will themselves to be subjects of history, as actors and agents, a people possessed of the idea of destiny as the minimum condition with which to aspire to sovereign nationhood.

The claim that Cuba had a past of its own, and that this past was proper to acknowledge and appropriate to act upon, and that indeed a separate history existed to which Cubans could turn and interrogate as a source of self-definition, suggested notions of sovereignty of far-reaching significance. Much had to do with a deepening awareness of the possibility of Cubans as a people apart, bound together by a common past, and to which to attribute common origins and shared sensibilities. This was a past imagined as properly belonging to Cubans as a matter of patrimony, at the very source of consciousness of Cuban, and more: a way to validate the propriety of agency and advance the logic of a separate nationality where "the mere claim to being *Cuban*," wrote essayist Antonio Duarte y Ramos in 1896, "was considered by the Spanish Government and its supporters as an unpardonable crime."[1]

That these sentiments contained within their very premise subversive possibilities was not immediately apparent or generally apprehended, of course. It would be unduly facile to attribute mischievous intent to the formation of nineteenth-century historical consciousness. In fact, it was more complicated. Historical narratives drew unabashedly upon sentimental attachments and heartfelt affections; they were wistful in tone and celebratory in purpose: all in all—at least at first glance—hardly more than declarations of devotion to place.

But that was precisely where the power of their appeal lay. Attachments fostered affinities, and affections produced allegiances: sentiments that were themselves experienced as the feelings from which the passion of nationality developed. Historical knowledge provided a way to draw distinction and define difference, to call attention to the things that the native-born population of the island shared in common as source of similarity and basis of solidarity.

The power of historical knowledge was contained within its capacity to foster consciousness of Cuban as a function of a newly discerned past, to enhance appreciation of shared antecedents as source of entitlement to nation, antecedents in which all creoles were potentially implicated and from which to advance the logic of a new nationality. Historical narratives propounded a point of view; they drew upon powerful emotions, those sentiments that often bestirred men and women to moral purpose and dramatic action. This was the past as prophetic, a means with which to use history to make history and forge a consensus around shared antecedents as the basis for collective action.

To invoke a separate past was to use history to validate the proposition of "Cuban," one more way to differentiate Cuba from Spain, to promote affection for and appreciation of the reciprocities of shared experiences by which to advance the claim to a separate nation. This was the stuff from which hazy yearnings emerged, of those earliest of dawnings in which people located themselves in time and place: a proper history possessed of the capacity to anticipate a past as a condition of the future. No longer was the Cuban past viewed as an extension of Spanish history, but rather of a people who possessed a different experience, distinct from Spain, and through which they had developed into a people dissimilar from Spaniards—but most of all as a way through which "memory" of the past could be shared and disseminated as source of consciousness of nationality and constituency for nation.

■■■

The Cuban historical narrative was imbued with a sense of purpose at its inception—indeed as a condition of its production. That its formal convention was determined by the intent for which it was designed to serve meant too that instrumental purport was inscribed into the very structure of the narrative, and thereupon deployed in the service of sovereign nationhood. The claim to nation thus produced a historical record, but it also produced a political need for a past, which in turn continued to produce and reproduce the nation. "The historiography of Cuba," historian Fe Iglesias rightly noted, "has evolved to complement the development of the nation and at the same time has contributed to the consolidation of this process."[2]

To have discerned the need at all for history was itself product and portent of a momentous shift in consciousness, evidence of an awareness of the utility of the past as a usable discursive framework through which to confer legitimacy on aspirations to nation. The historical narrative could not but reflect the ambivalence—indeed, the tension—with which temporal distance from Spain was drawn as a means to convey political distance from Spain. To propound a separate past could not but deepen Cuban estrangement from Spain, of course. A proper past enhanced the propriety of agency and promoted a sense of separate selfhood, a means through which to validate the claim of difference and divergence—of the very logic of separation: independence, in a word. This was the meaning of what essayist Jorge Mañach would later characterize as the Cuban "consciousness of being in history," the point at which historians first propounded the "transcendental concept of agency and a land of one's own."[3]

But it is also true that the formulation of coherent narrative structures of the Cuban past were themselves the product of specific historical circumstances. The narrative must itself be understood as a historical artifact, endowed intrinsically with documentary function in the service of an emerging but still inchoate national project. It was a product of its place, of course, and its time, imbued with purpose as a matter of discursive intent, designed to validate the very circumstances for which it was summoned. The narrative developed as a matter of need, a means by which Cubans addressed the circumstances of their times. "The history of Cuba does not begin to command real interest," observed poet Pedro Santacilia in 1859, nearly a decade after the rebellions of Narciso López, Joaquín de Agüero, and José Isidoro de Armenteros, "until these recent times, when its pages, bloodied by Spanish despotism, were bestirred by the warm winds of revolution."[4]

The historical narrative in this instance implied premonition of nation, which shared the premise of a new collective consciousness to which it contributed. Thus arose the need to historicize the narrative, for embedded in its premise—even without meaning to, and especially because it did not mean to—was the function of discharge of an inherently surreptitious purpose. Like all historical records, the Cuban narrative is possessed of multiple meanings in a constant state of flux, where the premise of interrogation often determines the insights it yields. It acts at once to provide an account of an earlier time, even as it serves as a document of its own time; it addresses the past within the analytical categories most readily available at the time, which means too that in construction and in content the historical narrative bears testimony to the circumstances of its own formation.

The Cuban historical narrative presumed the efficacy of nation as a condition of its structure. "It has always pained me as a good son [buen hijo]," Ignacio de Urrutia y Montoya (1735–95) acknowledged in 1789, "to see my beloved patria without its own history." Urrutia was entirely lucid in his purpose: "To learn the past, to make judgments on the present, and reflect on the future." Urrutia offered his history of Cuba—*Teatro histórico, jurídico y político militar de la Isla Fernandina de Cuba y principalmente de su capital, La Habana*—as a demonstration of his devotion to "my beloved patria" (mi amada patria) and insisted that knowledge of the past was essential to "the rights of the Island," adding: "It is disgraceful that a learned man ignore the common rights of his *patria* and even more so that they be not investigated in their origins."[5] Antonio José Valdés (1780–1836) studied the Cuban past, he explained, out of the "desire to give the *patria* the history that it lacks . . . in gratitude to the land in which I was born" (*agradecido al suelo en que nací*) and from the "simple effect of my disposition to be of service to the *patria*" (*útil a la patria*).[6] In exile far away in Rhode Island, Pedro José Guiteras (1814–90) completed his history of Cuba — *Historia de la Isla de Cuba* (1865) — out of a desire, he insisted, "to be of service to our beloved *patria* and to mitigate the sorrow of a long absence." The historian was duty-bound to write with objectivity, Guiteras acknowledged. But objectivity did not preclude objective. "This impartiality preserves the virtue of teaching future generations," Guiteras explained, "so that they may be inculcated with the spirit to imitate earlier ones. . . . Without this care history neither explains nor satisfies and what is worse, it has the tendency to demoralize and defile."[7] José Martín Félix de Arrate (1697–1766) explained that his "sole objective" for writing *Llave del Nuevo Mundo, antemural de las Indias Occidentales* (1830) — published posthumously — was to assure that the city of Havana did "not lack what cities of lesser prominence and reputation enjoy." Arrate was explicit: "I do not wish to come to the end of my life without offering my *patria* a modest demonstration of the love I have for it."[8] Historian Vidal Morales y Morales (1848–1904) was obliged to "reveal the genius of a people in its multiple manifestations in order to obtain exact knowledge of the truth."[9] This was the sentiment that informed Jacobo de la Pezuela's (1811–82) *Historia de la Isla de Cuba* (1868): a desire — he admitted — to respond to "a vacuum that the decorum of a national literature was obliged to fill."[10] It was inconceivable, essayist José Antonio Echeverría (1815–85) insisted, that Cuba could lack its own history. Echeverría contemplated the need for a history of Cuba with a sense of urgency. "In truth," he warned, "for a people to be without a history is like a child without parents, who does not know who he is, or where he comes from, because he has not been educated, and cannot contemplate his future." The importance of history, Echeverría affirmed, lay in its capacity to "inspire love of the *patria* and provide the strength to defend it." The stated purpose of his unfinished *Suma historial de la Isla de Cuba* was explained succinctly: "To know how this Island developed and to foster the greatest love [for Cuba] among its sons."[11] For Echeverría, historical knowledge served to "contribute to the advance of science and art, improve the customs of a people, and infuse a love of *patria* and convey the spirit with which to defend it."[12] Historian Eduardo Torres-Cuevas was indeed correct to observe in 2006 that "the first historians sought to establish the historical foundations of creole sentiment . . . and created the firm basis by which to convert the vague sentiment of the creole into the rationale of a new identity: the point of departure of Cuban nationality."[13]

■ ■ ■

It is thus possible to speak of a discernible nineteenth-century historiography, dedicated explicitly to advancing the proposition of nation and itself evidence of a deepening national consciousness: history as a means by which Cubans affirmed that they were indeed formed within a different experience, distinct from Spain, an explanation of how they had developed into a people dissimilar from Spaniards, but most of all a way to configure a specific epistemology as source of consciousness of nationality and the basis of nation.

Point of view was inscribed into the very premise of the historical narrative and fixed the perspective with which the history of Cuba was structured. This implied the development of historical knowledge explicitly as a surrogate narrative of nation, as a matter of individual remembrance and collective memory, of course, but also as a function of politics. Knowledge of the past contributed to the confidence with which Cubans inscribed themselves into history, that is, the proposition of a shared past as a necessary condition for a common purpose, a people bound together as a nationality in an inexorable reciprocity, dependent upon one another to make good on the promise implied in the idea of national sovereignty.

All through the nineteenth century, increasing numbers of Cubans consciously participated in the "making" of history. The men and women who participated in the nineteenth-century wars for independence had a past to share and lessons to teach. They carried history forward by example and experience, within themselves, self-consciously in the form of first-person testimony. The past and present collapsed upon one another, shaping consciousness and influencing conduct, and this too passed as history. "The past is the source of the present," insisted José Martí in 1889. "It is necessary to have knowledge of the past for the past is found within the present."[14] It was to history that Antonio Maceo appealed, and from which he fashioned the larger logic of liberation. He insisted on the right of peoples "to raise themselves into the subjects of history." History "authorizes the use of force when rights are trampled," Maceo was certain, and he concluded: "In accordance with the philosophy of history and reason, I will always defend the right of Cuba to establish a proper and free life [una vida propia y libre] over the impossibility of its union with and under Spain [con y bajo España]." Maceo affirmed his commitment to "the idea to make of our people [la idea de hacer de nuestro pueblo] masters of their destiny, to place in their possession the proper means adequate to fulfill their mission to reach the status of subject of History."[15]

■■■

At the center of the narratives on nation was the creole claim to Cuba as a place to possess. The proposition of nationality derived its internal logic first as an argument of nativity, expressed principally as a conviction that the island belonged to its people by virtue of their having been born there—los naturales de la isla de Cuba, as Spanish authorities were wont to say.[16] Attachment to place, with all its cultural and existential implications, assumed profoundly personal means through the experience of daily life from which to evoke the emotions often associated with memory in the form of sentimentality and nostalgia. Part of becoming Cuban was expressed as a deepening bond to place of origin and to come to an appreciation of how Cubans became who they were and of how being of Cuba implied entitlement to Cuba.

Vast numbers of men and women invested themselves deeply in a personal relationship to place, and that it was personal implied too the possibility of passion: attachment to and affection for the land, sometimes in the form of homeland (suelo natal), often as homestead (terreno), occasionally land as metaphor for country (tierra), at times a combination of all (nuestra tierra natal), and always as something to possess as site and source of community—tierra as "the basic formula of Cuban nationalism" (la formula básica del nacionalismo cubano), as journalist Eduardo Abril Amores insisted.[17]

To propound nativity was to proclaim a sense of self as one with source of self: patria as place of birth and setting of childhood, the site of forebears and formation, as place of kin and community to which one was bound through memories and modalities of everyday life. Writer Dolores María de Ximeno recalled the conventional wisdom of the nineteenth century in her memoirs: "[There existed] the natural tendency, the sacred right of man to make his own the land in which he is born and in which he has established himself for many generations."[18] Land symbolized resting place, as in burial ground, a place of one's past in the most personal of ways, often memorialized by cemeteries filled with monuments and markers of sacred purport, which obligated the Cuban, writer Rosario Sigarroa insisted, "to fight to defend his home and the sacred land containing the remains of his forefathers"[19]—land consecrated by the interment of the remains of forebears, as site to which personal history was inexorably bound. Attorney Mariano Aramburo y Machado wrote in 1901 of his return to Cuba precisely in these terms:

There is found my aging father who is awaiting my return, the coffin that contains the bones of my mother, the land in whose bosom the bodies of my ancestors await the Resurrection, the house of my grandparents that formed my earliest impressions and in which are still found the echoes of my earliest childhood cries, the church that received my earliest prayers, the school that nourished my understanding of the world and the teachers who provided me with rudiments of science and inculcated in my heart the foundations of virtue.[20]

Place as repository of memories gave meaning to being, which in turn served to intensify the desire to claim Cuba. The bonds reached deep into domains of popular consciousness, whereby a people could not imagine themselves without those attachments through which awareness of self had been formed. This was belonging as an essential facet of being, a way to give temporal meaning and spatial form to assumptions of antecedents and anticipation of descendants. To be denied claim to patria was to be deprived possession of place of formation, to be without those relationships from which the very meaning of being was derived.

Consciousness of Cuban developed as a deepening awareness of a collective condition as both means and end and acted to foster a longing for the kinds of associations not easily accommodated within the framework of Spanish colonial structures. The idea of nation provided reason for association and motive for mobilization, at once a means of empowerment and source of community, but mostly it offered Cubans the prospects of agency as protagonists in the creation of a nation of their own: the one eventuality to which the Spanish presence in Cuba was dedicated to preventing. Indeed, the proposition of nationality contained within its configuration properties incompatible with the premise of Spanish sovereignty. The meaning of nacionalidad cubana, José Antonio Saco insisted in 1859, implied the sum total of "our ancient origins, our language, our usages and customs and our traditions. All this makes up the actual nacionalidad that we call cubana because it has formed on and is rooted in an island called Cuba." Added Saco: "All people who inhabit the same land, and have similar origins, similar language, common usages and customs—those people have a nacionalidad."[21]

■ ■ ■

Patria as a place-bound source of collective identity expanded into realms of Cuban awareness as a series of cultural revelations, by way of artistic expressions—both highbrow and lowbrow—as classical genres and folk forms:

in the aggregate, sensory experiences through which to heighten awareness of place as source of consciousness of self and vice versa. Attachment to nation developed in multiple forms and developed most vividly by way of self-reflective aesthetics, the way that an expanding cultural imagination set a people on a course toward national integration. Sensory knowledge served to forge powerful local attachments, which when fulfilled often assumed the form of emotional exaltation and when thwarted produced visceral indignation. Much of what came together as properly Cuban formed around cultural-specific experiences. Precisely because consciousness of Cuban drew much of its early vitality from aesthetic sensibilities—both inchoate and intuitive, evoked often as a sentiment and at times as entitlement—it also served to transport much of what developed as national identity into deeply emotional domains, thereupon to summon and sustain the peculiar intensity and single-minded ferocity with which successive generations of Cubans mobilized in behalf of nation.

Long before the proposition of sovereign nationhood acquired political meaning, it had inspired deep sentimental attachments, those most powerful of susceptibilities by which cognitive structures of nation and intuitive meaning of nationality were charged with purpose and passion. Consciousness of Cuban obtained powerful emotional content as a source of social cohesion, principally as a moral system from which behavioral modes of duty and conventions of devotion were inscribed into norms of nationality. The proposition of Cuban was registered early as a matter of cultural revelation in the form of aesthetic production, at once as product and portent of a deepening mood, the stirring of cultural awareness of an emerging national temperament. This was not all art for art's sake, of course, but even when it was not produced for the sake of something else, the reach of its influence could not be contained by the intention of the artist. That moral purpose was not intended did not preclude the possibility that moral meaning was inferred.

It was through the medium of creole aesthetics that the proposition of Cuban was transformed from a source of self-knowledge into a means of self-determination. Poets and painters contributed evocative stirrings to emerging populist notions of nation. They propounded a point of view, very much a politics by another means; the language and symbols of nation directed Cuban aesthetics to outlets in new motifs. They elaborated upon idioms of nation and in the process added vernacular forms to popular aspirations very much conveyed in stylized images and symbols. Cultural production created new interior spaces from which to look out to imagine nation not—initially—as a politics but as a matter of sensation and sentiment, of emotion and passion, ways by which increasing numbers of men and women were drawn into an emerging consciousness of Cuban, where people began to "feel" themselves part of something larger than themselves.

Nineteenth-century aesthetics drew upon those creative impulses through which a people give expression to the concerns of their times: inscribed into the structure of literary genres, implied in the visual arts, and enacted in the performing arts. The creative impulses of the nineteenth century fused together into a new creole sensibility, one in which interior purpose assumed the guise of sentimentality, where the exaltation of Cuban formed and informed meanings of demeanor and disposition, all leading—although not always apparent at the time—to a new mode of politics. Artists strove mightily to efface their presence, to claim the role of presenting their work as reality for objective contemplation, but in fact forging bonds between the audience and the subject of their work. Creative forms contained discernible traces of the premonition of a redemptive vision, which shared something with the emerging collective consciousness to which they contributed.

Successive generations of Cubans arrived at the possibility of nationality by way of highly charged aesthetic genres as a matter of sensory susceptibilities. Cubans devoted to their tierra natal, determined to celebrate the nation through aesthetic representation, were inevitably drawn to the dramatic possibilities offered in literary forms, the plastic arts, music, and dance. Artists summoned sounds, sights, and images of nation with seeming objective specificity. It would be difficult to imagine who could better bring the emerging ideal of nationality "to life" than novelists, poets, musicians, and artists. Medium and message together acted to deepen appreciation for things Cuban and in the process fashioned usable aesthetic motifs from which an emerging sensibility of Cuban found expression.

Consciousness of Cuban deepened within the logic of successive cultural revelations, drawing upon tradition and custom, on folkways and popular forms, a people of diverse social origins and dissimilar racial identities coming over time to recognize themselves as part of and participants in a common national project. Notions of nation drew upon local fauna and flora in lyric poetry and landscape painting, in the elegies of folkloric writers, in the sentimentalized renderings of melody, in the verse of the ten-line décimas, in the choreographies of popular dance: all as new expressive genres that contributed to a heightened subjectivity of nation.

Attributes of nationality assumed multiple aesthetic forms, often the result of determined, self-conscious efforts to develop usable modes of self-definition. Poet José Jacinto Milanés called for the development of a creole idiom, one that eliminated the presence of Spanish influence in Cuban poetry. "Why cannot we in Cuba popularize poetry, making it a mirror of our usages and the many preoccupations contained therein?" Milanés asked rhetorically in 1836. "Of what use are those sonnets, those odes, those long serious compositions that are not understood by the Cuban *people* [*el pueblo cubano*]. . . . Do you not think that this type of [Cuban] poetry, in addition to the pleasure it brings to our compatriots for being entirely *criolla*, would also please foreigners who are interested in the true state of our usages and opinions at the present time?"[22]

Representations of nation drew freely upon the ways of the folk, in their most ordinary and commonplace forms: in recreational pastimes and leisure pursuits, as local custom and rural manners, always as celebration of things Cuban. Local motifs insinuated themselves into Cuban genres at about the time that the idea of nation was gaining currency, what historian Juan Remos described as the "imagery that depicted public and private life in Cuba, both in an urban setting and a rural ambience."[23]

The *costumbristas*, as the exponents of folkways became known, included Luis Victoriano Betancourt, Manuel de Zequeira, José María de Cárdenas, Gaspar Betancourt Cisneros, and Anselmo Suárez y Romero, among many others.[24] One of the early collections of published *costumbrista* essays, *Los cubanos pintados por sí mismo: Colección de tipos cubanos* (1852), featured a narrative exposition on Cuban "types" identified by occupations and associated with corresponding personality idiosyncrasies, including the milkman, the country doctor, the peasant, the midwife, and the country lawyer, among others. In the prologue to *Los cubanos pintados por sí mismo*, writer Blas San Millán drew the relationship between the celebration of *costumbrismo* and nationality explicitly as intimations of national character: "Cubans have also wanted to represent themselves [*pintarse á sí mismo*], for the same reasons that have impelled the French and Spanish . . . : to demonstrate their worth. Their intent is not to create caricatures but portraits of specific types . . . of the population. . . . Cubans have to know themselves to portray themselves faithfully, they have to value who they are and what they are." He concluded: "Within this context, the work they present has far more importance than appears at first glance and its completion is a true service to the country."[25]

The stirrings of national self-awareness found new expression in the development of distinctly Cuban musical idioms. It was not that music was politicized, exactly, but rather that politics was music in another form, the way a people began to assert agency in formation of themselves. Cubans adapted Spanish music and dance to local influences and idiosyncrasies and thereupon fused it with folk forms and African rhythms. A highly textured and multilayered idiom developed out of a process of cultural synthesis at a historic moment: the incorporation of new instruments, the fusion of new rhythms, and the development of new orchestrations, all drawn together selectively from what was at hand and most readily available.

Music was deeply implicated in the emerging consciousness of Cuban, itself an acknowledgment that received musical forms no longer fit the temperament of a new nationality in the process of formation. "The first reports we have of music on the island," early ethnographer José María de la Torre wrote in Lo que fuimos y lo que somos, o La Habana antigua y moderna (1857), "are very unpleasant; it is sufficient to note that black women sang in the church and among the instruments used was the gourd [güiro], used today in the vulgar dances [changüis] of the countryside." De la Torre continued:

> It is known that the provincial music and dance are the zapateo and contradanza. . . . The origin of the music of the zapateo appears to be from La Mancha in Castile. The origin of the dance is also from the Peninsula, but one and the other have experienced such variations that it can be said today to constitute a Cuban specialty [una especialidad cubana]. The contradanza music had captivated even foreigners and when it is composed by people of color, it has greater acceptance among criollos.[26]

By mid-century, local idioms had evolved fully into discernible Cuban genres — "the 'Danza Criolla' is the patriotic music of Cuba," observed traveler Walter Goodman in 1873[27] — as the embodiment of the creative energy with which a people invested themselves in something that was uniquely theirs, including the contradanza, the habanera, the danzón, the guaracha, the guajira, and the punto: all forms, Fernando Ortiz would later write, that evoked "our palm groves, the spirit of our history, the sentiment of love for the patria, and faith in its future."[28] The danza, journalist Ramón J. de Palacio insisted in 1883, "was nothing more than the old Spanish contradanza, modified by the warm and voluptuous climate of the tropics."[29] Few indeed were the number of travelers who visited Cuba during the nineteenth century who failed to take note of music and dance. "The Cubans are remarkably, and indeed passionately, fond of music, vocal and instrumental," Allen Lewis wrote in his travel journal in 1852.[30] "Never in my life have I seen such exciting and provocative dancing or listened to such enthusiastic and delicious music," Spaniard Antonio de las Barras exclaimed during his travels to Cuba in the early 1860s.[31] At mid-century, Fredrika Bremer similarly commented on the Cuban fondness for music, describing "that Cuban contra-dance, and its music so peculiar, so delineative of the Creole temperament." She added: "Wherever one may be, or wherever one goes in Matanzas, this dance-music may be heard. The time and measure are derived from the children of Africa, the peculiar music from the Spanish Creoles of Cuba."[32] Louisa Mathilde Woodruff visited Matanzas almost twenty years later and also noted "the celebrated Cuban dance, a strange, monotonous, half wild and half sad melody, which makes you doubtful whether it was intended to set you dancing madly, or to lull you to a dreamy sleep."[33]

There was a performative dimension to the emerging cognizance of Cuban: a people coming together to play music, to sing, and to dance, but most of all coming together self-consciously as Cubans, in the process fostering those solidarities around which the sense of nationality took hold. This was music as a language, in its own way substantiating the claim to the credibility of Cuban. Music and dance developed into one of the principal modes by which to articulate nationality, as aesthetic forms that insinuated themselves into an emerging national sensibility: another way to subvert the idioms by which culture sustained the colonial consensus.[34] The *danzón*, argued historian Manuel Moreno Fraginals, was "a palpable manifestation of national integration."[35] The compositions of Nicolás Ruiz Espadero ("Canto del guajiro" and "Canto del esclavo"), the *habaneras* of Manuel Saumell Robredo ("La amistad," "Recuerdos tristes," and "La celestina"), the *contradanzas* of Gaspar Villate ("La virgín tropical" and "Adios a Cuba"), and the *danzas* of José White ("Danzas para piano" and "Bella cubana"), among others, gave melodic expression to sentimentalized renderings of nation, to what historian Jorge Ibarra aptly described as "the new music of a national popular tendency."[36] The *danzas* of Ignacio Cervantes gave subtle and often haunting piano renderings of what was called *el criollismo romántico*, melodies that exuded reverence for and exaltation of things Cuban. Nothing captured better the idealized melodic images of *patria* than the *danzas* of Cervantes—in the brooding melancholia of "Adios a Cuba," written as he departed into exile, or the flushed joy of his return ("Vuelta al hogar"), or the spirited exuberance of "La camagüeyana." Novelist Alejo Carpentier was prescient to discern an "interior *cubanidad*" in the compositions of Cervantes, whose music "advanced the idea of a national character that could be best addressed by the composer."[37] A new music for a new nation was in the making, properly described by musicologist Elena Pérez Sanjurjo as "musical nationalism."[38]

The ten-line *décima* gained currency as a musical idiom all through the nineteenth century and indeed insinuated itself deeply into popular culture. Typically transmitted by itinerant performers traveling from one community to another, often improvised and always informative, the *décima* served as a source of news and a way by which people learned about each other—and themselves.[39] The verse was used principally, wrote historian Liliana Casa-nellas Cué, to sing to the *patria*, "in almost all times addressing political and patriotic themes, reaching their greatest notoriety in the exalted and well-known *décimas* of liberation [*décimas mambisas*]" and addressing what historian Antonio Iraizoz characterized as "that unquenchable yearning for liberty and national decorum."[40] Folklorist Virgilio López Lemus insisted that the *décima* early acquired separatist content and was "transformed into an instrument of war, a means by which to ridicule Spain and attack the morale of enemy forces [and] served as a means by which to raise popular consciousness into pro-independence sentiment."[41] The *décima* as a form of popular poetry, wrote Mariano Aramburo y Machado in 1901, served "to enliven the insurgent camps, and certainly under its influence the *mambí* felt more virtuous, more important, more Cuban, and more manly. We pay homage to the *décima*, because it is the voice of the people [*es la voz del pueblo*]."[42] Playwright Carlos Felipe gives voice to Pascual in the play *Tambores* (1943), who proclaims himself to be "the poet of the *décima*. We were the poets of the Cuban homeland [*la tierra cubana*]. We were loyal to the Cuban homeland."[43]

Consciousness of Cuban deepened within stylized—and subjective—representations of local fauna and flora, that is, Cuba as a physical environment to contemplate and celebrate. Landscape art presumed an observer for whom to evoke sentimentality of place: the idea of a geography which, when deployed as subject, implied nation in visual form. Loaded with ideological purport, the landscape evoked nation as a geographical entity, a visual image of *nuestra tierra natal* accessible to all to behold. It registered something of an identity politics as exaltation of place, suggesting a high moral ground, and once visualized suggested patrimony to possess and pass on, another way to foster attachment to place. The landscape artist "reconstructed" the image of the nation with concrete specificity and geographical verisimilitude. Art historian Narciso Menocal discerned in Cuban landscape art "an indication of the poetry and beauty of the national environment," which served as a means to "facilitate an assertion of national identity."[44] The landscape works of Federico Amérigo, Teódulo Jiménez, Miguel Arias Bardou, Valentín Sanz Carta, José Joaquin Tejada, and the three Chartrand brothers from Limonar—Esteban, Felipe, and Augusto—exuded a wistful tranquility for all to ponder. The landscape implied a truth and invited inference to what being and belonging meant, a way to envision—literally—a nation. There was consequence to this genre, perhaps not always by design but certainly by deduction. This was *patria* as a place to contemplate and celebrate, compositions based on the configuration of what nature had bestowed on the island and reverence for the natural world, one more way to differentiate the island from the peninsula. Romantic landscape artists (*los paisajistas románticos*) depicted the countryside by way of an intense visual realism, with a solemn semblance of presence achieved through the use of the brilliant light patterns of the tropics to render unabashedly sentimental paintings of pastoral tranquility, what ethnographer and novelist Miguel Barnet characterized as "romantic creole nationalism" (*nacionalismo romántico criollo*).[45] The paintings evoked all at once climate and ambience, terrain and sentience: geography as a matter of transcendental significance. The relationship between landscape and identity is imperfectly understood, but the sentimentality with which Cubans celebrated their geography must be considered as a source of the passion with which they contemplated nation: this was *patria* not as setting but as protagonist, where geography itself implied historical significance. Landscape was transformed into representation of national virtue, as something intrinsically Cuban, depicted variously as expansive groves of Royal Palms and expansive fields of sugarcane (*cañaverales*), set against breathtaking vistas of valley landscapes and sweeping mountain elevations—all in all, an art form that emerged at about the same time that consciousness of nation developed.

Nineteenth-century *paisajes* also took in wide panoramas of the *ingenio*, the towering smokestacks of the sugar mill against verdant fields of plumed sugarcane in muted tropical pastels. The graphic work of Federico Mialhe appeared in successive publications, *Isla de Cuba pintoresca* (1839) and *Viaje pintoresco por la Isla de Cuba* (1848). The lithographs of Eduardo Laplante that were used to illustrate Justo Cantero's *Vistas de los principales ingenios de Cuba* (1857) provided breathtaking expanses of *cañaverales* and *ingenios*. The mill as site of exploitative social relationships and execrable labor conditions was concealed, of course, and obscured from the history in which it developed. The depiction of the mill from a distant exterior view served to romanticize sugar production as subject to an aesthetic solemnity, celebrated as evidence of industry, technology, and enterprise that spoke to Cuba as a place of progress and prosperity: art as ideology in celebration of dominant production modes.

It would be unduly facile to suggest that nineteenth-century aesthetic forms, including the *décimas*, *danzas*, and *paisajes románticos*, propelled Cubans to rise up in revolution, of course. In fact, they served another purpose. They were themselves the means to affinities and attachments, possessed of the capacity of bringing ever-larger numbers of Cubans to sites of mutual self-recognition. They "worked" as sensory experiences and as forms from which feelings insinuated themselves into national identity; and insofar as they fostered development of identity with place, they contributed powerfully to the formation of the emotional content of nationality.

■ ■ ■

The possibility of sovereign nationhood also expanded into realms of the popular imagination through multiple literary forms and genres, perhaps most dramatically through the literary realism of the nineteenth-century novel. There was in fact a compelling relationship between political events that shaped the liberation politics and literary developments that formed the *independentista* sensibilities. "Nineteenth-century Cuban literature was dedicated principally to awaken[ing] the consciousness of Cubans," literary critic Max Henríquez Ureña correctly noted. "What do the poets and *costumbristas* do if not look inward, toward the essence of feeling Cuban [*sentir cubano*]? To what other purpose if not to seek the essence of lo *cubano*. . . . The history of Cuban literature represents in general terms the continual determination to enable the Cuban people to develop full consciousness of their historical destiny."[46]

The nineteenth-century novel provided an opportunity for Cubans to look in on themselves, as privileged insiders, but also with a spatial distance that could at the same time render them as outsiders, that is, the construction of perspective. The novel was at once representative and revelatory and served to set in relief the complexities of race relations, class contradictions, and gender hierarchies as a condition of a deepening disquiet of contemporary history, all explicitly situated within those unsettled domains of deepening colony-metropolis tensions. Daily life in Cuba was structured around multiple social layers, compressed tightly upon one another, interacting and interlocking, to be sure, but also separate and self-contained. The nineteenth-century novel presumed the formation of national character as intrinsic to its subject, and to which it bore witness, and indeed contributed to a shared content by which to forge the terms of unity. To depict plausibly the lives of men and women as subjects in circumstances of history as lived served to transform novelists into chroniclers of their times, as commentators and critics, often calling into question the very assumptions upon which the calculus of colonialism was based. Cubans all through the nineteenth century came to a deeper understanding of their times through the novels of Cirilo Villaverde (*Cecilia Valdés*), Ramón Piña (*Historia de un bribón dichoso*), Ramón Meza (*Carmela* and *Mi tío el empleado*), Domingo Malpica la Barca (*En el cafetal*), José Ramón Betancourt (*Una feria de la Caridad en 183 . . .*), Esteban Pichardo (*El fatalista*), Francisco Calcagno (*En busca del eslabón* and *Don Enriquito*), José de Armas y

Cárdenas (*Frasquito*), and Nicolás Heredia (*Leonela*). The antislavery novels of Anselmo Suárez y Romero (*Francisco*), Antonio Zambrana (*El negro Francisco*), Félix Tanco (*Petrona y Rosalía*), Gertrudis Gómez de Avellaneda (*Sab*), Martín Morúa Delgado (*Sofía* and *La familia Unzúazu*), Pedro José Morilla, (*El ranchea-dor*), Francisco Calcagno (*Romualdo, uno de tantos*), and Julio Rosas (*La campana del ingenio*) set the abolitionist narratives in wider circulation to a larger public and called attention to the iniquitous conditions to which men and women of African descent were subject within the colonial regime.

The novel served to acquaint the expanding middle class with a range of social knowledge often beyond its immediate experience and in the process prepared Cuban sensibilities for far-reaching changes in the offing. "[Cirilo Villaverde] has a purpose to accomplish," literary critic Roberta Day Corbitt wrote of the novel *Cecilia Valdés* in 1950. "He has pictured the epoch in almost every class of society in the capital and in the country; his is a photographic, not an artistic picture."[47] The nineteenth-century novel subsumed social com-mentary into emerging literary modes, as allegory and allusion, not always—to be sure—with the intent to subvert the moral authority of colonial conven-tions but almost always revealing the contradictions of colonial conventions as a condition of daily life. "With a plot that develops fully in Cuba," Max Hen-ríquez Ureña wrote of Gertrudis Gómez de Avellaneda's novel *Sab* (1841), "the author describes landscapes and customs [*paisajes y costumbres*] with which she was familiar since her childhood, and as the first novel inspired within slavery it acts at the same time to condemn and repudiate slavery."[48] It was a "sentimental novel," literary critic Luisa Campuzano affirmed, that "reveals and condemns the subjugated condition of slaves, women, and the poor."[49]

The nineteenth-century novel served as a source of self-reflection and a means of self-expression: knowledge that contributed to an evolving national consciousness. "The burst of inspiration [*el soplo de inspiración*] that informed *Cecilia Valdés*," journalist Diego Vicente Tejera wrote in 1886, "is the burst of patriotism, of compassionate affection for the abused colony, . . . of passion-ate love for a new Cuba that struggles to arise and to advance."[50]

Poets similarly rendered the abstract notion of nation into a readily acces-sible sensory experience. There is indeed a profound truth to the proposition that consciousness of Cuban obtained its greatest evocative resonance in the form of poetry—as José Lezama Lima mused, "The history of our Island be-gins within its poetry."[51] What gave the genre such enduring force had to do with its capacity to evoke affection, which, although not exactly political, cer-tainly possessed the possibility of politics as emotion. "The best productions of the Cuban mind," American tourist George Austin noted during his travels to Cuba in 1875, "must be sought in the realm of poetry. As in older lands, the poet, the morning-star of the mind, is also the patriot in the minstrel, and is recognized as such by the government."[52]

Poets proclaimed an unabashed love of place, a celebration of the sublimity of Cuban as a matter of emotional exaltation: the sights, scents, and sounds of the island evoked with poignancy and passion and subsumed in modes of sentimentality and solemnity. "My sweet Cuba," exulted poet Ignacio de Acosta in 1882, "the sweet scents of your breezes / the perfume of your flowers / the brilliance of your sky."[53] Poets summoned awe of Nature (la naturaleza cubana) and stirred a national imagination in wonder of what was Cuban, a poetry dedicated to the landscape (la poesía del paisaje): the products of the land, the fragrances in the air, the change of seasons, undulating fields of sugarcane (cañaverales), and expansive vistas of palm groves (palmares). "From this poetry," literary critic Raimundo Lazo insisted, "emerged in the nineteenth century the sentiment of nation [el sentimiento de la patria] . . . , conceived and experienced as a genuine love for the native land [tierra nativa]."[54] Poets Francisco Iturrondo, Juan Cristóbal Nápoles Fajardo ("El Cucalamabé"), José María de Heredia, Manuel de Zequeira, José Fornaris, Julia Pérez Montes de Oca, Miguel Teurbe Tolón, José Victoriano Betancourt, Joaquín Lorenzo Luaces, Luisa Pérez de Zambrana, José Jacinto Milanés, and Carlota Robreño, among many others, celebrated nation as a real place—not imagined, but experienced—as site and source from which Cuban sentimental attachments were derived, bonds that were themselves the source of an emerging national identity. "There was not a poet of any significance," historian Juan Remos correctly observed, "who did not contemplate liberty for Cuba. . . . On Cuban soil, they used symbolism; in exile, they were explicit." Nineteenth-century poetry, Remos suggested, provided "a powerful inspiration that mobilized the will and motivated personal decisions in support of the cause of patria, and maintained the flame of patriotism burning bright . . . and on more than one occasion pointed the way to realize the objective of the just and legitimate aspirations."[55] Diego Vicente Tejera expressed the same idea in slightly different terms: "The poet in Cuba has been an eternal rebel."[56]

The degree to which poetry influenced behavior is difficult to ascertain, of course, but that it did cannot be doubted. Not a few of the men who enrolled in the armed ranks of Cuba Libre—mambises, as they were known—commented on the influence of poetry in their lives. Eduardo Lores y Llorens recalled his military service years later: "It was the reading of patriotic poems that contributed to the forging of my desire to struggle against Spanish domination."[57] Poetry also summoned Horacio Ferrer to bear arms on behalf of Cuba Libre in 1895. He reflected years later: "I have always said that it was our poets who aroused the earliest spirit of combat in the generation of 1895."[58] This was poetry drawing on an aesthetic tradition given to an inherent—if not intentional—subversive exaltation. Subversive in the sense that it drew a people deep into those emotional realms where nation was experienced by way of feelings, what historian Ramiro Guerra y Sánchez characterized as "the gospel of the patriotism of the nineteenth century . . . that worked slowly in the national consciousness to prepare Cubans for the epic feats of 1868 and 1895."[59]

The nineteenth century was a time of tumult, successive decades of displacement and dispersal. Many tens of thousands of Cubans sought refuge in flight abroad. Poets played a vital part in the adaptive processes of expatriation, almost always with a fierce affirmation of nationality. Cubans were never more Cuban than when away from Cuba. "Distance," observed poet Cintio Vitier, "was the place of the myth of the island, and would always play a decisive role in shaping our sensibility."[60] It was out of a sense of place lost, from the experience of exile (destierro), that patria assumed its most compelling and indeed often its most impassioned representation. Place and past fused into remembrance of homeland not as an abstraction but as a real place: to return to, to reclaim, to redeem. Men and women of all classes, black and white—los emigrados, as they self-identified—departed and dispersed widely in foreign lands. They remained transfixed in their gaze homeward, ever so susceptible to the sway of nostalgia as the principal sentiment by which attachments to patria were sustained. Emigré Salvador de la Fe wrote in 1889 of his memories of "the leafy fronds of the perfumed sapota tree and the delicate caimito, the corpulent mango tree heavy with fruit, and the fragrant orange blossom."[61] Poet Belén de Miranda gave poignant lament to her eighteen years in exile: "One memorable and horrible day I found myself obliged to abandon my patria. . . . My soul filled with bitterness and pain, I left my beloved corner, where I left behind my youth, my golden memories, my cheerful expectations, and where the ashes of all those who I loved so dearly were laid to rest. . . . Goodbye Cuba! Goodbye my blue sky! Goodbye my sweet home!"[62] In "El desterrado," poet Pedro Santacilia wrote: "Far from my Cuba / Banished and in a foreign land / I have only tears in my eyes / And pain in my heart."[63]

The poetry of destierro—of exile and expatriation—dwelled on longing and the loss of place, on heartache and homesickness. It fostered powerful sentiments of nostalgia and melancholia, and it produced a highly charged emotional poetry of such distinction as to assume fully the form of a genre unto itself. The verse of exile contributed to the creation of community out of commiseration, for which remedy was to be found only in the redemption of the distant homeland, that is, a politics.

■ ■ ■

It would be a mistake to view the process by which deepening self-reflection contributed to consciousness of Cuban as limited to the celebration of folk culture and exaltation of fauna and flora. Cubans in the nineteenth century were a people deeply absorbed with multiple ways of learning about themselves, dedicated to the production of knowledge across broad fields of learning. They were engaged continuously in constituting themselves culturally, and in the process they forged a rich intellectual tradition that served to inform the meaning of nationality within well-established conventions of erudition and education. These were decades noteworthy for a rich literary production — in quantity and diversity of books and professional journals, as periodicals, pamphlets, and newspapers, dedicated variously to economy and education, literature and literary criticism, medicine, music, and meteorology, science, agriculture, religion, and jurisprudence. The number of newspapers increased across the island. Visiting Havana at mid-century, Robert Baird could not conceal his surprise upon learning "that there should be a considerable number of newspapers in Havanna. But such is the fact."[64] By late in the nineteenth century, nearly two hundred newspapers were in circulation across the island, published in all six provinces: Havana (ninety-nine), Las Villas (twenty-five), Oriente (twenty-five), Matanzas (twenty-one), Puerto-Príncipe (nine), and Pinar del Río (six), dedicated to politics, economy, literature, medicine, law, and the professions. The city of Havana had the largest number of newspapers, with eighty-five, followed by the cities of Santiago de Cuba (thirteen) and Cienfuegos (eleven).[65] "The character of some of these papers," observed traveler John Wurdemann during a mid-century visit to Havana, "in point of literary contributions, is . . . as good as that of many in the United States. . . . Metaphysical, scientific, and moral subjects are often well discussed . . . and rival in their excellence many of the contributions to our periodicals. Indeed, whoever takes up one of these papers will soon perceive that there is no lack of talent or learning in Havana."[66] A literary culture had indeed taken hold. Poet Julián del Casal took due note of the changing reading habits in Havana, observing in 1888 that "the merchant as well as the head of families can hardly begin their daily tasks without having previously read the newspaper. The reading of the daily newspaper has become one of their primary necessities."[67]

The nineteenth century was a time of population censuses, endlessly it seemed: in 1817, 1827, 1841, 1846, 1861, 1877, and 1887. Few indeed were Latin American countries that had, in the nineteenth century, as much census information as Cuba on topics as diverse as population, property, and production, fauna and flora, professions and occupations, the composition of households, and the demographics of race. Cuba had produced a corpus of interior knowledge unrivaled in the nineteenth century.

New knowledge about the island was produced continually by geographers, cartographers, economists, and naturalists, including an extraordinary number of treatises on political economy, geography, and cartography, in the works of Ramón de la Sagra, José García de Arboleya, Esteban Pichardo, Jacobo de la Pezuela, Miguel Rodríguez Ferrer, Felipe Poey, Francisco Javier Báez, Rafael Rodríguez, José María de la Torre, and Félix Erenchun, among others. "Serious study has a following far more numerous that commonly believed within the ranks of the young as well as among older and more mature men," observed Spaniard Dionisio Alcalá Galiano during a mid-century visit to Cuba. "Cubans read a great deal, especially in matters of political economy, and not only read but also understand and absorb its significance."[68]

These were years too in which Cubans acquired wider knowledge of the world at large, a world in which—often to the dismay of many—the place of Cuba seemed insignificant indeed. By the many tens of thousands, Cubans all through the nineteenth century traveled abroad, some as tourists and vacationers, others in pursuit of education, some in search of livelihood, many as disaffected exiles and displaced émigrés. Cubans "either live as outcasts in the land of their birth," wrote journalist Rafael María Merchán in 1896, "or they wander, like a people damned, over distant lands, spending their energies in foreign countries."[69] Emigration developed as a salient facet of the Cuban condition through much of the nineteenth century. The experience in the world provided Cubans with a vantage point from which to bear witness to far-reaching changes overtaking societies in Europe and the United States: societies in the throes of transition, transformed by advances in science and technology, by commerce, manufacturing, and industry, during decades of accelerating material progress and economic development.

These were not always felicitous experiences, however. Knowledge of the world at large often invited invidious comparison and could not but contribute to deepening Cuban discontent with the circumstances of daily life. Increasing numbers of men and women came to see their own society from the point of view of outsider—and did not like what they saw. Cuban self-esteem was often bruised by nineteenth-century encounters abroad. "Here is found all one can desire and even what one could not imagine existed," poet Federico Milanés wrote from New York at mid-century, adding: "It is difficult to understand how, after one has seen this, one can live in Cuba."[70] The experience abroad looms large in Domingo Malpica La Barca's novel *En el cafetal* (1890), where Leonor decries life in Cuba as "insufferable" and vows "to leave Cuba as quickly as possible and never think of it again."[71]

The experience abroad produced a peculiar Cuban angst, a deepening disquiet having to do with a sense of thwarted self-fulfillment, a people beset by a presentiment of exclusion from history, bearing witness to transformations to which they also aspired but sensed too that they were neither part of nor participants in. "I am reminded of Cuba and I weep for its backwardness," essayist Manuel Pichardo brooded during an 1893 visit to the United States[72] — a sentiment shared by Enrique Hernández Miyares, editor of *La Habana Elegante*, who wrote from New York one year later: "I think of Cuba with tears and in pain, despite how much I love her, because of how poorly it measures up in comparison."[73] Attorney Raimundo Cabrera visited the United States in 1892 and could only marvel at "the stupendous growth and development of the great [North American] Republic . . . and at the same time think with sadness that in our land, more fertile and perhaps with better possibilities for equal development, we live in conditions as poor as those peoples who inhabit barren lands."[74]

Encounters with the wider world could not but contribute to Cuban discontent. Cuban dissatisfaction with the prevailing order of things deepened, and the prevailing order of things was attributed almost entirely to Spain. "Cubans who had visited free countries," recalled Manuel J. de Granda years later, "Cubans who read and learned, those who shared a sense of common good, who analyzed and compared, could not tolerate the feeling of being subject to an archaic and retrograde nation [that is, Spain] . . . and were determined at all cost, exposing themselves to all sacrifices, to be free and independent, to govern themselves and not have to wait to receive everything from those who could give nothing."[75]

Cuba had produced a middle class fully imbued with aspirations of modernity and for whom the prospects for collective fulfillment were invested in the promise of the sovereign nation. This was an expanding middle class, of poets and writers, journalists, educators, physicians, dentists, attorneys, and engineers, small property owners and merchants, many educated abroad, bearing new ideas and returning as proponents of new ways. Their status was not necessarily derived from inherited property and family lineage, and they increasingly came to exercise decisive moral authority and intellectual influence over the expanding separatist movement. It was the result of years of travel in the United States and Europe, journalist Eduardo Machado Gómez later reflected, that made him determined "to awaken my people from the political lethargy in which they existed."[76]

Cubans invested themselves deeply in paradigms of progress and modernity. They thought much about a nation of their own, a sovereign nation whose destiny they would most assuredly direct, persuaded that Cuba had a rightful place among the advanced nations of the world. They thought highly of themselves, and indeed were unabashed in their patronage of high culture and pretensions to cosmopolitan respectability, dispositions so commonplace within creole sensibility as to appear as an attribute intrinsic to lo cubano. "From the personal communications of the many Cubans who have lived abroad," Enrique José Varona boasted in 1896, "and as a result of the marvelous facility with which today ideas are disseminated, there has emerged in Cuba an artistic, scientific, and judicial culture that while not general throughout the island is nonetheless extensive. In the cities and towns, the life that the Cuban is developing reaches very high on the scale of civilization."[77]

Middle-class Cubans were noteworthy for their vanity, and nowhere was this conceit more on display than in the affirmation of refined manners and tastes, in home furnishings and fashion, in demeanor and deportment, in style and social graces. "There is something strangely cosmopolitan in many of the Cuban families," American tourist Richard Dana observed of the Cuban middle class during a visit to the island in 1853: "education in Europe or the United States, home and property in Cuba, friendships and sympathies and half a residence in Boston or New York or Charleston, and three languages at command."[78]

The development of a creole aesthetic disposition provided one more way to affirm distinctions from things Spanish and in the process validate a claim to nationality on the basis of a superior cultural sensibility. These were years when the idea of progress assumed fully the form of an article of faith, where the very claim to inclusion among the civilized nations of the world was itself registered as an emerging creole temperament. Cubans never doubted they belonged. What added powerful cultural dimension to pretensions to sovereign nationhood was something of a haughty criollismo, expressed most typically as a deepening scorn for things Spanish. "There is no hatred in the world to be compared to that of the Cuban for Spain and all things Spanish," observed Italian tourist Antonio Gallenga during his visit to Cuba during the 1870s.[79] Traveler Richard Levis arrived at the same conclusion at about the same time:

"The hatred of the Cubans against their Spanish rulers is extreme. . . . I know from intimate communication with the people [of] its heart-felt intensity."[80]

Nothing undermined Cuban pretensions to cosmopolitan standing more than status as colony—and especially a colony of Spain: a country deemed hopelessly resistant to the promise of modernity and impervious to the possibility of progress. Simply put, to be a colony of Spain in the Americas in the late nineteenth century was a source of embarrassment. The mere existence of Spanish colonial rule in Cuba, journalist José Mayner y Ros insisted, was itself "in defiance of civilization and progress."[81]

For many Cubans, despair over colonial status often had less to do with *amor patrio* than with *amor propio*, less with political differences than with cultural ones. But there was always a politics to culture, of course, and a people feeling culturally compromised would also be susceptible to a political remedy to their discontent. A deepening self-esteem was itself very much a facet of an emerging sensibility of Cuban, one that could not be accommodated within the constraints of the colonial condition. Cuban identification with the idea of progress was total, from which corollary notions of modernity and civilization were derived and around which a specific paradigm of nationhood took decisive form. In this scheme of things, Spain was perceived as an obstacle to Cuban aspirations to self-determination and an encumbrance on Cuban hopes for self-fulfillment, conditions that persuaded increasing numbers of men and women that only by shedding the "weight" of Spain could Cubans realize the full potential of the promise of a separate nationality.

The proposition of Cuban as cosmopolitan resonated among proponents of sovereign nationhood precisely because it spoke to shared self-esteem as source of solidarity and means of common identity. Cubans drew the obvious moral. The faith in paradigms of modernity and the promise of material progress suggested that Cubans belonged and Spaniards did not and went directly to the heart of why Cubans were not Spaniards. Through much of the nineteenth century, Cubans defined themselves through denial and disavowal; they distanced themselves from Spain and differentiated themselves from Spaniards and strove mightily to discard and otherwise diminish the ways that served to identify them as Spanish.

Spaniards visiting Cuba at mid-century readily discerned the widening breach between the metropolis and the colony. "Between the Peninsula and Cuba," Dionisio Galiano observed in 1859, "there exists a complete and absolute divergence. The material civilization of this Island is in its essence [North] American, and radically opposed to values that rein over the provinces of our monarchy," and further: "Society in Cuba, exclusively mercantile and industrial in its tendencies, . . . is animated by the spirit of speculation that recalls the *go-ahead* of our North American neighbors."[82] Spanish tourist Antonio de las Barras visited Cuba two years later:

> The great mass of freight and steam ships promote the prosperity of this people [*este pueblo*]. It is wealthy as a result of its valuable products and commerce, always active and expanding. More than anywhere else in Spanish America, Cuba has been inoculated with the *Go-Ahead* progressive spirit of the United States, with which it is in very close contact as a result of education and commerce. Since the United States is without doubt the most advanced country in the world, Cuba, by virtue of a necessity that continues to expand on par with its fabulous wealth, meets its needs by way of the newest and most ingenious machinery and technology in every branch of science.[83]

The narrative of progress and modernity provided Cubans a compelling discursive framework in which to advance the proposition of the sovereign nation as a means of collective fulfillment. Manuel Linares anguished, "If we are to be Spaniards only to represent the Motherland as one of the most backward people in the world . . . , we must insist with devotion and resolution: at that cost, we do not wish to be Spaniards."[84] To remain with Spain was to remain hopelessly outside the mainstream of civilization and progress. Merchant Fidel Pierra gave voice to widely held sentiments: "If the Spanish have any virtues at all—and we do not deny that they have some—they are so enveloped and lost among their innumerable vices that to attempt to conserve the former we incur the risk of being contaminated by the latter." Spanish civilization was "pernicious," Pierra insisted, and it was necessary for Cubans, "at a very early date, to blot out even the last vestiges of it from the island." Spain had revealed its "incapacity . . . as a nation to evolve a civilization promoting and securing the well-being and happiness of those living within its folds." Cubans, on the other hand, were "endowed with those [qualities] of ready adaptability to new and more favorable media" and possessed "a great capacity for rapid and solid improvement and advancement."[85]

Continued association with Spain offered Cubans nothing. On the contrary, in the realms of industry, business, commerce, technology, and science, Spain was uniformly reviled as an obstacle to Cuban development. Advances of modernity in Cuba were proof of backwardness in Spain. "We had railroads before Catalonia," Juan Gualberto Gómez pointed out in 1890; "Havana had electricity before Madrid. . . . During the last thirty years Spain has provided us with little or nothing. As a result, our writers and thinkers, our men of science, have had to seek the elements of their knowledge and the source of their inspirations among foreigners."[86] Cubans were "vastly superior" to Spaniards, essayist Antonio Gonzalo Pérez insisted, for "quite early in the [nineteenth] century [Cuba] began to receive all the blessings of modern civilization." Spain, on the other hand, "situated in a corner of Europe, isolated by custom and tradition and by difficulty of approach, densely ignorant and fanatically religious, lay quite outside the current of progress." Pérez continued: "[Spain] is still saturated with the superstitions of the Middle Ages, which is equivalent to saying she is about five or six centuries behind the times. Therefore, it is not extraordinary that the Colony preceded the mother-country in the construction of railways and telegraphs, those valuable agents in the conveyance of modern ideas."[87] Fermín Valdés-Domínguez, collaborator of José Martí and officer in the Liberation Army, was categorical: "We owe nothing to Spain, who has despoiled us of our wealth and given us nothing in return: it has not attended to the education of our people, nor developed industry; nor has it even known how to promote commerce."[88] The protagonist in Tomás Justiz y del Valle's novel El suicida (1912)—set in the early 1890s—is adamant: "We are preparing ourselves to enter the twentieth century with dignity. . . . Cuba will never be truly civilized as long as one Spaniard remains. It is necessary to kill them! War without quarter!"[89]

Determinants of nationality originated from many sources, one of which had to do with thwarted pretensions to self-fulfillment. No difference was as sharply drawn or as clearly defined as the proposition of Cuba with a bright future and Spain with a dark past, of Cubans possessed of modern sensibilities and Spaniards burdened with backward mentalities. These were not entirely new issues, of course, for the antecedents of being "Cuban"—as compared to being "Spanish"—had their origins in the previous century. What was different in the nineteenth century was the invocation of nationality as identity based not only as a matter of nativity, but on the value assigned to what those differences implied. Cuban implied a different perspective, it presumed a different temperament, it portended a different way of moving about and being in the world. Simply put, to be Cuban was superior to being Spanish. "The Cuban," Enrique José Varona pronounced outright, "possesses characteristics that denote progress within his lineage [raza], and if he is not absolutely more intelligent than the Spaniard, he is certainly of quicker comprehension and less resistant to change. . . . He is more open, more modern, more cosmopolitan. . . . The Spaniard is ill-prepared for the higher necessities of civilization."[90]

The degree to which Spain lagged behind advances in science, technology, and industry, Cubans were persuaded, and the extent to which Spain appeared hopelessly inured to progress implied a larger malaise: that perhaps Spanish normative systems were incapable of accommodating a culture of modernity—and the corollary: to remain with Spain was to remain hopelessly in the past and forever outside the mainstream of progress and modernity. "If we want advance on the path of civilization and progress . . . it is necessary that we separate ourselves from Spain," *costumbrista* writer Gaspar Betancourt Cisneros insisted.[91] In Justo González's novel *Cubagua*, Arturo contemplates the larger meaning of the 1895 war for independence and explains: "This . . . is not a war between Cubans and Spaniards, but between the past and the future, between a spirit that renovates and another that petrifies."[92] The act of revolution was indeed necessary so as to redeem Cuban self-respect. "With a history so filled with ignominy," Rafael Merchán pronounced early in 1898, "Cuba would be a great stain on the Americas if it had not been revolutionary. Its future was to be found in the revolution. The revolution was its duty, its only hope."[93]

■ ■ ■

High culture provided a means of self-identity by way of self-esteem, a way for Cubans to be part of and participants in the world at large. "Knowledgeable economists," exulted María de las Mercedes de Santa Cruz y Montalvo in 1844, "distinguished writers, learned men who are fully equal to the level of European progress, writers and even poets: we have all this, and under the proper circumstances the fame [of Cubans] will circulate with splendor all across Europe."[94] Middle-class sensibility exuded a self-conscious cosmopolitanism, a setting of high society and highbrow culture—in theaters, in opera houses, in philharmonic societies, and in concert halls, where Cubans as both performers and patrons came together and obtained a sense of the ways that these shared interests were themselves at once source and outcome of community.

Cubans of means arrived at a sense of themselves as a people apart by way of sophisticated styles and enlightened sensibilities, represented in the development of an architecture that embodied an ideal into which increasing numbers of men and women invested themselves. Much creole wealth in the nineteenth century was allocated to the construction of concert halls and theaters, philanthropy as display of refined dispositions and cultivated instincts as affirmation of Cuban. Philharmonic societies expanded across the island, first in Havana (1824), and later in the provinces: Santa Clara (1827), Matanzas

(1829), Santiago de Cuba (1842), Trinidad (1842), Puerto Príncipe (1842), San Antonio de los Baños (1848), Cienfuegos (1849), and Sancti-Spíritus (1855).

Literary societies, artistic associations, and music conservatories flourished in Havana, Matanzas, and Cienfuegos, many with instructors recruited in Europe and the United States to teach music and dance in Cuba. "Many musical academies have opened up during the past few years," observed the *New York Times* correspondent in Havana, "to develop the taste for song and furnish the pupils with a knowledge of the technical part of music."[95] All through the middle decades of the nineteenth century, philharmonic societies and literary circles developed into sites of an expanding awareness of those things that men and women of the middle class shared in common: the consumption of high culture as source of shared sympathies and similar cultural predilections, loaded always with latent political purport.[96] The clubs included Liceo Artístico y Literario de La Habana (1844), Sociedad Liceo Artístico y Literario de Matanzas (1859), Liceo Artístico de Guanabacoa (1861), Liceo Artístico y Literario de Regla (1878), and Club Artístico de Santa Clara (1892), among others.

It is perhaps impossible to determine with precision the ways Cuban associations contributed to the development of national consciousness. The evidence is anecdotal but suggestive, and indeed the very existence of *liceos* indicates the presence of mobilized sectors of Cuban society. Gatherings at literary clubs and philharmonic societies served as occasions for discussions about art and literature, to be sure, but they also provided opportunities for conversations dealing with the politics of nationhood.[97] "In my humble opinion," Spaniard Antonio de la Barras suspected in the early 1860s, "these literary events that ostensibly have the appearance of literary functions . . . conceal a sentiment of a different type [related to] separatist tendencies. I have had an opportunity to confirm my suspicions, for every time I attend an event I notice the prominent presence of Cubans [*hijos del país*] known for their disaffection with Spain."[98] Revolutionary plotting in the Philharmonic Society of Havana prompted Spanish authorities to revoke its charter in 1849. The Sociedad "El Pilar" of Havana, founded in 1848, dissolved after 1868 when its members joined the armed ranks of the insurrection during the Ten Years War. The Spanish captain general closed the Sociedad Liceo Artístico y Literario de Matanzas in early 1869 due to suspected separatist sympathies.[99] Among the most prominent founders of the Philharmonic Society of Bayamo was Carlos Manuel de Céspedes.[100]

Cosmopolitan pretensions provided other ways to advance the claim to civilization, to establish Cuba as a respectable concert venue in the world of performing arts, a way to transcend the stigma of colonialism and participate in high international culture. Cubans derived great pride from their performance facilities, celebrated as rivals to the most famous concert halls and theaters of Europe and the United States. The construction of theaters—almost all privately funded—proceeded apace across the full length of the island all through the nineteenth century, what historians Hernando Serbelló, Pilar Ferreiro, and Carlos Venegas characterized as an "explosion of theater constructions":[101] the Coliseo Theater (1822) in Santiago de Cuba; the Principal Theater (1839) in Sancti-Spíritus; the Brunet Theater (1840) in Trinidad; the Centro Theater (1849) in Santiago de Cuba; the Fénix Theater (1851) in Puerto Príncipe; the Avellaneda Theater (1860) in Cienfuegos; the Sauto Theater (1863) in Matanzas; La Caridad Theater (1885) in Santa Clara; and the Terry Theater (1890) in Cienfuegos. The Diorama (Teatro Nuevo) of Havana was completed in 1827. The spectacular Tacón Theater was completed ten years later, claiming a seating capacity of 3,000 people. "One of the three finest theaters in the world," Richard Henry Dana pronounced it in 1859, and it was considered by American publisher Samuel Hazard as among "the largest and handsomest of the world."[102] Charles Rosenberg accompanied soprano Jenny Lind to Havana in 1850 and could hardly contain his exuberance over the Tacón Theater: "Compared with that of the Scala, the French Opera at Paris, or Her Majesty's Theater in London, it must decidedly have the preference."[103] British tourist Edward Robert Sullivan agreed, writing two years later: "The opera is really first rate, and the house, the most beautiful one I have seen in all respects; it holds five or six thousand people, nearly as large as the Queen's Theatre in London."[104] Spaniard Antonio de las Barras marveled at the "greatness of the public programs" in Havana, observing that "the best and most notable Italian opera companies have come and continue to come here, and in this regard [Havana] has no reason to envy New York, or London, or Paris, or Madrid."[105]

The opera had indeed captured the fancy of high society, certainly in Havana. "The opera house in Havana . . . is far more difficult of access than that in New York," wrote winter visitor J. Milton Mackie in 1864. "The Havanese mind seems to be smitten with a perfect rage for the opera. This is the grand and fashionable entertainment—the most expensive luxury of the town."[106]

Theaters served as venues of high culture and sites of high status, as historians María Elena Orozco and Lidia Sánchez characterized nineteenth-century Santiago de Cuba, where "theater, modernization, and city joined indissolubly together" to provide "a vector of modernity and the transformation of the

Tacón Theater, ca. 1870. From Samuel Hazard, *Cuba with Pen and Pencil* (London, 1871).

mentality of the people of Santiago [*mentalidad del santiaguero*]."[107] There was an ideology embedded in the architecture of neoclassical forms of nineteenth-century Cuba, to be sure, theater having to do with privilege and power. But it also had to do with display as definition, a way that consciousness of Cuban as a matter of civic virtue and cultural vitality insinuated itself into an emerging sense of nationality, another way that the drama of nation was unfolding. This too was a facet of Cuban, a shared cosmopolitan aesthetics as a source of national affinity. It provided alternatives to Spanish forms, and more: it served to give expression to Cuban aspirations to transcend the colonial and identify with the international as an attribute of the national. "The Havanese do not indulge in [Spanish musical programs] any more," observed the *New York Times* correspondent in Havana in 1867, "as they consider them out of date and no longer in fashion. Verdi and Bellini have assumed the right of preëminence, the time-honored Zarzuela has been cancelled to retire before its more fashionable competitor, the Grand Italian Opera."[108]

The proposition of nation gained adherents among multiple creole constituencies, sometimes in complementary relationship with one another, other times in competition, occasionally in conflict. What mattered most, however, was an emerging consensus on the primacy of Cuban, and what mattered more and more was how to translate the primacy of Cuban interests into a politics of nationality. Consciousness of Cuban developed in many ways, among Cubans of all social classes, middle class and working class alike, among men and women, white and black. It is not certain that they all came to an awareness of nationality in the same way, or at the same time, or by the same means, or with the same expectations. And not all who arrived at a sense of nationality enrolled in the ranks of armed separatism. What is certain, however, is that they shared in common the conviction of the propriety of the claim to a nation of their own. These were dispositions that informed the meaning of Cuban, a deepening dedication to the proposition of the sovereign nation from which the promise of nationality obtained plausibility.

National formation involved a complex process of negation and affirmation as one and the same imperative, often by way of the same set of acts, in discharge of the same sense of purpose. Aspirations to nation expanded simultaneously as an awareness of the past and a sense of the future, a process of both subversion and conversion, of displacement and replacement, of a people at one and the same time engaged in the development of a narrative of nation and absorbed with ways of inserting themselves into that narrative. The claim to a separate nation was acted upon as a commitment to a politics; it was actualized as a matter of cultural adaptation, in the form of changing tastes and changing patterns of conduct, as old practices passing into desuetude and new preference coming into being, and which when examined in the aggregate reveal a society in the throes of far-reaching social transformations.

The complexities of national formation were at work in many places: in concert halls and union halls, on the opera stage and in baseball stadiums, in Protestant churches and Masonic lodges. It is from this perspective that the nineteenth-century project of liberation must be understood: a multiclass, made up of men and women, and with biracial mobilizations, within shifting cultural sensibilities, to create a modern nation, the principal attributes of which were informed by notions of national sovereignty, progress, social justice, and democracy, a movement self-consciously embedded in a paradigm of voice and volition and which would not be reproduced in the world again until 1917.

3

TRANSFORMATION IN TIMES OF TRANSITION

A Republic organized on the solid basis of morality and
justice is the only form of government that promises to
guarantee citizens their rights and is at the same time the
best safeguard in pursuit of just and legitimate aspirations.
— Antonio Maceo to José Martí (January 15, 1888)

We demand the Independence of Cuba and of all Cubans. . . .
Our mission is to obtain Independence so that the Cuban
people can thereupon proceed to establish their political
institutions and organize the public administration that
best serve the needs of the nation.
— Consejo de Gobierno, "Manifiesto" (April 24, 1898)

The War was confused with the Revolution: the War was
a means, the Revolution was the end. The task was left
unfinished.
— Antonio Iraizoz y Villar, *Lecturas cubanas* (1939)

Almost from the beginning, from the point at which we
began to establish our national identity, the idea of nation
was associated with moral duty.
— Lisandro Otero, *Llover sobre mojado: Memorias de un
intelectual cubano (1957–97)* (1999)

The nineteenth century was a time of deepening discontent, mostly as an incremental condition, to be sure, but an inexorable one. Vast numbers of Cubans experienced daily life in a state of disquiet, borne principally as a circumstance to which men and women across the island accommodated themselves as a matter of course, conditions so commonplace as to pass for a normal state of affairs, without apparent recourse to remedy and certainly without immediate means of redress. This was discontent as a facet of daily life, discerned—if at all—as one's lot, often carried as grievance but borne in compliance, in accordance with the conventions of the natural order of things. Grievances deepened and widened and seemed never to get resolved. So they multiplied.

But these were also years of change, and what was changing most was the Cuban capacity to articulate discontent, accompanied with—or perhaps because of—a growing awareness of the possibility of agency—consciousness, in a word: that the condition of injustice was neither immutable nor unassailable and with the deepening conviction that the collective power of proponents of change was at least equal to the institutional strength of defenders of the status quo. The capacity to arrange consciousness of discontent into a coherent narrative implied cognizance of disaffection not as a personal and individual situation but as a social and political condition, itself a source of solidarity, where a grievance changed from the particular to the general, thereby drawing a people together to act in concert to seek remedy through collective means. More Cubans had more knowledge about more things, especially as it involved the circumstances in which they lived their lives. This too was part of national formation: all occurring in the ordinary course of events, sometimes as a matter of slow realization, other times in the form of sudden revelation, whereby the discontent with which men and women across the island lived everyday life was revealed as an untenable circumstance, and suddenly a system of oppression was exposed in full view and its vulnerability was revealed. It was often a matter of people simply sensing that things were not quite right, men and women living uneasily with their discontent, perhaps oblivious to the adaptations they had made because it was normal to adapt and because it was probably easier that way, in any case.

Changes of other kinds were under way, those types of changes that often release the great "forces" of history but whose consequences were neither readily apparent nor immediately experienced. Old allegiances were in transition and new attachments were in formation; loyalties were reordered and thereupon reconfigured around new categories of self-definition and self-interest. On all counts, and all at once, Spanish colonial rule was straining to contain the social forces transforming Cuban society—and increasingly revealing itself as incapable of doing so. That Cuban aspirations could no longer be accommodated within existing colonial structures was apparent, at least among Cubans; so too was the need for change—a powerful consensus indeed. To contemplate the need for change was itself a source of change, a way to induce thinking about how to "do" change: where the liabilities of colonialism became an ever-more-intolerable condition and where even the most fundamental assumptions of colonial relationships were called into question and increasingly lost credibility—all of which created a readiness for more change and suggested the need for faster change.

The implications of change were not always immediately apparent, of course, but the effects were at work always, inexorably and relentlessly. Gone were old certainties. Old habits of authority were no longer tenable; old assumptions of hierarchy were no longer sustainable. Commonplace truths seemed no longer to correspond to life as lived. The anomalies of time-honored deferential systems were exposed to be increasingly untenable—they had outlived their times and revealed existing normative systems to be ill-suited to Cuban needs. Long-standing conventions and customs were under challenge: everything, it seemed, and everywhere, it seemed, was subject to new scrutiny, an occasion to interrogate received wisdom and challenge conventional knowledge. Cultural displacements of far-reaching implications were in progress. Uncertainty was endemic, placing in doubt the very efficacy of the existing belief systems and inevitably raising new questions about their relevance, which contributed to further uncertainty. Each displacement was itself a symptom of a larger dislocation, and each provided an occasion to articulate discontent and act out dissent. New egalitarian notions were gaining currency. Systems of domination of all kinds were under increasing pressures from above and below, within Cuba and without. New ideas of selfhood, all very much about self-esteem and self-reliance, admitted the propriety of disobedience and defiance and could not but challenge prevailing conventions of entitlement and the practice of privilege.

Tensions within colonial society deepened and widened all throughout the nineteenth century, becoming ever more pronounced and sharply defined: between the colony and the metropolis, between *criollos* and *peninsulares*, between free and slave and black and white, among social classes and within the privileged classes, among whites themselves as cultural distinctions and ethnic divisions between Cubans and Spaniards increasingly hardened into multiple irreconcilable enmities, some social, others cultural, and eventually all political.

Economic good times served to deepen colonial contradictions; hard times acted to reveal them. Failed efforts at colonial reform in Spain seemed to make the need for colonial rebellion in Cuba more compelling. These were years of continuous movement: a people in motion, commodities in transit, new ideas in circulation. People and ideas moved so much more quickly: travel by steamship and railroads, communications by way of telegraph and telephone. Market forces were at work changing fundamental facets of daily life. Newspapers and magazines proliferated. Emigration from Cuba and migration within Cuba: workers emigrated abroad, peasants migrated to the cities, slaves escaped into the interior. All through the second half of the nineteenth century, Cubans—middle class and working class alike—traveled abroad, in pursuit of livelihood and learning, in flight from political repression and economic depression. They settled in New Orleans, Key West, Tampa, New Orleans, Philadelphia, and New York, among other cities in the United States. They took up residence in Europe, Mexico, Central America, and the Caribbean. Cubans organized: into trade unions and political parties, into baseball teams and literary societies, into *cabildos* and *cofradías*, in evangelical denominations and Masonic lodges, as outlaw gangs and insurgent bands.

At home and abroad, Cubans bore witness to the political transformations and social dislocations of their times. The challenge to the premise of power and practice of privilege unfolded in full view of successive generations of Cubans, even as they were self-consciously absorbed with the ways to assemble the meaning of nationality. What made these experiences especially momentous was that they were occurring simultaneous with deepening dispositions to change, during precisely the decades in which Cubans were engaged in the process of change, contemplating the raison d'être of nationhood, forging new social relationships in pursuit of new ways to form and inform nationality, searching for the means through which to articulate their separateness. Possibilities of remedy to social injustice were everywhere suggesting possibilities of the purpose to which the sovereign nation would be dedicated, and these possibilities acted to define much of what would shape the character of an emerging national sensibility.

The meaning of nationality—what being Cuban signified—bore discernible traces of the time and circumstances of its formation. A people engaged self-consciously in the process of national formation could not but have been susceptible to the transformations of their times, and indeed could contemplate the meaning of a nation of their own only by way of the normative systems most readily available to them. The *independentista* purpose drew upon multiple sources, some reaching deeply into the very antecedents of national consciousness, others influenced by circumstances of the times. It was informed by the moral philosophies of Cuban thinkers of the nineteenth century, including Félix Varela (1788–1853), José de la Luz y Caballero (1800–1862), and Antonio Saco (1797–1879). The project of nation expanded in the form of a moral imperative, one that shaped the purpose with which successive generations of Cubans evoked the idea of national sovereignty. It obtained meaning not as an abstract notion of freedom and liberty, however much those ideas aroused Cuban passions, but as something profoundly personal, very much inscribed in the interior histories of the many hundreds of thousands of men and women who invested themselves in the promise of nation. The process of national formation was experienced as a succession of paradigm shifts in which norms of nationality developed around shared normative attributes, where the claim to Cuban drew its proponents into a new moral order from which determinants of nationality emerged.

■■■

No idea shaped the meaning of nationality more decisively than the conviction of collective well-being and individual self-fulfillment derived from the promise of sovereign nationhood. Men and women in the nineteenth century committed their hopes for a better future to the promise of nation, with the expectation that a nation of their own would provide the means to remedy the sources of their discontent. The project of nation was a work in progress through much of the nineteenth century, an ongoing process of negotiation to accommodate competing interests and reconcile conflicting claims within larger consensual domains of nationality.

The constituencies for sovereign nationhood increased in number and diversified in kind, and in the process the meaning of national sovereignty itself broadened in scope and widened in purpose. The idea of nation took in notions of racial equality, universal suffrage, social justice, and representative democracy inscribed within narratives of progress, socialism, capitalism, nationalism, and romanticism: a complex dialectical exchange from which consciousness of Cuban developed. Everything would be better in the sovereign nation, Cubans were certain. "The Republic is the realization of the great ideals that consecrate liberty, fraternity, and equality of men," insisted Antonio Maceo. "And equality above everything else. . . . Let us establish a Republic on the unshakeable base of equality before the law."[1]

The proposition of nation evolved into multiple meanings all through the nineteenth century, changing with changing times, a process shaped by the very historical circumstances from which it emerged and to which it contributed, where the promise of sovereignty as a means of self-determination placed the possibility of desired outcomes within reach of increasing numbers of Cubans. Nation implied community, of course, a people bound together in a common cause for shared goals. But nation also contained within its premise a summons to ameliorate the divide of race and the distinction of class, a call for Cubans to surrender themselves to the transcendental ideal of nation. Nation was something to surrender to and to which to subordinate all competing identities and into which all were welcomed unconditionally. The solidarity of nationality formed around the ideal of sovereign nationhood—in part by design, to be sure, but also in part by necessity—for the very success of the independentista project depended on a purpose that privileged nation as the means with which to transcend class conflict, racial tensions, and gender hierarchies. Cubans of diverse backgrounds, men and women of different racial origins and dissimilar social status, joined together and in the process contributed to the development of a single national culture forged by the circumstances of its creation. The independentista project engaged successive generations of men and women in common purpose and deepening mutual dependency: that is, the very process by which Cubans fashioned the bonds of national solidarity. It had become appropriate to acknowledge—and indeed necessary—to accommodate within the expanding independentista polity grievances of multiple origins as the condition necessary to sustain the solidarity of national purpose. The proposition of sovereign nationhood as means of self-determination transformed the very meaning of nationality.

The nineteenth-century meditation on nationality developed around an emerging stock of social values, a process through which to inform belief systems, shape canons of self-representation, and influence norms of conduct: in the aggregate, the ways by which the collective sensibilities of a people found expression in a common purpose. This was a complex process. It lacked symmetry and uniformity and must be understood to have been an incremental development, over long stretches of time, implicating men and women of all social classes, black and white, at different times and in different ways, acted upon with the material resources at hand and within the moral systems most readily available.

The possibility of a people bound together as a separate nationality and a single people within a sovereign nation was itself a product of a deepening self-awareness of shared similarities as source of community and from which the logic of *lo cubano* obtained plausibility: a people coming to consciousness of collective self within a single nation. Its principal expression implied a re-flexive knowledge through which to register cognizance of sovereign nation-hood as the basis to link a like people together through shared experiences and common purpose. A powerful sense of collective selfhood formed around a deepening sense of self-worth, based on the conviction that Cubans had a destiny to pursue, that they had a right to independence, and most of all that they had a claim to national sovereignty as the means of self-fulfillment. "We will make independence for all," Maceo vowed, "and Cubans will be mas-ters of the future of their *patria*."[2] For the vast numbers of men and women implicated in the premise of Cuban, realization of nationality could not be imagined under any circumstance other than by way of national sovereignty: a people apart in possession of a nation of their own, central to which was the proposition of a sovereign nation as means of collective fulfillment, that is, nation in the service of nationality. "The objectives that we Cubans have ardently sought," Provisional President Bartolomé Masó affirmed, "are to be masters of the destiny of our country to attend by virtue of our own merits to the solution of its needs, and to meet public interests."[3] Antonio Maceo alluded often to "a free and sovereign *patria*" as the minimum condition of Cuban well-being. "With national sovereignty," he predicted, "we will obtain our natural rights, a quiet dignity, and the representation of a people free and independent." Repeatedly Maceo spoke of the Cuban purpose defined as the pursuit of "the national sovereignty of our people." Cuba possessed the right, Maceo insisted, "to move within the concert of free nations, that is to say, re-sponsible for its own destiny." On the matter of sovereign nationhood, Maceo was unequivocal: "What moves us is the idea of rendering our people masters of their own destiny, of placing them in possession of the means to fulfill their purpose as subjects of History."[4]

Inscribed into the properties of national sovereignty was the proposition of egalitarian purpose — nation as the means to enable redress of grievances, mediate social tensions, and ameliorate the sources of discontent — nation as a commitment to collective well-being, the promise of José Martí: "With all, and for the good of all."[5] Sovereign nationhood implied the possibility of allowing Cubans to become the people they wished to be: a better people, joined together through a shared faith in the promise of a better future for all. The promulgation of the Constitution of Guáimaro (1869) inspired poet/essayist Luis Victoriano Betancourt to lift his voice in celebration of the egali-tarian ideal to which the Cuban purpose was dedicated: "Cuba has a republic in which women are equal to men, in which the poor are equal to the rich, in which blacks are equal to whites. . . . Its constitution has made men into citizens, citizens into a people, and the people as sovereign; Cuba has the freedom of thought, the liberty of action, and the freedom of life."[6]

▪▪▪

The proposition of sovereign nationhood entered the Cuban imagination in multiple forms, charged with diverse functions and imbued with divergent meanings. It drew sustenance from many sources: some possessed of sentimental value and ends unto themselves and others invested with instrumental purpose as means to other ends. The boundaries among these categories were neither inalterable nor always discernible. They shifted often; sometimes they collapsed altogether, whereupon the promise of nation conveyed many things all at once. These elements coexisted in close proximity to one another, not always in congruent juxtaposition, to be sure, but rather as an amalgam of shifting representations by which to contemplate a frame of reference for affinity and affiliation.

The men and women who responded to the promise of nation brought with them multiple interior histories, bearing grievances of many kinds, experienced by different Cubans differently: some having been endured for many years, some of recent origins. It could hardly have been otherwise, for the sources of Cuban discontent tended to align along a wide arc of injustice, experienced as discrimination and disadvantage, having to do with color and class, gender and ethnicity, made all the more urgent by the deepening conviction that things did not have to be that way.

Multiple voices contemplated the meaning of nationality within different sets of value systems, corresponding to different hierarchies of moral imperatives and implying different modes of collective fulfillment; each privileged different attributes of Cuban, drawing upon a different ensemble of normative systems through which to propound different ways of political participation and imagine different forms of social inclusion. The constituencies of *Cuba Libre* represented a disparate and at first glance incongruous combination of class interests and political persuasions: capitalists and socialists, anarchists and Baptists, the intelligentsia and the illiterate, property-owning planters and propertyless peasants, former slaves and former slaveholders, workers on the sugar fields of rural Cuba and workers in cigar factories in Tampa. Interests of such diversity were not easily accommodated within the emerging *independentista* polity, to be sure, and indeed on more than one occasion the contradictions within the separatist movement erupted into internal disputes and plunged the project of nation into disarray.

But what appeared at the time as discord and dissension within the multiple constituencies of nation was in fact a process of complex negotiations among competing versions of Cuban. The character of the liberation project was forged as a continual state of adaptation and accommodation, intrinsic to its internal logic of an all-inclusive representation of the nation, given most of all to efforts to establish the basis of collective action as the means of a national polity. "The Revolution was organic," Manuel Sanguily wrote of the Ten Years War in 1893. "It was born of its antecedents, it had its reason for being, its logic, that is: its internal process. It consisted of multiple elements, and acquired a special structure. It developed and accommodated itself to its circumstances and its internal constituencies. It adapted . . . continually to changing conditions."[7]

On the matter of the primacy of nation, Cubans were nearly unanimous: a deepening awareness of devotion to place as source of common affiliation and shared purpose by which national solidarities took form. It was the perspective that sustained the emerging narrative of nation, indeed it was at the very core of the idea of the Cuban purpose, in the words of José Martí: "*Patria* is community of interests, the unity of traditions, the indivisibility of purpose, the sweet and consoling fusion of love and hope."[8] The founding of the Partido Revolucionario Cubano (PRC) by Martí in 1892 provided the institutional framework in which to integrate Cubans of all classes, men and women, black and white, into a single revolutionary project. The PRC dedicated itself to the preparation of a war of liberation even as it forged the consensual terms of nationality. Cubans bearing multiple forms of discontent joined together in a single unified movement for the specific purpose, José Martí announced, of mounting a "common revolutionary action" to obtain the liberation of Cuba, to unite all Cubans to wage war, and to provide the moral and material support necessary to secure the independence of the island.[9]

The enduring achievement of the *independentista* project was registered as the affirmation of a particular representation of Cuban, a version imbued with attributes that endured as the dominant embodiment of nationality deep into the next century. The emerging formulation of nationality acquired its definitive characteristics as much through means as ends, specifically through the conviction that the promise of nationality could not be realized in any form other than through national sovereignty, that any reconciliation with Spain on any basis other than independence was unacceptable, and that independence could be better secured by war and revolution than by negotiation and evolution: a new war to continue the war of 1879–80, which was a continuation of the war of 1868–78. "We were committed to the titanic struggle," General

Carlos García Velez reflected years later, "to realize the ideal of independence by force of arms with the knowledge that independence would have been impossible to achieve through peaceful evolution [*evolución pacífica*]."[10] Colonel Fermín Valdés-Domínguez was certain: "Cuba, my beloved *Patria*, cannot achieve its independence by any means other than war."[11] José Martí alluded variously to "the necessary war," to "the indispensable war," to "the inevitable war," and insisted: "War appears to be the only means with which to redeem the *patria*." There was "no other way to save our country except by war."[12]

Independence was far from merely political. The ideal of sovereign nationhood was the product of a particular version of Cuban, one deeply embedded within the proposition of national sovereignty not as an end but as a means, to enable self-determination as a way to well-being and source of self-fulfillment, of rising expectations lifting Cuban hopes for a better future and sustained by a commitment to the primacy of Cuban interests as the purpose for which the sovereign nation would be consecrated.

The challenge to the external sources of Cuban discontent in the name of liberty and freedom served to set in place a parallel discourse having to do with the internal causes of Cuban grievances, also in the name of liberty and freedom. Cubans aspired to end more than external forms of oppression, for which national sovereignty was the obvious end. They sought also to confront the internal sources of injustice, for which self-determination was the necessary means. Independence promised to make possible a new nation and a new order of things, the means to remedy Cuban discontent, a way to give Cubans a new place in society. The cause of Cuba was about the promise of political participation and social inclusion, about assembling a new value system as the normative basis of a new nation. The *independentista* purpose subsumed moral imperative into the idea of sovereignty, and in so doing transformed the meaning of nation from an abstract ideal to something real with actual consequences.

The ascendancy of the *independentista* ideal as embodiment of Cuban must be considered as a development of singular importance in the formation of nationality. If the liberation project was to have any prospect of success over the long run—and it was indeed over the long run that Cubans contemplated the pursuit of independence—it was obliged to render those attributes necessary to sustain Cuban resolve into properties of nationality. Inscribed into nineteenth-century formulations of nationality was the commitment to nation as a way to Cuban betterment—the creation of a nation possessed the capacity to ameliorate Cuban discontent and to provide collective fulfillment and individual well-being: a people who were persuaded they possessed the moral authority to make a history that met their needs. Aspirations to nation-hood were about making life better for all Cubans. "There is no salvation of Cuba other than independence," pronounced Antonio Maceo, "not as an end, but as an indispensable condition to achieve larger goals in conformity with the ideal of modern life."[13] As a means of self-fulfillment, liberation implied empowerment; as a basis of mobilization, it offered the prospects of mobility; as a movement, it promised membership.

National sovereignty implied the prerogative of power: power at the service of a national community without mediation, without intermediary; power to fashion the institutional structures of nation; power to assure the ascendancy of Cubans in Cuba; power to advance the primacy of nation as the basis upon which to constitute nationality. Aspirations to sovereign nationhood as a means of self-fulfillment implied making life better for all Cubans. That was the point: the creation of a nation entrusted with the defense of Cuban inter-ests as the very reason for existing in the first place.

■ ■ ■

Acknowledgment of Cuban discontent was not a novel insight. What was new was the idea that Cubans acting in concert and with common purpose could do something about the circumstances of their discontent, that they were indeed joined together by a shared past and dependent upon one another for a better future, that they could seize history and make it respond to their needs.

The capacity to articulate discontent as a matter of actionable grievances and to imagine the possibility of redress as an outcome of collective action were themselves evidence of a shift of consciousness, a revelation of sorts, whereby conditions of oppression could no longer be sustained as "normal" and the circumstances of inequality could no longer be defended as "natural." The act of agency, profoundly embedded in the ideal of national sovereignty as a means of self-determination, provided a way to contemplate the possi-bility of changes of other kinds, a people bound together into mutually depen-dent constituencies upon which the purpose of nation developed. Historian Lillian Guerra correctly characterized the liberation project as a movement of "popular nationalism," described as "a diffuse but radical set of principles for self-determination that included a commitment to racial (and, in some cases, gender) equality, socioeconomic access, and political justice through a grassroots-controlled democracy."[14]

The promise of independence was contained in the possibility of becoming and being someone, to be party to, part of, and participant in the creation of a new nation, for all Cubans, of course, but especially for the dispossessed and displaced, for Cubans who felt despised and disenfranchised: all in all, an entirely plausible formulation because it implied an all-encompassing paradigm of nationality, national inclusion as something real and important, a place in a community of agency, of collective well-being and the promise of a better future. José Martí envisioned a "moral republic," one that implied "not so much a mere political change as a good, sound, just and equitable social system, without the fawning of demagogues or arrogance of authority," and added: "We must never forget that the greater the suffering, the greater the right of justice."[15]

Solidarity of purpose was sustained by the proposition of nationality as the embodiment of virtue and value, by the promise of nation as a source of dignity and well-being, that is, national sovereignty possessed of the capacity to transport its adherents across new thresholds of political participation and social inclusion. The idea of national sovereignty seized hold of the Cuban imagination for its promise of agency as the exercise of voice and volition, of inserting Cubans as protagonists into their own history in the creation of a nation of their own. They lived the experience of the nineteenth century as self-conscious agents of their own history, a process that was itself source of the affinities with which they came to a cognizance of shared attributes of nationality. A sentiment of agency insinuated itself early into the emerging sensibility of Cuban, the idea of individual resolve as source of collective fulfillment. "Those of us who went into the field of battle," reminisced General Carlos García Velez, "were imbued with the idea that through our efforts we could contribute to the independence of Cuba."[16]

There was populist intent to the Cuban purpose, a commitment to national sovereignty conceived as political change as means of social betterment and economic well-being. "Without question," attorney Raimundo Cabrera wrote of the 1895 war for independence, "this has not been like the Ten Years War—not in its origins, or in its means, or in its expansion, or much less in its social, political, and economic aspects. Cuba today is revolutionary. . . . Everything is undone and in transition."[17] The premise of nation had fully expanded into a promise of social justice and racial reconciliation as the basis of national integration. "We do not undertake this revolution to expel the Spanish from the island in order to take their place at the banquet of shame and exploitation," affirmed Diego Vicente Tejera in 1897. "On the contrary, it is undertaken to bring an end to that banquet, so there will no longer be those who fatten and laugh at the expense of those who grow thin and cry, so that—in a word— there no longer exist neither exploiters nor exploited."[18]

The discursive structure of sovereign nationhood developed fully into a redemption narrative. To participate in the purpose of *patria* implied nation as a means of salvation. Fermín Valdés-Domínguez often wrote of the war for independence as "the redemptive revolution" (*la revolución redentora*).[19] José Martí repeatedly invoked the idea of a movement to join all Cubans around "the burning idea of decent redemption," as he proclaimed in 1891. "A war for the redemption and benefit of all Cubans" and "a nation redeemed" (*la patria redimida*), he reiterated the following year.[20] Nation as the basis of Cuban well-being, a means by which to fulfill the destiny of a people, the moral premise from which the ideal of nation expanded into the normative determinants of nationality: a conviction central to the rationale of the cause of Cuba, which meant too that it created expectations of nation.

The *independentista* appeal, with its commitment to collective well-being within the paradigm of nation, promised entrée into a national community as a means of a better life and drew vast numbers of Cubans into its purpose, especially Cubans of African descent. Contained within the formulation of the sovereign nation was a parallel narrative addressing the circumstances of the hundreds of thousands of Cubans of color and the means by which the emerging domains of nationality were to accommodate racial equality, what Diego Vicente Tejera insisted was to be "not solely equality before the law but social equality, the only equality that acts to promote and preserve fraternity among men."[21]

On the eve of the abolition of slavery (1886), African-descended people, both slave and free, constituted fully one-third of the total population of Cuba, approximately 500,000 out of 1.5 million inhabitants. The abolition of slavery raised as many issues as it resolved. Vast numbers of people of color, both men and women who had been born free and those who had been enslaved, were in a condition of transition and change even as Cuba itself was in the throes of transition and change. For the vast majority of Cubans of African descent, these were conditions in which the rules appeared to have changed—but not really: where the freedom implied by emancipation was often more apparent than real, and where the possibility of mobility and security was circumscribed at every turn by custom and conventions that revealed themselves resistant to change. "Freedom" in this instance meant mostly that many tens of thousands of black Cubans were not legally slaves. For many Cubans of color—perhaps most—the legal distinction was a moot point, for the material conditions and moral circumstances in which slavery had obtained validation persisted well after slavery itself had ceased to exist. No amount of "freedom" was sufficient to offset persisting conditions of injustice and inequality. The ranks of free people of color increased—and increased exponentially all through the nineteenth century. A vast constituency for change expanded across the island among the many tens of thousands of men and women of color who were "free" but subject to discriminatory policies and baneful practices. They had demanded the abolition of slavery and subsequently demanded recognition of rights to pursue a livelihood unmolested, to attain a standard of dignity, and to find a place of security in Cuba. "To arms!" Antonio Maceo exhorted Cubans of color. "Expel from Cuba the government that exploits you and oppresses your race. Yes—expel those enemies of the black humanity that are the source of your misfortune."[22]

The liberation project offered people of African descent the promise of entrée into the emerging national community, an opportunity to participate in the formation of nation and thereby claim access to the promise of sovereign nationhood. "We want liberty and independence from Spain and every other nation," proclaimed a manifesto of Cubans of color in Key West in 1881:

> We want to see a republican form of government established in our nation. We want positions of public office distributed on the basis of merit, and not favoritism and caprice. We want full political rights and civil liberties for all sons and daughters of Cuba. We want the establishment of schools across the island on the basis of free and obligatory education. We want education to serve as the means to eradicate the social inequality that still exists in our *patria*. We want an end to the obstacles that the Spanish government has imposed on the development of Cuban agriculture, industry, and commerce. In a word: we want an independent Cuba to embark on the path of prosperity and greatness that will lift our people to the same level as the most advanced nations in the world.[23]

The participation of men and women of color in the process of national formation was essential to complete the representation of nationality as the embodiment of Cuban—and more: to advance the proposition of nationality as a construct of racelessness. To the degree that people of multiple racial identities invested themselves in the transcendental category of Cuban, the *independentista* project served to underscore the power of the appeal of *patria*. The liberation movement, historian Ada Ferrer correctly observed, "gave rise to one of the most powerful ideas in Cuba history—the conception . . . of a raceless nationality."[24]

The project of liberation could not admit the formulation of racial purpose in any function other than in the service of nation: specifically, people of color subordinating racial identity to national identity. The intent was to

confer unanimity of purpose and unity of politics, to subordinate competing identities and potentially divisive attachments to the proposition of the
transcendental nation as source of solidarity, which implied too the promise — and expectation — of nation as means of redress and source of security.
Whatever divided Cubans from within and weakened them from without was
rejected as divisive, an obstacle to the fulfillment of the sovereign nation. The
moral was plain: unity of nation promised to transcend the division of race.
"There is happily no longer whites and blacks [in Cuba], pronounced Eusebio Hernández in 1895. "We are all sons of the same nation, all equal before
the law, which has no other purpose than to guarantee the rights of everyone
. . . to benefit the intellectual, moral, and social condition of the community."[25] To affirm color was deemed divisive and detrimental to the solidarities seen as necessary for the success of the *independentista* purpose. "Cuba
means more than whites, more than mulattos, more than blacks," José Martí
insisted: "To insist on racial divisions and differences of race among a people
already divided is to impede the attainment of national and individual well-
being, [goals] that are to be achieved by the unity of racial elements that constitute the nation."[26] This was the promise inscribed into the very premise of
nation. "We are going to work to remove obstacles that impede unity," vowed
Juan Gualberto Gómez, "and to strengthen our efforts with the maximum co-
operation possible so that equality may prevail and upon which we will fasten
permanent goodwill between blacks and whites."[27] As a transcendental category, the idea of sovereign nationhood could not admit the division of race.
"Ask for nothing as black," Antonio Maceo enjoined, but ask for "everything
as Cuban."[28]

To surrender to the promise of nation was to commit to the creation of a
new society which, by the very terms of equal participation and shared sacrifice with whites, was to guarantee people of color a place of equality in the nation. "The independence war," historian Tomás Fernández Robaina observed,
"in large measure contributed to the creation of a multiracial nation, in which
blacks could not be ignored and their claim of rights to public positions had
been more than adequately substantiated by their valor in the battles for independence." Further: "Expectations were virtually unanimous that in the imagined nation, the Republic of Martí, the bane of racial discrimination would be
eliminated."[29]

Vast numbers of Cubans of color responded, and many tens of thousands
enrolled in the military ranks and civilian positions of the liberation project,
adding their grievances with the prevailing order of things to the Cuban
purpose, confident that sovereign nationhood would provide remedy to the

sources of their discontent. And because they did, it would be to the nation that Cubans of color would subsequently make demands.

■■■

The plausibility of Cuban as a transcendental category of self-identity was understood early to be contingent on possession of nation, unmediated and unencumbered, sovereignty as the minimum for collective fulfillment. The liberation project developed within an all-encompassing paradigm deeply inscribed within the proposition of the sovereign nation as source of political integration and means of social unity. This implied first and foremost a deepening recognition of the need to relocate power within Cuba and reorder the purpose of power in behalf of things Cuban, but most of all the affirmation of the prerogative of Cuban in Cuba as the basis of future well-being: "Our independence is the basis of our future happiness," affirmed General Calixto García in 1878.[30] To the degree that Cubans invested selfhood into nationhood, the former could not be imagined without the latter. In late 1897, as Spain prepared to offer insurgent Cubans limited home rule, the Republic in Arms roundly repudiated any proposed settlements that did not include independence:

> We feel the need to affirm again in a loud and clear voice the firm and determined purpose that has motivated Cubans in this desperate struggle sustained against Spain. . . . Not special laws, not reforms, not autonomy—nothing that could under any circumstances and in any way continue Spanish domination of Cuba can bring an end to this conflict. Independence or death has been, is, and will be our determined and sacred precept. We have not taken up arms, or endured the ruin of our properties, or abandoned our homes, or risked our lives to settle for political measures that fail to resolve definitively the issue of independence. . . . We want absolute and immediate independence of the entire island. We wish to constitute ourselves as a free people, in an orderly manner, with prosperity and happiness. . . . Without independence Cuba will always be a site of discontent, a place of disorder, a theater of interminable convulsions. . . . We need to prevail—and we will prevail. Only with victory or through death will we leave the fields of *Cuba Libre*.[31]

Norms of nationality developed around a particular set of dispositions, a value system as a way of being, derived principally from the *independentista* purpose and proclaimed as the sum and substance of Cuban. These were complex formulations: national consciousness at once as cause and consequence of nation, even as the means used to create nation acted to shape the moral meaning of nationality. This implied a politics of national identity, of course, but it also had very much to do with the purpose for which the nation was conceived, which affected too the way that the norms of nationality formed.

By the latter half of the nineteenth century, the narrative on nationality had expanded beyond the category of simply "Cuban." The men and women who subscribed to the *independentista* project spoke of "true Cubans" (*verdaderos cubanos*), "good Cubans" (*buenos cubanos*), and "true sons of Cuba" (*verdaderos hijos de Cuba*)—as compared to those Cubans who supported Spanish colonial rule—in whatever form—variously characterized as "*espurios cubanos*," "*malos cubanos*," and "*falsos cubanos*"—those José Martí scorned as "weak Cubans" (*débiles cubanos*) and Antonio Maceo vilified as a "degenerate son of Cuba" (*degenerado hijo de Cuba*).[32] True Cubans were the men and women who by virtue of political persuasion and moral commitment had dedicated themselves to the purpose of sovereign nationhood as the means of collective self-fulfillment, and—at least as important—who subscribed to the proposition of sacrifice for *patria* as the duty of being Cuban. The expansion of the insurrection into western Cuba in 1896, Colonel Avelino Sanjenís remembered years later, "was when the true Cuban people came to believe in the cause of independence."[33] All "true Cubans," Colonel Gustavo Pérez Abreu insisted, were obliged to answer the summons of the *patria*, while Colonel Ramón Roa insisted that the "duty of every good Cuban" (*todo buen cubano*) was to the fulfillment of the sovereign nation.[34] "The cause of independence," affirms Tomás in Raimundo Cabrera's autobiographical novel, *Ideales* (1918), "is the only one that a good Cuban should have [*la única que debe tener un bueno cubano*]."[35] Poet Martina Pierra de Poo was lyrical about the need "To offer at the holy altar [of *patria*] / If necessary / The supreme sacrifice of life," adding: "And if there were a soul indifferent / To the call of his idolized *patria* / He could not be Cuban."[36] Emilia Casanova de Villaverde proclaimed that the "devotion of all true Cubans" centered on the cause of liberation.[37] José Martí alluded often to "all good Cubans" and "true Cubans of the nation."[38] Years later, Manuel Arbelo recalled enrolling in the Liberation Army, persuaded that "the time had arrived for every heartfelt-Cuban [*todo cubano de corazón*] to confront with determination all the sacrifices necessary for independence."[39] Antonio Maceo was unequivocal: "Honorable men and true patriots [*hombres honrados y verdaderos patriotas*] are those who above all other considerations love the independence of their country."[40]

The singular achievement of the *independentista* polity was to seize control of the master narrative of nation and thereupon to construct the terms through which—among other things—the "true" character of nationality—*lo cubano*—

would be measured. The standard of Cubanness was fixed in the proposition of *verdadero cubano*, one inextricably inscribed in the defense of the sovereign nation. Diego Vicente Tejera divided the island's population into "the true Cuban people," "heartfelt Cubans" (*los cubanos de corazón*), who supported the cause of independence, and "the bad Cubans" (*los malos cubanos*), those who supported Spain. It was necessary to choose sides, Tejera insisted, "to be with Cubans or with those who kill Cubans."[41]

The definition of *verdadero cubano* implied total commitment to the cause of sovereign nationhood as central to the normative content of nationality, explicitly as condition of entrée into nationality. Anything less implied disloyalty—or worse, it suggested treason. José Martí often characterized Cubans who by acts of commission or deeds of omission hindered the cause of independence as traitors to the nation.[42]

For the men and women dedicated to the *independentista* cause, proponents of anything less than sovereign nationhood—annexationists, for example, or autonomists—were suspect and indeed denounced as traitors. "All who by word or print express ideas contrary to the independence of the nation," proclaimed the Provisional Government during the Ten Years War, "will lose the right of citizenship and will be considered as traitors."[43] Cubans who supported Spanish rule, proclaimed the Republic in Arms, were deemed guilty of "treason to the *patria*."[44] The protagonist in Raimundo Cabrera's novel *Ideales* (1918) drew a stark dichotomy: "Between Spain that always oppresses us and the Cuba that rebels anew to remove its yoke, there can be no indecision: with our people to struggle and to die. Those who do not come with us will be [considered] in the future as traitors and cowards."[45] Autonomists who supported limited home rule within the Spanish colonial system "were not worthy of being called Cubans," the weekly *El Vigía* decried in 1897, "because they refuse to sacrifice, and openly and secretly serve the enemy," alluding ominously to the necessity "to cross the foreheads of these false sons [*hijos espurios*] of the *patria* with ashen marks for future action." *El Vigía* proclaimed outright: "They are traitors," men that the *Revista de Cuba Libre* similarly characterized as "a handful of traitors."[46] Autonomists were "false Cubans," insisted Fermín Valdés-Domínguez: "They are all simply traitors." The day of reckoning would come, Valdés-Domínguez vowed, for "those of us who fight for the independence of the *patria* with weapons in our hands must some day punish them for the statements they make. We would be cowards if we forgive those who in such a traitorous manner have aligned themselves with the Spanish and before our very eyes use insults and lies as weapons against us."[47]

The character of Cuban acquired specific moral attributes, all very much derived from the commitment sustained in behalf of the sovereign nation. The weekly El Cubano Libre was unequivocal about the meaning of Cuban:

> [Independentistas] are the only ones who can and should call themselves Cubans. [Autonomists] are without consciousness of their duty and throw themselves at the feet of tyrants. . . . Although sons of Cuba, they repudiate their patria, and their patria rejects them as unworthy sons. Those who kneel before tyrants to receive alms obtained from the pillage of the patria cannot be Cuban. Those who live in defeat, hiding their shame and cowardice in the shadows, do not form part of the Cuban people. Those who witness violence and pillage in silence, lacking the courage to raise their voice in protest, cannot be Cuban. That group of weak men, without faith and without hope, whose very pettiness makes them incapable of great aspirations, cannot be part of the Cuban people. The Cuban people are made up of those for whom the cry of "Patria and Liberty" kindled their dreams and who abandoned their homes and families and committed themselves to armed struggle.[48]

The mambises, insisted Raimundo Cabrera, "were the expression of the sentiment of rebellion of the country, and no one who is not blind or driven by ill-will can deny that they were the true representation of the country."[49] The independentista newspaper La República was categorical: "[The future of Cuba] will be determined only by those who are exposed to danger in the field of the insurrection, those who have shed their blood in combat after having been despoiled of what they owned, those who have sacrificed on the altar of the patria their family, their positions, and their possessions, those who by their own hand have reduced to ashes all their worldly belongings."[50] Only those engaged in the armed struggle — "those who have embraced the principle of 'Independence or Death,'" future president of Cuba Tomás Estrada Palma insisted — possessed the moral authority to speak as Cubans and to serve as "the representatives of the Cuban people, for they are the only ones who have the courage of their convictions, who endure danger and make the sacrifice of lives and interests on the altar of principles against the government of Spain," adding: "All Cubans [los hijos todos de Cuba] are situated between two extremes: either on the side of their compatriots in arms or on the side of those who kill their compatriots. . . . Simply put: who is not with me is against me."[51]

∎∎∎

The process of liberation advanced intermittently and haltingly. From a distance of more than 150 years it may appear to have progressed on a straightforward course, but it was not experienced in this fashion. Advances alternated with setbacks; defeats followed victories and were often followed by more defeats: all in all, progress so erratically registered as to have often been hardly discernible at all, decade after decade, and with prospects often in doubt and outcomes never a foregone conclusion.

Cubans undertook the nineteenth-century wars for independence with the presentiment of endless sorrow—"the history of the past insurrection has demonstrated indisputably that the war in Cuba may well be interminable," Antonio Maceo wrote in 1895.[52] They were resigned to the prospects of a vastly unequal struggle: Cubans over-matched and under-equipped, of civilians against soldiers, of *machetes* against *Mausers*, where the only advantage possessed by Cubans was the will to win and the willingness to die. "I am certain that our Independence will necessarily cost us much blood and many tears," Fermín Valdés-Domínguez confided to his diary.[53] Luis Rodríguez-Embil offered poignant musings of life within the insurgency in his novel *La insurrección* (1911): "It was composed of individuals the majority of whom had never thought of being soldiers, who had never known the meaning of constant danger, who had never experienced such hardship and suffering. And notwithstanding the rigors of this life and its dangers, had committed themselves unflinchingly with resolve to the cause. . . . Everything—jobs, home, family—everything had been abandoned heroically so as to commit themselves to sacrifice for liberty."[54]

The call to arms was a summons to sacrifice and struggle. "The revolution needs lives," exhorted essayist Ramón Céspedes Fornaris from within the ranks of the insurgent forces in 1871, "mass numbers of lives, it needs immense suffering in all forms, for the tree of liberty bears fruit only in those places where the tears of the good fertilize the soil."[55] To be Cuban—to be a *verdadero cubano*—implied unconditional devotion to the cause of the sovereign nation: to be among those "good and honorable Cubans [*buenos y honrados cubanos*]," José Calero explained, "who cherish their beloved *patria* and who are disposed to die for it gladly, with a smile on their face, with conviction and serenity."[56] The weekly *La Revolución de Cuba* commented at the close of the Ten Years War: "Without arms, without resources, without the material elements necessary to triumph, the Cuban people plunged into a cruel and bloody war . . . because much sacrifice and many lives given up as offerings are the price that freedom demands. The Cuban people have not hesitated to meet the cost."[57] Domingo Goicuría was succinct. "There is no choice but to prevail or perish," Goicuría wrote to his daughter on the eve of his execution for the act of rebellion in 1870, "and it is to this purpose that those of us with the Cuban heart [*el corazón cubano*] are committed." The destiny of the Cuban was set, Goicuría insisted: "We have come into the world to be martyrs."[58]

To be Cuban—*verdadero cubano*—implied conviction enacted as conduct, principally as dedication to duty and disposition to sacrifice, a way of being as means of becoming, proclaimed as the sum and substance of Cuban: briefly put, the way a people assemble the norms of national character. The *independentista* purpose acquired internal coherence by way of a set of beliefs and practices, shared among its proponents and transacted as an obligatory attribute of Cuban. "It is necessary to have faith and confidence in the holy ideals that enjoin us to suffer so that we may not lose heart," Fermín Valdés-Domínguez entered into his field journal on June 29, 1897, "in order not to lose patience, in order not to be frightened by a life—that in reality is not a life—that leads us to illness and perhaps death. It is necessary to be Cuban above everything else, to suffer and hope, the way we should all suffer and hope."[59] Carlos Loveira speaks through his protagonist in the partly autobiographical novel *Generales y doctores* (1920): "That's why we are Cubans. To endure all the suffering and the sacrifices necessary."[60]

The character of Cuban emerged out of the experience of a people who forged its meaning in the act of defining themselves, under specific historical circumstances, incrementally and over time, in response to the demands of their times and as a function of the requirements of their purpose. Nationality was endowed with specific attributes and attitudes, shaped within the experience of liberation as deeds and dispositions and thereafter transfigured into the terms of national self-representation. Much of the content of nationality developed as a matter of context and contingency, fashioned over the years of adversity—in part informed by the moral imperative of liberation, in part as pragmatic response to the needs of war, but mostly out of the realization that consensus of purpose and concert of action were indispensable conditions for the realization of Cuban aspirations. "We will accept nothing other than the independence of Cuba," vowed General Calixto García in 1897. "There is not a single man, however humble a soldier he may be, for whom the question of independence is negotiable, and since our cause is not the result of some improvised idea but of mature reflection, of a necessity felt for so many years [*una necesidad sentida de muchísimos años*] . . . we are disposed to prevail or perish in its behalf."[61]

Nationality developed within a value system, principally around discursive formulations conspicuous for their utility in the project of nation, out of practical need, deployed as moral strategies of mobilization, shaped into usable representational motifs, and thereupon subsumed into the larger cosmology of Cuban. For Fermín Valdés-Domínguez, it was the war of liberation itself from which the character of Cuban was to be forged and sustained: "Our war must serve as an example of virtue and principle of the new order of things that will summon into existence the stable and unifying great Republic." [62] The ways Cubans adapted to the necessity of struggle and sacrifice, decade after decade, transformed the very culture by which they were in the act of being formed. "Fortunate it is indeed," observed Diego Vicente Tejera in 1897, "that Spanish oppression—who would have believed it!—has had a salutary effect, for it has given the entire Cuban people a single soul, and as a result of the injuries suffered in common has forged a community of sentiments and ideas." [63]

Successive generations of Cubans came of age within a process of national formation, socialized in a moral system informed principally by the imperative of the sovereign nation. Historian Rafael Tarragó attributes "the cult of the recourse to violence" to José Martí, not sympathetically, to be sure, but in a manner that serves to underscore the formation of the character of Cuban:

> I suggest that we consider the effect on Cubans of those regular patriotic celebrations where Martí's words extolling physical courage and martyrdom have been read or explained, and those who disagreed with his methods have been condemned as traitors. Respect for diverse points of view cannot be developed where the population is steadily exposed to readings and speeches denigrating as inefficient the recourse of political negotiations and extolling war as necessary. It is inevitable that the population of that country will eventually consider civility to be pusillanimity. If the first hero of a nation is always quoted advocating intransigence, it is logical that the average citizen of that nation will value intransigence as a virtue. [64]

José Martí was formed by and he contributed to the normative system in which "physical courage and martyrdom" were deployed as dispositions necessary to obtain the sovereign nation. This was a value system in formation, to which Martí offered by word and deed prescriptive conduct as relevant to the imperative of nation. There was indeed something of a deepening intransigence to the Cuban purpose, a determination that developed into a celebrated attribute of the mambí ethos. It could hardly have been otherwise.

Deeds celebrated as heroic expanded fully into conduct corresponding to Cuban and from which to model behavior—and thereupon celebrated as an attribute intrinsic to nationality. This implied above all the need to inscribe into the normative structure of nationality behavioral norms in fulfillment of the independentista purpose, especially dedication to nation as an attribute of nationality, an assumption so taken for granted that it ceased to be apprehended in any way other than discharge of moral responsibility just by virtue of being Cuban. "Sacrifice for the *patria* was so commonplace," General Enrique Collazo later wrote, "that no one saw these efforts as anything extraordinary; to die for the *patria* was something so accepted by everyone that survivors saw nothing noteworthy in the deed, for it was understood that such a fate would befall everyone, sooner or later. The choice was clear: dishonor by joining the enemy or to die honorably."[65]

Decades of struggle and sacrifice registered deeply on the sensibility of a people for whom the process of liberation served as the circumstances in which the moral structure of collective selfhood developed. Cuban character, historian Ramiro Guerra y Sánchez suggested in 1921, was the product of "enduring and fervent efforts which Cubans have had the necessity to sustain [and] the suffering that they have had to endure in the course of the wars of independence." He added: "The tenacity and spirit with which the Cuban people defended their ideals during the last [nineteenth] century, with indomitable perseverance . . . engaged in the fundamental purpose of independence and liberty, have fortified and unified their character."[66] Nation was a cause to live for and, of course, to die for. But, more important, the process—of living and dying for the *patria*—was itself source of nationality and the purpose that shaped the people that Cubans became. Historian Sergio Aguirre was entirely correct in his observation that the Ten Years War was a phenomenon as much about an emerging nationality as it was "nationality consolidating into nation."[67]

For Cubans drawn to the promise of liberation, nation assumed something of sacral meaning, approached with reverence and devotion, for which the logic of sacrifice was a matter of discharge of faith corresponding to Cuban. Socialization into norms of nationality was transacted within an ethical system in which *verdaderos cubanos* were implicated by virtue of their claim to nationality. José Martí repeatedly invoked sacrifice as the central normative element of the condition of Cuban. Nationality was "a brotherhood of sacrifice," he insisted. "The *patria* needs sacrifice," Martí exhorted, understood always as the need "to rise, with nobility, at the time of sacrifice and die without fear as an offering to the *patria*." He was blunt: "A sincere patriot should sacrifice everything for Cuba."[68] Novelist Luis Rodríguez-Embil described in *La insurrección* (1911) the gathering of new recruits into the Liberation Army who looked upon the flag "as a symbol that belonged to them, and to which they had a duty imposed by they did not know who. And all, obedient to this mysterious duty raised their hands . . . to proclaim '*Viva Cuba Libre!*'"[69]

The measure of Cuban developed out of the narratives of nation, a combination of pragmatism and principle, means expressed as ends and ends exemplified as means, at one and the same time an affirmation of nationality as confirmation of nation. Cubans conferred on the cause of nation virtuous intent and honorable purpose, men and women fashioning a collective sense of nationhood within their understanding of the needs of their times, which meant too that nationality increasingly assumed the form of a moral system, an amalgam of attitudes and attributes assembled under specific historical circumstances given to the purpose of nation. Vast numbers of Cubans, over the span of three generations, came of age within a moral order forged by the circumstances of a war of liberation: planning for war, making war, recovering from war, and preparing for more war. General Carlos García Velez thought much about what he characterized as the Cuban "state of mind" during the nineteenth century, something he described as "a psychological state very similar to patriotic dementia [un estado psicológico muy semejante a demencia patriótica]," adding: "I myself experienced that admiration of those men [of 1868], and I rejected outright every argument contrary to the success of a new Revolution. Our patriotic faith rejected any possibility that we would be defeated, notwithstanding the fact that we knew we faced a superior army. . . . The independentistas persevered in the determination to realize the Ideal [of independence] against all logic, confident in their faith."[70]

Norms of nationality developed less from beliefs in abstract principles than from the lessons of lived experiences. For all who passed under its sway—and the numbers were considerable—the ideal of sovereign nationhood was the defining issue of their times. Patria was the purpose to which vast numbers of men and women dedicated their lives, what Raimundo Cabrera would recall decades later as "the supreme ideal of our youthful dreams."[71] Colonel Segundo Corvisón described himself as "obsessed by an ideal," and Ricardo Batrell Oviedo wrote of his "heart swollen with love for the sacrosanct Ideal and burning with faith for the reason of its Cause."[72] A notation in the field journal of Avelino Sanjenís reflected the sentiment prevailing among many mambises: "There is no one among us who is not disposed to continue for all eternity our struggle for independence."[73] Eduardo Rosell could only marvel at the Cuban capacity for sacrifices, confiding to his field diary: "What extraordinary power the idea of Patria has over us."[74]

These were powerful sentiments indeed, ones for which Spain was woefully unprepared. If General García Velez was only partially correct, "patriotic dementia" was an impossible collective state of mind to deal with in any way but one. "Spain has not been able to resolve the problem of Cuba except by force of arms," Spanish captain general Camilo Polavieja acknowledged in 1879, "and the guarantee of Spanish rule in the future may be possible only through the extermination of the majority of the inhabitants of the island."[75]

Cubans in the nineteenth century were a people in continual dialogue with themselves, men and women engaged in and fixed on the pursuit of sovereign nationhood, within the confines of literary societies and labor halls, at work and play, as a matter of political pronouncements, as public discourse and private correspondence, in song, verse, and poetry, texts circulated as printed matter and passed on by word of mouth.

■ ■ ■

But always—and always most important—this was a history that originated in private spaces, in the deep interior places of the intimacies of households, within conjugal relationships, between husbands and wives and parents and children, within networks of kin and across generations of family, sometimes within the context of gender conventions as they existed, at other times in adaptations of gender norms as required. Men and women found themselves in the ordinary discharge of gender-scripted designations during extraordinary times: women as mothers and primary caregivers and men as providers and protectors, in the process setting into place normative systems from which the terms of nationality took form.

The process of national formation, and specifically the circumstances under which the attributes of an emerging value system were inscribed as the normative basis of nationality, implicated men and women in distinctly gender-differentiated ways. That the commitment to nation was often enacted within the framework of received conventions of gender norms matters less than the degree to which gender functions were themselves informed by the purpose of liberation. Notions of manhood and womanhood were in a continual state of flux, changing to adapt to needs that were changing, and in the process setting in place a host of moral dispositions as attributes of Cuban.

Men and women jointly sustained the logic through which commitment to the duty of sacrifice developed as an attribute of nationality, albeit in vastly different ways. Sacrifice by men necessarily implied sacrifice by women and could not have been enacted without the disposition of women to uphold the very codes by which the determinants of duty were defined. Gendered concepts of duty situated men and women at different points along the spectrum of sacrifice, to be sure, but it is no less true that the assumptions derived from devotion to duty were themselves a shared source of solidarity.

The liberation project summoned into existence a complex system of social

Liberation Army camp, ca. 1898. Courtesy Biblioteca Nacional 'José Martí,' Havana, Cuba.

reciprocities and moral obligations, in the aggregate structured as a value system that acted to inform the meaning of nationality. Norms of manhood and
womanhood—idealized as they may have been—responded to the need to
foster those dispositions deemed indispensable for the realization of nation.
To understand the *independentista* polity as an expanding community inalter-
ably opposed to Spanish colonial rule, obliged continuously to replicate itself
as the minimum condition for success, is to appreciate the need for Cubans to
develop a cultural model of social action appropriate to the task of liberation.

The pursuit of nation drew upon an ensemble of gender-differentiated
codes of conduct, the multiple ways that Cubans arrived at an understanding
of duty demanded of them as men and as women. These were arrangements
in an ongoing state of change, always in response to circumstances of need as
experienced, that is, a process of cultural adaptation shaping the very meaning of Cuban: men and women acting not solely as agents but also conscious
of agency, aware of the purpose for which they acted, and in the process con-
ferring meaning on their acts. The realization of nation implied dedication
to values of duty and commitment to sacrifice, which were inscribed into an

all-encompassing paradigm of nationality and thereafter transmuted into the attributes by which nationality itself was gendered.

These were extraordinary times of far-reaching transitions, a time in which existing premises and practices of established gender norms adapted in the course of successive generations of Cubans to accommodate the needs of independence. The model of manhood as a standard of virtue expanded fully into a discursive construct of compelling purport: men as warriors who contemplated the prospects of death with equanimity and as a matter of a destiny foretold. Boys were conducted into realms of manhood by way of a moral system derived from idealized manly deportment, socialized into norms of a value system formed in function of liberation. The *independentista* discourse extolled ideals of sublime sacrifice, expected of all men by virtue of being male. Codes of manly conduct—"real men"—converged with norms of nationality—"real Cuban"—to celebrate qualities of valor and virility, honor and courage, but most of all the duty of sacrifice demanded of Cuban men. Masculinity in this instance was itself implicated in the cultural transformations attending formation of nation, specifically the construction of an ideal of conduct realized in the discharge of duty to nation.

Women experienced decades of war as an environment for an expanded public presence and participation. They developed new skills, discovered new self-worth, and found a new sense of freedom to participate in the creation of a new nation. The presence of women within the constituency from which norms of Cuban were in formation raised new issues about entrée into emerging nationality, about civic participation and political inclusion, about what women could plausibly expect in a Cuba for Cubans. Women were indispensable in assembling the moral order from which nationality developed. They were changed by change, by which their voices were added to the demands for change. Women entered the realms of nationality conscious of the need to participate in the process of nation, and, like men, they fully endorsed the necessity of sacrifice as a gender-determined attribute. "Women," historian Juan Remos correctly noted, "were the first and most powerful impetus to move entire families into the Revolution."[76]

Women transcended and transgressed existing gender boundaries to assume positions of leadership, in both public places and private spaces. They devoted vast amounts of creative talent to the cause of *patria*—as propagandists, poets, and essayists; as public speakers and political organizers. They proclaimed their devotion to the cause of nation—"to that beautiful Cuban flag," exults Lola in René Darbois León's two-act drama, *Un episodio de la guerra de Cuba* (1899), "the sacred symbol of our redemption, soaked and darkened with the blood of the martyrs of the Revolution."[77] The surviving correspondence, journals, and memoirs provide powerful testimony to the contribution of women to the moral environment in which the proposition of sovereign nationhood flourished and obtained validation. "The desire to serve the *patria* and contribute to its liberation is innate in me," explained Emilia Casanova de Villaverde. "Ever since I was a child . . . I vowed to myself that I would consecrate my life to that sacred and noble objective. To this day I have done little else except to work and dream of the redemption of my *patria*. . . . My love for the *patria* has always been greater than my love for anything else."[78] Years later, Rita María Suárez del Villar, a conspirator during the 1890s, reminisced about her childhood. "Knowledge of the oppression in which my beloved Cuba lived produced in me great anguish," she recalled. "This experience caused me to vow that as soon as I was old enough I would fight without rest until my beloved *Patria* became free and sovereign."[79]

The paradigm of arms-bearing men as defenders of the homeland and child-bearing women as defenders of the home drew upon dichotomies deeply embedded in the practice of received wisdom. The demands of nationality could not but implicate men in a gendered-scripted role as a matter of self-esteem and self-fulfillment: that is, what Cuban men were supposed to do by virtue of being male. But it was no less true—and no less important—that norms of nationality that propounded the ideal of male sacrifice as a function of nationality also required the collaboration of women, who were expected to bear the sacrifice of men with a resignation that was itself rendered as the duty of women. The proposition of sacrifice among men and the resignation to the sacrifice of men among women fused within a mutually reinforcing moral system and served to provide normative credibility to the commitment to necessary forms of collective conduct.

Men and women were drawn together into an accommodation to sacrifice as enactment of an ideal of Cuban, ineluctably, as indispensable for the realization of sovereign nationhood. "I am heartened by the certainty that in your strong angelic soul," Ignacio Agramonte wrote to his wife in 1872, "you bear everything with resignation, confidently awaiting a future filled with happiness that we will surely enjoy together after we complete the obligations that Cuba has imposed upon us."[80] Years later, Colonel Matías Duque would dedicate his book, *Nuestra patria* (1925), to his wife Mercedes Cortés for "having endured with sublime resignation the abandonment to which I subjected her upon incorporating myself into the revolution upon its outbreak. She faced that situation with an unparalleled patriotism, applauding and encouraging my conduct as Cuban. . . . Like other patriotic Cuban women, she held back her tears and proudly bore her *cubanismo*, and in this manner contributed to the triumph of the Republic."[81]

Women conferred moral vitality on the emerging norms of nationality by the discharge of gender-specific functions in the roles of wives and mothers. The ideal of Cuban womanhood bearing sacrifice stoically and enduring grief heroically acted to expand the consensual framework of nationality, the very process by which women contributed decisively to the formulations by which the meaning of Cuban was fashioned. Aurelia Castillo de González moved freely among separatist families and would write of the "noble mission" discharged by women during the Ten Years War, who "by virtue of their example strengthened the resolve of men, as examples of energy, abnegation, resignation, of patriotism," and who themselves contributed decisively to "preserving the sacred flame of the war of independence." She added: "Think that they swallowed their tears so as to not show weakness when their sons, fathers, brothers, husbands, and lovers were killed."[82]

The conventions of sacrifice were enacted as resigned acquiescence to the loss of men in the service of the *patria*. The ideal of wives disposed to suffer personal loss and sacrifice material well-being, to defer hopes for happiness and forgo the aspirations traditionally associated with family and home, assumed a place of prominence in the narratives of nationality. Mothers were drawn into the cause of nation with a special purpose, charged with the duty to form consciousness of Cuban as a central facet of child-rearing practices. The highest purpose to which motherhood could be given, José Martí insisted, was to instill in children love for the *patria*. Martí praised "the widowed mother who sees without tears her son depart for the wilderness in search of the grave of his father, to die to be worthy of his father, [and] provide with his body one more step toward the achievement of *patria*."[83] Indeed, this sentiment insinuated itself deeply into celebrated gender conventions of the time. Essayist Africa Fernández Iruela enjoined "mothers and sisters to encourage [sons and brothers] to support the struggle for Liberty, the way our grandparents encouraged their sons through word and deed during the glorious epoch of our Independence. It is not for nothing that we are a people among whom heroism has a throne and liberty a flag."[84] Dolores Larrúa de Quintana affirmed outright that the abiding aspiration of Cuban women was to contribute to the greater glory of the *patria*. She added: "However, Cuban women do not consider this aspiration as a duty; rather, it develops spontaneously out of her soul."[85]

The celebrated ideal of Cuban womanhood developed within the *indepen-*

dentista paradigm and readily inscribed itself as attributes by which the meaning of nationality gained currency. "I admire you, mother of mine," Consuelo Alvarez eulogized Cuban mothers, "and the superior spirit and sublime resignation with which you have endured the sad fate that has befallen you."[86] Juan Remos affirmed outright that "the pro-independence mother [la madre mambisa] was one of the most powerful defenders of the Revolution, whose support accounted for the filling of the ranks of the Liberation Army."[87] The weekly El Expedicionario in 1897 underscored the relationship between motherhood and nationhood:

> The Cuban mother, as a result of her particular way of being and feeling [por su modo particular de ser y sentir], above all other mothers, generally speaking, perhaps sacrifices herself with the greatest abnegation. . . . Look at the glorious revolution and see the Cuban mother, through her spirit and often through her material support, encouraging her sons . . . so that they are not disheartened, so that they fight until victory or death, until they redeem the enslaved patria and that they may enjoy the holy liberty that they deserve and which the despicable metropolis seeks to prevent. The Cuban mother is the soul of the revolution of Cuba, for from the time she put her sons to sleep in the cradle and later teaches them always to hate slavery and tyranny, [her sons] learn to love liberty and struggle to achieve it. Bless them![88]

Protocols of grief were assembled as attributes of Cuban womanhood as the culture of national formation adapted to accommodate the human cost incurred by the wars for independence. These were profoundly complex psychological adaptations and defy facile explanation, but that they were made cannot be doubted. Certainly the suppression of the public display of grief was vital to the morale and social solidarity of the independentista cause. But it is also true that the act of women bearing grief as exemplary carriage, in the form of pride and purpose, as a matter of public poise, served to confer powerful validation on an undertaking that Cubans knew from the outset would cost them dearly.

The model of stoic bearing, of women discharging the duty of sacrifice as affirmation of Cuban, loomed large in the nineteenth-century narratives of nationality. It suggested a standard of conduct women were enjoined to comply with and expected to conform to—what essayist Concepción Boloña (pseudonym Coralia) characterized at the end of the war as "expressions of sublime abnegation and suffering borne with heroic resignation."[89] There could be no more powerful vindication of the ideal of duty than through the conduct of wives and mothers who commemorated the death of husbands and sons as exemplary deeds in the service of *patria* and who in the anguish of their bereavement lent the moral force of their grief to consecrate the higher purpose for which sacrifice was rendered. "And our women?" asked Luis Quintero in 1875. "Could we ask for any greater abnegation?" He continued:

> Are they not rivals of the daughters of Sparta? Have they not surpassed [Spartan women] in resignation and in suffering? . . . There is no task they have not performed, no misery they have not suffered, no sorrow that has not afflicted their heart. They have lost their dear brothers, their beloved husbands, their adored sons. Their sons! We who know how much a Cuban mother loves her son can appreciate the intensity of her sorrow. And yet these women suffer their exile and their misery and their pain without the slightest complaint against the revolution, and they encourage and support the patriot who wishes to share with his brothers the horrors of war. The sons of such women cannot but know how to be free.[90]

José María Izaguirre remembered *criollas* during the Ten Years War possessing "extraordinary commitment and abnegation: from what I saw then I was fully persuaded that Cuban women are truly heroic."[91]

The process was dialectical, of course, gender conventions acting on and being acted upon, a complex ensemble of moral dispositions insinuating themselves into the meaning of nationality. The process of national formation was itself the means of the transformation of a value system shaped by the circumstances of liberation. The power of gender conventions to shape meanings of Cuban must be considered as factors of far-reaching consequences and were themselves facets of the larger cultural transformations through which an emerging moral order insinuated itself into the broad consensual norms of nationality.

Men and women together fashioned mutually reinforcing bonds by which they held each other to the task of liberation. Purpose often operated as assumptions so thoroughly understood that they need not have been apprehended at all. In ways perhaps all too imperfectly understood, the role of women in the formation in men of the will to liberation cannot be overstated. The commitment with which men dedicated themselves to the cause of Cuba was very much fashioned within the conventions of intimacies exchanged with women. It was the love and tenderness of women, reflected Francisco Gómez Toro in 1894, that "induces us to give our lives to the *Patria*."[92] Gender determinants of nationality were negotiated not as a matter of abstract formulations but within realms of complex interpersonal relationships, under circumstances of life as lived, men and women making their expectations of each other known, sustaining one another, each looking to the other for clues and cues as guide to comportment and carriage, seeking to fulfill the hopes they held of each other, and in the process forging the solidarities from which the meaning of nationality developed.[93] "I will always acknowledge your Superiority," Provisional President Carlos Manuel de Céspedes wrote to his wife from insurgent headquarters in 1871, "and accept the example you represent and the reprimands that you provide."[94] Colonel Fermín Valdés-Domínguez provided a poignant chronicle of the relationship between love of patria and love of wife. "I serve only to fulfill my duty as Cuban and to be worthy of your love," he wrote in March 1896 while on military operations, and two months later: "I have been formed by this life of [military] honor in which—for you—I serve Cuba to make myself worthy of your affection," adding, "I know you know: I serve Cuba so that I can return to you proud and at peace for having fulfilled my obligations." In August, he wrote again from the field: "Oh! You know that I would not deserve the affection of those who struggle here by my side for the honor of Cuba; that I would not deserve the honor of dying for the liberty of our patria . . . if I did not feel you within me like the light of heaven, as a source of strength and life of my life. . . . For me you are not only the woman who I adore with the passion of man: you are more. You connect me to life and make me think of virtue. You make me dignified and strong, and give me the courage to feel Cuban."[95]

To be worthy of the admiration and affection of women was indeed very much a part of the moral sustenance with which men enrolled in the armed ranks of Cuba Libre. The call to revolution was often embedded in complex gender codes, of the need to acquit oneself honorably in the eyes of men, of course, but also and especially in the eyes of women: self-respect among men was obtained by earning the respect of women. Indeed, the esteem or contempt of women was a powerful moral force. "With what profound scorn," Carlos Manuel de Céspedes exhorted in an 1870 manifesto to the Cuban people, "would a wife look upon a husband who refused to join the insurrection, would a mother view a pusillanimous son, would a girlfriend look at her fiancé. And with what pride would a woman in any of these three situations look upon a husband, a son, and lover, covered with the dust of combat and bearing the laurels of battle. . . . Every man is a soldier."[96]

The interior lives of successive generations of Cubans were shaped decisively by personal experiences within a polity organized single-mindedly around a purpose to which almost everything else was subordinated. The surviving correspondence, journals, diaries, and memoirs of men provide powerful testimony to the contribution of women to the moral environment in which the project of nation expanded into a collective undertaking. Women inserted themselves decisively into the lives of men as agents of cultural formation, which is to say, as proponents of an ethos of nation. This was a complicated process, in which a people took in and acted out the larger social meanings of their times. All through the nineteenth century, women embraced the proposition of *patria* with unabashed sentimentality and unwavering dedication. They engaged the issues of their times, inserted themselves consciously into history, and contributed powerfully to the normative foundations of nationality. Women defined the moral currency of duty and in the process forged the ethical framework in which established codes of manhood were enacted within the emerging conventions of nationhood. Consciousness of male was inscribed within consciousness of Cuban, principally by women. Historian José Abreu Cardet was entirely correct to note that women "arrived first at the sense that [Cubans] were making history."[97]

How to take the measure of the central importance of women in the formation of nation is indeed a complex matter and perhaps impossible to accomplish with any precision. It is to invite attention to the interior workings of the creole household as the source of an inchoate national history, to connect the internal lives of family relations with the historical forces of national formation. Much of the history of Cuba had its origins within the everyday intimacy of the family, as a matter of conventions of kinship and within conjugal intimacies, and especially in those child-rearing practices by which offspring were inscribed into the emerging moral premises of nationality. Children were agents of a family, bearing traditions and values, sent into the future to carry on. It may in fact be impossible to determine exactly the workings by which the idea of nation insinuated itself into the domain of the domestic, to be transmuted into facets of child-rearing practices and transmitted as sentiments by which to shape the sensibility of children coming of age under specific historical circumstances. What is certain, however, is that these attachments were produced and reproduced within extended kinship systems, and in the process they set in place the purpose around which successive generations of Cubans organized their lives. They facilitated the realization of new possibilities by the very act of imagining them.

The experience of the household of a *peninsular* father and *criolla* mother was particularly noteworthy. The evidence is anecdotal but suggestive and does indeed serve to corroborate historian Victoria de Caturla Brú's contention that Cuban mothers "constantly instilled in their children love of things of the land . . . and created an ambience of new customs that acted continually to sever the traditional ties to the Metropolis—something that the Spaniards themselves recognized by observing that they could do anything they wished in Cuba except have Spanish children."[98] Dolores María Ximeno moved freely within the Cuban middle class of the nineteenth century, always an astute observer of the conventions of household intimacy, particularly as it involved *peninsular-criolla* families. "The suffering of the *criolla madre* was beyond belief," Ximeno wrote years later, "who very much in secret and without her husband's knowledge, resisted the weight of the cruel humiliation inflicted [upon Cubans] by Spain. . . . She demanded justice, a more responsive [colonial] government, [and] equal rights." The family as constituted was overwhelmingly creole, and the home was filled with the presence of children, grandparents, aunts, and uncles—"relatives all of the *madre criolla*," remembered Ximeno.[99] The loyalties of the children of *peninsulares* especially rankled Spaniard Mariano Benítez Veguillas. "Do you think they would honor us with the decorous public conduct?" he asked rhetorically in 1897. "Wrong! Upon completing their education, paid by their fathers, those young men shame their fathers and their dignity as Spaniard. Of every 100, no doubt 98 are conspirators against Spain."[100] Correspondent Grover Flint met two aides to Cuban general José Lacret Morlot in 1896—"sons of Spanish officers of rank," he learned—which "proved the saying 'from Cuban mothers Cuban offspring.'"[101] Spanish captain general Camilo Polavieja despaired over the prevalence of "the separatist tendency," what he characterized in 1892 as "an integral and principal characteristic of the nature of nearly all the creoles of the Island of Cuba, including the children of the resident *peninsulares*."[102] George Clarke Musgrave would later write about his service with Cuban insurgent forces: "Hatred to Spain seemed to be imbibed in the air of Cuba, and Cuban-born sons of Spaniards proved invariably rebels, especially when born of Cuban mothers. 'Take a Cuban wife for a rebel son,' was a pertinent Spanish aphorism, and the revolution caused houses to be divided, son against father, the mother and daughters usually siding with the son."[103] Fermín Valdés-Domínguez wrote of Spanish colonel Angel Pérez, who planned to enroll his two Cuban-born sons in a guerrilla military unit to fight against the *mambises*, and whose *criolla* wife upon learning of her husband's plan protested, "with tears in her eyes, and told her sons that she preferred to see them dead than dressed in the uniform of a *guerrillero*."[104]

The influence of women reached deep into those psychological domains of personality development, to the very source of national consciousness and the site of formation of gender roles deemed necessary to consummate nation. Women conferred moral validation on the project of nation and, at least as important, contributed to the passion of purpose with which Cubans committed themselves to the project of nation. "No one complains of the heartache associated with the departure of loved ones to join the campaign in the west," observed General José Miró Argenter of the women in Holguín. "On the contrary, they exude pride that their men have the good fortune to participate in the conquest of Spanish-held territory in the western provinces. They share in the glory that will accrue to the invading army." Concluded Miró: "Examining these and similar deeds, themselves indications of incomparable virtue, the historian of the future will be baffled in seeking to determine upon whom to confer the greatest credit for patriotism: the man who for political ideals abandons family and treasure to risk all in the war, or the woman who remains resigned in an empty and uncertain home, a prisoner of nostalgia."[105] Demoticus Philalethes observed during mid-century travels to the island that "the patriotism of the Cuban ladies is far greater than that of their countrymen; they manifest a more intense hatred to the Spanish government, and have more courage to evince it."[106]

These sentiments were even more pronounced during the Ten Years War. "Women are responsible for the insurrection in Cuba," Spanish correspondent Antonio Pirala reported. "If they were not the first to feel rage of offended dignity, they were the first to express it. The opinion that women form is irresistible among men. They spoke with clarity and with honesty, fearlessly: to us they spoke of [Spanish] abuses and to their men they spoke of rights and duties. . . . Like the women of Rome and Sparta, they pointed their men to the battlefields and told them, 'There is your place.' . . . When women think and act in this manner, men are invincible."[107] Women contributed decisively to Cuban success, Rodolfo Bergés recalled in 1905: "They helped us make the Revolution and obtain Independence, for they harangued their sons and husbands in behalf of their beloved Cuba."[108] The *Diario Cubano* suggested that men "played a secondary role" in the insurrection, with "women as the will and men as the muscle." Spanish colonel Eusebio Sáenz y Sáenz of the Guardia Civil also took note of the role of the wives of insurgents during the Ten Years War, observing that "they surpassed their husbands in [revolutionary] ideas . . . and exercised such superiority that the husbands obeyed them blindly."[109] Cuban general Federico Cavada wrote early on in the Ten Years War:

Our women in particular deserve the praise and sympathy of all generous and sensible souls. Having taken refuge in the depths of the forests, they endure hunger, nudity, and illness. . . . They suffer, weep, and pray for the liberty of Cuba. There is much truth to the view that this is the war of the women [*es la guerra de las mujeres*]. They are the principal objective of Spanish strategy. . . . An effort was recently made in our Representative Assembly in behalf of the emancipation of women and to ratify social equality with men. In Cuba, women do not need the intervention of men in this sense. Women have known how to equal men through their heroism and abnegation. The insurgent woman [la insurrecta cubana] has liberated herself not of the tenderness and decorous attributes of her sex but against the slander that would tempt the vanity of men to characterize her as cowardly and weak.[110]

Whatever else the emerging consensus on nationality may have drawn upon for sustenance, it was profoundly sentimental, possessed of moral intensity derived unabashedly from a stock of highly charged emotional commitments. This implied the presence of a powerful metaphysics, of course, one that insinuated itself deeply into the formative elements of nationality, the way the moral order that informed the terms of Cuban was acted upon, susceptible always to the passions stirred by certainty of purpose. There was something of a redemptive imperative to the exhortation to nation, one that reached deep into a sublime sensibility. Mothers contributed powerfully to the moral purpose by which the ideal of nation inscribed itself into the consciousness of sons. "The Cuban mother taught her son about the greatness of the men who fought for their *patria*," comments the narrator in Juan Maspon Franco's autobiographical novel of the independence war, *Maldona* (1927). "Cuban women dispatched their sons, weak or strong, with these heroic words: 'Go die defending liberty.'"[111] Certainly this is what Manuel J. de Granda remembered. "Women were the most determined and the most fervent supporters of liberty for the *Patria*," he recalled in his memoirs.[112] The evidence is anecdotal, to be sure, but highly suggestive. "I have seen [Cuban] children playing with their mothers," observed Ramón Céspedes Fornaris in 1871, "jumping up and down with joy, suddenly become angry. I have inquired into the cause of this behavior and have discovered it to lie in the horror their mothers experience at the approach of a Spaniard. There is something in a mother's look of love or look of contempt that immediately changes the mood of her children."[113]

It is entirely plausible to contemplate the formative ethos of nation as the product of female sensibility. This is not to suggest that men were incapable of conveying sentiment and emotion to their children, of course, but rather to suggest that women acting within the received conventions of gender-scripted conduct were far more "authorized" to dwell in realms of sentiment and emotion, especially with sons, and indeed must be considered as one of the principal means by which males were conducted into the moral realms of nationality. This is to ponder, further, the means by which women were themselves socialized to act as agents of the nation and, conversely, the degree to which the very proposition of nation was invested in women. Gendered formulations of Cuban were assembled into highly complex moral hierarchies from which to fashion prescriptive conduct out of ascriptive codes, a process that served to implicate men and women alike in the validation of those formulations upon which the realization of sovereign nationhood depended. In no other way could the commitments that held men and women together over successive generations in the pursuit of nation have been sustained.

Few themes recur with greater frequency in the memoirs of the *mambises* than the wistful reminiscences of mothers shaping among sons consciousness of nation and inducing commitment to duty. Antonio Maceo reflected nostalgically upon the death of his mother: "It was with the tenderness of her soul . . . that she obliged us to fulfill our political duties."[114] General Enrique Loynaz del Castillo recalled years later a childhood birthday present from his mother: "On one birthday she made me a small altar to the coat of arms of Cuba for my room . . . and adorned it with small Cuban flags. She gave direction to my life."[115] General Carlos García Velez remembered years later the women who contributed to the development of his consciousness of Cuban. "I have never been able to forget," he confided to his journal late in life, "the stories [of the Ten Years War] that my grandmother recounted to us in Key West and New York every night before going to bed. . . . My deepest preoccupation ever since my childhood was the independence of Cuba. I was raised in an environment of heroic women . . . of my grandmothers, my mother, and my aunts, on both sides of the family. In exile, with them, at home listening with religious respect and intense attention to the stories of the misfortunes of the Cubans who had taken refuge in Key West and New York."[116] Colonel Horacio Ferrer similarly reflected on a childhood moment: "In the bosom of my family . . . we would often exchange impressions about the subject of liberation." He continued:

> I was five years old and was very close to my mother. . . . She began to teach us, inculcating in us love of the truth and of study and of honor. And in talking about history, she told us there was a man named Máximo Gómez, who fought for ten years [1868–78] to make Cuba independent. I also heard from her lips the very first mention of the names of Carlos Manuel de Céspedes and Ignacio Agramonte. She inculcated in us a love of the *patria*. . . . The seed of [my] love for Cuba, instilled in my spirit by my mother during my childhood, flourished during my adolescence. . . . On one occasion, my devoted mother, overcome with emotion but with total

presence of mind, concluded one of those discussions by affirming: "My sons have two mothers: the *patria* and me, and they should attend to the one that needs them the most!" On that day, for my brother and me, our fate was sealed.[117]

The process of national formation developed within the complexities of personality formation, with its origins located within the intimacies of the creole household. That family was so fully understood to exist as the domain of the "domestic"—and, per established gender conventions, as the purview of mother/wife—suggests the central role women played in the formation of consciousness of Cuban. How utterly natural it was for the women's club of Güinía de Miranda to affirm in 1869 that "the woman is the home, and the home is *patria*."[118]

Creole disaffection took hold first and foremost within the family, the central social unit of the colonial society, itself a measure of the depth and breadth to which subversive sentiment had insinuated itself into the intimate spaces of daily life. The household must be considered as the site of origins of national consciousness, where the sensibility of Cuban acquired emotional content, whereby the private interworkings of familial systems acted to inform the public purpose of political engagement. The powerful moral authority of the family, with its complex codes of kinship and gender relationships by way of established hierarchies of authority and norms of reciprocity, must be seen as the point of origins of nation.

The creole household was a highly politicized environment, a site of initiation and place of transmittal, where the idea of nation entered realms of shared values in the experience of everyday family life. "With the struggle for liberty across the full expanse of a century," observed historian Mercedes García, "the spirit of the Cuban family cohered, for there was no greater source of common purpose than shared suffering."[119] Dispositions by which the meaning of nationality developed, no less than conduct necessary to make good on the claim to national sovereignty, emerged from the most intimate spheres of creole family life, within those long-standing conventions and well-established customs.

Conventions and customs more than adequately institutionalized the practice of narrative engagement in multiple forms of family reunions: at wakes and weddings, on birthdays and baptisms, on anniversaries and holidays, on *nochebuena* (December 24) and *Reyes Magos* (January 6). Children listened to and listened in on adult conversations—and learned; they entered domains of nationality by way of established conventions of kinship, on occasions of family gatherings and reunions, the times when multiple generations of the same family engaged each other, what Flora Basulto de Montoya later recalled as those special occasions when "large numbers of family members, spanning three or four generations, would come together in each house."[120]

Children were socialized within the household even as the home was itself politicized, subject continually to changing historical circumstances. The household served as an environment in which culture and custom served as the means through which to reveal the reality of life as lived. "The Creole's hatred for the Castilians," observed one mid-nineteenth-century traveler to Cuba, "and consequently of the government to which he feels constrained to submit, is nourished from early childhood."[121] The household was the setting in which discontent and disaffection were first articulated, in the security offered in those private spaces of the home where remedies could be contemplated and redress plotted. "After dinner," Benito Aranguren Martínez remembered decades later, "papá would read to us accounts of episodes of the Ten Years War and the biographies of its leaders. His idea that Cuba, for its own well-being and prosperity, would be independent, instilled itself into our hearts [and] influenced us in a decisive manner, fostering a firm love for our flag and a desire to see it flying over the beloved land in which we were born. From the time when we were very young we began to feel the necessity to contribute . . . to the great project of obtaining Independence." And to the point: "That is how I became a soldier, a mambí, that is how I began to discharge the debt that my father instilled in me and that my stoic mother helped me realize."[122] Mambí officer Alberto de la Cruz Muñoz recalled vividly his coming of age in a creole household. "In the privacy of the household," Cruz Muñoz wrote soon after the war for independence ended, "during the silence of the evening, the events of the war [Ten Years War] were discussed, always with admiration of the valor of the liberation warriors [los guerreros mambises], whose deeds were recounted in low voices and made a deep impression on my soul, creating in my child's heart and filling my spirit with a hatred of tyranny and all its defenders."[123] Colonel Segundo Corvisón recalled a childhood listening to stories of the "fabulous war of ten years, of the heroic legends, [which] had for us—the next generation of warriors—the effect . . . of awakening a love of danger and the desire for privation and suffering at the altar of liberty."[124]

It was during those moments of intimacy and on those occasions of private conversations, in which parents and grandparents sought to explain the world to their children and grandchildren, that the meaning and measure of Cuban assumed mythical proportions as the model of being, serving as something of a currency of childhood. The larger moral imperative of nationality moved from public domains into private realms, from the outside to the inside, from general to specific, from collective to individual—and then reversed. The pursuit of nation was densely packed with moral certainty, which meant too that this same sense of moral certainty informed the narratives through which children learned their history. The memoirs and reminiscences of scores of men and women involved in the *independentista* project are filled with accounts of formative childhood experiences. "I was born in Cuba when it was ruled despotically by Spain," Manuel Sanguily wrote in 1888. "I grew up in a dense atmosphere in which one breathed only hatred of Spain and even of the Spanish people."[125] Memory passed as history, and vice versa. Knowledge of the past conveyed in family settings was the stuff of Cuban childhood memories, suggesting history received in the form of household intimacy, thereupon to assume deeply personal and emotional meanings, associated with family and remembered with sentimentality, and always loaded with point of view. Generations of men and women came to their knowledge of the meaning of Cuban by way of firsthand sources and first-person ruminations, through the lives of loved ones, a telling and retelling of history by which multiple generations bonded together in a running narrative of a nation in formation. "We came of age with the certainty of our triumph," General Carlos García Velez remembered, "a conviction nurtured from our childhood through the stories of veterans of 1868 and 1879, from our parents, from family members, and friends."[126] History was indeed one way Cuban families organized themselves into a national community. Historian Blancamar León Rosabal was correct to discern in the memoirs of the *mambises* of 1895 the influence of "the epic events of the Ten Years War . . . which were received as legends of 1868, in well-known heroic figures and at times relatives."[127]

Historical knowledge was transmitted across generations as reminiscences and recollections received from loved ones, often remembered as stories of childhood. Girls and boys bore witness to their history, and girls no less than boys were shaped within the household environment and thereupon implicated in the very value system that was shaping the meaning of Cuban. "The legend of the heroism of the ten unforgettable years of war," Fermín Valdés-Domínguez wrote in 1896, "was the lesson children learned that formed the sacred worship of the *Patria* that parents transmitted to their children in their daily conversations. These lessons are the basis of the insurrection of today."[128] Rita María Suárez del Villar recalled her household during the Ten Years War, when her "father's brothers and friends gathered in my home to conspire against the Spanish government." Years later, she recalled vividly: "I listened to their conversations about the outrages committed by the oppressor of my *patria* [and] the injustices committed against the poor patriots . . . and that experience affected me to the core of my being."[129]

Vast numbers of the *mambises* of the 1890s were shaped by the first-person stories of their history. Serafín Espinosa reached the rank of colonel during the war of 1895 and recalled a childhood listening to "the accounts of the incidents of the war of 1868, told in the intimacy of the home by my father or by my uncles who had participated in the war." These accounts made a lasting impression, Espinosa remembered, "for they lifted my spirits and, for that reason, at a very early age, the love of the land [*amor a la tierra*] and the devotion to its flag took permanent hold of my soul."[130] Manuel Piedra Martel recalled coming to "consciousness of his duty as a man and as a Cuban" during those occasions of family reunions and gatherings at which as a boy he listened to accounts of "Cuban victories and heroism, from the mouth of one or another veteran," adding: "It made a powerful impression on me and stimulated in my soul the powerful desire to imitate the combative spirit. These were the first moral factors that began to act on the development of my patriotic sentiments."[131] Angel Rosende y de Zayas attributed his decision to join the insurrection in 1895 to "the accounts of the ten-year-old conflict learned from relatives . . . who gave us an idea of what that past signified: the seed of the future."[132]

Spaniards long suspected the creole household as a place of subversion, almost always with an abiding sense of betrayal. Mariano Benítez Veguillas denounced Cuban women who raised their children with wages paid by Spanish-owned enterprises—"while the father is mixed up in the liberation hordes [*hordas libertadoras*] . . . and who repay our generosity by teaching their children, by way of play, running to and fro in their humble households, simulating the killing of Spaniards with the use of a broomstick."[133] Play was indeed a serious matter. Childhood games and play served easily enough to socialize children into the emerging normative systems of Cuban, thereupon shaping those dispositions toward behavior and conduct. Correspondent Grover Flint visited Cuban-held territory (*prefectura*) during the war for independence and observed children at play:

> The children's games were all warlike. They played Spain and Cuba with sticks for guns, and carried on skirmishes in the underbrush. Sometimes it was a game . . . where one child hid a broom horse in the thicket and another played Spaniard and scouted about with a wooden *machete* to find and kill it. The first sound the babies mastered was "*Alto, quien va? Cuba*," and "*Pah, Pah*," "*Poom, poom, poom*,"—for often sounds of shots came from

the high-road, and the infants learned to distinguish between the bark of the *Mauser* and the slow detonation of the Remington.[134]

Colonial authorities were not unaware of the depth of disaffection that had taken hold inside creole homes across the island but could respond only with a deepening sense of helpless foreboding. Spanish fiscal agent Mariano Torrente early discerned the widening estrangement between Cubans and Spaniards. "The Cubans," he wrote in 1852, "however painful it may be to confess but necessary to convey discreetly to the Government, are all with few exceptions heartfelt proponents of independence [*adictos de corazón a la independencia*], with the only difference being that some are open proponents of these sentiments while others conceal these sentiments with studied dissimulation."[135] Little had changed in six years. "However much it pains me," Spaniard Dionisio Galiano acknowledged in 1858, "the great majority—perhaps the near unanimity—of the native-born population [*los hijos del país*] look upon the continuance of Spanish rule in Cuba with displeasure and even contempt."[136] Spanish captain general Camilo Polavieja acknowledged expanding Cuban discontent with a deepening sense of urgency. "[Creoles] wage an implacable campaign against us . . . within their domestic households," Polavieja brooded in 1892, and he elaborated on another occasion:

> Here there is only passion carried to the ultimate extreme on the part of those . . . who aspire to the ideals of independence. . . . These groups thrive on a . . . hatred of us. They do not reason. Every means that contributes to emancipation from Spain appears to them to be legitimate, even moral. They wage a war without quarter against us, as much in the press as in public meetings, in private conversations within the innermost intimacies of their families. They educate their children in hatred of Spain. . . . They see themselves as enslaved by us and hate us the way that a subjugated people hate their conquerors.[137]

Spanish wartime measures were often directed explicitly against the Cuban household. Early in the Ten Years War, the Spanish army command in eastern Cuba mounted operations specifically against women. A Spanish war proclamation in April 1869 was explicit: "Women who are not in their respective farms and dwellings, or in the homes of their parents, must relocate to camps in the towns of Jiguaní and Bayamo, where they will be cared for. Those who do not voluntarily obey this proclamation will be escorted to [Jiguaní and Bayamo] by force."[138] To view Captain General Valeriano Weyler's reconcentration program in 1896–97 as a wartime measure designed only to deny the insurgency of material support of the *pacífico* population is to overlook the far more insidious intent of the Spanish purpose: to shatter the Cuban family as source of moral subsidy of the insurrection. George Clarke Musgrave interviewed Captain General Weyler in 1896 and asked about the release of *reconcentrados*, and particularly women, to which Weyler answered: "Ah, but these Cuban women have borne rebel sons and will encourage them."[139]

Horatio Rubens remembered years later the conventional wisdom during the war of 1895: "There was a saying that if a loyal Spaniard married a Cuban woman his children would be Cuban at heart, not Spanish. Thus if the Cuban breed was to be destroyed, the women, as the breeders, must be destroyed."[140] Weyler's purpose, recalled Cuban colonel Avelino Sanjenís, "was to exterminate Cuban families which, by virtue of being Cuban, could not but produce Cubans."[141] By the tens of thousands, grandparents, parents, and the wives, siblings, and children of Cubans bearing arms were purposefully singled out for internment — and extinction, in what must be viewed as an act of immense depravity. "The reconcentration arrived [in rural Havana province]," remembered María Josefa Granados years later. "The villages were abandoned. The women and children of the insurgent families [*familias mambisas*] filled the [reconcentration] settlements, where they died by the thousands of hunger and beriberi."[142] Poet Juan Jorge Sobrado remembered the reconcentration at war's end: "It made me believe that the intention was to exterminate all Cubans."[143] This belief was perhaps not too far from the truth. Recalled Spanish captain Enrique Ubieta: "I remember that the mayor of Güines presented himself before General Weyler telling him that he had more than 6,000 women and children dying of hunger in his town and that he begged him for resources with which to support them. Weyler answered him that he had effected the reconcentration precisely with the object that all might die, and the mayor went back to Güines and there in the streets of Güines I saw women and children die of hunger."[144]

∎∎∎

The history of Cuba developed fully into the history of a cause, in the form of a heroic narrative and rendered as a chronicle of sublime sacrifice and steadfast purpose. And this too was a vital facet of national formation. Contained within its discursive boundaries was the understanding of a history very much in progress, of Cubans living within the very history they were making. Most of all, it was understood all through the nineteenth century as an unfinished history, a purpose pending for which the deeds and deportment of the men and women of 1868 served all *verdaderos cubanos* as the standard of duty. Cubans took their legacy to heart, which served to infuse passion of purpose into their politics. "The new generation [of the 1890s]," observes the narrator in Gustavo Robreño's autobiographical novel, *La acera del Louvre* (1925), "did not wish to be any less valiant than the previous generation."[145] Speaking through the narrator in the novel *La insurrección* (1911), Luis Rodríguez-Embil drew upon memory to recall the telling of tales of the war: "The history of the [Ten Years] war, a war that had ended seventeen years earlier, had little by little acquired fully the dimensions and overtones of legend for everyone in the villages all over Cuba." Continues the narrator:

> The accounts of the suffering endured by the *insurrectos*, of their amazing deeds, of their endurance that seemed superhuman: a small handful of men taking on the forces of an entire nation, filled Cubans with a natural sense of pride and induced a veneration of those men who had scaled the heights of such heroism. . . . The stories of horrors of the lives of the patriots—their marches under the blistering sun, their thirst and desperate searches for water to relieve their misery, their wounds, the fatigues, the dangers, the pain. These horrors and many others, far from scaring the listeners, served in fact only to make them wish for the day in which they could too prove that they knew how to sacrifice themselves for the *patria*.[146]

Historical knowledge served as a source of socialization, the means with which to convey a value system very much inscribed in an emerging cosmology of Cuban: ideals, to be sure, but ideals by which entrée to nationality was obtained. This was history as a source of moral sustenance, at once legend and legacy, a people inspired by the very history they created. Years later, Santiago Rey would reflect on his participation in the war of 1895: "We were imbued with the patriotic enthusiasm inspired in us by the glorious legends of 1868 [and] possessed of the firm resolve of making sacrifices equal to those made by the glorious and giant figures during the Ten Years War who had so aroused our imagination and seized our soul."[147] This was history to learn, of course, but mostly it was history to learn as something to reenact, history engaged self-consciously as a lived experience: at its essence, didactic; in its premise, prescriptive. "With the continuing lessons of our history," reflected Gonzalo de Quesada only four years before the start of the third war for independence in 1895, "with the accounts of its glories, we will prepare the youth of today for their predestined mission." Quesada continued:

> We will speak to them of the men who challenged the colonial power at La Demajagua [that is, the Ten Years War]; we will speak to them of

him who died as liberator, the martyr of San Lorenzo, Carlos Manuel de Céspedes. . . . If we need virtue in those times in which it appears to be in short supply, we will remember our past. . . . To teach young Cuban men how to die, we will remember all the martyrs. . . . Honor means war. We, the youth born of 1868, those of us who render homage to the *patria*, vow never to dishonor the history written in sublime blood; we vow to resume armed struggle with the dignity and honor with which our fathers fought: we vow to struggle, alone or accompanied, to die if necessary, they way they died, to create a free *patria*.[148]

The *independentista* narratives evoked history as a continuum in which Cubans were expected to discharge their duty as a matter of legacy, to commit to continue the cause of sovereign nationhood. The Ten Years War continued the struggles of the 1850s; the Little War of 1879–80 continued the Ten Years War; the independence war of 1895 was a continuation of all previous wars. José Martí exhorted Cubans to fulfill the commitment to historic continuity, "to complete the task inaugurated by our fathers at Yara on October 10."[149] The Manifesto of Montecristi signed by José Martí and Máximo Gómez in March 1895 proclaimed the war of 1895 as a process of continuation: "The revolution of independence, initiated at Yara [that is, in 1868], has now after glorious and cruel preparation entered a new period of war."[150] History was being recorded as it was being made, principally by participants who proceeded to fuse first-person accounts with third-person narratives. Juan Arnao, a co-conspirator with Narciso López, published his *Páginas para la historia política de la Isla de Cuba* (1877). The participants in the Ten Years War who published their memoirs included Enrique Collazo, *Desde Yara hasta Zanjón, apuntaciones historicas* (1893); Ramón Roa, *A pie y descalzo, de Trinidad a Cuba, 1870–1871 (recuerdos de campaña)* (1890); and Manuel de la Cruz, *Episodios de la revolución cubana* (1890). This was history in the making. "We are passionate converts to the religion of our past," proclaimed Manuel de la Cruz in *Episodios de la revolución cubana*.[151] The *Album de 'El criollo'* (1888) published a collective biography of the principal leaders of 1868: the Cubans of "that great generation that acted to break the chains of slavery, who set their rich plantations ablaze, and who struggled for ten long and bloody years against a formidable power, and who surprised the civilized world by displaying super-human energy in one of the most horrific wars for independence. . . . Because of them the valor of the Cuban people has rapidly risen and, as a result of their bravery, Cubans have become one of the most heroic people on earth."[152]

These were momentous years, during which the pursuit of sovereign nationhood as experienced in the lifetimes of its protagonists produced legacy, and where legacy passed almost immediately as history, and vice versa, the way Cubans used history to make history. It was drawn from those deeply personal experiences of the many hundreds of thousands of men and women implicated in the project of nation. This was history as word of mouth and memory: recounted, remembered, and recorded, inherently subjective, to be sure, but itself the source from which the past reached out to shape the future. "The revolution of the Ten Years [War] in which you and I participated," pronounced Julián to a friend in Raimundo Cabrera's novel *Ideales* (1918), "is not a mere memory; it is the experience and the guarantee of the future."[153]

The Ten Years War had a decisive impact on the development of national consciousness. "The Revolution [of 1868] failed only in the sense that it did not in fact fully realize its program," observed Manuel Sanguily in 1894. "But it succeeded in infusing the entire country with its democratic spirit, its egalitarian purpose, and its restorative justice."[154] The war resulted in "the definitive creation and consolidation of Cuban nationality," historian Ramiro Guerra y Sánchez correctly noted. "A nation is in its essence a historical essence, a moral entity with a past and a future. It needs to possess a spiritual patrimony of glory and heroism, of epic and legend. There does not exist a strong people or robust nationality that does not possess it. Before 1868, Cuba in large measure lacked this patrimony, and the Ten Years War created it in magnificent fashion. After [the Pact of] Zanjón, and notwithstanding defeat, Cuba possessed a rich patriotic tradition to revere and cherish."[155] Autonomist Eliseo Giberga recognized in 1897 that the Ten Years War had contributed decisively to forging a Cuban identity. "Every insurrection," Giberga wrote, "leaves in its wake, in addition to the passions that are the natural consequences of resistance and repression, a condition favorable to the political ideal to which it was dedicated. The Ten Years War has conferred on Cuba its proper history, different from the history of Spain, which until then it did not possess."[156] This was the conclusion that historian Leví Marrero reached almost one hundred years later: "Those ten years [1868–78] forged a people, unified with an unmistakable identity from that time on."[157]

A generation of Cubans came of age formed by the memory of the experience of the Ten Years War, history to be sure, but made all the more personal and poignant by the fact that for vast numbers of Cubans this was the stuff of family lore, transformed into a purpose that passed from mothers and fathers to daughters and sons. "History is something more than a random story, without transcendental significance, without influence," insisted Manuel Sanguily in 1893. "Either it is a moral institution—History as a mirror of the past and a means of education, by way of imitation and suggestion — or it is nothing, useless, without significance."[158] It is certainly an arguable proposition that there were far greater numbers of Cubans disposed to break with Spain in 1895 than there were in 1868, and that this was itself a product of a generation coming of age within the experience of their history. "I am sorry to report," wrote Captain General Camilo Polavieja in late 1890, "that from the time of the Peace of Zanjón [1878] to now, rather than decrease, the numbers of separatists have increased."[159]

■ ■ ■

Nationality implied solidarity around attitudes and attributes conspicuous for the efficacy with which they served the cause of sovereign nationhood, not always by choice — often not even by design — but rather out of need, as a matter of moral strategies of mobilization, shaped into usable representational motifs of the cosmology of Cuban. The process spanned fully the second half of the nineteenth century and gave shape to the moral system from which norms of nationality formed and thereupon transmuted into the norm of Cuban.

The liberation project has been most commonly understood as a political process, as indeed it most assuredly was. But the process of national formation was also very much about cultural change, in which the experience of liberation acted to forge consciousness of nationality within a larger moral order. This was a revolutionary movement sustained within an evolutionary process, a cultural transformation within political transformation, gradual and uneven, to be sure, but acting inexorably to define the character of the cause of Cuba from the inside out. The proposition of nation as a historical outcome is not fully comprehensible unless it is also understood to imply an all-encompassing cultural system by which the meaning of Cuban was consolidated. The liberation experience contributed decisively to the development of a moral system central to a cumulative process through which culture formed. The emerging moral order adapted to the needs of collective effort, as a matter of a people determined to ascertain the meaning of a new nation and differentiate values of a new nationality. This was culture as the means through which normative systems were dialectically constituted and reconstituted in the process of national formation. The cause of Cuba was experienced as cultural accommodation to political aspirations, and vice versa: to "normalize" the values that informed collective purpose and — perhaps more important — render them as attributes of Cuban. "The war should serve to moralize," Colonel Fermín Valdés-Domínguez insisted, "an example of virtue and principle of the new order of things that will emerge in the stable and great Republic."[160] This was a complex process, fully spanning the second half of the nineteenth century and occurring simultaneously in the form of cognitive representations and affective responses, and indeed it must be understood as central to the ways that Cubans shaped themselves into a national community. To discern dispositions to act—or not—as a matter of historically conditioned patterns of conduct is to identify the circumstances that contributed to the development of nationality as a value system. Such dispositions were shaped within those moral-forming and action-guiding cultural realms, where a people came to know the cues and learn the codes that governed socially sanctioned behavior—and acted accordingly.

National formation implied the need to forge a new value system, one that corresponded to the purpose for which Cubans joined together as a single people. Between the expeditions of Narciso López, the uprisings of Joaquín de Agüero in Puerto Principe and José Isidoro de Armenteros in Trinidad in the early 1850s, and the end of the war for independence in 1898, three successive generations of men and women had come of age within an all-inconclusive logic of liberation. The experience served as the moral environment in which they were formed and in which they proceeded to raise their children, the purpose to which vast numbers of men and women dedicated their lives. It shaped the defining purpose into which successive generations of Cubans were socialized. To be immersed in the task of liberation as a matter of daily purpose, decade after decade, in the form of a lifelong commitment of personal involvement and political engagement, was to fashion the normative determinants from which the salient elements of nationality developed. "The movement of national liberation," historian Jorge Ibarra correctly noted, "was of such a nature and of such magnitude that its impact radically transformed the customs, the habits, the traditions, the psychology, and, in the end, the very national character of the Cuban people."[161]

The moral determinants of Cuban were configured into coherent narrative order by way of patriotic speeches heard and read, from manifestos, pronouncements, and proclamations, through the telling and retelling of heroic deeds, and through exemplary meanings assigned to heroic deeds—disseminated by word of mouth, sometimes transmitted through poems and song, often as legend and lore, sometimes as fully blown myths, all directed to one overriding end: the triumph of the Cuban purpose. That the narratives would later serve as a "historical source" should not obscure the power of their appeal in their own time, principally their capacity to fix the value system from which the meaning of nationality developed. There was no inherent conflict in assimilating myth and reconstructing historical reality, for "myth" was as essential a facet of the historical record as "truth." The result was a running narrative of a new nationality in the throes of establishing itself, a way to summon and sustain a people engaged in a process of national formation, at once binding and integrative: as source of inspiration and a way of inclusion, of bringing together the multiple elements of discontent into an expanding voluntary association around the emerging consensus of Cuban. The narrative of liberation developed a coherent vernacular of collective ideals around which to sustain Cubans of diverse social origins to act together in concert for common cause.

National formation was very much about the development of a moral system through which to expand the terms of popular inclusion: interlocking reciprocal ideals extolling the virtue of Cuban, speaking to aspirations and expectations, to be sure, but also to obligations to assume and purpose to discharge as a function of being Cuban. To be Cuban—*verdadero cubano*—implied an obligation to a set of normative imperatives, propounded within a new ethical system accessible to everyone who embraced the premise of nation. It was to confer moral purpose on the meaning of sovereign nationhood as both means and end, from which to forge canons of collective conduct and convey modes of individual comportment, celebrated as the all-inclusive cause around which the logic of Cuban formed. The process of liberation involved the development of ideals of culturally patterned modes of behavior, assembled into a more or less coherent moral system to which Cubans subscribed and from which conduct was prescribed—that is, a deepening insight informed by the awareness that the actualization of nationality could not be realized without a value system appropriate to the purpose for which the sovereign nation was conceived. Certainly this required the development of a usable political framework to sustain the means. But it required too the development of a value system through which to validate the ends. The celebration of the Cuban purpose served to consolidate the normative foundation of nationality as a cultural condition and established the premise by which the meaning of Cuban obtained plausibility. Its principal expression implied a reflexive knowledge through which to register consciousness of nation as an affinity of a like people linked together through the experiences of a shared past and aspirations for a common future.

The numbers of Cubans who extended moral support and provided material assistance to the armed cause of *Cuba Libre* cannot be ascertained with precision. Not all Cubans subscribed to or enrolled in the project of liberation, of course. However, the numbers of Cubans who did participate must be presumed to have been vast. Certainly, Spanish authorities believed so. "Creole are divided into three groups," explained Spanish captain general Camilo Polavieja in a confidential communication to Madrid in 1881. "The smallest group is openly pro-Spanish and supports everything that guarantees our control. The next group in size is made up of good people, loyal and honorable, who desire union with Spain but who, because of their ideas, goodwill, and ties of friendship and family, desire many important things that favor only the separatists, who are the third and the strongest group." Ten years later, Polavieja wrote again: "The sentiment of nationality . . . is held by the masses, led by educated men of true intelligence. . . . We cannot prevail in the face of these circumstances. One should not enter combat without at least the minimum expectation of victory. We would be engaged in a monumental self-deception not to recognize that everything favors our adversaries."[162] Traveling between Santa Clara and Bayamo during the early months of the war for independence in 1895, Captain General Arsenio Martínez Campos conveyed his "sad impression" that "all the inhabitants hate Spain."[163] In December 1895, as the expanding insurgency reached the jurisdiction of Sancti-Spíritus, Santiago Rey recorded in his field diary that virtually every male fifteen years of age and older had joined the insurrection. "Young and old," he recorded, "rich and poor, black and white, all contributed to the swelling ranks of the Liberation Army."[164] The expansion of the insurgency into Havana and Pinar del Río provinces in early 1896, wrote Autonomist Eliseo Giberga the following year—and Giberga was no friend of the independentista cause—had galvanized local support for the insurrection. "Entire towns welcomed the insurrectos," he wrote. "The towns offered their weapons as contributions. They received the insurrectos as liberators. . . . The town councils [ayuntamientos] convened official sessions to welcome the invaders. Banquets, dances, serenades, and other fiestas were organized. Thousands of men joined the insurrecto ranks. Entire towns were left with only old men, women, and children. Entire families passed over to insurrecto camps. There was no lack of women who took up arms and participated in the fierce combats." By 1897, Giberga wrote, "Few indeed are the number of families in Cuba, without distinction of social class or position, that do not have a participant in the Revolution. Even the brothers, sons, and other relatives of Spanish generals and officers . . . have enlisted in the armed ranks of the insurgency or joined the revolutionary clubs or in some other form support the separatist cause."[165] Years later, General José Lachambre, Spanish military commander in Oriente province during the 1895 war, would look back on the insurrection with lingering bewilderment. "The Government was, in fact, taken by surprise," Lachambre remembered, "and was quite unprepared to meet such a formidable revolution, and this condition was very seriously increased and intensified by the fact that almost the entire population, especially the rural population, including that of the small villages and towns, was with the insurrection."[166]

On the other hand, it is also arguable that numbers are perhaps not the real issue. What matters at least as much is the process by which national formation evolved as a matter of cultural transformation, influenced by the moral imperatives and ethical purpose by which the men and women engaged in the liberation project were themselves transformed and the development of a value system that expanded into the dominant normative framework that served as the model of the ideal of nationality. That the proposition of a discernible Cuban character was advanced within the context of narratives of nation suggests how Cubans thought about themselves, which in turn implicated them in conduct corresponding to their self-identity. Shifting value systems acted on attitudes, of course, and new ideas induced new behavior. No less important, changing attitudes also implied new ways of perceiving and evaluating the world, which necessitated the need to consider new forms of conduct: briefly put, new ways of being. Values took form and accrued over time, given purpose under specific historical circumstances, in response to experience: all in all, a necessary cultural means with which to achieve political ends. "In the final analysis," noted historian Joel James Figarola, "the revolution [for independence] was a revolution in the culture, that is to say, of mentalities."[167] Once culture became important, the nature of the behavior that was available to imitate was strongly affected by what Cubans learned from each other—as a matter of survival, of course, but also as a means of success.

Nationality evolved in the form of a value system summoned to sustain Cuban resolve through decades of struggle and setbacks and years of sacrifice and suffering, subsequently transfigured into the discursive framework of Cuban. The character of Cuban developed as an ensemble of normative structures, acted out and acted upon by the historical circumstances of national formation, to produce commonly shared dispositions and demeanors: that is, nationality as a cultural condition. National identity in this instance served as the context in which to integrate a people around the value system from which collective conduct was derived and subsequently deemed "normal": historically determined attributes emerging as pragmatic adaptation to the necessities of the Cuban purpose.

Liberation imposed demands on all who were implicated in its assumptions: to do what had to be done to prevail, at whatever cost, for however long, as discharge and display of Cuban. This was devotion to an ideal and dedication to a task that, once inscribed into the norm of nationality, served to fix the moral boundaries in which the consensus on the meaning of Cuban was formed. The process of national formation fostered social integration in function of moral purpose and contributed decisively to the very construction of Cuban, principally in the form of a value system summoned to sustain the solidarity necessary for success of the liberation project and which endured as the moral source of Cuban. It was the way by which a people arrived at a consensus among themselves on the standard by which the meaning of nationality would be enacted.

Cubans fashioned the moral environment deemed necessary to sustain collective purpose, that is, culturally patterned norms that insinuated themselves into realms of the commonplace and thereupon became an integral part of the emerging value system. It could not have been otherwise, for culture was necessarily the context in which consciousness of Cuban formed as a value system, the way a people acquire the attitudes and adopt the behaviors deemed necessary to the realization of their purpose. Perhaps the enduring significance of the liberation experience was the transformation of a political ideal into a cultural condition, as shared ideas and patterns of behavior, to shape the moral order that expanded into the character of a people. "A national culture," Frantz Fanon discerned, "is the whole body of efforts made by a people in the sphere of thought to describe, justify, and praise the action through which that people has created itself and keeps itself in existence."[168]

4 NATION IN WAITING

As a man, as a Cuban, as a patriot, I am filled with anxiety
in the face of the horrible and universal bewilderment
produced by the American intervention. It has contributed
to the dilution of the political consciousness of my nation.
The moral consciousness of the nation has dissolved almost
instantly, before my very eyes. And it appears to me in this
moment of unbearable moral anguish that the soul of
Cuba—that *our soul*—is threatened with extinction.
— Esteban Borrero Echeverría to Nicolás Heredia
   (March 25, 1900)

José Martí lived, dreamed, suffered, and died for Cuba.
Antonio Maceo, [Ignacio] Agramonte, [Francisco Vicente]
Aguilera, and [Carlos Manuel de] Céspedes died for Cuba. We
will not debate if they died for a dream or for a utopia: they
died for Cuba. And although everything has been an illusion,
it is necessary to close our eyes and continue dying for that
illusion, which is our dignity, with which we live among the
other countries in the world; and even among the most
powerful and the most arrogant countries we can maintain
our heads high and our hearts disposed to love.
— José Antonio Ramos, *Manual del perfecto fulanista:*
   Apuntes para el estudio de nuestra dinámica
   político-social (1916)

The great leaders of the liberation wars of 1868 and 1895 struggled to sever the political ties that bound us to the government of Madrid, not solely for the purpose of placing in Cuban hands the capacity to direct the national destiny but also with the goal of fundamentally renovating the bases of our collective existence and transform the manner in which all the national institutions were to function.
— *Carteles* (March 29, 1925)

Cuba possesses a unity in its tradition, and by virtue of a commonly shared destiny affirms its historical unity [*unidad histórica*]. And such unity has been intense, sufficiently strong to shape a common psychology within the population which—notwithstanding its diverse origins—allows one to speak of a "Cuban character."
— Programa de la Organización Joven Cuba (1934)

The truth of the matter is that Cuba has been waiting for a long, long time to become a nation.
— Luis A. Sanjenís (October 12, 1959)

The republic was inaugurated on May 20, 1902, an occasion celebrated on a grand scale: a national holiday, in fact, given over to acts of public ceremony and popular revelry. "The greatest day in the history of Cuba," *La Lucha* pronounced.[1] Cubans across the island surrendered themselves joyfully to public displays of euphoria and elation. Years later, Havana resident Tomás Villoch remembered May 20 as "a day with a splendid blue sky, almost as if God himself had come down to participate in the ceremony," with street dancing, strolling musicians, and everyone dressed as formally as their means allowed. "There wasn't a window, a door, a roof, a balcony, or a lamppost on a public thoroughfare without a Cuban flag."[2]

But the national mood was not unmixed. General Máximo Gómez was inconsolable. The republic had indeed arrived, Gómez brooded, but "not with the absolute independence we had dreamed about."[3] Thoughtful observers understood that something had gone terribly wrong. "I knew many people who remembered May 20 [1902]," Graciella Pogolotti reminisced years later, "and preserved in their memory a sensation of confusion, of contradictions. On one hand, they experienced—finally—the joy of seeing the raising of the Cuban flag, but, on the other hand, they were not unmindful of the fact that this was a limited independence, an independence only half achieved, that there yet remained much to do and much to realize."[4]

■■■

Much was made about the transition from colony to republic. But it was not entirely clear that the notion of transition accurately reflected the circumstances of Cuban independence. Just how much had changed and what had changed was difficult to ascertain. Some things had changed, of course, but much had not. And therein lay the problem, for much of what had not changed was precisely what Cubans had set out to change in 1895.

Cuban pretensions to national sovereignty had challenged more than the propriety of Spanish colonial rule. Cuban aspirations had also threatened the presumption of North American succession to sovereignty. For nearly one hundred years, the United States had laid claim to Cuba as a matter of vital national interest, "of the highest importance as a precautionary measure of security" and "essential to the welfare . . . of the United States," pronounced Secretary of State William Marcy at mid-century.[5] The U.S. military intervention in 1898—"the Spanish-American War"—was directed as much against

Cubans as it was against Spaniards, a means by which to neutralize the two competing claims of sovereignty and establish by force of arms a third one. The Americans did not start a war, they joined one in progress. They inserted themselves between weakened Spaniards and weary Cubans, to complete the defeat of the former and obstruct the victory of the latter, and thereupon advance claim of sovereignty over the island as a spoil of war.

The Americans took up the war and took over the peace. They were true to their proclaimed interests, if false to their professed purpose. They had arrived in the guise of allies and remained in the role of conquerors. American troops entered Cuban towns and cities as self-proclaimed liberators, to the acclaim and accolades of the local citizenry; Cuban soldiers followed, disarmed and dispersed, often arriving—if at all—at the rear of the victory procession. Serafín Espinosa y Ramos, a colonel in the Liberation Army, remembered years later the bitter-sweet end of the war for independence: "Due to the way that the war ended, the joy of the victory was doled out little by little, in small dosages. . . . On the occasion of the formal entry of the Cuban forces into Santa Clara, I did not experience the enthusiasm or exhilaration that I had long expected to occur on this occasion."[6] General Máximo Gómez confided his disappointment to a diary entry dated January 1, 1899:

> Sadly the Spanish have departed and sadly we remain, for a foreign power has replaced them. I had dreamed of peace with Spain. I had hoped to bid the valiant Spanish soldiers farewell, those with whom we had long faced on the field of battle. . . . But the Americans, with the tutelage they have imposed by force, have soured the joy of the victorious Cubans. . . . It is possible that the Americans will dissipate all sympathy here.[7]

Popular memory passed into popular culture and fashioned a parallel historical narrative. "The [Cuban] liberators entered Havana," comments the narrator in Gustavo Robreño's novel La acera del Louvre (1925), "but as individuals, dressed in civilian clothing, without arms and without any of the military attributes with which to corroborate the sublime victory obtained at such great cost."[8] Years later, novelist José Soler Puig gave voice to what many Cubans remembered, in Un mundo de cosas (1989): "It was as if the war had been between only the United States and Spain, and not one between Cuba and Spain. . . . And at the entrance to the town of Caney, the inhabitants saw the mambises arrive, entering the towns from the field of operations, dirty and tattered in rags, disarmed and without military formation. . . . It seemed impossible to believe that the mambises had gone to war to free Cuba from Spain."[9] Memory transmuted as fiction to pass as a facsimile of history.

Depiction of "enthusiastic welcome extended to the United States' troops by the inhabitants of a Cuban village" in 1898. From *Illustrated World News*, 1898.

But it was more complex still. The master narrative of a "Spanish-American War" as fashioned by the victors—and corroborated by the vanquished—served to preclude any possibility of Cuban participation in postwar arrangements. The inference was as self-evident as it was self-confirming. The Americans—and not the Cubans—had ended Spanish colonial rule, for—and not with—the Cubans: Spain had been defeated through the resolve and resources of the United States, the Americans insisted, as a result of American efforts and through American sacrifices, at the expense of American lives, and through the expenditure of American treasure. Cubans had contributed nothing.

The claims reflected more than displays of national hubris. In fact, the American claim to have unilaterally ended Spanish colonial government was the basis on which the United States advanced its authority to regulate the terms of Cuban self-government. In simple terms, the United States claimed the island as territory conquered from a vanquished Spain. Secretary of War Elihu Root was blunt: "We acquired title to Cuba by conquest."[10] The United States had defeated Spain and seized sovereignty over Spanish territories in the Caribbean and Pacific, inherent in which was the authority to determine the disposition of the newly acquired colonies. In the case of Cuba, this was registered as authority to supervise, regulate, and otherwise mediate the scope and substance of self-government the Americans would concede to the Cubans. "The United States," pronounced Root in 1901, "has . . . not merely a moral obligation arising from her destruction of Spanish sovereignty in Cuba, and the obligations of the Treaty of Paris, for the establishment of a stable and adequate government in Cuba, but it has a substantial interest in the maintenance of such a government," and to the point: "We have, by reason of expelling Spain from Cuba, become the guarantors of a stable and orderly government in the Island."[11]

For the duration of the U.S. military occupation (1899–1902), Cubans were relegated largely to the status of audience, transformed from active to passive, cast as spectators rather than participants, from agents of liberation to subjects of occupation. They were converted into supplicants in their own country: as applicants for jobs, as claimants for reparations, as mendicants for alms. Nor were Cubans oblivious to the circumstances of military occupation. "The intervention today is a dictatorship at its apogee," protested Rafael Fernández de Castro in 1899, adding: "The replacement of Spanish sovereignty on January 1 by the American military occupation did not result in a period of transition given to the preparations for a free, independent, and sovereign Cuba. Rather we have regressed to the regime of military personalism, the elimination of which was the true reason for the struggles, the sacrifices, the pains, the heroism and the martyrdom of generations of Cubans."[12] "Those who raised the first cry of liberty for Cuba," General Agustín Cebreco protested the following year, "confided in the expectation that upon their death others would continue with the work of liberation." He continued: "This task has not ended. Cuba is separated from Spanish domination, but has not been emancipated from foreign tutelage. It is necessary to die before allowing the betrayal of the vow given to the oppressed *Patria*. In order to be a good Cuban [*para ser buen cubano*], it is not sufficient to have participated in the battlefield. It is necessary to cooperate in everything that serves to obtain absolute independence. . . . Liberty should be our first religion."[13]

Independence—when it did arrive on May 20, 1902—was not without conditions. In fact, the United States did not fully relinquish its sovereignty over Cuba. The prerogative of U.S. interests in exercise of that sovereignty were embedded directly into the political structure of the new republic and served to fix the purpose to which the republic was to respond as the very logic of its creation. The exercise of North American sovereignty was institutionalized through the Platt Amendment, written into the Cuban Constitution (1901) as an appendix and subsequently ratified in treaty form as the Permanent Treaty (1903): all properly disguised as the rule of law as a means to obscure the role of force. The republic was divested of properties of national sovereignty and self-determination: Cubans were denied authority to enter into "any treaty or other compact with any foreign power or powers," deprived too of the authority to contract a public debt beyond its normal ability to repay and obliged to relinquish national territory for the establishment of a North American naval base. Cubans were required to cede to the United States "the right to intervene" for the "maintenance of a government adequate for the protection of life, property and individual liberty."[14] The military occupation would not end, the Americans warned, until Cubans incorporated the Platt Amendment into their constitution, that is, until Cubans renounced their claim to national sovereignty as a condition of self-government.

Cuban opposition to the Platt Amendment erupted into anti-American demonstrations across the island. Municipal governments, civic associations, and veterans' organizations cabled protests to Governor General Leonard Wood.[15] Newspaper editorials denounced the Platt Amendment. The amendment, protested Juan Gualberto Gómez, had rendered Cuba "a conquered country in which the conqueror, as a requirement of evacuation, imposed conditions that had to be met, otherwise it would continue to be subject to the laws of the conqueror." He continued:

And those conditions are very difficult, onerous, and humiliating: the restriction of independence and sovereignty, the [acquiescence] of the right of intervention, and the relinquishing of national territory. . . . If instead of declaring war on Spain to assist the cause of Cuban independence, the United States had declared war on Cuba itself, for whatever reason, what other conditions would the Americans have possibly imposed on Cubans, except perhaps outright annexation? . . . A people occupied militarily are asked prior to constituting their own government, prior to the removal of a foreign army from its territory, to concede to the military occupier who came as a friend and ally rights and faculties that annul the sovereignty of said people.[16]

The new republic was thus compromised at the moment of its creation: indeed, as a condition of its creation. The Platt Amendment rendered meaningless all but the most cynical definition of independence. The Americans had fixed the limits of Cuban sovereignty at the point of its origins, institutionally, and made the future of self-government contingent on the efficacy with which Cubans accommodated U.S. interests. The republic was denied at the point of its origins the capacity to defend Cuban interests as the primary purpose of its existence. "There is, of course," Governor General Leonard Wood wrote privately to President Theodore Roosevelt toward the end of the military occupation, "little or no independence left in Cuba under the Platt Amendment. It is quite apparent that she is absolutely in our hands."[17] The republic was organized as an extension of the North American national system, designed to accommodate American interests as the principal purpose of its existence. "Although technically a foreign country," Elihu Root acknowledged years later, "practically and morally . . . we have required [Cuba] to become a part of our political and military system, and to form part of our lines of exterior defense."[18]

■ ■ ■

Cubans had obtained independence without sovereignty, self-government without self-determination. Something had gone terribly wrong. For half a century, successive generations of Cubans had dedicated themselves single-mindedly to the pursuit of sovereign nationhood, to expand the scope of political participation and enlarge the terms of social inclusion, an effort committed to the cause of national sovereignty as means to remedy the sources of Cuban discontent and attend to the needs of the men and women who had sacrificed to make the republic a reality.

¡En paz descanse!

Tras medio siglo de incesante lucha,
cuando alcanzar creyó la ansiada meta,
ve frustrados sus puros ideales
nuestro pueblo infeliz.—¡Triste contempla
el sepulcro do yace para siempre,

víctima de traiciones y torpezas,
la dignidad de Cuba soberana,
sin la cual es falaz la independencia!
¡Ya que no pudo defenderla viva,
él se conforma con llorarla muerta!

Rest in Peace: "Here lies the sovereignty of Cuba, gift of Mr. Platt and his accomplices."
From *El Mundo*, June 6, 1901.

The outcome of their efforts did not live up to the hopes of their expectations. The republic as constituted could not discharge the tasks for which it had been imagined or meet the needs of the people in whose name it was constituted. The sources of Cuban discontent in the nineteenth century continued largely unabated into the twentieth century, the only difference being that the United States had replaced Spain as defender of the prevailing order of things. "The Platt Amendment," historian Enrique Gay-Calbó wrote in 1934, "subverted the *independentista* plans, dampened enthusiasm, disrupted and debased the political system, gave rise to the bane of interventionism, and encouraged incapacity."[19] "A humiliation," proclaims Fernanda in Ofelia Rodríguez

GALLO TAPADO

EL PUEBLO CUBANO.—Pero amigo D. Guillermo, ¿qué quiere usted que haga con ese gallo después de mutilado tan cruelmente por su *compae* Platt?

The deplumed rooster. Depicting Senator Orville Platt and President William McKinley offering the rooster (that is, independence) to the Cuban people, who respond: "But friend William, what do you want me to do with that rooster after having been so cruelly mutilated by you and your buddy Platt?" From *El Mundo*, April 13, 1901.

Acosta's novel *Sonata interrumpida* (1943), "without whose forced acceptance the transfer of power to Cuban hands in 1902 has not been realized."[20]

Cuban disillusionment verged on despair. The United States, disheartened *mambí* colonel Manuel Piedra Martel was persuaded, "whose only claim to authority in Cuba was force," had defrauded the Cuban people of their sovereignty: "The source of our sovereignty continues to be foreign. The American government considered the Cuban government subordinate to its interests, and the Republic was a simple juridical fiction without a real existence."[21] Manuel Arbelo was in despair. "That after the immense sacrifice of life and treasure," he brooded, "of indescribable moral and physical suffering, sustained with extraordinary heroism and sublime resignation at the altar of liberty and independence of Cuba, a foreign power, ignorant of the rights which

¡¡El verraco está en la yuca!!

Depiction of the United States as a boar devouring Cuban independence. From *El Mundo*, April 21, 1901.

we claimed to our *patria*, denied us all the principles of justice with which we protested Spanish rule. . . . We felt despised and treated as pariahs."[22] The aging *mambí* in Marcelo Salinas's novel *Un aprendiz de revolucionario* (1937) reflects: "Every day I become more disillusioned: in the War we were told one thing only to experience something else. The Republic is the same or worse than the government of Spain"—at which point the narrator comments: "It was the pained grievances of the soldiers of the revolution of liberation, of those who went to war against Spain out of the desire for an era of justice and liberty, and who saw their ideals defrauded the day the republic was established."[23]

Vast numbers of Cubans had emerged from the war in various conditions of indigence and impoverishment. They had sacrificed property and possessions

El Nuevo Prometeo

¡Burlando las promesas, los halagos;
Ante los manes de Martí y Maceo,
El buitre "redentor" produce estragos
En la entraña del Nuevo Prometeo......!

The Cuban people as Prometheus betrayed by the United States, with José Martí and Antonio Maceo looking on. From *El Mundo*, May 28, 1901.

in the hope that, in the end, in a nation of their own — in a Cuba for Cubans — conditions of daily life would be better than before. Collective purpose had formed around the promise of nation as means to enable Cubans to recover their losses, reoccupy their homes, and return to their livelihoods: to resume their former lives under improved circumstances, always with the expectation of a future with better things to come. They had endured wars of ruinous proportions, in whose behalf they had willfully laid waste to the land and willingly impoverished themselves. "The majority of the Cuban people," wrote General Enrique Collazo in 1905, "have dreamed — and still dream — of absolute independence, in pursuit of which they have sacrificed everything: their wealth, their well-being and entire generations of their children. To achieve independence, Cubans have not hesitated in sacrificing life and family." [24]

Tens of thousands of impoverished Cubans wandered aimlessly about the island asking, "What have we gained by this war?" [25] Men and women all across the island took stock of the meager results their sacrifice had wrought. They gave more to free Cuba than they expected to receive from free Cuba — and they received less. They had won, but they had lost everything in the process. Nothing could have prepared them for the impoverishment that their success had produced. As Cubans surveyed the result of their efforts, not a few contemplated a cruel denouement indeed: perhaps they had created a future in which there was no place for them. "Where do I start?" a soldier ruminates in Salvador Quesada Torres's partly autobiographical short story "El silencio" (1923). "I have suffered much, a great deal, so much that were I to describe my suffering in detail it would result in a sorrowful book. . . . It is the story of humble men like us who liberated Cuba and today have nothing to eat. In my own land . . . I find myself without protection or assistance."[26] These were the circumstances in which General Alejandro Rodríguez found himself at war's end. "You know," he confided to a friend in 1899, "that abandoning my interests and family, I was among the first to reach for arms and support the revolution." He added: "I who have served my country, for which I have sacrificed everything, cannot even have my family at my side for a lack of means to support it. I cannot embark on any business or reconstruct my farm due to a lack of funds. I see myself perhaps forced to emigrate in search of bread in a strange land."[27]

The war had shattered the world as known by most Cubans. Many returned to peace in worse condition than when they began the war. Ramón Roa "had struggled and suffered without ever allowing my spirit to falter," he reminisced years later, to return home to Sagua la Grande "only to understand that I had gone to war to lose everything."[28] The fortunate few returned to doing what they were doing before the war, grateful to be doing something but more than slightly bewildered by how little seemed to have changed. Esteban Montejo returned to Cruces after the war "without a penny in my pocket," he recalled years later, and "began to work in the San Agustín Maguaraya sugar mill. To work at the same old job. Everything seemed like I was back in the past all over again."[29] Mambises in vast numbers fell upon hard times, cast aside in the republic they had sacrificed to create. "With painful frequency," lamented Santiago Rey in 1931, "on the public paseos and the principal streets, one is aware of the painful presence of a founder of the nation [fundador de la patria]." He added: "An old invalid black man, with medals of the war for independence pinned to his chest, peddling lottery tickets or selling boxes of matches, an indirect means to defend his dignity, and imploring generosity from those he liberated. Blacks and whites, old men, filled with memories and pain, thus negotiate daily their very subsistence."[30] Years later, mambí Feliciano González would look back on the republic and lament: "I did not ever think that things would be so bad. I had figured the republic would be a great thing for us. But it turned out differently."[31]

Cubans of African descent had welcomed the end of Spanish rule with high expectations. Martín Morúa Delgado celebrated the Cuban purpose as a triumph for all Cubans, black and white, for "the democratic spirit that had reigned in the insurgent camps has taken hold, and nothing and no one will be capable of reversing that spirit of equality and justice that informed the program of Montecristi and which was ratified in the fundamental objective of the Revolution."[32] The participation of Cubans of color had been decisive to the success of the liberation project. They had emerged from the war with standing and status, many with military rank and political position, with authority and prestige acquired by way of heroic comportment during decades of armed conflict, all of which seemed to suggest a favorable future indeed for the much-promised raceless nation. Historian Alejandro de la Fuente was entirely correct to note that "Afro-Cubans had emerged from the war with a public presence and prestige they did not enjoy before the struggle began."[33] For the vast numbers of men and women of color who had enrolled in the *independentista* ranks, sovereign nationhood held the promise of dignity and respect, racial equality and political participation. Cubans of African descent had suffered and sacrificed on behalf of independence in the belief of the promise of the sovereign nation.

In fact, the end of Spanish colonial rule brought little relief to the condition of vast numbers of Cubans of color. During the years of the U.S. military occupation and into the early republic, Cubans of color, including many of the most prominent leaders of liberation, were cast aside and passed over. *Mambí* Ricardo Batrell Oviedo returned to Matanzas and bore witness to the systematic discrimination against blacks: "The war ended, and the Spanish dominion over Cuba came to an end. It was with sadness that I saw the rise of the practice of intrigue and injustice in the province of Matanzas, where the war against Spain was sustained by men of color. No sooner than the armistice was proclaimed that the few white officers who passed the war without fighting began to emerge from their hiding places. Positions that properly corresponded to us, those of us who had fought without respite during the war, were distributed to those cowards [*majases*] who avoided engaging the enemy in the field of battle."[34]

Cubans of color realized early on that something had gone terribly wrong. "Unfortunate indeed would be the fate of black Cubans," protested essayist Rafael Serra as early as 1901, "if the only thing to which they are allowed to aspire to as just remuneration for their sacrifices for the independence and liberty of Cuba is hearing the National Anthem and receiving the false adoration dedicated to our illustrious martyrs." Serra continued:

Blacks were told to suffer a little more, for discord among Cubans would imperil the success of the redemptive [liberation] project from which we all would benefit equally. The black Cuban agreed. The war began. Blacks had to endure injustice in the émigré communities abroad and on the fields of combat in Cuba. . . . The war ended. Spaniards and Cubans embraced. The people of Montoro [that is, the Autonomists] kissed and made up with the people of Martí [that is, the independentistas], and blacks remained in virtually the same condition as they were under Spain. But still they were told: suffer a little more for now, because what is presently happening is the fault of the Yankees, and any conflict among Cubans would imperil the redemptive project from which we all would benefit equally. We should all join together as one people so that these Yankee lynchers depart and leave us alone. But tomorrow the interveners will leave, and we know the lesson: the tyranny will continue. Suffer a little more for now because whatever conflict among Cubans could imperil the redemptive project from which with *the passage of time* . . . we will all benefit equally. If we are not united, the Yankee lynchers will return to this land to intervene in our affairs, where there is some tyranny, but—we are all Cubans.[35]

The meager distribution of public positions and political appointments among Cubans of color early on bode ill. In 1902, a committee headed by General Generoso Campos Marquetti and representing Veteranos y Sociedades de la Raza de Color met with newly inaugurated president Tomás Estrada Palma to protest the shabby treatment of blacks in the new administration. The small number of blacks and mulattos in the Rural Guard and police, Campos Marquetti insisted, as well as the systematic discrimination against Cubans of color in the civil departments of the government, was an affront "toward a race that had valiantly spilled its blood in defense of the Cuban cause." Campos Marquetti concluded: "The truth is, Mr. President, this is not what we expected from the Revolution, and things cannot continue like this."[36]

Little changed in the years that followed. "The revolution for independence brought to Cuba a civilization that made us a better people," *mambí* colonel Miguel Balanzó wrote on the eve of the rebellion organized by the Partido Independiente de Color in 1912:

But I doubt that all Cubans would consider themselves happy. I hear all around me voices that speak of the humiliations experienced among those who are descendants of those unhappy blacks who were driven by the whip of white men. . . . Have we forgotten that all were redeemed by the tears of

Cuban women and the blood of the martyrs and heroes of our wars for independence? All of these poor souls are the sons of the same *patria*. . . . They too deserve the right to receive the best collective treatment and enjoy the felicity that the clarion announced to the civilized world on May 20, 1902, with the establishment in Cuba of an independent Republic.[37]

■ ■ ■

The promise of nation had implied a change of relationships, among Cubans themselves, of course, but especially between Cubans and their government, with the presumption of the prerogative of Cuban as a condition of sovereign nationhood. "Why so much struggle?" Fernando Ortiz asked rhetorically. "Why so much blood spilled?" He continued: "Was it only for a coat of arms and a flag? No. Our bloody national effort was not a mere desire for independence, only to continue, in our own country and without foreign control, the same values of daily life that had been imposed upon us by oppressive norms. Our war was for independence, but it was also in its essence a separatist project. A war of separation from the past, separation from the colony, separation from despotism."[38]

The proposition of sovereign nationhood had seized hold of the Cuban imagination as a way to a better future, not as an abstract idea but as a means to actualize the promise of "with all, and for the good of all." It was about an egalitarian purpose that evoked expectations of common good, social justice, and collective well-being, conditions the republic was charged to bring into being. "The revolution [for independence]," José González Lanuza explained to Governor General John Brooke in 1899, "fought Spain in order to overthrow the entire past; its men went to war in order not merely to secure a flag for our soil, but to see that they became masters of their own land."[39]

The promise of nation had summoned Cubans to dramatic action with the expectation of dramatic change. They had imagined a sovereign nation dedicated to the betterment of life for all Cubans, to the defense of Cuban interests, as the principal purpose for its existence. National sovereignty implied self-determination—the capacity for agency—consecrated in the ideal of nation as a source of security, certainly from external adversary but also from internal adversity. Three generations of Cubans had dedicated themselves to the project of liberation, affirmed Ramón Alfonso, "not merely to change flags but to create a more perfect society on the remains of the defunct colony."[40] Cubans had entered into a covenant, as they had understood the terms of their commitment, a moral contract in which they had devoted themselves to bringing into being a republic dedicated to the defense of their interests. "The

Republic," observes the narrator in Arturo Montori's autobiographical novel *El tormento de vivir* (1923), "affectionate and paternal, was obliged to care for its children, the Cubans, who had suffered so much to create it." And more:

> Especially the poor, the émigré workers who took bread from the mouths of their loved ones to raise money for the Revolution, the peasants who abandoned their families to all sorts of horrors and misery to join the insurgent ranks, and all . . . who endured humiliation and were prepared to take whatever risk was required for the cause of liberty. They would now be, surely, the pampered children, the favored ones of the new situation, in which their needs would be met with affectionate solicitude, against the abuses of the strong, merchants, bourgeois, planters, owners of enterprises, all the new owners of the wealth, mostly foreigners.[41]

Norms of nationality had developed within the lived experience of national formation under specific historical circumstances, a process very much inscribed in the promise of nation as a means of individual well-being and a way to collective advancement, around which all were expected to subordinate coexisting—and competing—identities to the all-encompassing paradigm of Cuban. It is from the distance of more than 150 years that the influence of the nineteenth-century process of liberation reveals its impact on national sensibilities. The experience reached deeply into the moral order from which Cubans came to a recognition of themselves as a single people, of what they could reasonably expect of each other by virtue of being Cuban.

The nineteenth-century process of liberation had acted decisively to shape the moral framework of nationality, as an experience and as an expectation: as an experience, it provided Cubans with celebratory narratives of heroes and heroic deeds, a testimonial of a people joined together for noble purpose; as an expectation, it fixed the promise of national sovereignty as means of shared fulfillment. The project of nation forged the values around which the attributes of nationality were assembled, as ideals, to be sure, but as ideals so central to the terms of self-representation as to make them the standard by which the character of Cuban would thereafter be measured. The expectation endured as a purpose to pursue—that is, a promise to fulfill, and this too developed into a facet of the character of Cuban. The "heroic gesture" of independence, historian Antonio Iraizoz wrote in 1939, was expected to produce "a change in mentality, in disposition, in spirit: in short, to fulfill the desires and legitimate hopes of those rebels and dreamers [*rebeldes y soñadores*] who sacrificed themselves for the good of Cuba. . . . It was to produce new conditions and new commitments to which the Republic would be dedicated."[42]

All of which served to set the shortcomings of the republic in stark relief. Simply put, the purpose for which the republic was organized was incompatible with the ideals by which nationality had been shaped. The normative determinants of Cuban had formed around the proposition of nation as a means to mediate inequity and ameliorate injustice, to remedy the sources of Cuban discontent and redress Cuban grievances. "No one can think," wrote newspaper publisher Carlos de Velasco in 1924, "that the men and women who initiated the Cuban Revolution believed that achieving political separation from Spain would signal the fulfillment of the *independentista* ideal. No. They possessed a higher concept of their purpose and their people; they wished to transform the country in every way: in the political, the moral, and the social. . . . The revolutionary ideal has not been realized."[43] The commitment to sovereign nationhood developed as a devotion to faith, a belief in the promise of nation as the source of the common good. Historian Ramiro Guerra y Sánchez understood the promise of *patria* as the basis of a "moral community," dedicated—he wrote in 1921—to the creation of "the essential conditions for collective well-being," obliged to "create the quality of life for national well-being," including "health care, without which life is toil and torment; security for life, property, and honor; public recreational facilities; education; public transportation; charitable organizations to aid and protect children, the elderly, the ill, and the needy."[44]

The idea of nation had been imagined as something to believe in, to belong to Cubans, to do the things Cubans believed needed to be done: the nation as something to revere as an act of faith. Cubans had long ascribed sacral properties to the ideal of nation: indeed, a purpose of redemption as means of deliverance. *Patria* was rendered variously as altar, as hallowed ground— "the *patria* is sacred," proclaimed Martí.[45] It was site of worship and source of grace, at once transformative and transcendent. "Everything should be sacrificed at the altar of the *patria*," enjoined novelist Anselmo Suárez y Romero.[46] Carlos Manuel de Céspedes alluded to "the holy war of our independence" (*la santa guerra de nuestra independencia*).[47] Emilia Casanova de Villaverde paid homage to Cubans who were "disposed to sacrifice themselves on the altar of the *patria*."[48] Salvador Cisneros Betancourt enjoined all Cubans "to join us and sing together with us the hymn of redemption that we raise in fervent veneration at the sacrosanct altar of the Patria."[49] And Antonio Maceo celebrated "our national sovereignty" as the "holy ideal of the independence of Cuba" (*el ideal santo de la independencia de Cuba*).[50]

Nationality implied integration into community on the basis of well-being and security, as source of status and dignity, to draw Cubans together into shared normative systems, an ethic from which shared moral purpose was derived. In a society where status was often the prerogative of property, nationality offered the possibility of self-respect and pride, available to all, openly and equally. These were the terms by which national identity assumed form, as ideals, to be sure, but as ideals so central to the terms of self-representation as to make them the standard by which the character of Cuban was enacted.

▪ ▪ ▪

History had not turned out the way it was supposed to. Achievements fell short of aspirations. The expectations that had sustained Cuban hopes yielded to disappointment and disillusionment, then to demoralization and eventually cynicism. The promise of nation persisted as a hope unrealized, for the historic sources of Cuban discontent continued unremedied. Years later, a disheartened Manuel Piedra reflected on the outcome of Cuban efforts and could only wonder what might have been if Cubans had obtained independence "without a foreign intervention, and been spared four years of a foreign military occupation and many years of national subordination, which resulted in deforming the natural process of the Revolution and the deflecting of the course of aspirations to which we committed ourselves to the battlefield."[51] The protagonist protests in Antonio Penichet's novel ¡Alma rebelde! (1921): "This is what the republic was for? This is why so many innocent people perished?"[52] Julio Antonio Mella was severe in his judgment: "The Revolution for Independence has been a farce."[53] Loló de la Torriente lived through the years of the early republic and recalled vividly the disillusionment that had seized hold of the popular mood. "Everyday discontent increased . . . in the face of the thwarting of the ideals of Martí," she remembered. "There was no doubt among the Cuban insurrectos that 'something' remained unattained."[54]

The realization that "something" had remained unaccomplished did not reveal itself in a single dramatic moment, but slowly, over time and in turns, each new revelation adding to the frustration attending the unrealized sovereign nation. Cubans seemed to have been overtaken by forces they could neither control nor comprehend, unable even to render the sequence of events into coherent narrative order. Many did not know what had happened, or how it had happened, or why.

The passage of time served to reveal how little influence Cubans exerted over the government constituted in their name. The end of the U.S. military occupation in May 1902 was followed by more U.S. armed interventions, in 1906 and 1917, to end Cuban protests of electoral fraud, and in 1912, to aid in the suppression of the uprising organized by the Partido Independiente de

Color to protest the persistence of racial injustice. The Americans intervened continually in the conduct of Cuban internal affairs. It seemed to have no end; it was a self-perpetuating process. More intervention required more intervention. Anything that seemed to impinge on American interests—which soon came to include almost everything—was the object of U.S. concern—and was acted upon. "And then there were the Americans," as novelist José Soler Puig speaks through his protagonist in *Bertillón 160* (1960). "It was impossible to sustain a good government in Cuba. Good government meant one that would address the eternal problems of Cuba: unemployment, peasants without land, public service monopolies, monoculture, the sugar mills."[55]

Between the early 1900s and the late 1950s, a succession of American diplomats arrived in Havana to exercise breathtaking authority over the management of the internal affairs of the republic, including Frank Steinhart, William E. Gonzales, Boas Long, Enoch Crowder, Harry Guggenheim, Sumner Welles, Jefferson Caffery, Arthur Gardner, and Earl E. T. Smith, among others. The Cuban government, observed the British minister in Havana in 1910, "though nominally independent, is so fully aware of its subordination to the will of the United States that it never ventures to take any step of importance which might displease Washington, and in most cases consults and acts upon the advice it receives from the United States."[56] It was left to former president Gerardo Machado to offer insight into the workings of North American hegemony. "The specter of intervention was of such potency," Machado observed, "that no one ever dared to oppose it. It was believed . . . that the act of rejecting an unjustifiable [U.S.] supervision could bring to Havana harbor warships and marines from the United States."[57] Former U.S. ambassador Earl E. T. Smith acknowledged as much in 1960, if in slightly different terms: "The United States, until the advent of Castro, was so overwhelmingly influential in Cuba that . . . the American Ambassador was the second most important man in Cuba; sometimes even more important than the President."[58]

Cuban political leaders and officeholders brought further discredit to the republic. That political office lacked substantive public purpose fixed the function of politics principally as a medium of exchange among power contenders, a source of sinecures and a system of spoils, a means of personal aggrandizement and individual enrichment. "Here politics means personal gain," planter Manuel Rionda observed tersely in 1909.[59]

All through the first half of the twentieth century, a succession of presidential administrations, with hordes of hangers-on in tow, proceeded to lay siege to the public treasury and lay waste to public trust. A total of twenty different parties competed for political office in the republic, and, with few exceptions, nothing distinguished one from the other except personalities. "In Cuba," attorney José Antonio González Lanuza pronounced wryly, "nothing more closely resembles a liberal than a conservative, and vice versa."[60]

Corruption seemed to have no limits, and political malfeasance appeared to have no end—all through the administrations of Tomás Estrada Palma (1902–6), José Miguel Gómez (1909–12), Mario Menocal (1912–20), and Alfredo Zayas (1920–24), the dictatorship of Gerardo Machado (1925–33), the extralegal military rule under Fulgencio Batista (1934–40), the sordid years of Auténtico administrations (1945–52), and dictatorship under Batista (1952–58). Corruption acquired structural form, as far reaching as it was widely practiced; bribery, graft, and embezzlement developed into the principal means by which to conduct the affairs of state: "Politics as an endless filth [un asco perpetuo]," poet Agustín Acosta remarked in 1924.[61]

A yawning moral void settled over the civic realms of the republic. A reading of the national press during the 1920s provides a dismal view of the state of the republic. Smuggling was rampant in the customhouses and among port police officials. Allegations of graft in the post office had become commonplace. The Department of Treasury was rocked by recurring scandals, including the disappearance of retirement pensions, misappropriation of tax revenues, and padded payrolls. Graft and corruption were especially rampant in the Department of Public Works, where kickbacks and rake-offs were the normal methods of doing business. So were bidding irregularities, misappropriation of funds, and cost overruns. Vast expanses of state-own land passed illegally from the public patrimony to private possession.

These were years of political malfeasance transacted in full public view with utter impunity—and immunity: ballot stuffing, vote rigging, and electoral violence, endlessly, it seemed. Scandal after scandal and no readily available remedy, what Francisco José Moreno remembered as "the barracks-rabble, old cronies, and reprobate politicians [who] grabbed public offices and sinecures with equal contempt for both form and substances of public decorum."[62] With few notable exceptions, Cuban political leaders were successful at little more than self-aggrandizement. Politics in the republic was sordid stuff, corrupt and corrupting: all in all, a pervasive condition of moral squalor. Cynicism developed into the currency of conventional wisdom and took hold as received knowledge, with politics commonly reviled and widely vilified. U.S. ambassador Spruille Braden was aghast at "the widespread and shameless corruption existing in all walks of life, but permeating the Government from top to bottom." Warned Braden in 1945: "The persistence and further growth of the unbelievable corruption is sapping the moral and physical strength of the nation and [there will] eventually be an explosion by the Cuban people into revolution and possible chaos. This development would necessarily create disagreeable and difficult consequences for us."[63]

This is not to argue, of course, that had the United States not denied the republic the capacity to exercise national sovereignty Cubans would have discharged the functions of public office with moral probity and ethical virtue. These are obviously matters of unknown outcomes. It is to suggest, however, that without the capacity for national sovereignty, Cubans lacked the means of self-determination, and without the capacity to exercise collective agency, whether as a matter of persuasion or a circumstance of power, Cubans lacked the means to hold public officials to the task of advancing national well-being as the principal function of political power. Which was the point: in fact, the republic was structured principally to meet American interests, not Cuban ones. On those occasions in which Cubans bestirred themselves to protest political fraud and electoral violence—as in 1906 and 1917, for example—the United States intervened in support of the status quo. Fernando Ortiz understood the forces at work in the early republic and commented in 1932:

> We Cubans are aware of our own serious responsibilities resulting from the acts of successive corrupt governments, but there is one great extenuating fact, namely, that every time the people of Cuba . . . have attempted to eradicate the abuses of a despotic government by resorting to the only available means, the efforts to restore justice and freedom have been frustrated by the diplomatic policy in Washington. . . . American diplomacy has supported the culpable government and has prevented the Cubans from restoring a government in accordance with their laws and civilization.[64]

For Cubans to overturn the norm of malfeasance that had seized hold of the public life of the republic and, further, to force local power holders to defend Cuban interests as the principal function of government would have inevitably challenged the primacy of North American interests, that is, the purpose for which the Americans had designed the republic in the first place. Cubans had very limited means with which to seek remedy of the sources of their discontent, for, most assuredly, to challenge the regimen of the republic as a means to advance nation also implied a challenge to a political system in which the primacy of foreign interests had been institutionalized.

The republic could neither serve Cuban needs nor represent Cuban interests. It was overtaken by an utterly circular logic: without power to govern on behalf of national interests, government lacked the capacity to advance the well-being of the people in whose name it was presumed to have been constituted, and inevitably to forfeit the credibility necessary to maintain the legitimacy of government. "Cubans have always been in fact a people debarred from self-determination," literary critic Jorge Mañach wrote in 1933. "The Cubans have not been able to shape their destiny according to their own will, because that will has been lain in semi-subjection." The Platt Amendment had "resulted in crushing the Cuban sentiment of self-determination, when it imposed expressed limits on the exercise of collective will"[65]—what historian Luis Aguilar would call this a "deep wound" (herida honda).[66]

The republic developed into a source of embarrassment, in disrepute and out of favor, incapable of inspiring popular confidence, unable to command political credibility. Cubans lost control of the means with which to define themselves, on their own terms, in their own forms, and were still unable to affect the forces that governed their lives. Disappointment begot disillusionment. "We are not independent," despaired poet José Manuel Poveda. "We are nothing more than a colonial factory, obliged to work, and offer its harvest and crop, forced by the whip. We are disorganized and debased, like a bad entourage: we cannot defend ourselves. A gust of dispersion [un soplo de dispersión] has swept away conscience, and [with it] everything that there was of dignity, purity, and valor. . . . We are a shadow of a people, the dream of a democracy, the longing for liberty. We do not exist."[67] The aging mambí general Carlos García Velez was despondent. "I will die with the regret of not having done more for the future of our children, left defenseless in an immoral and mercenary society," he wrote in his journal on April 19, 1951. And four months later: "The social cancer has developed such profound roots that any effort to extirpate the disease will necessarily place the life of the republic in danger." In a published interview three years later, García Velez was no less candid— and no less despondent over the state of affairs: "There is no Republic. There is nothing. I do not believe in anything."[68]

Thoughtful observers could not conceal their disquiet over the Cuban condition. "In truth," essayist Manuel Bisbé brooded, "we have not discharged our debt. . . . The men to whom fell the task to realize in the Republic the unrealized program of 1895 were not all far-sighted, responsible, and honest as the circumstances required." He concluded: "We have failed to become masters of our destiny."[69] Years later, poet Heberto Padilla looked back on these years with a deep sense of anguish: "Cuba was a country for sale, a parody of a country."[70] This was precisely the same imagery used by the 26 July Movement in its "Program-Manifesto" of 1956: "The Republic is a sorrowful caricature, through the fault of Cubans."[71] In Dreaming in Cuban (1992), novelist Cristina García has her protagonist given to plaintive musings: "Cuba has become the joke of the Caribbean, a place where everything and everyone is for sale. How did we allow this to happen?"[72]

The demoralization was palpable. Through much of the first half of the twentieth century, vast numbers of men and women had come to question the value of being Cuban, frustrated by the inability to achieve the nation upon which the fulfillment of nationality was contingent. The national memory had internalized disparate facets of the past, difficult to reconcile and especially difficult to accommodate within the discursive realms of nation as imagined at the time of its formulation. Self-interrogation produced self-reproach and inevitably a loss of self-esteem. "What is our nationality?" novelist José Antonio Ramos asked in despair as he brooded over the corruption of public life in the 1910s. "I feel a terrible shame at being Cuban."[73] Jorge Mañach frequently alluded to a national condition of "inferiority complex" and "pessimism," and essayist Juan Marinello identified a debilitating "disquiet" that had produced among Cubans a persisting "inferiority complex."[74] Twenty years later, physician Gustavo Pittaluga arrived at a similar conclusion: "Our country has long suffered—from the times of its very founding—from an 'inferiority complex.'"[75] It perhaps could not have been otherwise. "The colonial structure survived under the factitious symbols of the national anthem, the coat of arms, and the flag," Raúl Roa reflected years later. "Out of that frustration developed the inferiority complex that characterized our republican life."[76] U.S. State Department officials often characterized Cubans as "sometimes influenced by a sense of inferiority, which promotes exaggerated nationalism."[77] Novelist René Vázquez Díaz's narrator in La isla del Cundeamor (1995) described Cubans as a people "driven by that nationalism that lies latent in the subconscious of every Cuban and makes them prone to the strangest excesses."[78] Psychiatrist José Angel Bustamante identified "the Platt Amendment and the constant fear of intervention by a foreign country, as well as the resulting disquiet attending the frustration created by the governments of the Republic" as salient factors in "the structure of the basic Cuban personality," expressed principally as "insecurity and the feeling of inferiority."[79] The Tenth National Congress of History concluded its 1952 proceedings with a "Declaration of Principles," approved as the Final Act, affirming that "the imposition of the Platt Amendment upon the new Republic created among our people a terrible inferiority complex, of skepticism and lack of confidence in their own destiny, and lack of faith in the Republic."[80]

Men and women of goodwill could only look about with numb incredulity, to bear witness to recurring spectacles of scandal, each more spectacular than the one before, alienated from a succession of governments unresponsive to Cuban needs. "There is not a single Cuban who is not disillusioned by the farce that is today the republic," broods the protagonist in José Antonio Ramos's novel, *Las impurezas de la realidad* (1929).[81] So many had given so much. The republic seemed unworthy of the sacrifices made on its behalf. For the vast numbers of men and women for whom independence had been about sovereign nationhood, about the fulfillment of collective well-being contingent on the realization of Cuba for Cubans, the republic stood as a mockery of the very ideals that had informed the meaning of nation. Demoralization developed into one of the salient characteristics of civic culture in the republic. "Our nation is passing through a horrendous crisis," brooded Raimundo Cabrera in 1923. "It is not crisis of a government, it is not a crisis of a party, it is not crisis of a class. It is a crisis of an entire people."[82]

Without the capacity to exercise national sovereignty, without the means to fulfill the purpose for which the idea of nation was conceived and which had given the proposition of nation the power of its promise in the first place, the republic lacked the means to advance the primacy of Cuban interests. Historian Ramiro Guerra y Sánchez bore witness to his own times: "The disillusionment is great, the sorrow of the great mass of the Cuban people is sincere, while a wave of cynicism subdues and almost extinguishes the enthusiasm of the early days. But the Nation does not lose faith in the patriotic ideals."[83] Fernando Ortiz could hardly contain his despair. "After that noble national project on behalf of the liberation ideal [*la idealidad mambisa*]," Ortiz wrote in 1912, "into which we poured our last drops of blood, . . . we have descended shamefully into the muck of immorality, of ignorance, of passions, and most of all of indifference, of the most horrible national apathy." And he continued: "Our descent has been so rapid, our political failure so frightful, that the Cuban people are on the verge of losing — if they had not already done so — what was their most precious achievement, the only thing that encouraged their personality and gave them stamina and life: faith. Poor us. . . . What is completely incontrovertible . . . is the absolute discredit into which political activity has fallen, considered among us today totally as ineffective, futile, and what is more pernicious."[84]

Essayist Waldo Medina attributed the sources of the Cuban angst to the dashed hopes of liberation. "Everything has been a failure, frustration, a loss of confidence in the national destiny, an erosion of the sentiment of nation and nationality," a dispirited Medina wrote. "The redemptive revolutions of 1868 and 1895 were subverted, the genuine ideals of the old liberators were betrayed. The last war organized by Martí was won, but for others, not for Cubans, who continued to live without land, without bread, without peace.

Bread and peace that signified justice and democracy." Medina described the fate of the *mambises*, who endured "the mediated peace of the first foreign intervention—a national humiliation . . . and [source of] the great Cuban frustration." The "valiant defenders of the . . . *patria* meditated in silence with the shame of knowing that they were vanquished even though they were the victors: without land and without resources. . . . Poverty was transformed into the sole virtue of many of the men of the war."[85] Lamented José Enrique Varona in 1917: "The generations of Cubans who preceded us and who gave so magnanimously at the hour of sacrifice would look at us with astonishment and pity, and ask themselves incredulously if this is the result of their efforts, of the cause into which they put their hearts and lives. . . . Cuba of the republic is the twin sister of Cuba the colony."[86] The differences between generations were also on the mind of the protagonist, *mambí* colonel Damaso del Prado, in Luis Rodríguez Embil's short story "La impurezas de la realidad: Carta respuesta" (1932). "We made the Republic," Colonel del Prado writes to his son. He continues:

> At the time no one thought about identifying the meaning of action because the action was the meaning. At the time one simply acted, because one *had* to act. . . . Everything at the time was very clear and simple in our eyes. . . . My generation did something, because it *believed* in an ideal—the ideal of absolute independence—and its fulfillment. The generation that immediately followed mine, more intelligent and less instinctive and intuitive, in comparison, achieved nothing, for seeing the ideal of the previous generation totally mutilated upon its realization lost the *faith* that had characterized my generation. . . . The difference between one generation and another is to have faith—or not—in an ideal.[87]

■■■

Cubans lived with the presence of their past as part of daily life, packed with purpose, a history that had a reason for being: sometimes as a moral lesson, at other times in the form of prescriptive purport, and always as a point of view and perspective. The past insinuated itself into the popular imagination in the form of an unfinished history, the past as a calling, a summons to Cubans susceptible to the promise of nation. The past was where the virtues around which the attributes of nationality had formed, as ideals, to be sure, but as ideals so central to terms of self-representation as to make them the standard by which the character of Cuban was measured. Cubans were obliged to remember, insisted Ramiro Guerra y Sánchez in 1923, "the great deeds realized by our fathers in defense of our homes, our liberty, and our rights." He added: "The Cuban who comes to know the history of our past will feel heir to a rich patrimony and will discover in that very legacy the means to make it greater." Guerra was succinct: "Our history is the only thing that we possess that is genuinely ours."[88]

The past was preserved as a monument to commemorate a heroic deed—a statue to honor a patriot, a plaque to mark a place of historical significance, a tomb of a martyr, a birthplace, or the site of conspiracy. The anniversary of a patriot's birth date elicited testimonials; the commemoration of a death date evoked tributes. The past was memorialized in stamps, coins, and currency, in the construction of statues and sculptures as "public works of historical utility," wrote historian Miguel Varona Guerrero, "in remembrance and honor of our heroes and martyrs of freedom and independence."[89] Monuments, markers, and mausoleums in honor of the martyrs expanded across the island—what one Cuban commentator characterized as "the representation of our nationality in marble and stone."[90] That monuments were not designed specifically with political intent does not reduce their political impact, for they developed into one more form by which historical knowledge entered domains of popular awareness. They occupied public space and presumed to provide a specific interpretation of a decisive aspect in the Cuban past. "Since the war ended," observed Frederick Ober during his travels across the island in 1904, "the Cubans have nearly impoverished themselves erecting marble memorials and monuments of other sorts, to their brothers slain by Spaniards."[91] Visiting Havana almost twenty years later, Joseph Hergesheimer characterized Cubans as "morbidly sensitive about their land, their monuments and martyrs."[92]

The mambí memory passed into memoirs, some as chronicles of campaigns, others as diaries, and almost all in the form of first-person testimonials. Between the 1900s and 1950s, the publication of first-person accounts of the nineteenth-century wars of liberation, including the diaries, campaign journals, reminiscences, and autobiographies of the veterans of the wars of independence, developed fully into a genre of Cuban historical writing.[93] This was history as word of mouth and memory, recounted, repeated, and recorded, inherently subjective, to be sure, but itself the source from which an understanding of the past acted to shape the terms of Cuban. The literature of memory, observed historian Diana Iznaga, was characterized "by its function in the service of a cause which, in the final analysis, was the cause of the Cuban people: the struggle for the right of national independence and rescue from oblivion their heroic tradition of combat and victories. . . . It was valuable because by virtue of reading the memoirs we see develop before our very eyes the emergence of a people."[94]

Mambises also turned historians, to bear witness and chronicle the history that they themselves had contributed to producing. Officers of the Liberation Army published historical studies of the war for independence, including Colonel Matías Duque, Nuestra patria (Lectura para niños) (1925); Captain Aníbal Escalante Beatón, Calixto García: Su campaña en el 95 (1946); Colonel Manuel Piedra Martel, Campañas de Maceo en la última Guerra de Independencia (1946); Major Miguel Varona Guerrero, La Guerra de Independencia de Cuba, 1895–1898 (1946); Colonel Cosme de la Torriente, Calixto García cooperó con las fuerzas armadas de los EE. UU. en 1898 (1952); and General Enrique Loynaz del Castillo, La Constituyente de Jimaguayú (1952) and Maceo, héroe y carácter (1952). Captain Joaquín Llaverías inaugurated the publication of the Boletín del Archivo Nacional in 1902 and served as the director of the Cuban National Archives between 1913 until his death in 1956.[95] The founding of the Asociación Pro Enseñanza de Hechos Históricos in 1939, under the direction of Captain Luis Rodolfo Miranda, was dedicated to the dissemination of knowledge of the nineteenth-century wars for independence. "It is our desire," explained Miranda, "to make known the achievements of the men who, with a smile on their face, were happy to die for Cuba Libre. We wish our youth of today to learn of the sacrifices and glory of the past, knowledge that serves as a source of pride to our people so that they will continue to struggle to complete the noble work begun by those men."[96]

Legacy was honored in national acts of remembrance. A presidential decree in 1903, subsequently ratified in the Constitution of 1940, established October 10 (Grito de Yara), February 24 (Grito de Baire), and May 20 (independence day) as national holidays. Towns and cities across the island observed annual dates of local historical significance: January 12 for the burning of Bayamo; January 22 in Mantua for the completion of the 1896 invasion; April 14 for the commemoration in Guáimaro of the Constitution of 1869. The value of patriotic holidays, exhorted one primary school manual, lay in their "profoundly educational" function: "They serve to contribute to ideas of social solidarity and foster and strengthen a national spirit. . . . Through these observances children learn that patriotism does not consist only of shouting vivas to the patria on a given date, in May or October, but also in learning to fulfill their duty . . . [and] that the best way to demonstrate love for the patria is to meet our obligations."[97] Years later, General Harry Villegas Tamayo vividly remembered his adolescence: "[Patriotic commemorations] created a patriotic sentiment among the youth. The celebration of October 10 represented something very important. For me it was decisive in the later development of my life."[98]

1895 1868

Céspedes y Martí: ¿Qué has hecho de la República?

La sombra del Generalísimo: — Y yo todavía no tengo estatua.
La sombra del Apóstol: — Yo siquiera tengo el pisa-papel del parque

History hovering: Depicting the looming presence of the *próceres* standing in judgment of the conduct of public affairs of the republic. Left: José Martí and Carlos Manuel de Céspedes condemning President Tomás Estrada Palma for having invited U.S. intervention in 1906. From *La Lucha*, October 10, 1906. Right: Caricature by Conrado Massaguer depicting Máximo Gómez and José Martí condemning the corruption of President Alfredo Zayas. From *Carteles* 8 (April 19, 1925).

The national calendar filled with dates to commemorate the death of *próceres*—the *mambises* and martyrs of the nineteenth century—always an occasion to remind the living of the debt owed to the dead: February 27 for the death of Carlos Manuel de Céspedes; May 11 for Ignacio Agramonte; May 19 for José Martí; December 6 for Antonio Maceo. Provincial towns and cities across the island honored the martyred *hijos predilectos*—local favorite sons and daughters—and thereby established a civic claim to participation in the cause of national liberation: Calixto García in Holguín, Magdalena Peñarredonda in Artemisa, Serafín Sánchez in Sancti-Spíritus, Pedro Díaz in Yaguajay, Isabel Rubio in Guane, Francisco Carrillo in Remedios, Eusebio Hernández in Colón, Juan Delgado González in Bejucal, Rita Suárez del Villar in Cienfuegos, Francisco Leyte Vidal in Mayarí, Adela Azcuy in Viñales, and Emilio Núñez in Sagua la Grande, among hundreds of others.

The presence of the deceased *próceres* hovered symbolically over the conduct of civic affairs in the republic, something of a specter understood to stand in judgment of political comportment. The living were in continual dialogue with the dead, the dead residing in the present in the form of moral authority, to be addressed and asked—rhetorically, of course—to render judgment on some aspect of public life. It was from among the dead, and specifically those who had perished in pursuit of *patria*, that the living were enjoined to seek inspiration and a standard of conduct. "The voice of the martyrs—those who sacrificed to create the *patria*—must be heard," exhorted elementary schoolteacher Francisco Rodríguez in 1910. "The martyrs will live on in the legend of their virtuous actions and their example will inspire us to imitate them."[99] The example of the dead imposed on the living the obligation of duty to the *patria*. "The dead will save Cuba . . . against the thieves who corrupt and violate Cuba," journalist Eduardo Abril Amores insisted in 1922. "The bones of our heroes will come out of their tombs to attack the wretched. . . . Those who died for the liberty of Cuba will have to continue to defend the *patria*; like El Cid, they must continue to win battles from the glorious tombs. . . . They created the *patria* with their lives and from death they preserve it."[100]

The celebration of the past drew Cubans into direct and indeed often personal engagement with their history. It was both programmatic and performative. Historical knowledge was diffused by way of commemorative participation as a collective experience in a national context. "The patriotic holidays were celebrated with fervor," José Juan Arrom recalled of his childhood in Mayarí. "I remember the program of one February 24 celebrating the beginning of the war for independence. [The event] began early in the morning with a reveille played by the municipal band, marching along Leyte Vidal Street. All the children awoke with enthusiasm to see the parade. We later had breakfast and dressed in our finest clothing, some even wearing new shoes for the occasion. We gathered at the school from where we departed with our teachers in a children's parade until reaching the Veterans' Center."[101]

Children in primary schools participated in weekly patriotic commemorations. Every Friday, teachers and students participated in "civic acts," explicitly as a means to foster affinity with the *patria*. In 1910, the administration of President José Miguel Gómez introduced a "patriotic act" known as the "Allegiance to the Flag" (*Jura de la Bandera*) for all public elementary schools, whereby children pledged loyalty to the flag.[102] A large Cuban flag and the national coats of arms were placed on display, attended to by a student honor guard selected for good grades and exemplary conduct. The assembled students would salute the flag and sing the national anthem. Speeches would be given, variously discussing love of nation, the poetry and political thought of José Martí, and the deeds of Antonio Maceo, Calixto García, and Carlos Manuel de Céspedes, among others. For the commemoration of February 24, children previously selected as the civic act guards were honored to receive the "Kiss of the Patria" (Beso de la Patria), whereby the cheek of each child was brushed with the Cuban flag. Recalled Tania Quintero: "Every week one of us would assist in the preparation for the Acto Cívico on Fridays: to set up the stage and raise the flag, to be a presenter to read compositions and poetry. The high point was the award of the certificates to the winners of the Beso de la Patria, which I received in the fifth grade."[103]

Teachers organized field trips to historic sites and monuments, to museums and commemorative events. Affirmed the manual La enseñanza de la historia de Cuba (1951): "In this way, the civic consciousness of Cuban children will be strengthened, from the earliest grades through the completion of primary education, by way of an appreciation of patriotic values and knowledge of their duties as children of a nation whose liberty was the result of the sacrifice of its most eminent men, to render homage to these men and the symbols of the Patria."[104] Years later, the father of Camilo Cienfuegos reminisced how much the young Camilo liked Cuban history: "It was his favorite subject. He always showed great interest—I would say passion—to learn about the lives of our patriots, and especially about the lives of Martí, Maceo, Máximo Gómez and others." The future comandante of the Rebel Army, recalled his father, learned that "the Cuba in which we live was not the one that Martí dreamed about and for which so many mambises had sacrificed their lives."[105] Cienfuegos received on several occasions the Beso de la Patria award.[106] Huber Matos similarly recalled his childhood: Every Friday, the end of the week was celebrated "with a ceremony called la Jura de la Bandera, where we had to take flowers and scatter them about the Cuban flag. We recited patriotic poetry. All very magisterial, by which the people were convinced of the need to make the effort to make our republic a reality."[107] Carlos Franqui later recalled the origins of his affection for the Cuban past: "In La Duda public school I met an exceptional teacher . . . who explained the history of Cuba to me; she introduced me to its martyrs, its poets, its struggles."[108] The education system of the early republic, literary critic Luisa Campuzano insisted, played a decisive role in the development of a sense of nation among the members of the next generation. "The school," Campuzano observed, "formed Cubans within knowledge and love of their country, of its customs and its culture."[109]

Memory assumed multiple forms, thereupon transmitted from one person to another, from one generation to the next, the way that legacy often passes into legend and takes hold as a matter of received wisdom. Across the island, all through the years of the early republic, the names of towns, schools, parks, and streets were changed to honor the deeds and dead of the wars for independence. Among the towns to change their names were Recreo (Máximo Gómez), Hato Nuevo (José Martí), Corral Falso (Pedro Betancourt), Lagunillas (Domingo Méndez Capote), Paso Real (Isabel Rubio), Cuevitas (Ignacio Agramonte), and Cimarrones (Carlos Rojas). In Havana, the streets Tacón, Concha, and Cánovas were changed to Martí, Maceo, and Gómez, respectively; Dolores was renamed Jesús Rabí, and Maloja was changed to Francisco Vicente Aguilera. In Sagua, Tacón was renamed Carlos Manuel de Céspedes. In Alquízar, the names changed from Calle Real to Antonio Maceo; from Calle de la Iglesia to Pedro Díaz; from Paseo Juana to Paseo Rius Rivera; from Barrio de Chafarinas to Barrios de los Mártires. Few indeed were the number of towns larger than 10,000 residents that did not have streets named after José Martí, Antonio Maceo, Máximo Gómez, Ignacio Agramonte, and Carlos Manuel de Céspedes. In 1922, the Cuban Congress decreed January 28—the birth date of José Martí—a national holiday. A bust of Martí was placed in every public school in the republic. Each municipality of the republic was required to designate "one of its principal streets with the name 'José Martí'"; every municipality was required to dedicate "to the memory of the Apostle a statue, a bust, an obelisk, a commemorative column, a bronze plaque or marble plaque memorial in the most prominent public place."[110]

Historical knowledge assumed multiple forms, rendered as legend and lore, preserved in popular memory as purpose, received as heritage, and passed on as legacy to live up to and make good upon. The past persisted as a presence, observed and celebrated, in the form of fact and fiction: in the classroom and on the pages of daily newspapers and weekly magazines, in popular *décimas* and political discourse. Historical themes developed into a staple of film, produced on stage, sung in song, and recited in poetry.

The ideal of sovereign nationhood insinuated itself deeply into the aesthetic sensibilities of the first generation of the republic as Cubans sought new ways to articulate aspirations of national sovereignty. "Culture in the republic," José Antonio Portuondo observed, "developed under the specter of our political frustration."[111] The novels of Carlos Loveira, José Antonio Ramos, Miguel de Carrión, Graziela Garbalosa, Luis Felipe Rodríguez, Ofelia Rodríguez-Acosta, and Jesús Castellanos, among others, and the poetry of Regino Boti, Agustín Acosta, José Manuel Poveda, Mariano Brull, Regino Pedroso, and Nicolás Guillén, among others, mounted a withering assault on the character of public and private life in the republic.[112] "It is important to emphasize," writer José Antonio Grillo Longoria wrote in regard to the con-

Los Mártires de la Patria

¡Tanto muerto para que viva tanto "vivo"!

Conrado Massaguer, "Martyrs of the *patria*." A veteran of the war for independence (*mambí*) paying homage to the grave of deceased veterans, commenting: "So many dead so that so many can live in debauchery." From *Carteles* 7 (December 7, 1924).

ventions of Cuban fiction in the republic, "that writers and artists have an important role in the task of rescuing the past, to awaken interest in the history of their country, and to preserve for eternity and with gratitude the memory of the martyrs and heroes of the past."[113]

The principal periodical literature of the early years of the republic, most famously *Cuba Contemporanea*, as well as the weekly magazines *Bohemia*, *Carteles*, *Gráfico*, and *Social*, were relentless in their criticism of the political culture of the republic, denouncing the corruption, malfeasance, and graft that had undermined public confidence in government. Caricaturist Conrado Massaguer, a member of the Grupo Minorista and founder/co-founder of the magazines *Gráfico*, *Carteles*, and *Social*, provided graphic indictment of the malaise of the republic, to what he later described as his "disillusionment with [the politics] of early republican years."[114]

The world of the plastic arts conveyed the angst of frustrated nationality in memorable artistic achievements. The vanguard painters of the 1920s and

Conrado Massaguer, "My God! The Dead always end up so all alone!" Depicting the "death" of *cubanismo*, patriotism, nationalism, altruism, civic pride, heroism, idealism, abnegation, and sacrifice. From *Social* 8 (November 1923).

¡Dios mío! ¡Qué solos se quedan los muertos...!

1930s immersed themselves in the representation of the nation, very much about the politics of *patria*, a people very much immersed in the history in their own time. The landscapes of Domingo Ravenet, Lorenzo Romero Arciaga, Arístides Fernández, Amelia Peláez, Antonio Gattorno, and Víctor Manuel celebrated scenes of rural communities, the fauna and flora of the countryside, and the idealization of the *guajiro*, evoked as highly sentimental renderings of the meaning of Cuban. Themes of the liberation of the nation informed the art of Carlos Enríquez and Jorge Arche. Graciella Pogolotti maintained that the works of Víctor Manuel, Amelia Peláez, and Carlos Enríquez, among others, "were divested of their decorative function and dedicated to constructing the image of an incipient nation."[115] Artists contributed powerfully to consciousness of Cuban by way of "their symbolization of national identity," suggested art historian Juan Martínez: "Emphasis on national independence, rejection of old colonial practices, affirmation of new and modern ways, and attention to neglected sectors of Cuban society such as the peasant and the Afrocuban were expressed in various ways in the art of the *vanguardia* painters. . . . These painters' consistent interest in expressing the national ethos and their choices of land, creole tradition, and the common people as symbols of *cubanidad* . . . and the acclamation of the *patria* was given symbolic form in [their] art."[116]

■ ■ ■

Cubans acquired much historical knowledge as a matter of inherited wisdom, knowledge so fully assimilated in the collective being of a people as to assume fully the form of intuition as a matter of feeling and sentiment. Knowledge of the past developed principally as narratives possessed of didactic function and instrumental purpose, presumptively actionable and loaded with political purport: an agenda, in short, to make good on legitimate aspirations thwarted, which meant too that vast numbers of Cubans carried within them a readiness to remedy.

The meaning of the past gained popular currency principally as a morality tale, learned at home and taught at school, given sensory embodiment in aesthetic forms and assigned political meaning as a discourse of dissent. A brooding sense of something gone wrong insinuated itself into the character of republican politics. The nineteenth-century project of nation developed early on into a usable politics, a framework in which to articulate opposition, as a set of ideals immediately recognizable and inherently revolutionary: more than simply challenging political power, the project of nation challenged the premise of the republic. To be a revolutionary as an agent of history was an honorable calling, a purpose amply validated as a matter of a past pending, an ever-present and long-standing summons to complete a history begun in the nineteenth century. "Everyone wanted to confer on himself the title of revolutionary," affirms the narrator in Enrique Serpa's novel *La trampa* (1956).[117] In those interior places where deeper truths dwelled, Cubans in the early republic understood the presumptive condition of independence as fiction and the claim to national sovereignty as false. The past pointed the way forward. It was necessary for Cubans to reclaim "the sense of our history" (*el sentido de nuestra historia*), historian Enrique Gay-Calbó insisted in 1934, and thereupon "resume our march toward the future."[118]

The power of the past to serve as a source of inspiration and means of fulfillment increased in direct proportion to the disillusionment with the republic, for contained in the promise of its moral lay the presumption of redemption. A heroic past consecrated as a matter of an unfinished history could not but implicate Cubans in the premise of their history as a purpose to pursue. The past developed into a guarded site, a sanctuary of sorts, where the values that had conferred meaning on Cuban could be protected and preserved—in reserve—as a fount for future generations to draw upon as a matter of perspective and purpose. The salvation of the nation depended on the defense of the past, Cubans sensed—that is, the past as a circumstance about which Cubans could still do something. The history—in its diverse forms and its multiple functions—was what remained of the people that Cubans had wished to become, with the conviction that fulfillment of the ideal of nationality could be realized only by the enactment of the past, that is, a commitment to the purpose that had informed the meaning of nationality. "We cast a retrospective glance to those bright days of our past," essayist Pedro Sotolongo wrote in 1911, "not solely to pause to contemplate the heroic achievements, but also to seek to understand the disinterested motives that motivated those generous hearts and the purpose that impelled them with such fervor to prolonged war in pursuit of a plausible ideal. . . . We are obliged to study our history conscientiously to demonstrate who we once were, to prove our capacity for the heroic [and] good faith, jealous of our own self-worth and worthy of our times and deserving of the respect of the world at large."[119]

Cubans dwelled in the past as a place of moral clarity, a past structured as a point of departure from which aspirations of national fulfillment necessarily obtained orientation. They were deeply sentimental about their past, and because sentimentality implied feelings and emotions, the past was something about which Cubans were passionate. Therein lay the source of the Cuban angst: living with a wrong that needed to be righted, as both a state of mind and a condition of the heart: the prospects for the future well-being of the nation depended upon the fulfillment of the past. Historian Roberto Pérez de Acevedo insisted that the study of the past engaged Cubans in an endeavor of consequence, for "it was by way of history that a nation is prepared for the future."[120] Much of the theater of playwright José Antonio Ramos was informed by a deepening awareness of the past as means of national redemption. "The historian today has resting upon his shoulders perhaps the most important and most decisive mission in the task of consolidation and contributing to a definitive national coherence," Ramos insisted in 1917. "Of primary necessity, as the first step, must be a History of Cuba, a history . . . that is emotional, suggestive, and philosophical, that is something more than a recounting of deeds, to serve the new generations, today disoriented and without the slightest idea of the road traveled [el camino recorrido]." Concluded Ramos: "Our History is beautiful, a powerful greatness upon which rests all our rights to liberty."[121] Thirty years later, Emilio Roig de Leuchsenring summoned the historian to national service. "We know that all people need to understand their true history," Roig insisted, "for within that truth exists the reason of their existence and the rich source of future rectification and orientation." Cuban historians were morally obligated to apply "the lessons and orientations applicable to our *patria* to correct past errors, find new avenues of inquiry, and apply better political and administrative methods in the search for the consolidation and ennoblement of the Republic," and, further, "to prevent the use of concepts and forms that act to demoralize [Cuban] nationality." History was obliged to serve as the means to develop "respect of Cuban sovereignty, among its citizens and as well foreigners and their governments."[122]

The Cuban historian was charged with the role of conscience, not simply with chronicling the past, insisted Roig de Leuchsenring, "but with the duty vital to the Cuban people: to expunge the sense of inferiority from which the Cuban people suffer, a cancer that has plunged them into a condition of a devastating defeatism," and, further, "to prevail over defeatism, to destroy the inferiority complex that our people suffer, and to revive and instill in our people faith and confidence in their own abilities, those virtues possessed by the four great leaders of our war of liberation of 1895: Martí, Maceo, Gómez, and García. This patriotic task is incumbent upon us in a special way, precisely in our capacity as historians, because in the distortions of the true history of our last war of liberation are to be found the sources of our republican defeatism."[123]

Historians had a special responsibility to foster civic pride and patriotic virtue, Roig de Leuchsenring affirmed in 1956. "The first thing that all children should know," he insisted, "is the history of their country, in all grades. . . . All teachers of the History of Cuba and all authors of history texts used in the classroom should be Cuban by birth [as a way to combat] the inferiority complex from which so many Cubans presently suffer."[124]

Historians of the republic studied the past with a purpose, an endeavor that was itself a project to preserve and pass on the ideals that had served to substantiate the Cuban claim to sovereign nationhood, something akin to a commitment to remembrance as an act of resistance. This was historical knowledge as it always had been: informed with instrumental purport and possessed of political utility. Historians dedicated themselves to the idea of the past as a purpose to pursue, task to complete, and hopes to realize. "Few countries can wear the crown of thorns of martyrdom in defense of exalted and pure ideals of liberty and independence like Cuba," insisted historian Elio Leiva in 1953. "Among us, in effect, the idea of the *patria* emerged upon unspeakable

pain, upon enormous sacrifice of life and treasure, upon extraordinary heroism, upon a sadness of such profound dimensions that it is impossible to
conceive that it can be contained within the human spirit without shattering
the oppressed souls in small pieces. The act of recounting this history would
tire even the most intrepid historian."[125] Historian Juan Leiseca explained the
purpose of his textbook, Historia de Cuba (1925): "I wrote it inspired with the
sole purpose of offering Cuban children one more means by which to enrich
their minds and spirit. . . . I wish to put in [their] hands a weapon for struggle
[un arma para la lucha], but not a weapon only to advance historical awareness,
but one that, reaching deeply into the hearts of the children, invigorates their
capacity to admire the greatness of the patria and arouses in them the desire
toward emulation and the awareness of the purest nationalism." Leiseca appealed directly to the classroom teacher to insist that "we can have a strong
and free patria only when Martí is considered as Apostle and redeemer in every
corner of the nation," adding: "The teacher should be above everything else a
patriot who ardently loves his country; who sees in his students the citizens of
tomorrow engaged in the national life; and who especially believes that when
he teaches history, he engages in an eminently nationalist task."[126] Elio Leiva
and Edilberto Marbán dedicated their co-authored Historia de Cuba (1944) to
the dissemination of knowledge of "a long, tenacious, and painful struggle
courageously mounted by men and women endowed with an elevated concept
of patriotic duty that their times imposed upon them and knew how to bequeath to us lessons that should serve always as the norms of our civic duty.
To remember the virtues of that generation who sacrificed itself to offer to us
the legacy of a better nation is the task given to the Historia de Cuba."[127] Historian Fernando Portuondo del Prado expressed the hope that his Historia de Cuba
(1953) "would contribute to the development among young Cubans today of
an understanding of the deeds of previous generations of Cubans and to the
feeling of solidarity with a common past."[128] Ramiro Guerra y Sánchez was
categorical:

> We must teach our children to admire everything that is worthy of ad-
> miration in our history: the indomitable valor displayed during our epic
> struggles for independence; the perseverance of sacrifice in pursuit of lib-
> erty that engaged us during the second half of the nineteenth century; the
> heroism of our wars; of the greatest of the soul that revealed the beauty
> of women who served as an inexhaustible source of tenderness and love
> of Cuban mothers, always disposed to the sacrifice by husbands and sons
> for the patria. We must make our students understand the rich patrimony

to which they are heir, and by way of love of the past they will also love the present and the future.[129]

It was necessary to celebrate the *Grito de Yara* (1868) and the *Grito de Baire* (1895). The future well-being of Cuba, historian Herminio Portell Vilá insisted, depended on collective faith in the promise of the past. "The first duty of every Cuban who truly wishes to rescue Cuba from the ills of today," he wrote in 1949, "is to believe in the epic history of Cuba and in the heroes, martyrs, and patriots who created Cuba."[130]

The proposition of duty to sacrifice as attribute of Cuban had established itself as a historical truth. The generation of liberation, insisted *mambí* colonel Matías Duque in his text *Nuestra patria (Lectura para niños)* (1925), was obligated to teach children "the way of duty, the path of sacrifice," adding: "The children of today, taught by us as examples, will love Cuba the way the *mambises* loved Cuba, and if necessary they too will defend it the way of the soldiers of Céspedes, Agramonte, Máximo Gómez, Maceo, Martí, and so many others who offered to the *Patria* the sacrifice of their treasure and lives in order to realize the ideal of liberty, decorum, and honor."[131] Sociologist Ciro Espinos assigned particular importance to the ideal of sacrifice in the formation of personality among adolescents:

> The integral ideal of *cubanía*—central to the formative period of adolescence—originates from the patriotic past. Because many Cubans heroically sacrificed their lives to obtain liberty for their contemporaries and for later generations; because the greatest Cubans of the past, the most intelligent, the bravest, Cubans of wealth and social standing, immolated themselves as martyrs in the redemption of the enslaved *patria*; because many Cubans of modest backgrounds, workers, peasants, artisans, young and old, all of the most humble social origins, also immolated themselves anonymously with unparalleled heroism on the altar of redemptive ideals of the *patria*, . . . later generations [now] possess and enjoy a free *patria*.[132]

This was the past conceived as legacy bequeathed to children in the form of collective trust. Children were conducted into domains of nationality, implicated in those dispositions around which self-awareness as Cuban was fashioned. "Look at sea breeze as it gently caresses the star of my flag, your flag, our flag," exults the narrative voice in Luis Ricardo Alonso's novel *El palacio y la furia* (1976). "The blue and white, the triangle of red blood, the ideal and the reality. What made us cry as schoolchildren when we listened to the national anthem: 'To die for the *patria* is to live.'"[133]

In classrooms across the island, from primary school through university, historical knowledge was intended to forge consciousness of Cuban. In *Enseñanza de la historia* (1940), pedagogue Pedro García Valdés emphasized the importance of history "to the formation of national consciousness and national character." To be Cuban implied a disposition to discharge duty derived from a historically determined value system. "The failure to prepare our youth to commit to the fulfillment of the national past," García Valdés warned, "is to leave our grandchildren without *patria* and leave our children without love. It is to extinguish the patriotic flame." And to the point: "It is necessary to nationalize our youth [by way of the sacred legacy of the past], for a people who lack national ideals and aspire only to base materialism are a people who proceed to lose the liberties that others have obtained for them." Historical education was designed to develop a sense of shared memory, to develop within children the desire "to feel, think, and love in Cuban [*sentir, pensar y querer en cubano*]."[134] Ramiro Guerra y Sánchez was lucid in the purpose he assigned to historical knowledge: "The history that forms and perfects the love of *patria* . . . is not only political history that deals with heroes, wars, and revolutions . . . but a far more profound and comprehensive history of who we are and how we have become who we are."[135]

Emphasis was placed on the celebration of the life of José Martí as the exemplary Cuban, with attention given to the lives and deeds of the *mambises* as models of behavior, including, and especially to deduce duty to sacrifice for the *patria* as the ethic of nationality and obligation that corresponded to Cubans by virtue of being Cuban: a people "over whom," observed María del Carmen Boza, "the image of Martí hung as a burden of example."[136] The teaching of history encouraged "appreciation of the sacrifices of the founders of the nation to secure liberty and progress"; to "promote knowledge of the personality of José Martí, exemplary patriot that all Cubans should imitate for his sublime virtues"; to "develop patriotism and sense of duty"; to "learn proper Cuban conduct according to the principles of Martí [*principios martianos*]"; and to "identify the attributes the child should have in order to follow the example of the Apostle [Martí]."[137]

The teaching of history in the primary grades, the manual *La enseñanza de la historia de Cuba* (1951) stipulated, was to emphasize "love of the *Patria*, its national symbols, the national holidays, and the achievements of notable Cubans." The 1930 manual for primary-school teachers of history—*La enseñanza de la historia en la escuela primaria*—emphasized the need "to develop interest and affection for history, to facilitate its study, and to strengthen the sentiment of nationality [*fortalecer el sentimiento de la nacionalidad*]." Particular attention was given to teaching history through the biographies of the "great men of the nation, for by this method the student will be formed in behalf of national solidarity in support of noble and valuable ideals"[138]—what history teacher Carlos Valdés Codina insisted in 1905 was the need "to provide children with the models of those great men who made the *patria*."[139]

Biography served as model tales for Cubans, who were exhorted to live their lives in discharge of the obligations of nationality. "The historic figures who bequeathed to us this beloved *patria*," columnist Isabel Carrasco wrote in 1925, "emerge from the pages of History immortalized by the affection of all Cubans, and should serve to stimulate and inspire by their example, uniting everyone under the beneficent shadow of the flag of beautiful colors, sustained by one ideal and one purpose: to see the patria great, beautiful, and always free."[140] The virtue of Cuban was discerned in the lives—and deaths—of *mambises*: celebration of heroic individuals who embodied devotion to the nation and the ideal of nationality. *Mambises* endured as examples through which to make history anew. "We must continually remember the lives of our dead," enjoined historian Néstor Carbonell y Rivero, "to make altars of their tombs [as] spiritual bridges between today and yesterday. . . . We must always remember our heroes and our martyrs. They constitute the life of the nation in what represents the most pure and the most noble. They are, in sum, the glory of who we were, the truth of who we are, and the faith of what we can become. . . . There is still much history to make in our nation: we must bring together in a continuum those who died for the nation with those who live for it."[141]

Biography assumed the form explicitly of a genre of didactic purpose. At least as important, biography evoked a history told as a narrative of human agents, shaping the course of events and pointing the way for others to follow. "The life of Antonio Maceo," insisted biographer Luis Rolando Cabrera, "is a lesson, an example which should be studied by all Cubans as source of exemplary inspiration through which to fulfill our civic duty. . . . Maceo was the sum of all virtues, a worthy example of valor and integrity."[142] The life and death of Guillermo Moncada, pronounced biographer José Mesa Vidal, was an example "to glorify for all eternity the need to sacrifice for the greater glory of the *patria*."[143] In his prologue to the 1928 biography of Ignacio Agramonte, Francisco de Arredondo summoned "good Cubans" (*los buenos cubanos*) to "follow the glorious examples set in 1868," adding: "Today, as we seek to purify the Government and Cuban Society, as we seek to escape definitively from the social and political corruption to which the colonial system accustomed us, there is no better example for Cuban youth than the life of Ignacio

Agramonte."[144] Matías Duque completed a biography of his *mambí* brother Antonio, he wrote, because it was "necessary for youth to appreciate those magnificent examples of virtue so that they be imitated and to understand that there is nothing greater in life than service in behalf of these earthly virtues."[145] "The central idea that has inspired the writing of this book," explained Benigno Vázquez Rodríguez in his preface to *Precursores y fundadores* (1958), "was to offer to the generations of Cuban youth of the present and the future the beautiful example to be derived from these lives."[146]

The study of the past assumed multiple institutional forms. The Academia de la Historia, founded in 1910, served as the principal center of historical scholarship and included Fernando Ortiz, Enrique José Varona, Emeterio Santovenia, and Enrique Collazo, among others. The founding of the Sociedad Cubana de Estudios Históricos e Internacionales in 1940 provided the forum in which the principal historiographical developments were registered. In collaboration with the Office of the City Historian of Havana, the Sociedad Cubana organized annual National Historical Congresses. In 1945, at the urging of the Second National Congress of History, the Cuban Congress enacted legislation decreeing the official name of the 1895–98 conflict to be "Spanish-Cuban-American War." The scholarship of a cohort of historians, most born within several years of each other, shaped the dominant thematic and interpretative perspectives of the historiography in the early republic and contributed decisively to the collective self-understanding of the nation: Ramiro Guerra y Sánchez (1880–1970), Emilio Roig de Leuchsenring (1889–1964), Emeterio Santovenia (1889–1968), Enrique Gay-Calbó (1889–1977), Jose Luciano Franco (1891–1989), Leopoldo Horrego Estuch (1892–1989), Herminio Portell Vila (1901–92), Elías Entralgo (1903–66), Fernando Portuondo del Prado (1903–75), Hortensia Pichardo (1904–2001), and Julio LeRiverend (1912–98).

Cuban efforts in the nineteenth century failed to produce national sovereignty, but they did result in a rich twentieth-century historical literature, and it was in response to the former that the latter developed. This was a scholarship that served to bear witness to the national angst, historians bearing grievances and seeking redress. Most of all, this was a scholarship filled with a sense of thresholds not crossed. The publication of hundreds of titles of books and articles between the 1920s and the 1950s fixed the dominant purpose of Cuban historiography: to advance Cuban claims to national sovereignty and self-determination. That Cubans addressed the past largely within the conventions of historical scholarship should not obscure the inherent political purport that informed much of the twentieth-century historical literature. There was a purpose in the point of view to which Cuban historiography was dedicated, a literature that strove relentlessly to enter its times. It was the place to work through the grievances of the past, and inevitably grievances developed into a way to remember the past. To engage history offered the possibility of enabling agency: to preserve and perpetuate memory as usable historical knowledge. This was the past as a point of orientation, what the narrator in Ofelia Rodríguez Acosta's novel *En la noche del mundo* (1940) contemplates as a means of "proper direction by way of History."[147] Historical knowledge was very much structured around the norms of nationality, by way of assumptions of a destiny due to Cubans by virtue of their past. Purpose was self-evident: to call attention to an unfinished national project and to propound the propriety of the Cuban claim to sovereign nationhood.

But it is also true that this was a history that existed simultaneously outside the canons and conventions of the formal historiography of the republic: principally as historical knowledge that dwelled in realms of the public domain. Its meanings developed analogously to the ways that popular memory remembered the past. A sense of wrong was inscribed into the premise of historical knowledge, always with intimations of frustration from which to draw the inference of a past still pending.

Memory of what was widely understood as an injustice had become intrinsic to the founding narratives of the republic. An unfinished history implied an incomplete nation, a people forged into a community without the means to actualize the purpose that had provided the rationale to nationality. Pretension to agency in the form of sovereign nationhood persisted as an ideal around which to organize — and precisely because it embodied the value system from which nationality had developed, it informed a politics that could not be readily repudiated. This too was the legacy of liberation, passed on as an unrealized ideal to which subsequent generations were obliged to respond as duty of Cuban. "It can be said," poet Cintio Vitier commented in 1957, "that for us frustration has been transformed into something of a dark duty. He who is not frustrated . . . is a traitor who deserves to be stoned."[148] Poet José Manuel Poveda was moved to brooding introspection during a 1918 visit to the ruins of the sugar mill La Demajagua, the site at which Cubans inaugurated the Ten Years War in 1868. "There may have been differences among them," Poveda reflected, "but all wanted the same thing, and to obtain it, they sacrificed life and home. *They wanted the same thing, and that was their greatness.* . . . They dreamed the same dream of heroic liberation and patriotic abnegation." He concluded: "The national conscience turns in onto itself, and understands that its present is not different from its past, and that today it is obligated to heroism in defense of liberty owing to the heroism of the founders of [Cuban] nationality, and that our responsibility is no less than theirs."[149]

Cuban historical narratives acquired discernible structure around the proposition of an interrupted history, mostly as an unrealized purpose from which—indeed, as a result of which—the dashed hopes of a people originated. Cubans entered the twentieth century with a sense of an unfinished history, of a purpose unachieved and a nation unrealized, and most of all with the historic sources of their discontent unremedied. An unfinished past seemed to imply history in progress, awaiting completion, a process to join up with and take part in. To contemplate the past was to confront an unsettled history, to ponder where things went astray, and how, and why, and always to brood about so much sacrifice offered for so little gain. Historical knowledge entered into the mainstream of public life, a living history, present and relevant at every turn. This was a history that could be acted upon, from which to derive a politics and deduce a purpose as a duty to fulfill. It is indeed entirely arguable that the turn-of-the-century generation of historians more than adequately contributed to the intellectual environment with which the Cuban revolution in 1959 was received. "I believe that there was a decisive moment for all of my generation: the triumph of the Revolution in 1959," reflected historian Eduardo Torres-Cuevas, and he continued:

> Its significance was contained in the fact that this event was understood by way of our national history. It is not that the Revolution developed a new interpretation of history, but rather we assimilated the revolutionary processes as a consequence of the historical education we had received by way of the works of Emilio Roig de Leuchsenring, Fernando Portuondo, Ramiro Guerra, Leopoldo Horrego. . . . That is to say, this was a disposition derived from a culture of history that was at once an incentive and an element basic to the formation of Cuban revolutionaries in the 1950s and 1960s.[150]

The men and women who enrolled in the ranks of armed resistance during the 1950s were formed principally during the 1930s and 1940s, representatives of the second generation of the republic, coming of age during the ascendancy of a critical national historiography. Nicolás Rodríguez Astiazaraín, a member of the Civic Resistance during the 1950s, later reflected on his own intellectual formation. "We read everything," he recalled, "although we had a particular interest in the first-person accounts of our history. . . . We were assiduous readers of the serious books like those of Hortensia Pichardo, Fernando Portuondo, Emilio Roig [de Leuchsenring], among others." He added:

"Although patriotic sentiment is not forged solely by way of study, it certainly helped in the development of political ideas and assisted in understanding the continuity of the revolutionary processes that our ancestors inaugurated. At that moment, we understood that the Republic, born in 1902, had nothing to do with the Republic that Martí and other founders [*forjadores*] of our independence had envisioned."[151]

■ ■ ■

The idea of an interrupted history insinuated itself deeply into national sensibilities and could not but invite the inference of a legacy as a matter of redemptive purpose which all *verdaderos cubanos* were obliged to fulfill. This was history in the form of burden as inheritance. "He recalled the sad history that he had studied in high school," the narrator describes Sebastián in Edmundo Desnoes's novel *No hay problema* (1961). "History had weighed Cuba down. . . . Cubans could laugh and dance the *conga* and *rumba* while a powerful sentiment of frustration simmered below the surface, the frustration of a country without a future."[152]

The proposition of thwarted nationhood acted decisively on the political culture of the republic, which meant too that the discourse of political opposition derived purpose as a politics of continuity in pursuit of the nineteenth-century ideal of nation. The past flourished in the political imagination of the early republic: the ideal of the sovereign nation as a highly charged sentiment, at once a frame of reference and a point of view to which Cubans were highly susceptible. Cubans bore the "weight" of the knowledge of a nation unfinished, of a republic compromised at its inception and impaired in its function: a past denied the denouement to which three generations of men and women had dedicated their lives. The ideals that had informed the normative content of nationality assumed the form of legacy to live up to and passed into the dominant political discourses of the republic as purpose to pursue and ideals to realize. The cause of Cuba was deeply embedded in the memory of the ideal to which vast numbers of men and women in the nineteenth century had dedicated their lives—without the desired outcome: memory as a factor of the Cuban condition, observed Cintio Vitier, as "a longing for a familiar heroic yesterday."[153] The future to which they had dedicated their efforts had eluded them, and what remained was the past to contemplate, always as a point from which to begin anew and reclaim their bearings. "It is necessary to learn to appreciate historic deeds," wrote Julio Antonio Mella in 1926, "not with the fetishism associated with the fatuous worship of the past but for their importance to the future, that is: for today."[154]

Cubans lived with a brooding sense of history having gone awry, given very much to pondering the course not taken and the cause not achieved, of what might have been if the ideal of sovereign nation had been realized. The practice of the counterfactual—of what might have been if—developed fully into a mode of historical writing and a moral of political discourse in the early republic. The ideal was the enemy of the real and in no small measure contributed to the political environment in which the republic was divested of moral authority. Past and present remained locked in a relentless dialectical relationship. The nineteenth-century ideal of nation served as the standard with which to take measure of the twentieth-century republic and could not but invite invidious comparison, continually—and of course the republic fared poorly every time. The very act of comparison contained within the purport of its premise the moral basis with which to challenge the existing order of things, and most assuredly with the result—if not the intent—of discrediting the republic.

Memory mattered, and the Cuban preoccupation with history suggested a people clinging to the past as a means of collective continuity. History was something to hold on to, or perhaps more accurately, something that could not be let go of, for this was a past as repository of the value system that had given meaning to Cuban: the way a people sense that they had lost their way and gone astray, that they had not fulfilled the task for which they had come together as a single people, and that it was necessary to attend to their past as if it were still in front of them. Simply put: to persevere with their past. There was purpose to the past, a purpose that shaped the function to which historical narratives were put, something akin to the past as a calling. "The frustration of the central objectives of the war of 1895 as a result of the North American intervention," Cintio Vitier suggested, "made the generation [of the republic] think that the only way to start up Cuban history again [*echar a andar de nuevo la historia cubana*] . . . was to reclaim the legacy of Martí."[155]

Remembrance of the past acted to structure historical knowledge as a moral narrative around which a politics formed and a purpose developed. The idea of a *Cuba irredenta* insinuated itself deeply into Cuban political culture: to revive and redeem the promise of sovereign nationhood and thereby fulfill the ideals around which nationality had formed. "The Cubans of the republic," essayist Julio César Gandarilla wrote in 1913, "the Cubans of honor, have the right to struggle for the sovereignty of Cuba, the way the martyrs of 1868 and 1895 struggled," adding, "The vow of 'independence or death' remains to be fulfilled by all Cubans." Gandarilla distinguished between "the bad Cubans" (*los malos cubanos*), whom he characterized as enemies of Cuba, and "the good Cubans" (los buenos cubanos), who were committed to the redemption of the ideal of nation.[156] The United States was "a usurper of a victory that was ours," insisted playwright Pedro José Cohucelo in 1925, "first through the military intervention of the Island and then through the odious Platt Amendment, [and] proclaimed that it was not Cuba which, through the efforts of its sons and blood spilled by its martyrs and heroes, had obtained the independence and sovereignty sought for half a century." The duty of all Cubans, Cohucelo insisted, was to end "the 'appendix' [the Platt Amendment] that demeans our very conscience and humiliates us in the eyes of foreigners who commonly look upon us as slaves in a North American colony that is called Cuba. . . . The Platt Amendment is an affront to Cubans, and we cannot call ourselves free and independent as long as this appendix serves to embarrass and shame us."[157]

All through the first half of the twentieth century, political contenders of almost all ideological persuasions defended—some more, some less—the ideal of the sovereign nation, something of an article of faith to which almost all aspirants to power professed devotion and thereupon proselytized as a politics. There was no higher source of moral validation to political purpose in the early republic than the claim of discharge of duty imposed by history: fulfillment of nation transmitted as legacy and received as duty of Cuban (el deber del cubano).

The past formed and informed the purpose with which virtually all political contenders in the early republic aspired to power, thereby rendering history as the basis of a politics of national fulfillment. The cause of unfinished purpose developed as the principal discursive mode of political opposition in the early republic, especially noteworthy for its claim to continuity with the nineteenth-century independentista project. History offered a readily accessible political purpose, widely shared and commonly held reference points with which to summon indignation with the prevailing order of things. Historical narratives as political discourse served to establish the moral framework for oppositional politics of the republic: fulfillment of the independentista project as the alternative to the status quo. The possibility that the past was prophetic must be considered central to the logic with which it held Cubans in its thrall.

That Cubans were deeply invested in the anticipation of their past as a condition of nationality also meant that they were especially susceptible to the moral of its meaning. A politics claiming a mandate from the past, in the name of the unfulfilled nation, developed into a powerful challenge to the legitimacy of the republic. The past entered the realm of politics because politics seemed to offer the only way to redeem the past: Cubans increasingly turned to history to give purpose to their politics. The way to summon Cubans to make history was through history; the way to realize the expectations of a better future was to fulfill the aspirations of the past.

Domains of selfhood and nationhood closed in upon one another, acting upon each other—that is, nation as an ideal to surrender to as frame of reference and source of self-esteem, always as something to live up to and do right by. This was the transcendental nation to which all Cubans were joined as the basis to the claim to being a single people. "The *Patria* is to be loved above everything else," exhorted Matías Duque in his 1925 history text for children, *Nuestra patria (Lectura para niños)*:

It guarantees our life and our dignity. It allows us to live respected by foreigners; it confers splendor on the home and in the family; it cares for us and is with us as we move about the world. . . . For a man to be respected by other men he must love the *Patria* and be disposed always to make sacrifices, whatever sacrifices may be required. . . . Without *Patria* there is no honor, there is no family, there is no happiness. The *Patria* is everything and everything should be for the *Patria*. Nothing can be withheld from the *Patria*. One has to be generous and noble with it; nothing can be denied to the *Patria* at any time: not life, not family, not wealth. Everything is from the *Patria* and everything should be for the *Patria*. When the *Patria* asks valor of its sons and daughters, it should be given unconditionally, even if it is necessary to die. When the *Patria* asks for the destruction of the home, it should be destroyed. When the *Patria* asks for one's property, money, and well-being, that too should be given.[158]

■ ■ ■

The first republican-born generation came of age during the 1920s, formed within the contradictions of the ideal of the nation and the reality of the republic—a generation that Luis Araquistain characterized as having been "born and nurtured with a new social spirit and a new historical consciousness, restless with a sense of duty and responsibilities toward a nation in danger."[159] The young men and women of the early republic bore witness to an endless spectacle of malfeasance and misgovernment. There seemed to be no limit to the practice of political abuse, no end to revelations of graft, no constraints on the reach of North American power. They mobilized for change, to protest political abuse and denounce graft and corruption. Continual popular disaffection with conditions in the republic was expressed with the organization of the Partido Independiente de Color (1907), the Federación Nacional de Asociaciones Femeninas (1921), the Federación Estudiantil Universitaria (1922), the Asociación de Buen Gobierno (1923), the Falange de Acción Cubana (1923), the Protesta de los Trece (1923), the Grupo Minorista (1923), the Movimiento de Veteranos y Patriotas (1923–24), the Confederación Nacional Obrera de Cuba (1925), the Partido Comunista de Cuba (1925), the Liga Anti-Imperialista (1925), the Directorio Estudiantil Universitario (1927), and the Liga contra la Enmienda Platt (1928).

A new generation of Cubans discerned a politics in the past, all very much as a matter of principles and program contained within a larger paradigm of continuity with the nineteenth-century *independentista* project. To remedy the republic implied the need to reclaim the historical project for which Cubans had first organized as a united people in behalf of sovereign nationhood. Raúl Roa reflected on his coming of age during the 1920s and 1930s: "New generations, historically driven to complete the unfulfilled feat of 1895, introduced a new spirit and new expectations into the Cuban people. José Martí was reclaimed for living and for struggle."[160]

The generation of the republic revived aspirations of the nineteenth-century liberation process and committed itself to the promise of the past in the form of a leap into the embrace of faith in its history. Cubans looked inward and backward to make themselves in their own image. The model of exemplary conduct was contained in the lives of the *mambises* of the nineteenth century. "I would like to see the noble youth of today," Enrique José Varona urged in 1930, "of civic culture, prepared, and committed, confront the problems of today and meet the issues of tomorrow with the same noble heroism with which the glorious youth of 1868 and 1895 met the challenges of their time."[161]

Cubans disaffected with the prevailing order of things inserted themselves consciously into the continuity of their history. They found in the past a purpose to fulfill and a program to propound, but most of all a legacy to fulfill. "A noble people with knowledge of their history know how to honor their past," affirmed Rubén Martínez Villena in the "Exposition" of the Falange de Acción Cubana en 1923.[162] He contemplated the commemoration of February 24— the beginning of the 1895 war for independence—with a sense of purpose of a task unfinished. "It is time to have a real *patria*," he reflected, "with a firm foundation, strong and coherent. . . . It is time to have a true nation [*tener Patria de verdad*]. . . . *Patria* is political independence and an orderly functioning of the State; honorable household and virtuous government; the national treasury filled and a clean civic conscience."[163]

The organization of the Junta Cubana de Renovación Nacional in 1923 included many of the most prominent representatives of the public life of the republic, including anthropologist Fernando Ortiz and historians Ramiro Guerra y Sánchez, Emilio Roig de Leuchsenring, and Fernando Figueredo y Socarrás. The 1923 Manifesto of the Junta Cubana de Renovación Nacional proclaimed its purpose: "To consolidate the Republic and complete the task begun by the revolution of liberation." In a wide-ranging denunciation of the conditions in the republic, the Junta warned that "the nation is plunging headlong into disaster" and insisted that "the people demand the public life of the republic be worthy of the dignity and honor of the Cubans who made its existence possible."[164]

Abuses in the republic often recalled abuses in the colony. The 1925 National Assembly of the Movimiento de Veteranos y Patriotas denounced the Liberal, Conservative, and Popular parties' support of Gerardo Machado, insisting that Cuba in 1925 was "in the same situation as the year 1895, when three political parties then—the Constitutional Union, the Reformist, and the Autonomist—acted contrary to the interests of Cuban people who in 1895 understood the necessity to do away with the three existing parties in order to have their legitimate interests respected."[165]

Political opposition to the government of Gerardo Machado during the late 1920s and early 1930s was increasingly articulated within a paradigm of continuity with the nineteenth-century liberation project. Indeed, almost all opposition groups dedicated themselves to the fulfillment of the larger historical project of nation. The Directorio Estudiantil Universitario demanded "the complete independence of the Cuban people": "That members of the Constituent Assembly in 1901 preferred a mortgaged republic to no republic at all does not prevent us from rebelling against the denial of our sovereignty and against every act upon which that denial is based."[166] The young men and women of the Directorio Estudiantil Universitario proclaimed themselves to be "the worthy sons and daughters of that handful of heroes, that small group of titans, who scaled the summit of immortality and glory in the legendary [battles of] Peralejo, Las Guásimas, [and] Mal Tiempo." The Directorio affirmed its commitment to the "consolidation of our institutions, bequeathed as legacy of those who committed themselves to the struggle in pursuit of an ideal and a free nation [una patria libre]," and vowed: "This revolution is more formidable than those of 1868 and 1895." Alluding to the need to redeem "la Patria irredenta," the Directorio invoked "the glorious pages of Cuban history and the sublime examples of abnegation, sacrifice, patriotism, and virtue of that history, from which emerges the sentiment of nationality, which is the supreme synthesis of all the elements that influenced the formation of the nation." It was now the turn of a new generation to join "the struggle for an ideal and for a *patria libre*."[167] The Directorio, Justo Carrillo recorded in his memoirs, propounded far-reaching objectives, "aspiring to the discharge of a historic role through and for the strengthening of consciousness of nationality in order to achieve economic and political independence."[168]

Cubans of almost all political persuasions drew a common moral from the past. "The cry of six generations of Cubans," exhorted Julio Antonio Mella—a founder of the Cuban Communist Party—in 1928, "from the time of [Joaquín] Agüero through our times, has been '*Cuba Libre.*' What does it mean? A great desire to secure liberty: yesterday from the Spanish regime; today from *machadista* despotism and American imperialism." It was necessary for Cubans to renew their commitment to the nineteenth-century ideals of egalitarian politics, social justice, and political democracy, Mella insisted, to act together to honor "the symbols of Yara [1868], Baraguá [1878] and Baire [1895]," and he declared that "all of Cuba is today a Baire."[169]

The organization of the ABC Revolutionary Society in 1931 developed as a cellular resistance group to undertake armed struggle, including sabotage, bombings, and assassination, as methods of a larger campaign against the government of Gerardo Machado. Its corporatist structure notwithstanding, the ABC, like the opposition of the left, consciously acted as a historical actor in pursuit of national fulfillment. The ABC Manifesto-Program of 1932 demanded economic reform as an outgrowth of "the liberation struggles that had a principal economic objective: to achieve political independence as a means to pursue the material development of the nation. This was the purpose for which the [1868] war against the Metropolis was launched." The ABC celebrated "the generation of 95," which "through its liberation efforts had fulfilled its glorious historical mission." The task of liberation had passed to a new generation. "Martí had predicted that after independence," the ABC affirmed, "it would become necessary to wage a new war for liberty. This is that new war!"[170] Historian Francisco Ichaso, a founding member of the ABC and author of the ABC Manifesto-Program, reflected on the revolutionary struggles of the early 1930s and denounced the progovernment Liberal and Conservative parties as having "deserted history," adding that it was "precisely in that painful moment when the two political parties deserted history that the ABC was founded." He continued:

As our Manifesto-Program of 1932 affirmed: we came to continue and complete the work of the liberators. Cuba obtained its independence at a cost of extraordinary and cruel human and economic sacrifice. The *independentista* enterprise had a defining Numantian characteristic [*un marcado sello numan-tino*]: Cubans did not hesitate to endure all manner of material sacrifice, determined to free themselves from a metropolis that could not fulfill the desire for liberty, democracy, and progress that was bestirring the island.

The founding of the ABC responded to the logic of legacy, Ichaso insisted, to uphold the ideals that had summoned Cubans to dramatic action in the nineteenth century. "At the time we confronted mentalities similar to [the sentiments in 1878] of the Autonomists," Ichaso recounted, "the [defeatist] people who assumed that 'all was lost,' that 'nothing could be done to over-throw tyranny,' and that there was no other remedy than to compromise and sign a new [Pact of] Zanjón [that is, to surrender]. [They charged] that we revolutionaries were idealists and dreamers if not crude troublemakers that no one should take seriously." Continued Ichaso: "The ABC was the Protest of Baraguá of the new Cuban revolution . . . and it proceeded to situate itself on the straight line of history. For the historic deed consisted in not entering into shady negotiations with the despot, but to remove him and to structure a more just future atop the ruins of the repressive apparatus."[171]

The reform movement of the 1920s and early 1930s culminated in 1933 with the overthrow of Gerardo Machado and the subsequent short-lived govern-ment of Ramón Grau San Martín. For one hundred days, between Septem-ber 1933 and January 1934, the Grau government devoted itself to the task of transforming Cuba with exalted purposefulness, a combination of improvised populism and systematic reform. The overthrow of Machado represented an act of agency, popular indignation channeled into a deed of popular will. Cer-tainly, this was how the fall of Machado in August 1933 was celebrated: a re-pressive government unable to meet the needs of the Cuban people removed in response to popular revulsion. "For the first time since the war of indepen-dence," exulted Jorge Mañach, himself a founding member of the ABC, "the people of Cuba experienced during those August days the emotion of control, the feeling that they were the masters of their own destiny."[172]

Under the injunction of "Cuba for Cuba," the Grau government proclaimed its commitment to the ideal of nation based on the "lines of modern democ-racy [and] upon the pure principle of national sovereignty" and abrogated—if only symbolically—the Platt Amendment as an act of national sovereignty and self-determination.[173] Cuban aspirations for sovereign nation had been realized, proclaimed the new government: "Sixty-five years after the sepa-ratist revolution of 1868, the first fundamental declaration of the Provisional Government . . . [is] to proclaim and sustain above all other interests and ideas the absolute and immaculate Independence of the *Patria*, the preservation of which all Cubans today, like Cubans of the past, are disposed to sacrifice their lives and treasure, which mean nothing when such glorious ideals are at stake." The new Provisional Government affirmed its commitment to "absolute independence and national sovereignty and the defense of the principle of self-determination in the resolution of its internal conflicts."[174] The Cuban people, proclaimed the Directorio Estudiantil Universitario, "aspire to obtain our political independence, the task that the *mambises* of 1895 left uncompleted." The Directorio affirmed its "complete satisfaction with the achievements of the present historical moment . . . presiding over an independent and sovereign Republic, without ignominious international tutelage, and presiding over the development of the moral forces found in the soul of our nationality."[175]

Cuban aspirations to national sovereignty were no more acceptable to the United States in 1933 than they had been in 1898. Washington was implacable in its opposition to Grau. That this was eminently a reformist government—rather than a revolutionary one—mattered less than that it had committed itself to the defense of Cuban interests as the principal purpose of the public policy. The reforms of the Grau government had indeed challenged the premise of the primacy of North American interests in Cuba. "Respect for us is diminishing," Ambassador Sumner Welles warned on September 25, "and the belief is rising, sedulously fostered by the radicals, that the United States can be flouted with complete impunity." Three weeks later, an alarmed Welles warned again that the new government was engaged in a "deliberate effort . . . to show its intention of minimizing any form of American influence in Cuba."[176] In the months that followed, the U.S. government withheld diplomatic recognition and coordinated plans of internal subversion in collaboration with local opposition groups and the army under the command of Colonel Fulgencio Batista.

The Grau government appealed for hemispheric support. In December 1933, it presented its case directly to the Seventh International Conference of American States held in Montevideo, convened—as events would have it—to ratify a proposed convention on the "duties and rights of states," central to which was the proposition that "no state has the right to intervene in the internal or external affairs of another." Cuban demands for national sovereignty were presented in the form of a historical narrative by historian Herminio Portell Vilá, a member of the Cuban delegation. Cuba "wishes to be free, independent, and sovereign," the Cuban delegation pronounced, "and aspires and insists upon the exercise of self-determination."[177] "You know how the Platt

Amendment was incorporated into the Constitution of Cuba," Portell Vilá recounted. "My country had just emerged from a bloody war in which it had expended all its energies and laid waste to all the resources of the nation." The Platt Amendment, Portell Vilá insisted, was designed as a "substitute for the annexation of Cuba to the United States." Cubans were warned in 1901 "that the Platt Amendment was a legislative ultimatum: either the Platt Amendment was accepted or Cuba would not be independent." He concluded: "The Platt Amendment and the Permanent Treaty are iniquities of coercion, for the Cuban people never freely accepted either the Platt Amendment or the Permanent Treaty, for my country was occupied by North American bayonets."[178]

Even as the Cuban delegation made the case for the principle of nonintervention in Montevideo, the United States had completed preparations to remove Grau from power. In January 1934, acting with the support of and in behalf of the United States, Colonel Fulgencio Batista ousted Grau from power and thereupon emerged as the new power broker of the republic.

The reformist coalition of 1933 subsequently divided into two principal tendencies. One month after his removal from power, Grau organized a new political party: the Partido Revolucionario Cubano, named after the party of José Martí, committed to the realization of the "authentic" goals of Martí. One year later, Antonio Guiteras, previously the secretary of the interior in the Grau government, organized Joven Cuba. A revolutionary organization, Joven Cuba vowed to realize the promise of nation. "Cuba possesses all the indispensable elements to constitute itself as a nation, but it is still not a *Nation*," the program charter of Joven Cuba affirmed, adding: "Cuba remains in a *colonial state*."[179]

■ ■ ■

Efforts at national sovereignty and self-determination had failed again. Some things did change, to be sure. The Platt Amendment was abrogated in 1934, although the United States kept control of Cuban territory on which it had established the Guantánamo naval base. The subsequent promulgation of the 1940 constitution was received with enthusiasm and expectation that perhaps the new constitutional order would provide a way to fulfill Cuban aspirations. The election of Ramón Grau San Martín as president in 1944 raised hopes of better things to come. These hopes did not last long.

The events of the 1930s passed into the collective memory as *la revolución frustrada*. The men and women of the 1920s and 1930s had committed themselves to the fulfillment of the nineteenth-century ideal of nation. The past had informed the purpose to which their politics was put and shaped the program to which their efforts were directed, but to no avail. The mobilizations of the 1920s and early 1930s ended in frustration, and another generation was thwarted. "I confronted the tyranny in my nation in 1933," reflects Ricardo in the José Antonio Ramos play FU-3001 (1944). "And from the failure of the revolution to this very day, I have lived without a sense of purpose."[180]

The reform project of the 1930s had failed, but the purpose of the past persisted: a people awaiting fulfillment. "It is worth remembering," Pablo de la Torriente wrote from New York in 1936, "now more than ever, that the revolution for which we struggle is exactly the one that fell mortally wounded with the fatal bullet of Dos Ríos" (that is, the death of José Martí).[181] The struggle of the 1930s — "to be who we wish to be" — Raúl Roa reflected years later, "had its roots in the process of the previous century." Roa added: "Our perspective and our attitude were sustained . . . in the enduring example and the unfulfilled ideal of 1868 and 1895, that continues to act as the driving force in shaping our destiny. Each generation has its proper task. The task of our generation was — and continues to be — to transform into a historical reality the revolutionary principles that the generations heir to the liberation legacy [el legado mambí] repudiated and trampled upon." Cubans were obligated, Roa insisted, to pursue the nineteenth-century project of nation as a matter of "historic duty," and "the fate of that revolution [of independence] is our fate," bearing as much relevance to Cubans in the 1930s as it had to Cubans in the 1890s. "It is in being a revolution of this type," Roa insisted, "that it derives its nationalist tenor and anti-imperialist character. . . . From this condition, to revive the pursuit of the thwarted objectives of the revolution of 1895 and [from which] it obtains its battle cry: 'Cuba for Cubans' . . . it seeks respect for our sovereignty and the independent development of Cuban life."[182]

5 ANTICIPATION OF THE PAST

History is cumulative. One never begins from zero, for
every revolutionary experience—including failed ones—
contributes to the collective consciousness of a people and
serves as the basis for the inauguration of new processes.
— Jesús Arboleya, "El saber del socialismo y el socialismo
   del saber" (2007)

Nothing is more central to Cuban revolutionary ideology
than a sense of history. The nationalist "Generation of 23"
and the anti-Machado forces looked to the Cuban past for
inspiration. . . . It is not merely that the Moncada attackers
knew and identified with Cuban history, but that they
perceived that their actions were in themselves events,
events that counted, actions that made history. The attack
and aftermath greatly reinforced this self-perception as
historical actors.
— C. Fred Judson, *Cuba and the Revolutionary Myth* (1984)

Cuba has a history, and for that reason Cuba has a
revolution.
— Armando Hart, *Obra revolucionaria* (December 7, 1962)

We believe we are history / Because we know we are history.
— Olga Alonso, *Testimonios* (1975)

History is often what you believe.
— Herbert Matthews, *The Cuban Story* (1961)

On January 1, about 2:15 A.M., Castro returned to the
balcony. . . . His mind was already rushing far ahead, and
he decided that he didn't want this moment to be wasted
by merely gloating in the defeat of the Batista dictatorship.
. . . It was important the people realized all the work, all
the Cuban history that had led up to this moment.
— John Dorschner and Roberto Fabricio,
    The Winds of December (1980)

Cuba has returned to the future.
— Raúl Roa, *En pie, 1953–1958* (1959)

The past was a presence everywhere: learned at home and taught in the classroom; eulogized in poetry and celebrated in song; dramatized in film and narrated in fiction; memorialized in the form of monuments and statuary, commemorated on national holidays, and observed on patriotic anniversaries.

But this was also a living history. The past persisted as a presence precisely because it had not fully passed—literally. Not that many years had elapsed between the conclusion of the war for independence in 1898 and the fiftieth anniversary of the founding of the republic in 1952. Cubans at mid-century continued to live closely with their history—often in intimate proximity—with surviving *mambises* very much in their midst. The census of 1953 recorded an estimated 142,000 inhabitants over the age of seventy, a population that included vast numbers of men and women who had participated in and lived through the *independentista* experience.

Almost everywhere across the island, memory passed for history, or to be more exact, memory served as a representation of history, susceptible always to the passage of time and the changing times, of course, but enduring over time: deeply personal narratives of the men and women who remembered themselves as protagonists in a history of their making. This was remembrance as reverence, memory of the nation in formation passed on by word of mouth, a means by which knowledge of the past passed from one generation to the next. The parents, grandparents, and great-grandparents of the 1950s were the *mambises* of the nineteenth century, a link to the past in the form of living voices with which successive generations of children came of age in the twentieth century. The historical imagination of the twentieth-century Cuban childhood was nourished within familial intimacy, by way of received memory, as first-person reminiscences and remembrance of heroic deeds and the noble cause of the *independentista* effort. "My mother kept our Cuban history alive," María de los Angeles Torres remembered fondly.[1] Gladys Marel García-Pérez acquired a "*sensibilidad mambisa*" from her grandmother. "I learned to be a patriot from my *mambisa* grandmother," she reminisced, "who always recounted to me stories of the war of 1895."[2]

Narratives of memory developed into one of the principal sources of historical knowledge, offered in the form of testimony and received as a matter of testament, always possessed of the capacity to render the past as something profoundly personal, a way that successive generations of Cubans came to claim direct lineage with their past. This was history structured around retellings. Rodolfo Sotolongo recalled the adult conversations of his childhood: "My father and several other veterans would come to the farm and from time to time sit around to reminisce about the war and how some of them were members of the insurgent cavalry and how they used the *machete*, which was their favorite weapon."[3] Writer Alicia Hernández de la Barca, the daughter of a colonel in the Liberation Army, recalled that "almost every day at home, during lunchtime, there were always discussions of some episode of our wars for independence."[4] Jorge Domínguez was among the many Cubans who learned history through the memory of a parent: "My father spoke to me a great deal about the War for Independence and Martí."[5] As did Giraldo Mazola Collazo, who remembered his mother "recounting with pride stories of my grandfather who had been a captain in the Liberation Army."[6] Carlos Franqui recalled visits with his grandfather, who "would tell me stories about the wars for independence."[7] Novelist Dora Alonso acknowledged that her writing was influenced by "the histories of the war that my great-uncle, who fought for Cuban independence, recounted to me."[8] The narrator in Alvaro de Villa's novel *El olor de la muerte que viene* (1968) recalls "memories of his own childhood, the summer evenings on the old porch of the farmhouse, when his father recounted stories of his struggles in the War for Independence."[9] Lourdes Gil wrote of her "old Cuban family," through which she "acquired a sense of history, of continuity, as a child, a notion of our presence in the world." She added: "So I grew up with a particularly loaded cargo—all of that is transmitted in the bosom of an old family, a family with great respect for the life of the country. It was a very strong influence, a sort of initiation rite. It endowed me with a notion of who I was—or, at least, of where I came from."[10]

That these were personal reminiscences meant that the aspirations that informed the hopes of a generation contained within their telling deeply emotional content: a people learning history through the lives of loved ones. Vast numbers of young men and women of the republic sat in the presence of their history, privy to the past as a matter of first-person experiences and through which they developed emotional bonds to their history. Two generations of Cubans had come of age between the 1920s and the 1950s with *mambises* in their midst, as residents in their communities and as members of their own families. Flor Fernández Barrios recalled ninety-eight-year-old Salvador Gutiérrez in Cabaiguán:

> The ninety-eight-year-old used to tell stories about the turn-of-the-century war of independence against the Spaniards. In the evenings, we children

sat around him with great anticipation, waiting for another colorful tale of the old days. Salvador's repertoire seemed unlimited, and every night he had a new story for us. . . . I learned more about Cuban history from Salvador Gutiérrez than from any textbook. His stories were filled with anecdotes and vivid images of the people who gave their blood for the freedom of our country and people. . . . The old man's raspy voice transported us to the battlefields, capturing our attention with imaginative sounds and images: I could hear the old shotguns and the *machetes* of the Cuban independence fighters, and see the *morros* and the *cañones* firing at the enemy. . . . To me, Salvador was the wise old man, the one who remembered the link between the ancestors and the soul of our town.[11]

These were personal memories, to be sure, subjective and selective, different things remembered differently. But it was also true that these were memories inscribed into an all-encompassing narrative that assumed the form of a history understood as something pending and unfinished. "To remember is not to know what happened, but rather being capable of living it again," the narrator in Aida Bahr's short story "Ausencias" comments on the meaning of history.[12] The remembered past was indeed relived as a reference point of national origins, something to transport the imagination, of course, but also the means through which history acted to shape the sensibility of Cuban.

Memory served as a means to integrate Cubans in a historically informed conception of nation: a body of historical knowledge disseminated as first-person narratives to celebrate heroic deeds and which in the aggregate fashioned the moral context in which a people came to an understanding of the ways they were bound together as Cubans. Francisco José Moreno recalled a childhood listening to "conversation, references, and arguments . . . always couched in terms of war or its political variants: struggle, strife, confrontation, rebellion, insurrection, revolt, revolution," and discussions bearing on the "mutilated independence" and "the colonial tutelage of the Platt Amendment."[13] Guillermo García lived his childhood in the remote interior of the Sierra Maestra, without schools, without access to radios, books, and newspapers, where illiteracy was considered normal and isolation was a way of life. But García was fully conversant with the history of the nineteenth-century *independentista* struggles, a knowledge that included the Ten Years War, in which his grandfather had served in the Liberation Army. "The stories that our parents recounted when my brothers and I were small," remembered García, "provided a way passing the time."[14] At the other end of the island, Neill Macaulay recalled his experience in the late 1950s with Cubans at the guerrilla front of Pinar del Río: "Although few had gone beyond elementary school, all had absorbed a great deal of Cuban history. They enjoyed telling me about the Cuban War for Independence and the march of the great mulatto general, Antonio Maceo, through Pinar del Río."[15]

Many of the men and women who had participated in the nineteenth-century liberation project—in the army, as members of the Provisional Government, or in the patriotic juntas abroad—were among the persons who subsequently filled the ranks of public schoolteachers, a living link to the past for successive generations of schoolchildren. Juan Marinello remembered his elementary schoolteacher, "who very much influenced my formation because he was truly a *mambí* who had fought in the revolution for independence, . . . a veteran of integrity and profoundly Cuban."[16] Years later, Giraldo Mazola Collazo wrote of his *mambí* schoolteacher, "who inculcated in me a devotion to the history of our great leaders of the independence wars."[17] Enzo Infante Uribazo remembered being schooled by two aunts: "My aunts had been formed as teachers in the very early Republic, and they still preserved that patriotic aura [*halo patriótico*] of the struggles of 1868 and 1895. They began to teach at the beginning of the twentieth century, and they transmitted to us all those traditions that were still fresh in their memory."[18] Rita Suárez del Villar, a conspirator during the war for independence, was appointed an elementary schoolteacher in Cienfuegos at the conclusion of the war, and she dedicated herself to the consecration of the memory of the *mambises*. "I spoke of the glorious deeds of such brave patriots as Antonio Maceo and Panchito Gómez," she recalled years later, "and what the Pact of Zanjón signified. When I spoke I could see the tears well up in the eyes of the girls. This was all such recent history, that to remember was to be overcome with emotion. Many of the family members of those girls had perished in the effort to win liberty for our *Patria*."[19]

The presence of *mambises* was a facet of everyday life, celebrated and commemorated across the island in multiple performative acts of tribute and testimonials, on patriotic holidays and historic anniversaries, one more way that remembrance of the past acted to implicate Cubans in the moral of their history in very personal ways. "Remember that when I was born in 1910," José Juan Arrom recalled his childhood in Mayarí, "the war for independence had ended a mere twelve years earlier. As a result, there were many veterans in Mayarí who had participated in that war." The death of each veteran provided an occasion for solemn commemoration of the past:

When one died, the coffin was transported across the river . . . en route to the cemetery, brought by a black hearse tied to two horses. The municipal band followed the hearse, playing a funeral march. The band was followed by family members and dignitaries of the town, and they were followed by a squadron of soldiers as an honor guard prepared for a military salute for the deceased veteran. Later all the farmers [campesinos] arrived on horseback, forming two very long single files on each side of the Street. And I, who felt very patriotic, always wished to pay honor to my [deceased] compatriot.[20]

In the years that followed, Cubans organized a myriad of associations dedicated to remembrance of the wars of independence. These included the National Association of the Veterans of Independence, the National Association of Revolutionary Cuban Emigrés, and the National Association of the Daughters of the Liberators. Veterans organized into provincial associations, and almost every town had a local veterans' association. In cities and towns across the island, Centros de Veteranos and the Hogares del Veterano—part retirement home, part recreation center, and part museum—developed into sites of living history and the preferred locations to commemorate events of national and local historical significance. *Centros* and *hogares* provided a powerful moral presence, fully engaged in the civic life of the community. Distributed across the island, the local centers were themselves organized into the larger National Association of the Veterans of Independence dedicated to "honoring national sentiment and sustaining devotion to the memory of those who gave their lives for the freedom of the *Patria*."[21] Against a national landscape noteworthy for the squalor of public life, the veterans were increasingly looked upon—Jorge Mañach commented in 1952—"as the only real moral authority that remains to us in the nation."[22]

As sites of first-person history, the Centros de Veteranos were visited often by families with small children and by primary-school classes, and they served as centers of local reunions and public gatherings on occasions of patriotic holidays. Tania Quintero recalled one February 24, in 1952, on which as a third grader she visited the local Hogar de Veteranos in El Cerro "to present cigars to the old *mambises* who were residents in the home."[23] Filmmaker Juan Padrón remembered vividly his childhood in Cárdenas, and he especially recalled the local veterans center: "In Cárdenas there was a Centro de Veteranos, something of a meeting place reunion of the old *mambises*. As can be imagined, during the 1950s they were of advanced age. But one had to see them so dignified in their humility, recalling their experiences in the war. What I most appreciated were the photographs of the last war for independence and the first years of the twentieth century that were hanging on the walls. On display

Veterans of the 1895 war for independence (*mambises*) on the occasion of the centennial of the Ten Years War in 1968. From *Cuba* (Número Especial) (October 1968).

were the field uniforms, the *machetes*—in sum, for me an elegant portrait of the men who had taken up arms in the fields of Cuba."[24] Julio Carreras recalled growing up within a family of *mambises* fully immersed in the memory of the veterans: "My uncles were active in the Consejo de Veteranos. I always over-heard conversations there in the Centro de Veteranos that was located on Zulueta Street. . . . I lived within the world of the liberators [*dentro del mundo de los libertadores*], among the officers of the *insurrecto* army and the enlisted men."[25]

■■■

Cubans all through the first half of the twentieth century lived with and within their history. The past was remembered—relentlessly. The meaning of nationality was itself fashioned largely by way of memory, through remembrance of experience and expectation, deeply personal and individual and forged into a shared historical sensibility. What was personal and individual was transmuted into something national and collective. Memory joined past and present together by way of published memoirs and autobiographies, as reminiscences and recollections, men and women looking back on their lives and recalling themselves in a history of their making: a way through which to bequeath a legacy of agency from one generation to another and in the process shape the knowledge with which children came to an understanding of the meaning of their past. These were the conventions of a culture given to remembrance, enacted as canons in discharge of oral traditions, within kinship systems and across generations, between teachers and students, among friends and families. Memory—selective as it indeed often was—"worked" powerfully to inform the values and influence the dispositions of successive generations of Cubans, a way to carry the past forward into the future in deeply personal terms.

The remembered past also recalled thwarted aspirations and dashed hopes, which meant too that twentieth-century sensibilities were eminently susceptible to the purpose that informed the Cuban understanding of the past. Cubans fixed on the decisive moments and the defining deeds from which the idea of nation took form, a people in constant exaltation of a past from which to derive pride and—as important—a past to which they were inexorably bound as a matter of duty, what the narrator in Lorenzo García Vega's novel *Rostros del reverso* (1977) characterizes as "the responsibility of history."[26] In claiming lineage from their history, Cubans also contracted obligations. They carried their history within themselves, and they understood too the need to live out and live up to the moral of their past, to make history happen.

Historical narratives achieved something of mythical proportions, highly sentimentalized and intensely idealized, the way that heroic deeds and righteous purpose are often transmuted into legend and then into legacy, thereupon celebrated as model of conduct and standard of comportment which all were enjoined to uphold: in sum, those values that inform and influence the character of a people.

These are hallmarks of national histories almost everywhere, to be sure. But in Cuba there was added complexity. Cubans indulged their history, rich with heroes and filled with heroic deeds, of righteous purpose and noble conduct: nothing unduly remarkable in these tendencies to celebrate, of course, for this was the stuff of founding myths of many national histories. But there was a dark side to this history, for the sense of a people wronged deepened in direct proportion to the exaltation of the past: the greater the idealization of the Cuban purpose the greater the resentment of the outcome, for in the end, there was no "founding" — not at least the way Cubans had imagined the founding of the republic. A popular undertaking of heroic proportions for a righteous cause had failed to realize the task around which the normative structures of nationality had developed.

Cubans had been formed within a moral system that had failed to realize a corresponding moral republic. The proposition of sovereign nationhood had fixed itself as the mooring of nationality, an ideal from which consciousness of Cuban had formed: the very purpose for which Cubans had committed themselves to one another. This was a past that could not be let go of, for it was the principal means through which to preserve the value system from which the terms of nationality had derived meaning. Commonly shared knowledge passed on as received wisdom, a people living with a reality of a condition of dashed hopes and thwarted aspirations, with a brooding sense of an inability to move history along the desired course.

Because knowledge of the past had insinuated itself deeply into the collective memory, Cubans could construct something of a vernacular based on a history-specific vocabulary with which to converse with one another, a language that carried within it the metaphysics of remembrance — not exactly in code, but through tacit insinuation inscribed in a shared knowledge of the past, transacted by way of figures of speech, as a matter of analogy and allegory, through the use of metaphor and symbols. All in all, it was a stock of common reference points by which a people addressed the pending purpose of their past as legacy. This involved nuance of phrasing and word choice, a way that Cubans were conditioned to look and listen beneath the surface: history as the language with which to sustain the politics of nation, something of a culturally privileged discourse loaded with figurative allusions to the past whose interior meanings were readily discerned—intuitively—among the men and women formed within that history. "Our identity," novelist Noel Navarro suggested through his protagonist in El nivel de las aguas (1980), "is not only theoretical—it is eminently intuitive."[27] By the mid-twentieth century, historical knowledge had indeed passed into realms of intuitive familiarity, to know something without having to think about it: a history that could be felt well out of proportion to what was known.

The past could not be undone, of course, but it could be understood. There was prescriptive purpose embedded in Cuban historical narratives, a summons to verdaderos cubanos to honor legacy that contained within its very logic the imperative of redemptive purport. This was the past at once as patrimony and as purpose. It propounded duty of such compelling moral force as to command compliance, an honorable purpose which Cubans were obligated to pursue by virtue of being Cuban. Successive generations of Cubans were formed within the conventions of their history, so that consciousness of Cuban was inscribed in consciousness of the past and its legacy as matters of duty and responsibility. "Our civic education," Fernando Martínez Heredia recalled of growing up in Yaguajay, "was formed with the help of narratives and the exaltation of the revolutionary struggles for independence. Almost every facet of local life was given to this task: family, school, childhood games, commemorative events, regional historical narratives, and the local media. All Cubans considered themselves heir to that patriotic tradition."[28]

It is important to emphasize again that not all Cubans inferred a sense of duty from their past, or fully lived up to the ideals by which the standard of verdadero cubano was measured. Many engaged their history as a matter of passing interest, certainly conscious of their past, more or less conversant with its course and content, but otherwise absorbed in the overriding demands of daily life, getting by and getting ahead, preoccupied with concerns of family and friends, in pursuit of security and happiness, making a living and making ends meet. History was something to study and learn, certainly, dutifully as required: dates to commemorate and deeds to celebrate. The conduct of politics—past and present—was often observed from afar with detachment and disdain, but until and/or unless political developments disrupted established patterns of daily life, politics was something to stay away from. Indeed, vast numbers of Cubans lived estranged from a politics that seemed incapable of serving their needs. Politicians were deemed corrupt, and politics was considered corrupting. That was the way things were: unchanging and unchangeable.

But it is also true that Cubans had been formed within a historically determined moral environment as a condition of nationality, imbued with didactic meaning and prescriptive purpose. To a lesser or greater extent, all Cubans lived within their history, implicated in the proposition of *verdadero cubano* as an ideal, to which all were expected to aspire even if not always meeting aspirations. In circumstances of adversity, on those occasions when the routines of everyday life plunged into disarray, the model of the ideal could be relied upon to serve as the standard of conduct by which men and women would acquit themselves as a matter of duty as a Cuban. What is especially compelling to contemplate is the degree to which at times of national crisis, like the early 1930s or the mid-1950s, when the political became personal, the past suggested paradigm—something with which Cubans were familiar—possessed of the moral capacity to summon a people to dramatic action by example, as a matter of principle and in the form of precedent, as ideals that had been learned by heart and borne as faith.

Cubans disaffected with the circumstances of their times, disposed by political conviction and moral persuasion to take action to remedy the sources of their disaffection, found more than adequate inspiration in their past. This was a history possessed of an inherent moral warrant with which to challenge conditions of iniquity and injustice. The past implied a purpose, celebrated as a cause to make good on, which, when rendered as a moral imperative, imposed on all Cubans in the thrall of its meaning a duty to discharge. *Verdaderos cubanos* could not be insensible of the responsibility to which they were heir as a matter of being Cuban. That the past persisted as an unfinished condition in which fulfillment of nationality had foundered suggested that remedy to the sources of Cuban discontent was to be found where it had always been: in the past.

Cubans bore the weight of their history in the form of a quest, as a wrong to right and aspirations to realize. The Declaration of Principles approved as the Final Act of the Tenth National Congress of History in November 1952 revealed the persisting angst that was itself symptomatic of the national mood all through the first half of the twentieth century. Denouncing the American decision to deny the Cuban Liberation Army entrance to Santiago de Cuba and exclude Cuban participation in the postwar treaty negotiations in 1898, the Final Act affirmed that the "Spanish-Cuban-American War of 1898 was the final phase of the Thirty Year War of Cuban Liberation, the rightful triumph of which belongs to those who since 1868 had struggled with purposeful determination to win their independence," and continued:

The Republic established on May 20, 1902, was without doubt not the one that several generations of Cubans had envisioned and for which they fought and died, [not] the one they had fully achieved by their efforts during the Thirty-Year War of Liberation. . . . The nation of [Félix] Varela and [José de la] Luz y Caballero, [Carlos Manuel de] Céspedes and [Ignacio] Agramonte, [Máximo] Gómez and [Calixto] García, [José] Martí and [Antonio] Maceo, was thwarted by the shameful intervention of the United States in the larger conflict between Cuba and Spain. Immediately upon the end of the war, the ideals of liberation were suppressed by force as a result of a foreign intervention. The departure of Spain notwithstanding, Cuba was neither independent nor free.[29]

This was historical knowledge shaped purposefully with instrumental intent, history as a means of change, a wellspring from which to draw inference as a matter of argument—history used as a frame of reference for political discourse designed to authorize change and possessed inherently of moral mandate with which to challenge the status quo. Knowledge of the past was inscribed within a discursive framework of oppositional politics, within a narrative structure that privileged the proposition of the unrealized nation as a means to condemn the failings of the republic. The moral was clear. Things were bad because the hopes that had given meaning to nationality had been betrayed in the republic. Historical narratives contributed to the collective disquiet of the national condition, sometimes more, sometimes less: a facet of a political culture in which the ideals of the past served as a readily available means to discredit the conditions of the present.

But if the past contributed to dissatisfaction with the republic, it also offered the possibility of redemption: the past as a summons to complete the project of liberation as envisioned by the *próceres*. Raúl Roa spoke for a generation in exhorting Cubans "to complete the unfinished project of José Martí and realize ourselves in a manner consistent with our history, without foreign interference."[30] The past offered a way forward. It served as a reference point from which to take measure of the degree to which the twentieth-century republic had fulfilled—or not—the nineteenth-century ideal of nation. That the project of nation remained "unconcluded" and pending—in multiple representations and characterized variously as an incomplete history, or an unrealized nation, or unfulfilled ideals, or an unfinished liberation project— served as an ever-present reminder that Cubans lived within the interstices of an interrupted national project. The proposition of "unfinished" gave decisive shape to the political culture of the republic, where the ideals of the past served as the means to envision a better future and political contenders aspired to power as proponents of a historical purpose to consummate. That the republic was almost universally perceived to have fallen short of expectations implied a standing mandate for change, for indeed at issue was the republic itself. Cubans had acted in concert, with a sense of purpose and commitment to cause, but without effect: they had been denied the outcome from which consciousness of Cuban had formed. Everything seemed to have come to nothing.

∎∎∎

It is possible that the structural tensions of the republic could have persisted unresolved, perhaps indefinitely. These were profoundly complex issues which in the ordinary course of events did not lend themselves to simple solutions and even less to obvious remedies. Electoral politics provided something of an outlet, raising hopes that were soon dashed, only to be repeated in the following election cycle. The election of Ramón Grau San Martín in 1944 was one such occasion. The rise of Eddy Chibas was another. Cubans addressed their discontent through imaginative if often ill-fated strategies, mostly as acts of personal perseverance and individual resolve. They did all the right things. They showed enterprise, they studied and resisted discouragement, they persevered with determination and spirit. They responded to historical conditions as a matter of individual circumstances, doing the best they could. Failure or success was understood as private misfortune or personal triumph.

A national crisis could change everything, however, an occasion of disruption and disarray in the established patterns of daily life, experienced simultaneously by a people as a shared revelation in which accumulated grievances were discerned as a commonplace and collective condition. Discontent previously endured as a matter of individual disgruntlement found expression as collective disquiet. Multiple currents of dissatisfaction with the status quo converged upon one another with startling force, thereupon to gather momentum as powerful impetus for action and catalyst for change.

Such a crisis occurred on March 10, 1952. A military coup led by General Fulgencio Batista ended twelve years of constitutional legality—a seizure of power, the general explained at the time, that was necessary to halt the chronic abuses of civilian government.[31] Civilian rule had indeed been characterized by years of malfeasance and misconduct, of disclosures of shameless graft and shoddy scandals, of venality so all-inclusive as to implicate almost everyone at the highest levels of government.[32] Perhaps the only virtue that civilian government could have plausibly offered in its defense was respect for constitutionality. March 10 ended that too. The constitution was suspended. Elections were canceled. Congress was dissolved. Censorship was imposed. A military dictatorship was installed for three years, and through fraudulent elections in 1955 it perpetuated itself in power for another four-year term.

Cubans across the island experienced the 1952 coup with a mixture of incomprehension and incredulity. Mario Coyula recalled March 10, 1952, as "a tremendous blow," one that "caused me surprise and confusion."[33] This sentiment was shared by poet Rubén Darío Rumbaut, who wrote at the time: "The first reaction I had when I learned of the coup was uncontrollable indignation. . . . The republic had been taken over by a military dictator whose favorite pastime, it seemed, was to make and unmake history. And now: what to do, I asked myself, filled with a sense of rage and impotence in the face of other nations of the world, of my fellow citizens, before my very children."[34] Cubans were bewildered. "I will tell you," playwright Raúl González de Cascorro spoke through his protagonist in El mejor fruto (1958), "all of us were surprised. It is like when you are taken by surprise and you are left stunned and helpless. I don't know. It was something that no one could have imagined. . . . We were left indecisive, not knowing how to react."[35]

A pall of uncertainty settled over households across the island. The murmurs of discontent were everywhere audible; the signs of disquiet were everywhere visible. "Whoever lends an ear to public opinion," columnist Ernesto Ardura despaired in 1953, "can appreciate the state of uncertainty and confusion in which the Cuban people live. There is something of a sensation of shipwreck. That psychological state of desperation can be observed in all social classes: among workers, industrialists, and merchants, in the suffering middle class. The common psychological denominator of the national moment is lassitude and profound disillusionment. . . . There is no enthusiasm, there are no great plans with an eye to the future, for the future is a huge cloud and offers security to no one."[36] Lisandro Otero remembered the national mood in the 1950s as a condition "between disquiet and bewilderment, between anxiety and shame."[37] Jorge Mañach agreed. "We are a disoriented people," he wrote in 1954. "More correctly, a people without orientation."[38]

The March 10 coup changed everything, and what changed most was how Cubans saw themselves: with embarrassment and humiliation, with deepening doubt and diminished confidence. Auténtico Party candidate for the presidency in 1952 Carlos Hevia wrote of "the humiliation of [Cubans] losing their right to elect their Government." U.S. ambassador Arthur Gardner reported that the coup had "wounded the pride of many Cubans."[39] John Dorschner and Roberto Fabricio would later write that Cubans joined the opposition "out of a sense of embarrassment, a feeling that while they could boast of their air conditioners and TV sets that seemed to put them almost on a par with Americans, they had as government a shabby military dictatorship that seemed more worthy of an old banana republic than a country aspiring to join the modern world."[40]

Things were never quite the same after March 10. "Cuba ceased to belong to the world," writer Andrés Felipe Labrador later reflected.[41] Columnist Hernández Travieso was filled with self-doubt and wondered if "we are incapable of exercising democracy and, as a result, spiritually we have gone back to the colonial era, where our grandparents lived reconciled to law being the caprice of a Captain General."[42] The moral was only hinted at and alluded to, by way of insinuation and innuendo, but it was on the minds of many. "Control of the country was taken in such an illegal manner," journalism professor Arnaldo Ramos Yániz lamented, "as if Cuba were a country where the laws of the jungle prevailed."[43] The military coup, Herminio Portell Vilá reflected, "makes one wonder if perhaps it would be preferable not to have laws that will be violated, even though by not having them we would find ourselves in regard to civilization below the savage tribes of New Guinea and the Amazon. . . . The foreign visitor departs from our country thinking that the gloss of civilization has not penetrated very deeply."[44]

■ ■ ■

The illegal seizure of power served to expose all that was wrong with the republic, all at once, and all in plain view. Rule by force begot opposition by violence. Resistance increased, and so did repression. The economy stalled, and when it began to move again it was all downward.

The character of the republic was again subjected to scrutiny, and again it was found wanting. These were troubled times, unsettled conditions as a facet of daily life calling attention to the larger malaise that was the republic. Writer José Lezama Lima despaired privately, confiding to his diary in September 1957: "We are now in the chaos resulting from the disintegration, confusion, and inferiority of Cuban life of the last thirty years. (It could be equally said: of the entire period of the republic.) On one hand, fear, bewilderment, confusion. On the other, desperation."[45] Three months later, Cintio Vitier brooded: "It is obvious that within a very few years of the founding of the Republic, what remained of the political inspiration of the founders [los fundadores] . . . was hardly anything more than a grotesque phantasm. Today, not even that."[46] To interrogate the character of the republic was to confront conditions with origins in the nineteenth century. "The colony has survived in the Republic," lamented Joaquín Martínez Sáenz.[47]

These conditions could not be attributed entirely to Batista, of course, but his illegal seizure of power made everything so much worse. He brought Cuban discontent into sharp focus—in political terms, an objective; in moral terms, a cause—and in the process drew upon himself the wrath of a people bearing grievances decades in the making. Batista represented all that was objectionable about the Cuban condition. He was both symbol and symptom of the failure of the republic, the corruption of public life, the venality of political leaders, the futility of political institutions. The political reaction that followed could not but identify the historical origins of the demise of Cuban constitutionality. The deepening crisis of the 1950s implied more than a military coup, what the narrator in Noel Navarro's novel El nivel de las aguas (1980) says about the protagonist: "He was convinced that Batista, the army, all their minions, and all that, were nothing more than one aspect—a grim one, to be sure, but only one aspect—of the problem."[48] This was understood at the time by Francisco José Moreno. "The Cuba in which we lived was not Batista's doing," he later recalled, "but the doings of Batista were the results of the Cuba we lived in."[49]

Men and women across the island were coming slowly to question the assumptions of everyday life, uneasily, and they despaired, becoming ever more predisposed to break with the prevailing order of things. The Batista coup acted to "push" Cubans further along, deeper into those realms of solutions that incline a people to dramatic action. The possibility that the removal of Batista would provide the means to address larger—that is, historic—issues was very much inscribed within the calculus of resistance all through the 1950s. Rufo López-Fresquet was indeed correct to observe that the Batista government "converted nearly every Cuban into a revolutionary."[50]

■ ■ ■

It happened too that Batista governed during years of recurring historical commemorations, a convergence of circumstances and coincidence, to be sure, but one that provided poignancy to the Cuban angst: years of remembrance in times of grievance. The 1950s were years dense with history. The year 1952—the year of the coup—was the fiftieth anniversary of the founding of the republic—under the circumstances, a singularly portentous occasion to take stock of half a century of nationhood. No less portentous an occasion, in 1953, was the centennial of the birth of José Martí. Indeed, the 1950s were noteworthy for centennial celebrations. Towns and cities across the island commemorated the birth centennials of men and women of local origins who had distinguished themselves during the wars for independence: Víctor Ramos Hernández in Guisa (1852), Alejandro Rodríguez in Sancti-Spíritus (1852), Vidal Ducasse in El Cobre (1852), Bernarda del Toro in Jiguaní (1852), Juan Gualberto Gómez in Sabanilla (1854), Agustín Cebreco in El Cobre (1855), Emilio Núñez in Sagua la Grande (1855), Demetrio Castillo Duany in Santiago de Cuba (1856), and Tomás Padró Griñán in Santiago de Cuba (1856), among many others.

In an environment of deepening political tensions, public acts to honor heroes and commemorate heroic deeds provided occasions for protest, to make the meaning of the past relevant as a moral for the times. The organizers of the centennial commemoration of Martí's birth in January 1953, Alba Martínez Fernández acknowledged years later, used the centennial occasion to distribute pamphlets containing quotations of Martí selected explicitly as allusions with which to attack the Batista government. "We determined," Martínez Fernandez reminisced, "that in all public acts the ideas of Martí would be prominent not only to render homage to the distinguished teachings of the Apostle, but also as a means to combat the insolent and backward dictatorship that had made a mockery of the centennial anniversary of Martí's birth."[51] Gloria Cuadras de la Cruz remembered that on December 7, 1952, the anniversary date of the death of Antonio Maceo, women in Santiago de Cuba organized a commemorative march that resulted in "a protest that proclaimed 'down with the dictatorship' that resonated throughout the entire city."[52] Observance of December 7 in Manzanillo in 1954 was marked by the affirmation that "those us who sincerely love the *Patria* . . . mourn this date as a time of a loss of liberty."[53] Organizers of the Maceo commemoration in December 1957 summoned "all Cubans of dignity" to continue the patriotic task inaugurated by Maceo: "There is not a single true Cuban [*cubano verdadero*] who does not demand the restoration of liberties and who does not call for a return to the road leading to a democratic government."[54] Belarmino Castilla Mas later remembered Santiago de Cuba during the 1950s: "The entire student movement of Santiago de Cuba . . . converted every historic date—January 28, February 24, November 27, and December 7—into an opportunity to take to the streets and use the occasion to protest against the [Batista] tyranny."[55]

∎∎∎

The deepening crisis of the 1950s called attention—again—to the persisting condition of malaise that Cubans seemed unable to undo and overcome. The shortcomings of the republic seemed to reveal themselves in magnified form during the 1950s: the problems seemed so vast, the solutions so beyond reach. All in all, a people overwhelmed by seemingly persistent circumstances of adversity, not certain they knew where to begin, or how.

In search of direction, Cubans increasingly turned to the past for signs and solutions, a way to understand the circumstances of their times by way of their history. Because it was a past without end, accessible and always usable as a politics, its moral and meaning seemed to possess something of a timeless relevance. The past offered perspective and purpose, a way to articulate a politics of change readily accessible to all.

No less important, the past also offered methods of remedy and means of solution. The historic manifestos, the pronouncements, and the programs—that is, the texts by which the nineteenth-century liberation project had fixed itself in the popular imagination—retained their relevance precisely because they addressed grievances with origins in the nineteenth century, almost all of which persisted unremedied in the twentieth. José Martí served as an inexhaustible supply of truths, for all occasions, on all subjects. So too with the foundational texts of the independence movement—the Constitution of Guáimaro, for example, or the Bases of the Partido Revolucionario Cubano, or the Manifesto of Montecristi: all, it seemed, could be revived to address the ills that continued to afflict the island. "The revolution [against Batista] as a historic intent," proclaimed the Federación Estudiantil Universitaria in 1956, "has its roots in the wars for independence. The Manifesto of Montecristi is our basic document."[56] The organizers of November 30, 1956, in Santiago de Cuba invoked "the Revolutionary Proclamation of Demajagua [the Ten Years War], the Manifesto of Montecristi, and the words of José Martí . . . in discharge of a debt to our generation and to the History of Cuba."[57]

The power of the past to inform the politics of protest and influence a course of action is, of course, a profoundly complex phenomenon. The very invocation of the past as purpose implied a challenge, as it always had, less to a person than to a political system, less to a government than to a national condition. The desired outcome was inscribed in the premise. Cubans experienced their times as a history in progress, understood as a commitment to the ideal from which the meaning of nationality had originated and into which they self-consciously inserted themselves.

Across the island, all through the 1950s, men and women joined an expanding insurgency as a matter of legacy, disposed to discharge duty long consecrated in the narratives of nation. For many, the act of resistance responded to an outpouring of indignation and offended sensibility, the need to do something: to act. The protagonist in Luis Ricardo Alonso's novel *Los dioses ajenos* (1971), comments the narrator, "joined the revolutionary movement in order to maintain self-respect."[58] The desire "to participate in concrete deeds [*participar en hechos concretos*]" was how Conrado del Puerto remembered his decision to join the Civic Resistance in Matanzas.[59] "What is important," pronounces the protagonist in Marcos in Julio Travieso's autobiographical novel *Para matar el lobo* (1981), "is to do something, and not just stand there doing nothing"[60]—what Guillermo Jiménez of the Directorio Revolucionario recalled years later as "the need to do something—something, anything."[61] Many joined the resistance, General Harry Villegas remembered, "out of a sense of justice, to struggle against the status quo, that which had been imposed upon us, and to fight existing ills. Many people did not know exactly why they joined."[62]

The resistance included men and women motivated by the moral of their history, conscious of an obligation to live up to legacy, a summons drawing them into a flow of continuity with their past, acting on the determination—articulated often during the 1950s—to enter into history (*entrar en la historia*). "I loved the history of the wars of independence of my *patria* with a passion," as Giraldo Mazola Collazo, a member of the Civic Resistance in Havana, reminisced about his secondary-school years. "At the time I thought it to be a bygone era, not to be repeated again, without realizing that within a few years I would be incorporated into a movement that would signify continuity with that process."[63] For Roberto Hernández Zayas, the decision to join the Civic Resistance was a matter of devotion to the purpose to which the past had been given. "When the Cuban people launched the war for liberty and independence on October 10, 1868," Hernández Zayas later wrote, "a long process of struggle was inaugurated, one distinguished by historic phases and milestones, one that still continues." Hernández Zayas wrote of himself in the third person, a young man who took up arms to redeem the "*patria* envisioned by Martí: free, independent and sovereign, honorable, noble, proud, united, and just," and added: "That young man proceeded to develop his love for the *patria* while immersing himself in the history of Cuba, in its wars for independence of the nineteenth century, in its legendary figures, their heroic acts, and the nobility of their cause. Accordingly, his spirit was nurtured and his consciousness strengthened. The words of Martí influenced him profoundly and through them fostered an attachment to noble sentiments and human values."[64] Gladys Marel García-Pérez remembered being drawn into the armed struggle against Batista out of the desire "to be like the patriots of the nineteenth century. I was conscious of acting in the role of the *mambisas*, like my grandmother."[65] Enzo Infante Uribazo later reflected on the effect of studying history: "Something very curious happened to me. When I read and heard about our heroes of independence, I always asked myself if I would someday have the opportunity to do something like they did. Maybe that was the stuff of childhood, but I always did dream with doing some heroic deed in order to change the situation in which we lived our lives."[66]

These were historically conditioned sentiments, very much what made for consciousness of Cuban, a people acting in accordance with what they understood the moral of their history required of them. For many Cubans, historical knowledge was integral to the moral calculus of nationality, understood as the need to participate in a historical process, to live history and more: to participate in a living history understood as legacy. Blanca Mercedes Mesa recalled the despair to which she succumbed as a result of the 1952 coup, and it was to the past that her thoughts turned: "It was almost a physical blow, and brought me to tears and indignation. . . . What to do? Seemingly, nothing. Nothing to do against brute force. But the lesson of 1868? And the lesson of 1895?"[67] This was similar to the experience of Vilma Espín, who remembered March 10 "as something that for me was explosive. . . . It was for me almost a personal offense. . . . [But] I jumped for joy thinking about the prospects of joining an armed protest. In reality, I always had romantic longings of being able to participate in heroic struggles like the War for Independence, the struggle against Machado, etc. At that moment I truly believed that armed protest was the only recourse. I was as happy as a child in a party, and wanted immediately to pick up a rifle and go to fight."[68] Mario Coyula experienced the 1950s through knowledge of the 1890s. "From the outset," he recalled years later, "in accordance with the lessons I had learned at home based on patriotic traditions, for my ancestors had fought in the wars for independence, I understood that this was an utterly intolerable situation."[69] Julio García Olivares of the Directorio Revolucionario later reflected that "something impelled us to seek in the past the connection that would link us to the frustrated revolution that began with the War for Independence and which would at the same time serve as a point of departure in the process of struggle against the tyranny of Batista."[70] The illegal seizure of power of March 10, Guillermo Jiménez remembered years later, gave "definition to a life of action based on the deeds of the nineteenth century, in fulfillment of the legacy of independence [el legado mambí]."[71]

The logic of armed struggle obtained its most compelling validation in the form of discharge of duty as Cuban. This implied conduct and commitment to enact the ideals upon which the nation had been conceived. The men and women who joined the armed resistance during the 1950s looked back as much as they looked forward, and they understood too the former as a means to the latter. They drew inspiration and motivation from the past and inserted themselves consciously into their history as a matter of legacy. The combatants of the Sierra Maestra, recalled Arnaldo Rivero, were imbued with the "precise discipline and clear concept of duty to the *patria*," for Cubans could not "remain downtrodden when confronted with the names of Maceo, Martí, Agramonte, Céspedes, and Guiteras."[72] The past contemplated a purpose pending in which all Cubans were implicated by virtue of being Cuban. Asked by Jules Dubois in 1958 to explain the political philosophy of the Movimiento Revolucionario 26 de Julio (MR 26-7; the 26th of July Movement), Raúl Castro responded, "the doctrines of Martí," and added: "We consider ourselves followers of his unfinished work. If we cannot conclude it we will nevertheless have fulfilled our historic role, sustaining until the end the standard of his ideological principles. Behind [us] will come new generations, which rising anew will know how to carry it forward another step."[73]

Historical knowledge had insinuated itself deeply in realms of received wisdom, in widely accessible and readily comprehensible narrative forms, celebrated as those understandings from which a people derive the values they feel represent their best qualities, a way to comprehend being in the present as a condition of the past. The men and women who took up arms in resistance during the 1950s drew freely upon what were already well-established narratives of the unrealized nation and unfulfilled aspirations as the larger rationale of the armed struggle. They spoke to a purpose with which vast numbers of Cubans were sympathetic, and to which they were eminently susceptible.

Once the premise of the legacy insinuated itself into the logic of resistance, the duty of armed struggle seemed as obvious as it was obligatory. It signaled resumption of the project of nation, of Cubans inserting themselves into the continuity of their history as a matter of moral obligation inscribed in Cuban. The decision to participate in the insurrection, Belarmino Castillo Mas remembered, was a matter of "loyalty to the legacy of our predecessors."[74] Luis Saíz Montes de Oca took up arms as a matter of "duty as Cuban" (*deber como cubano*), in "the firm belief that the duty of our generation [was] to fulfill our destiny and realize the revolution that Cuba has awaited for a century, whatever it may cost."[75] The commitment to struggle and sacrifice, Camilo Cienfuegos insisted, "is our duty [*es deber nuestro*], and if not, we were ill-born as Cubans."[76] The assailants of Moncada, Pedro Miret explained years later, "participated in fulfillment of a debt,"[77] while Faustino Pérez remembered returning to Cuba aboard the yacht *Granma* "conscious that I was fulfilling a duty of Cuban [*cumplía un deber de cubano*]."[78] Mario Lazo Pérez participated in the attack on Moncada to uphold "the revolutionary tradition of our people, [which] pointed to the course to follow and allowed the vanguard of Cuban youth to follow the example of Céspedes, Agramonte, José and Antonio Maceo, Gómez, Martí, Mella, Trejo, and Guiteras."[79] Enzo Infante Uribazo later characterized his participation in the revolution in modest terms: "I was an idealist person who joined the revolution because I deeply believed that it was my duty as an honorable citizen [ciudadano honrado]."[80] "A free man," the narrator in José Soler Puig's novel En el ano de enero (1963) comments on the meaning of Cuban, "is the one who knows that he has a duty to fulfill and fulfills it entirely of his own volition, without having to be told, because he knows he has to a duty to fulfill."[81]

Armed resistance drew its principal rationale from the past, a sentiment with antecedents in the nineteenth century, to act as a matter of common task in a manner consistent with the obligation of shared duty. The resort to arms was understood not only—and perhaps not even principally—as a reaction to Batista, but as a response to historically determined imperatives with antecedents in the nineteenth century. "We are determined to liberate Cuba," a barbudo (guerrilla) says to seventy-year-old mambí Panteleón Núñez in Bernardo Viera Trejo's short story "El precio," "the same way that you and men like you liberated Cuba in 1895."[82] The narrator in Juan Almeida Bosque's autobiographical novel La única ciudadana (1985) reflects on the continuity of purpose implied in the armed struggle during the 1950s: "Just like those heroic men [of the nineteenth century], today we too struggle to see our flag waving in the breeze, as symbol of the real independence for which so much noble Cuban blood has been spilled."[83] This was the point Camilo Cienfuegos made explicitly: "We cannot but recognize the difficulty of the insurrectionary war, that war to realize a free patria, to see the patria liberated and to realize the great patria that Martí had dreamed about."[84] Huber Matos was among the many Cubans formed within the logic of the unfinished nation. "I embraced the commitment to continue with the task of founding the Republic of Cuba," he reflected—"that we were a republic, but incomplete; that we were a republic, but debased. . . . My generation and the generation of the first half of the twentieth century were formed within that commitment." Matos was lucid in recalling his decision to join the insurrection: "Others had sacrificed themselves to break the chains of the colony, forging step by step the Republic . . . at the end of the nineteenth century. It was the result of several generations at a cost of many thousands of lives and indescribable suffering. It is now our turn to defend the rights and well-being of the Republic that they bequeathed to us."[85] Julio García Olivares joined the resistance "determined to sweep away once and for all the corruption and immorality that had characterized the political life of the country and organize the Republic on the basis established by José Martí: to achieve the objectives for which the *mambises* had striven since 1868, to improve the conditions of life of our people. . . . We were simple students, but the moment had arrived to bear arms, the way we had learned from our ancestors in the wars for independence. . . . We were mindful of our duty, if not to consummate the task inaugurated at Yara [the Ten Years War], at least to advance further toward that purpose."[86] The protagonist in Benigno Nieto's novel *Los paraísos artificiales* (1999) affirms this: "To sweep away once and for all the ignominious past."[87]

∎∎∎

The ideal of national fulfillment, even as—especially as—dashed hopes, inscribed itself deeply into the consciousness of Cuban. As a sentiment—as a feeling—it "worked" within those intuitive realms of presumed certainty. It needed neither justification nor explanation. On the contrary, it was an outcome Cubans claimed as a matter of faith in their history. The redemption of "the oppressed *patria*," a coalition of opposition groups affirmed in the unity Pact of Caracas of July 1958, "will be achieved by all of us who believe deeply in the historic destiny of our nation, its right to be free and to constitute within a democratic community . . . the magnificent future to which our people have a right by virtue of their History."[88]

The master narrative of the nation, loaded as it was with aspirations as anticipation, readily drew Cubans into the plausibility of revolution as remedy, largely as a matter of culturally determined dispositions, for these were the articles of faith from which the normative determinants of nationality were derived. It was in this sense that the historical knowledge by which a people came to a sense of themselves was revelatory, for it evoked the promise of a past to fulfill as a premonition, at once prescriptive and prophetic, an ideal Cubans had been enjoined to pursue as legacy in the form of destiny. Columnist Agustín Tamargo called for new political leaders "who will confront the problems of Cuba the way that Martí faced the truth."[89] The weekly *Carteles* concluded in 1953 that "what we do know is that the process of deterioration appears unstoppable. On the contrary, it is accelerating. What is the possibility that men like those of 1868 still exist, who desire that Cuba dignify its national life and seek the culmination of its most promising destiny? Where are they?"[90]

Fulfillment of the promise of the future was possible only through the realization of the aspirations of the past, Cubans were certain. It was a way that many came to see Fidel Castro. "I would say," affirmed René Díaz in 1957, "that Fidel Castro is the Apostle of the new generation. He possesses sublime ideals and the dignity of Martí [*vergüenza martiana*]. It was with men like him that José Martí dreamed of our *Patria*."[91] Alfredo Guevara later remembered these years as a time when "our generation dreamed of José Martí, that José Martí was needed" and that Fidel Castro was looked upon "as someone who could perhaps become the José Martí that my generation was awaiting, had searched for, wished to discover."[92] Rafael Rojas was entirely correct to note that the plausibility of the revolution was in part derived from a susceptibility to a messianic moral embedded in Cuban history.[93]

The Batista coup provided a new generation of men and women with the opportunity to join their history. Almost all the revolutionary groups that emerged to oppose the Batista government inscribed themselves explicitly within the framework of historical legacy. Only days after the military coup, the Federación Estudiantil Universitaria (FEU) proclaimed its determination to resist the Batista government as a matter of solemn duty based on a covenant with the past. "Cuban students," the FEU affirmed, "will maintain respect and reverence only for the symbols that the *mambises* provided us, soaked in the blood of the battlefield for liberty: our national anthem, our coat of arms, our flag. Never before have those symbols had as much historical meaning as they do now. We want a Republic free of foreign intermeddling and internal deception."[94] In its Declaration of Principles, the FEU proclaimed its commitment to "the defense of the *Patria* bequeathed to us by the *mambises*."[95] José Antonio Echeverría, president of the FEU, alluded often to "the historic destiny of our Nation" and expressed confidence in the realization of the "revolutionary ideals that constitute the very essence of our Nationality."[96] With the founding of the Directorio Revolucionario (DR) by the FEU in 1956, students committed themselves to armed struggle to complete "the revolution inaugurated by Joaquín de Agüero [1851] and which to this date remains unfinished and yet to be realized" as a means to "honor our martyrs."[97] The formation of the DR guerrilla front in 1958—the Second Front of Escambray—the DR pronounced, was to keep faith with the duty that the past imposed on all Cubans. The Proclamation of Escambray (1958) was explicit:

The men who enroll in the ranks of the Directorio Revolucionario are conscious of the role that we play in the historic process of our people. . . . "The war that today we initiate"—affirmed José Martí in 1895—"is the continuation of the one begun by Céspedes in 1868 in La Demajagua." We know that our generation is connected to the generations that preceded us yesterday. For that reason it is the same cause. . . . That is the dialectical process of our history, which is the history of the Americas. This is our understanding, and it is the process of history into which we integrate ourselves.[98]

The Movimiento Nacional Revolucionario (MNR), organized within one year of the 1952 coup, inserted itself directly into the larger narrative of nation as the basis of principles and from which it affirmed its claim to "historical continuity" in the form of "true revolutionary spirit." The MNR proclaimed its determination to fulfill long-deferred national aspirations: "All the great cycles of historical developments," the MNR reminded the nation, "have ended without achieving the fullness of purpose: the Ten Years War ended in defeat, that of [the Pact of] Zanjón; the war of 1895 ended with a mediated and semi-intervened republic that did not resolve the fundamental problems of the Cuban people." The new generation, the MNR vowed, would realize the "historic destiny" of the nation: "The Movimiento Nacional Revolucionario is organized to bring to a completion the work that the Cuban independentista conspirators initiated at the dawn of the last century, continued by the patriots of 1868, carried on by the liberators of 1895, and which the revolutionaries of the 1930s sought to bring to fruition: to realize the definitive integration of our nationality."[99] The MNR, affirmed its founder, Rafael García Bárcena, was prepared to assume the duty imposed by history: "The national history of Cuba has been the history of a prolonged revolution, to whose fulfillment diverse generations of Cubans have been entrusted . . . and to which the MNR was committed."[100]

No group more fully adopted the past as purpose of politics than the Movimiento Revolucionario 26 de Julio (MR 26-7). Under the leadership of Fidel Castro, the MR 26-7 elevated the historic narratives of nation into an all-encompassing paradigm for revolution. This was the past used as source of actionable knowledge, a narrative structured as a continuum which Cubans were enjoined to insert themselves into: a leap of faith so central to political purpose as to assume fully the form of moral imperative, precluding and preempting all outcomes not given to the realization of the ideal of sovereign nationhood as means of fulfillment of Cuban.

The genius of the leadership of the MR 26-7 was its ability to inscribe itself into the past and to reemerge as its proponent, to represent itself as the bearer of nineteenth-century truths—in part conscience, in part consciousness—to summon Cubans to dramatic action as a matter of duty inherent in the meaning of nationality. The sentiments were themselves a sensibility possessed of a proper history, and indeed it was precisely this condition of the past that made for the efficacy of history as a politics. The political culture of the republic had formed within a history understood as unfinished, imbued with a sense of expectation intrinsic to which was the possibility—and precedent—of agency: a condition that invited "participation" in the deliverance of the promise of the past as a matter of redemption.

Fidel Castro brought passionate intensity to the pursuit of political change, profoundly steeped in and sustained by a conviction of historical purpose based on the premise that the sources of Cuban discontent could be addressed only through the realization of the promise of sovereign nationhood. The past offered a moral of portentous purport. To claim legacy of the past as the basis of a politics was to demand duty as a matter of nationality, a way to inscribe Cubans into a historical continuum as means of legitimacy of purpose.

History had been Fidel Castro's passion.[101] That he was clever, even brilliant, manipulative and shrewd, cunning and calculating, are all undoubtedly true, but he was effective principally because he was of the history that he propounded. He fashioned a larger vision of political purpose in the form of a claim in discharge of historical legacy. "He was determined to insert himself in history in whatever way possible," as Heberto Padilla remembered the young Fidel Castro.[102] Fidel Castro espoused the past explicitly as the rationale of political purpose, discerning within the normative determinants of nationality a relentless moral logic of revolution. He was properly reverential of the *mambises* as symbol and source of validation. As early as November 1947, on the occasion of the anniversary of the 1871 execution of University of Havana medical students, Castro—then a student at the University of Havana—organized a campus demonstration to protest government corruption, for which he invited the participation of surviving *mambises*. He addressed the purpose of their presence:

> It is necessary to set in relief the miracle of this moment. The liberators who fought for our independence from Spain still, after fifty years, retain the same rebellious spirit that propelled them into the battlefield of redemption [*la manigua de la redención*]. It is a momentous occasion when the veterans of our independence struggle ally themselves with the students in pursuit of the liberating aims of our past. The liberators of yesterday trust the young students of today so that we can continue their goal of achieving independence and justice.[103]

The MR 26-7 leadership understood the power of the past to inform political purpose. This was to use history to make history: to exhort Cubans to live up to legacy as an obligation implied in the meaning of Cuban. The "Manifiesto de los revolucionarios del Moncada a la nación," distributed on the eve of the assault on the Moncada barracks in July 1953, affirmed the determination to fulfill "the revolution of [Carlos Manuel de] Céspedes, [Ignacio] Agramonte, [Antonio] Maceo, [Julio Antonio] Mella, [Antonio] Guiteras, [Rafael] Trejo, and [Eduardo] Chibás, the true revolution that has not yet been completed." The Manifiesto proclaimed the year 1953—the centennial of the birth of José Martí—as "the culmination of a historical cycle marked by progress and setbacks in the political and moral realms of the Republic: the bloody and vigorous struggle for liberty and independence; the civic contest among Cubans to attain political and economic stability; the shameful practice of foreign intervention; the dictatorships; the unrelenting struggle of heroes and martyrs to make a better Cuba." The assault on Moncada was planned in the "name of the determined struggles that have characterized the summit of glory in Cuban history," and further: "The Revolution identifies with the roots of Cuba's national sentiment [and] recognizes and bases itself on the ideals of José Martí contained in his speeches, the program of the Partido Revolucionario Cubano, and the Manifesto of Montecristi."[104] Asked at the trial what the purpose of the Moncada attack was, Raúl Castro responded: "To make the revolution that Martí and Maceo wanted, to make the revolution of our mambises."[105]

It was to history that Fidel Castro appealed for absolution during the Moncada trial, and it was history from which he claimed the mandate to discharge the duty of Cuban. Castro's trial speech, subsequently expanded and distributed as the foundational text of the MR 26-7, "History Will Absolve Me," invoked the legacy of the past to validate the moral propriety of revolution. Moncada responded to historically conditioned attributes of nationality, Castro explained, acted out as behavior modeled on the example of heroic comportment associated with the mambises. "All doors for peaceful struggle being closed to the people," he insisted, "there is no solution other than that of [the revolutions] of 1868 and 1895." Castro invoked the duty to "exercise the right" of the Cuban people to revolt against oppression as a matter of "historic continuation of the struggle of 1868, 1895, and 1933." Castro appealed explicitly to obligations deemed intrinsic to the character of Cuban. "We are Cubans," he exhorted,

> and to be Cuban implies a duty: not to fulfill this duty is a crime, it is treason. We live proud of the history of our patria; we learned it in school and we have grown up hearing of freedom, of justice, and of rights. We were taught early to venerate the glorious examples of our heroes and our mar-

tyrs. Céspedes, Agramonte, Maceo, Gómez, and Martí were the first names inscribed in our minds. We were taught that the Titan [Maceo] had said that liberty is not begged for, but rather conquered through the edge of the *machete*. . . . We were taught that October 10 [1868] and February 24 [1895] are glorious anniversaries . . . on which Cubans rebelled against the yoke of infamous tyranny. We were taught to . . . sing an anthem every afternoon, the verses of which say that "To live in chains is to live in shame and dishonor" and that "To die for the *patria* is to live."[106]

The men and women of the MR 26-7 immersed themselves in the history of Cuba as a matter of political education in preparation for armed struggle. Years later, Mario Llerena recalled a conversation with Castro in Mexico in 1956: "Castro told me over and over that, in addition to military and guerrilla training, the soldiers of the revolution were required to read and discuss a variety of books of historical and political significance, especially, he emphasized, the works of the Cuban liberator José Martí."[107] This is also what Teresa Casuso remembered, explaining that she was persuaded by Fidel Castro to join the MR 26-7 with the argument that "in dealing with Batista and his army there was no other way but to wage 'the necessary war,' as Martí had called the one waged for our independence. Fidel showed that he had read a great deal of José Martí, who seemed, indeed, to be the guiding spirit of his life."[108] Haydée Santamaría often recounted that the preparations for Moncada involved "giving ourselves to reading Martí in depth," with particular attention "to the Manifesto of Montecristi and the statutes of the Partido Revolucionario Cubano."[109]

Between 1953 and 1955, the years of imprisonment, Castro conducted daily classes in Cuban history. "The desire to know more about our past, our people, our great men of the past," he wrote from prison in 1954, "has been preying on my mind for some time. The enthusiasm, love, and interest I put into all my reading on this subject is a source of comfort for me."[110] Patriotic holidays in particular offered occasions for history lessons. "On every patriotic date of Cuban history," Castro wrote, "we have gathered together to commemorate the occasion and hold discussions on the subject."[111]

Vast numbers of men and women sustained devotion to nation as a matter of belief in their past. They bore their history with a sense of purpose, conscious too of the duty that their history imposed upon them. This was a history dense with narratives of martyrdom and heroic deaths, honored as deeds noble and noteworthy, to be sure, but also as conduct represented as model and measure of Cuban: this is what Cubans did by virtue of being Cuban. "If what is needed at this time," Castro proclaimed in 1955, "are Cubans willing to sacrifice themselves to redeem the civic sensibility of our people from shame, we offer ourselves with pleasure."[112] The duty "of sacrifice [and] of honor is honest, useful, worthy, heroic, and is part of our glorious tradition." This was validated by invoking a passage from Martí: "Great moments require great sacrifices."[113] To do less implied dereliction of duty and dishonor to the ideal of Cuban. Those who perished at Moncada, Fidel Castro affirmed, "learned to die when the *patria* is in need of heroic immolation to lift the faith of the people . . . [as] the inevitable realization of their historic destiny."[114] The narrator in Luis Ricardo Alonso's novel *El palacio y la furia* (1976), based on the abortive 1957 assault on the Presidential Palace to assassinate Batista, comments: "Many were ashamed that they had escaped with their lives. Perhaps it was the influence of religion, of so many years hearing talk of the glory of martyrdom. And for those who did not believe in God, twelve years in school hearing talk of the martyrs of the *patria*: Martí, Maceo, hundreds of others. Since everyone was going to die anyway, we used to say in school, better to die like the great heroes. There wasn't a single boy who wanted to die in bed."[115]

The MR 26-7 claimed history as source of redemptive purport, having as much to do with overturning the conditions that had produced Batista as overthrowing Batista. To invoke the nineteenth-century *independentista* project as the discursive framework of revolution implied the use of the past as a way to contemplate solution to the historic sources of Cuban discontent. The MR 26-7 insisted outright that "the dictatorship can only be toppled by those who seek something more than its simple removal. . . . Those who pretend simply to 'topple the dictator' will not even achieve that, since they lack both serious motives and support from the social forces necessary to oppose regime embodying the most negative aspects of Cuban society. . . . The current government is not the cause but the result of the republic's fundamental crisis."[116]

The politics was embedded in the history, which meant too that the men and women of the resistance acted consciously as agents of their past. History served as a way to give context to commitment. The men and women of the MR 26-7 adopted the past as source of purpose and assumed the role of agents of history in fulfillment of the long-deferred project of nation. "Today we see [the martyrs of liberation] more alive than ever," exhorted *El Morillo* in 1958, the official publication of Column 9/Third Front 'Antonio Guiteras' of the Rebel Army led by Hubert Matos, "a presence [*sombra*] that drives us forward and guides our arms tirelessly to struggle against the enemies of the *patria*."[117] Virtually all the principal texts prepared and disseminated by the MR

26-7 during the years of the insurrectionary war characterized the process of armed struggle as a matter of historical continuity. The "Manifiesto Número 1 del 26 de Julio al pueblo de Cuba" (1955) affirmed:

> The Cuban revolutionary movement is today organized and prepares for its great task of redemption and justice. . . . The streets and parks of our cities and towns bear the names and display with pride the statues of Maceo, Martí, Máximo Gómez, Calixto García, Céspedes, Agramonte, Flor Crombet, Bartolomé Masó, and other illustrious heroes who knew how to rebel. Our glorious history is taught in school, and the dates of October 10 and February 24 are venerated with devotion. These were not dates of submission or of resigned and cowardly acceptance of existing despotism. . . . In adopting again the line of sacrifice we assume before history responsibility for our acts.[118]

The Manifesto-Program (1956) provided the clearest exposition of historical sensibility as the logic of armed struggle. "The 26th of July Movement proposed fundamentally to reclaim the unfulfilled ideals of the Cuban nation and bring them to fruition," the Manifesto-Program began. The MR 26-7 proclaimed itself as the "continuation of the revolutionary generations of the past" and insisted that it was "in reality the resumption of the unfinished Revolution of Cuba. It is for that purpose that we commit to the same 'necessary war' propounded by the Apostle [Martí], and for the same reasons." The Manifesto-Program insisted that armed struggle was "at least as justified today as it was in 1868 and 1895, perhaps more so. In reality, we are resuming the unfinished revolution of Martí." It continued: "Cuba fully possesses the geographical, historical, political, economic, and sociological justifications to constitute itself as a sovereign and independent nation. This is the first and basic affirmation of our struggle. Without it, the historical progress of the Cuban people in the last one hundred years would be totally devoid of any sense." Indeed, the document proclaimed,

> the Revolution is the struggle of the Cuban nation to fulfill its historical objectives. . . . The Revolution is not exactly a war or an isolated episode. Rather it is a continuing historical process represented by distinct moments and phases. The landings of Narciso López in the mid-nineteenth century, the wars of 1868 and 1895, the movement of the 1930s, and the struggle against the outlawry of the Batista regime are all part of the same and only national Revolution. . . . The principal objective of the Revolution is to affirm the full sovereignty of Cuba.[119]

The MR 26-7 reaffirmed this theme one year later: "The Revolution is based on the historical ideal of the *Cuban nation*. . . . This is the basic and foremost affirmation of our struggle. Without it, the historic process of the last one hundred years would be devoid of meaning," adding:

> That the struggle has not yet been brought to a successful conclusion means that the nation has not been fully consummated. . . . The Revolution is the struggle of the Cuban nation to achieve its historical objectives and realize its full integration. The Revolution seeks full national sovereignty and economic independence. The Revolution is not exactly a war or an isolated episode. It is a continual historical process that develops in different moments and through different stages. The conspiracies of the last century, the wars of 1868 and 1895, the movement of the 1930s, the struggle against the terror of Batista are all parts of the same and only Revolution.[120]

■ ■ ■

Not for the first time was the past deployed as a politics. But never before had the discursive framework of opposition been so fully transacted as discharge of historical purpose. The MR 26-7 inscribed itself into the past as a matter of context and continuity, to claim the fulfillment of the ideal of the sovereign nation as reason for revolution: the past as a shared reference point of memory and remembrance, of aspirations that were themselves at the very source of nationality. "Having won the war of independence, after the defeat of the colonial regime," the MR 26-7 explained only weeks before the triumph of the revolution, "our people had earned the right to their independence. But almost immediately the sovereignty for which we so yearned was abrogated by the opprobrious Platt Amendment. . . . That was how the Republic was born." The MR 26-7 pledged its determination "to conquer for our *patria* its legitimate right to be present in history as a nation free and democratic . . . [a commitment] that derives its inspiration from the thought of the Apostle [Martí]."[121]

From the outset, the MR 26-7 inscribed the meaning of armed resistance within allusions and analogies to the past: a continuation of the cause for which generations of *mambises* in the nineteenth century had sacrificed. Insurrection in Oriente province was itself possessed of intrinsic historical significance, an opportunity for Cubans to incorporate themselves into the historic geography of the nation, the very region associated with the origins of the wars for *Cuba Libre*. "[Oriente] is the land of the invincible heroes," proclaimed the MR 26-7, "for it represents the spirit of sacrifice and love of the

Patria of the Liberators of 1868 and 1895, of the struggles against Spain and Machado . . . and always to emerge triumphant."[122] All through 1957 and 1958, the insurgency in the Sierra Maestra was likened to the wars for independence. The clandestine newspaper *Sierra Maestra* proclaimed that "today in the mountain ranges of Oriente, a war for the freedom of Cuba is being waged in precisely the same way that the *mambises* fought in the war of 1868 and the war of 1895."[123] Enzo Infante Uribazo joined the insurgency, he remembered, inspired by the knowledge of "the prestigious combatants in Oriente who filled the pages of our history with acts of heroism," noting: "All these things conferred on Oriente a great tradition of epic struggles and events."[124] "Young Cubans today," wrote Armando Villa in 1957, "fight like the *mambises* of 1868 and 1895," and further:

> The way that sunlight originates from Oriente, once again light will arrive in Cuba from the indomitable region of its Liberty. First it was Maceo, who in his triumphal march brought the Light of Justice and Democracy, with all the *mambises*, from Maisí to San Antonio [that is, from one end of the island to the other]. Now it is Fidel Castro, the leader of the present generations, who has taken control of our highest mountain, to start a fire that will serve as the beacon of redemption of our martyred *Patria*. . . . The flame of liberty has been set ablaze again in Oriente and it will reach across the entire island.[125]

But it is also true that the armed opposition to the Batista government extended far beyond the confines of the Sierra Maestra. Across the island, in small towns and large cities, a vast underground network expanded to mount clandestine operations against the Batista government.[126] The resistance involved vast numbers of Cubans, mostly ordinary men and women, of all social classes, who made a choice to act on what they believed to be the moral of their history. "We workers," proclaimed *Candela*, the clandestine newspaper published by laundry and dry cleaning laborers, "faithful to the ideals of 1868 and 1895, appeal for the support of the *mambises* of today, to the revolutionaries who are truly committed to the construction of the Republic that Martí had dreamed about."[127]

A new generation had taken up the cause of fulfillment of nation as a function of historic purpose. It identified itself as the "Generation of the Centennial" and would thereafter claim direct ideological lineage from José Martí, who was thereafter identified as the "intellectual author" of Moncada.[128] The assault on Moncada, proclaimed the "Manifiesto de los revolucionarios del Moncada a la nación," was planned with the "desire to honor with sacrifice and victory the unrealized dream of Martí."[129] Fidel Castro invoked the centennial of the birth of Martí as the occasion to redeem the ideal of nation: "[Martí's] dream lives on. It has not died. His people are rebellious. His people are worthy. His people are faithful to his memory."[130]

Many of the facets of the insurrection were modeled on the war of independence. "The similarity of the situation," Castro wrote from prison in August 1954, "reminds me of the efforts made by Martí to unite all honorable Cubans [*todos los cubanos dignos*] in the struggle for independence. Each [person] had his history, his glories, his achievements; each believed to possess more rights than the others, or at least as many rights. . . . I am certain that without [Martí's] magnificent effort, Cuba would still be a Spanish colony or a *yanqui* dependency. Perhaps that is the reason that I so admire the pages of Cuban history. They are not so much about feats on the field of battle as about that vast, heroic, and quiet effort to unify Cubans for the struggle."[131] Like the Partido Revolucionario Cubano in the 1890s, the MR 26-7 organized revolutionary clubs abroad in the 1950s. Like José Martí, Fidel Castro traveled to the United States to enlist support among Cuban communities in New York, Tampa, and Key West. Speaking to a Cuban audience in New York in 1955, Castro drew the obvious parallel: "We are realizing anew with the émigrés those things that our Apostle Martí taught us in a similar situation."[132] To have landed on Playa Las Coloradas in 1956 aboard the yacht *Granma* was to reenact the arrival of Antonio Maceo at Duaba and José Martí and Máximo Gómez at Playitas de Cajobabo in 1895. Castro's invitation to correspondents Herbert Matthews, Robert Taber, and Andrew St. George to the Sierra Maestra reenacted the Cuban invitation to U.S. correspondents to insurgent camps in the nineteenth century. The establishment of the newspaper El *Cubano Libre* in 1957 in the Sierra Maestra replicated the establishment of the newspaper of the same name by Antonio Maceo in 1895. "El *Cubano Libre* was the official newspaper of the *mambises*," proclaimed MR 26-7. "Today El *Cubano Libre*, in the mountain ranges of the Sierra Maestra, is the voice of those of us . . . who struggle to reclaim the liberty that forms the legacy that the *mambises* bequeathed to us."[133]

Many of the guerrilla operations were influenced by the war for independence. The battle of Guisa in November 1958 was inaugurated on the same date that General Calixto García had laid siege to Guisa in November 1897. The dispatch of guerrilla columns to Havana in late 1958 under the command of Ernesto Che Guevara and Camilo Cienfuegos was designated as "the Invasion," the same name given to Antonio Maceo's march westward in 1895–96. Camilo Cienfuegos designated his command as Column 2 'Antonio Maceo.'

Recalled Dariel Alarcón Ramírez, a member of Column 2: "Camilo always had an extraordinary love for General Antonio Maceo. . . . He lived in passionate admiration of the principal actions and battles directed by Maceo. . . . Ever since the nineteenth century, he has been one of our most admired warriors as a result of his courage and dignity. That was the reason Camilo gave Column 2 the name 'Antonio Maceo.'" These were historic associations that informed the sense of moral purpose with which Cubans joined the insurrection. Recalled Alarcón Ramírez: "When we received orders to undertake the march westward . . . and reached the historic site Peralejo, Camilo explained to us the significance of [Maceo's victory at the battle of] Peralejo. For an hour he spoke, with a fervor so pure and so revolutionary that I came to feel myself like one more Maceo in the invasion of the West. I believe that it helped me enormously, for I always remembered the beautiful words spoken by Camilo. This strengthened my resolve."[134]

In 1957, the MR 26-7 declared war on the economy in imitation of the tactics adopted by the mambises in the nineteenth century, that is, sabotage as enactment of historical mandate: "Work is a crime against the revolution," General Máximo Gómez had proclaimed in 1896.[135] "The economic war against the Dictatorship has commenced," proclaimed the Rebel Army command in 1958. "The 26th of July Movement has decided to use against the Tyranny the same method that Máximo Gómez used with success against the Captain Generals of the colonial regime."[136] The purpose was clear. "We will burn the sugarcane fields," vowed the MR 26-7. "We will not hesitate a single moment to destroy the cane, the way the mambises did not hesitate to burn the cane during our wars of independence. There will be no harvest with Batista in power."[137] To burn sugar was raised to the level of historic duty. "The burning of the sugarcane fields," proclaimed the MR 26-7, "signified today what it meant in 1868 and 1895: the revolutionary obligation of the Cuban people."[138]

The concept of armed struggle gradually transformed from a rebellion against the Batista government (la lucha contra la tiranía) and the overthrow of the dictatorship (derrocar a la tiranía) to a war of national liberation, a momentous if perhaps not readily discernible change in an environment dense with the rhetoric of revolution—but one with far-reaching implications. By late 1957, Fidel Castro was characterizing the guerrilla columns as the "Liberation Army of the 26th of July Movement" (el Ejército Libertador del Movimiento 26 de Julio). Radio Rebelde inaugurated transmissions from La Plata, the Rebel Army headquarters in the Sierra Maestra in 1958—on February 24, the anniversary date of Grito de Baire: "Aquí Radio Rebelde transmitiendo desde la Sierra Maestro en Territorio Libre de Cuba!"—liberated territory: exactly the terms that the mambises had used to refer to territory under their control during the war for independence.[139] All through 1958, the broadcast transmissions of Radio Rebelde repeatedly invoked the proposition of national liberation as the purpose of the armed struggle.[140]

■■■

The triumph of the revolution on January 1, 1959, was the triumph of history. Certainly that was the claim advanced by the victors. It seemed plausible—and persuasive. For a people who believed in the prophetic power of their past, the triumph of the revolution was received as vindication of their faith in their history—"la llegada," many Cubans believed—a revolution that "had come out of the past," Herbert Matthews wrote at the time.[141] This was a history that had insinuated itself deeply into multiple domains of the popular imagination, what Cubans had been reading in fiction, viewing in film, singing in song, reciting in verse, all bearing the moral of a nation awaiting fulfillment. Historical knowledge had reached deep into the national imagination, a process that must be understood as one of the principal means by which the claim of the revolution as redemption of the nation obtained popular currency and political credibility.

Memory lingered in places of unsuspected profundity. In this moment of unmediated triumph, on January 1, Cubans found themselves immersed in their history, self-consciously reclaiming their presence in their past as protagonists, fully imbued with a sense of agency and expectation of fulfillment. A joyful María de los Reyes Castillo was reunited with her two sons in early January 1959, both combatants in the Sierra Maestra, and greeted them through the eyes of a woman of her history: "How beautiful they were! With their olive green uniforms, and long hair and beards; one, an officer. They were dignified successors to the *mambí* tradition of my ancestors and my father."[142]

Sixty years after the defeat of Spain, as the victorious Rebel Army prepared to descend from the Sierra Maestra into the city of Santiago de Cuba, as the government of Fulgencio Batista crumbled, the parallels were far too compelling to allow them to pass without comment. Something significant was happening, Cubans sensed, although certainly the dimension and depth of what was happening could hardly have been suspected on January 1, 1959. But the presentiment of momentous was everywhere. It was palpable. "Something big is happening here," comments the protagonist in January 1959 in José Soler Puig's novel *En el año de enero* (1963).[143] Reflects Adriana in Freddy Artiles's play *Adriana en dos tiempos* (1972): "I realized that something fundamental had changed. I didn't quite fully comprehend what it was, but I felt that it was something new, and above all something different. Even the people seemed different. Public life entered into the home, even entered into one's self."[144]

Momentous times indeed, for which the larger narrative rendering of the armed struggle as liberation—certainly in its discursive structure—had more than adequately prepared national sensibilities. This is not to suggest that the revolution was a matter of inevitable outcome, of course. But to acknowledge that the Cuban revolution was not inevitable should not be understood to mean that it lacked an internal logic, one derived from the very history from which it emerged. The MR 26-7 had fashioned a politics of the unfinished project of nation into a revolutionary metaphysics of powerful appeal. To address Cuban discontent as a historical condition, possessed of solution in the fulfillment of the promise of the past, was to confer on the proposition of revolution the achievement of redemption. "Fidel Castro with the support of the revolutionaries who followed him," novelist Lisandro Otero reflected years later, "assumed the task of realizing the project of nation that had been conceived at the very origins of Cuban identity," and added: "They were prophets of the new era, preachers in a new-found Arcadia. They discharged the mission that had been conferred upon them by history: the hour of our genesis was at hand."[145]

The triumph of the revolution was a defining moment, not only—and perhaps not even principally—because it was a historical event in its own right, but also because it lay claim to the purpose of all the history that had preceded it. For many of the men and women "inside" the revolution, that is, those who had contributed to the triumph, the revolution did not come from history—it was history. This was an exquisite existential moment, when the past and present collapsed in on one another and in that instant revealed the power of the past to give meaning to the present. Filmmaker Julio García Espinosa recalled January 1, 1959, vividly: "We felt finally that our interior lives could now be reconciled with our public life. Time had become one and indivisible. The present had become the past and the past, the present and future. The image we now saw in the mirror was not that of a stranger, but of ourselves."[146]

But the triumphant revolution came bearing another message, one of portentous purport, precisely because it had so fully inscribed itself into the historic project of nation. The men and women of the revolution discerned in the past a politics of radical reach, as a program and a purpose, conveyed principally in the proposition of national sovereignty as means of self-determination. The revolution summoned Cuban indignation against the prevailing order of things, to be sure, but with the understanding that the sources of Cuban discontent were the product of historical circumstances that could be remedied only by the realization of the purpose that had given meaning to the idea of nation in the first place. "There is a common view in Cuba," Fidel Castro warned pointedly in January 1959, "that in destroying the tyrant we destroy tyranny. But tyranny is not a man; tyranny is a system."[147] The overthrow of the Batista government implied more than a restoration of pre-1952 constitutionality; it signified rejection of the post-1902 republic.

In the exaltation of triumph on January 1, fresh and flushed with victory, Fidel Castro chose that moment to recall the past. This was the past as a means with which to arrange the present into coherent narrative order, of acts and actors of almost impenetrable complexity rendered as history in actual time, but mostly a way to confer continuity on discontinuity and introduce memory to anticipate the future. At dawn, Castro addressed the nation by way of Radio Rebelde: "Cuba is not free yet. . . . The war has not ended because the murderers remain armed. The military men . . . insist that the rebels cannot enter Santiago de Cuba; we have been prohibited from entering a city that we could take with the valor and courage that our fighters have taken other cities. They wish to deny entrance to Santiago de Cuba to those who have liberated the *patria*. The history of 1895 will not be repeated!"[148]

The comparison was plausible; the meaning was purposeful. The celebration of liberation obtained in 1959 called attention to liberation obstructed in 1898. The long-deferred liberation was at hand, an unmediated victory achieved through war, with the victors entering the cities to receive the adulation of a grateful people: at once an act of catharsis and consecration, a process by which a people affirmed reintegration into their history. Not like 1898, when the Cubans, disarmed and displaced, marched into the cities behind the Americans and saw foreigners receive credit for the victory that properly should have been—minimally—shared with the Cubans. Not in 1959. José María Cuesta Braniella remembered well the symbolism of Fidel Castro entering victoriously into Santiago de Cuba. "It was to vindicate the Liberation Army [el Ejército Mambí]," he wrote years later, "that was not permitted to enter Santiago de Cuba after the victory of the War for Independence in 1898."[149]

These were men and women acting consciously as agents of history, determined to make good on their past and driven single-mindedly to bring an unfinished history to a conclusion. "This time the *mambises* will enter Santiago de Cuba! This time the revolution will not be thwarted," Fidel Castro thundered on January 1, 1959, effacing all distinction between the *mambises* of 1898 and the *barbudos* of 1959. "This time, fortunately for Cuba, the revolution will be consummated. It will not be like the war of 1895, when the Americans arrived and made themselves masters of the country; they intervened at the last minute and later did not even allow Calixto García, who had been fighting for thirty years, to enter Santiago de Cuba."[150] Later that day, Castro spoke at Céspedes Park in Santiago de Cuba. "The republic was not freed in 1895 and the dream of the *mambises* was frustrated in the final hours," Castro recalled. "We can say with joy that in the four centuries since our country was founded, we are for the first time entirely free and that the work of the *mambises* will be fulfilled." The Cubans who had struggled for thirty years only to see their dreams denied, Castro was certain, would have rejoiced at the realization that the "revolution that they had dreamed of and the *patria* that they had imagined had finally come to pass."[151] Castro reflected upon a private pilgrimage he had made to Baraguá a day earlier:

> A profound sense of devotion compelled us to stop at the monument com-
> memorating the Protest [of Baraguá]. At that late hour, with only our pres-
> ence there, thoughts of the daring achievements of our wars of indepen-
> dence, the idea that those men would have fought for thirty years and in the
> end did not see their dreams fulfilled because the republic was thwarted,
> and our anticipation that very soon, the revolution that they dreamed of,
> the *patria* they yearned for, would be transformed into a reality, made us ex-
> perience one of the most powerful emotions that one could ever imagine.
> I saw those men relive their sacrifices, sacrifices which we experienced so
> recently. I could conjure up their dreams and their aspirations, which were
> the same as our dreams and our aspirations, and I reflected that this gen-
> eration of Cubans must render and has rendered the most fervent recogni-
> tion of loyalty to the heroes of our independence. The men who perished in
> our three wars of independence now join their efforts to those of the men
> who perished in this war, and to all those who perished in the struggles for
> liberty. We can tell them now that their dreams are about to be fulfilled.[152]

Thoughtful observers sensed that Fidel Castro was saying something else, something more—that the moral of the idea was greater than the meaning of the words. These were, after all, acts and allusions with far-reaching im-
plications, by design and with a purpose, something that Cubans understood intuitively: the visual and the verbal registered as a sensory moment whose advent had been anticipated long before its achievement. Signs of what was to follow were, in fact, all there, and everywhere portentous. The past was indeed prophetic. To evoke memories of aspirations thwarted sixty years earlier implied a larger purpose, of course. It was left to the literary imagination of

novelist César Leante to grasp the mood of the moment in his short story "El día inicial," as the narrator listens to Fidel Castro's radio broadcast from Santiago de Cuba and ponders the meaning of those allusions to the past:

> Finally, at dawn, . . . the voice of Fidel Castro. It is not a deep voice, not as full as many have expected, but thin, tense, a little forced, that does not construct brilliant paragraphs, that speaks in everyday language, that gets entangled in clauses that remain incomplete, and that, most of all, already, from this early moment, sounds troubling. . . . "This time the revolution will not be thwarted"—predicts the distant orator. "This time, fortunately, for Cuba, the revolution will be consummated." And in continuation, a warning, the sounding of an alarm that should have made the contented well-to-do slightly uneasy—only slightly, for the time being. "It will not be like the war of 1895, when the Americans arrived and made themselves masters of the country; they intervened at the last minute and later did not even allow Calixto García, who had been fighting for thirty years, to enter Santiago de Cuba." That allusion to the United States . . . that allusion . . .[153]

In the days that followed January 1, Fidel Castro and an entourage of hundreds of victorious *barbudos*—the *caravana de la libertad*, as it became known—made their way slowly westward to Havana. All along the way Castro stopped to speak, and again and again he alluded to the past as something of an uncontested—and incontestable—moral warrant of the revolution, always to the roaring approval of many thousands of Cubans. He rendered the meaning of *patria* in deeply sentimental terms, unabashedly nostalgic, recalling the nineteenth-century promise of nation as remedy to the historic sources of Cuban discontent, and especially *patria* as meeting Cuban needs—the very proposition that had given meaning to nation in the first place. "The tragedy of our people has been the lack of *patria*," he affirmed on January 4 from Camagüey: "How can we say, 'This is our *patria*,' if from the *patria* we have nothing. 'My *patria*'—but my *patria* gives me nothing, my *patria* does not sustain me, in my *patria* I die of hunger. That is not *patria*! . . . Patria is a place in which one can live, *patria* is a place in which one can work and maintain an honorable livelihood and earn just wages for one's labor."[154] Two days later, in Santa Clara, he proclaimed that "our Revolution has triumphed for something. It has triumphed because the people have understood from the outset that this is not a mere change of men but a change of purpose," adding: "Our people long ago lost faith in our *patria*." But things had changed: "For the first time in our history the nation is truly free." History was very much on Castro's mind: "The glory of the revolutionaries, of all who have fought, belongs to the people and

Fidel Castro in Santa Clara, January 1959. From Luis Báez and Pedro de la Hoz, *Caravana de la libertad* (Havana, 2009).

to history! The dead who have fallen, whatever their affiliation, belong to the *patria* and to history! The sacrifices that have been made belong to the *patria* and to history."[155] Later that day, in Sancti-Spíritus, Castro affirmed purpose in fulfillment of the past: "The struggle was not only to overthrow the dictatorship," he proclaimed. "The struggle was for something more: to build on the ruins of the toppled dictatorship a new *patria*, that must be different from the *patria* which has existed up to this day." He continued:

> The triumph of this Revolution is contained within a moral renovation, not only for those who have fallen in this struggle. It is with enormous satisfaction to think that this Revolution will be the realization of the dreams not only of the men of this generation, but also the realization of the dreams of the generation that struggled against the dictatorship of Machado and the realization of the dreams of our liberators which still have not been realized.... We pay homage and will continue to honor the fallen of today, and the fallen of yesterday, and the fallen of our wars of independence.... They are men who have perished struggling for a dream, a dream that has not been realized, but a dream that we will fulfill.[156]

The next day, in Matanzas, Castro elaborated further: "A people determined to defend their rights are invincible, no matter how small they are. For that reason, I believe that our people, this time, the first occasion when a revolution has fully triumphed—the revolution that did not triumph in 1895 because it ended in an intervention, and the revolution of that did not triumph in 1933 because it was thwarted by a military coup—this time there is and cannot be an intervention or a military coup. ... This time the people will achieve the goals that have so often been denied to them."[157] All along the way to Havana, Castro repeatedly invoked the idea of liberation, of the triumph—he insisted—of a revolution that represented the completion of a struggle for national liberation begun more than one hundred years earlier. In Santa Clara, he praised the new "veterans of the war of liberation [*veteranos de la guerra de liberación*]." In Matanzas, he expressed appreciation to the Cuban people for their support of the "*ejército libertador*" (liberation army).[158]

Across the island, the scenes of popular euphoria that anticipated the arrival of the triumphant Fidel Castro and the officers and soldiers of the Rebel Army were those of a people receiving their liberators in a collective mood of deliverance. Guillermo Vincente Vidal recalled the arrival of the *caravana* in Camagüey: "A celebratory procession that would have rivaled any Caesar's triumphal entry into Rome. For days, offices and shops everywhere were shut down. Throngs of people spilled out into the streets, and virtually every Cuban

THE HAVANA POST

CUBA'S ONLY ENGLISH-LANGUAGE DAILY OLDER THAN THE REPUBLIC

| Vol. LXI No. 6 | Havana, Cuba, Friday Morning, January 9, 1959 | Price: Five Cents |

Castro Receives Liberator's Welcome

Roaring Multitude Lines Havana Streets to Greet Rebel Chieftain

By WILLIAM L. RYAN
Of The Associated Press

Before a Wildly Cheering Crowd of 30,000

Castro Warns Cubans They Must Guard Liberties Won

In Accordance With Smith's Recommendations

US Ready to Grant Generous Aid to Cuba

Headline of the *Havana Post* announcing the arrival of Fidel Castro in Havana on
January 8, 1959. From *Havana Post*, January 9, 1959.

tried to find a way to see and cheer our revolutionary hero. . . . People threw
flowers, confetti, freed doves into the festive air. . . . It was a wonderful time
to be alive."[159] Marcia del Mar vividly remembered the arrival of the *caravana*
in Havana: "There was drinking and singing in the streets. The green-clad soldiers entered the city accompanied by cheering mobs. Women threw multi-
colored flowers into the happy crowd from wrought-iron balconies. Everyone
felt miraculously saved from tyranny. . . . The crowds went wild with joy. . . .
The savior and his disciples had emerged victorious. . . . Our neighbors held
'liberation parties,' flying torn, mildewy flags insolently out their windows.
Fireworks went off for weeks."[160] Hiram González, a young officer in the
Rebel Army in the *caravana*, remembered entering the capital: "As we moved
toward Havana, our guerrilla columns were mobbed everywhere we went. Old
women hugged us, young girls kissed us and gave us flowers to adorn our

jeeps and hats. When we stopped, townspeople brought us containers of hot food, gifts. Little children asked us for autographs. It was a time of joy, of incredible happiness. I was twenty years old, a lieutenant in the army of liberation. I felt on top of the world."[161] Observed the British ambassador in Havana on January 10: "[Castro's] triumphant progress throughout the length of the island during the past week, culminat[ed] in what the press with some justification termed the apotheosis of his entry into Havana. . . . Romantically bearded, with his cohorts of battle-scarred veterans recalling the liberation fighters of sixty years ago, it is neither blasphemous nor exaggerated to assert that for the great majority of Cubans, intoxicated by recent events, Castro represents a mixture of José Martí, Robin Hood, Garibaldi, and Jesus Christ."[162]

"Never in the history of Cuba," *New York Times* correspondent Ruby Hart Philips confided to her journal, "has anyone received such a welcome. The ovation was of such magnitude that it was a little frightening. The majority of Havana's one million inhabitants must have turned out."[163] *Chicago Tribune* correspondent John H. Thompson, wrote Jules Dubois, "who was in Paris when it was liberated in World War II, compared the welcome accorded to Castro with that historic event."[164]

■ ■ ■

Contained within the proposition of the revolution as liberation was a claim as irresistible as it was irreversible: the presumption of continuity with the nineteenth-century wars for independence, and more: the triumph of the revolution as consummation of nation. The revolution claimed the mandate of change as a legacy, the promise of the past fulfilled. A people seemed to have been revived to reclaim control over their history. The idea of rebirth took hold. Manuel Urrutia recalled Castro's entrance into Havana as the moment "the country was being reborn."[165] Rufo López Fresquet looked upon the revolution as signaling "the rebirth of the nation."[166] Jorge Mañach discerned Cubans as a changed people. "We are living in Cuba a brilliant moment of profound renovation," Mañach wrote in 1959. "Renovation . . . of the spirit of our people, of hopes and of will; most of all, of faith in ourselves. . . . What has been reborn in Cuba is not as much faith as the confidence of Cubans in themselves."[167]

How difficult indeed it would prove to be to challenge the moral propriety and political legitimacy of the men and women who declared themselves to have realized the nineteenth-century project of liberation and who, in the process, proclaimed the revolution as fulfillment of historical destiny. The victorious Cubans, Tony Santiago García of the Directorio Revolucionario proclaimed in January 1959, had "consummated the Third War of Independence of our misfortunate patria."[168] By early 1959, the idea of national liberation had expanded fully into the master narrative of the revolution and had obtained discursive ascendancy across the island: the new *mambises* had realized the long-deferred liberation of Cuba. In the euphoria of victory in the early weeks and months of 1959, in the exaltation of triumph, Cubans across the island celebrated the triumphant revolution as liberation and the resumption of the history interrupted in 1898. Journalist Waldo Medina celebrated "the liberators of the 26th of July who, in the voice of its outstanding leader . . . Fidel Castro—Martí reborn—has set Cuba on a new course."[169] Roberto Fernández Retamar insisted that "it was with perfect clarity that the objectives of Fidel Castro represented continuity with the republic propounded by José Martí."[170] In 1959, the Cuban people surrendered themselves joyfully to their history. "January 1959," Cintio Vitier remembered years later, "was an ecstasy of history." He continued:

> An ecstasy in the sense of a suspension of time: it appeared as if a vision had revealed itself, not an image or metaphor, but a vision of something that had been realized but seemed impossible. . . . And everyone who experienced this moment—something very difficult to convey to young people—will never forget it. A moment that not Martí, that no one lived to witness: not Céspedes, not Agramonte, not Maceo, not Gomez, not [Julio Antonio] Mella, not Rubén [Martínez Villena]—not anyone. We were witness to that vision in which history was aligned on the side of the good in absolute terms. That cannot be forgotten.[171]

The triumph of the revolution was received as the fulfillment of national liberation. The weekly *Bohemia* celebrated the MR 26-7 as "the soul of this project of national liberation."[172] In announcements and advertisements published in newspapers and magazines, merchants, manufacturers, and financiers were exuberant in their congratulations to the victors and further ratified the proposition of the triumphant revolution as redemption of nation. "Our eternal gratitude to the heroes who liberated us," proclaimed Fin de Siglo department store. La Filosofía department store paid its respects to "the new liberators . . . who have gloriously emulated the immortal deed of the War of Independence: the liberation invasion [*la invasión Libertadora*]."[173] Beer manufacturer Tropical congratulated the "glorious army of liberation," and the Association of Merchants and Industrialists proclaimed its support of the "army of liberation and its maximum leader Fidel Castro."[174] "We wish to congratulate the people of Cuba for its liberation," affirmed the Shell Oil

Advertisement welcoming the arrival of
the liberators in Havana, January 7, 1959.
From *El Mundo*, January 7, 1959.

Company, "and we welcome with open arms the liberation army with its maximum leader Dr. Fidel Castro Ruz."[175] The Rice Growers' Association of Sancti-Spíritus pledged its support of the "revolution of liberation," and the American Sugar Company expressed its gratitude to the "young generation at this time of liberation."[176] Affirmed the Social Security Bank of Cuba: "We can now sing victory for now that the chains that impeded our complete political, social, and economic liberation have been broken, Cuba can now determine its own destiny! Now we can legitimately proclaim: 'Viva Cuba Libre.'"[177] January 1 was proclaimed the "Day of National Liberation." The year 1959 was proclaimed the "Year of Liberation." The insurrection was henceforth designated as the war of national liberation.[178]

The proposition of the triumphant revolution as culmination of the nineteenth-century process of liberation drew unabashedly upon the value system from which nationality had formed and indeed developed early into the master narrative with which the victors claimed power. It served to transport a people into realms never before visited with a confidence that only a faith in their history could sustain. "The present revolutionary process," affirmed Camilo Cienfuegos in early 1959, "to which our generation has fully given its soul, its heart, and its valor to the cause of liberty, is nothing more than the continuation of the liberation process initiated in 1868, resumed in 1895, and frustrated during the Republic. The ideals of liberation, of social, political, and economic justice for which our Apostle [Martí] gave his life, are the reasons for our struggle."[179] "The *mambises*," proclaimed Fidel Castro in February 1959, "initiated the war for independence that we have completed on January 1, 1959."[180] He did not hesitate to draw the obvious moral: "Finally, the dreams of the men who for more than one hundred years struggled to have their own *patria* have been fulfilled. They struggled so that our people would be masters of their destiny, to have a place of dignity among the countries of the world, and to have also a space in the history of the world."[181] Raúl Castro made the same point: "Now, with this Revolution . . . we have done nothing less than finish the War of Independence that was begun nearly one hundred years ago by our *mambises*. On January 1 of this year we completed our War of Independence. We inaugurated the Republic on that date."[182]

The imagery of the victorious *barbudos* as *mambises* seized hold of the popular imagination. "Our dark past has remained behind," reflected historian Leví Marrero days after the triumph of the revolution, "spurned by the rifle fire of the new *mambises*. . . . The admirable troops of the liberation army replicated the heroic feats of the *mambises*."[183] Columnist Carlos Todd celebrated the men and women of MR 26-7 as "living embodiments of the famed '*mambises*' of the revolutionary past of Cuban's beginnings as a free nation. . . . They appeared before the cameras, a reincarnation of the men led by Maceo, Máximo Gómez, and Calixto García, bearded, long-haired, bristling with bandoliers and rifles and carbines."[184]

■ ■ ■

Fidel Castro was not the first Cuban to aspire to the role of redeemer of the nation. But he was different in that he appealed to the logic of a history that was as self-implicating as it was self-confirming. The power of the appeal to the past lay where it had always been: in the promise of nation as the premise of nationality, central to which was the demand for national sovereignty and self-determination as the minimum condition for fulfillment of Cuban. Few political leaders in the twentieth century were—as a matter of intellectual formation and political persuasion—as fully conversant with the Cuban past as Fidel Castro. He understood intuitively that to inscribe a politics of change into well-formed and widely shared historical sensibilities was to appeal directly to the very aspiration by which Cubans had arrived at an understanding of the people they wished to be. "Castro has become the most genuine representative of the Cuban youth," Jorge Mañach had concluded only months before the triumph of the revolution, "and indeed of many older citizens who share the views of youth—which has inherited all the accumulated sense of betrayal of several republican generations."[185] Precisely because Cubans were conversant with the moral of their history as a matter of received wisdom, the use of allegories, analogies, and allusions to the past as the logic of change could be easily encoded into a metaphor of revolution. That it would threaten the status quo and especially challenge the premise and the propriety of privileged power contenders, including and especially the Americans, was not immediately apparent. A careful reading of the meaning of the sovereign nation in its nineteenth-century formulation would surely have laid bare the implications of the Cuban purpose in the mid-twentieth century—although, no less surely, even after such a careful reading, few would have thought Cubans capable of sustaining a project of such radical reach in defiance of North American power. That too was the conventional wisdom. "No sane man undertaking to govern and reform Cuba," the Central Intelligence Agency had reasoned, "would have chosen to pick a fight with the U.S."[186]

That the summons to revolution was inscribed within the narrative of a familiar history served to conceal the radical portent of the nineteenth-century ideal of nation: powerful in the late nineteenth century, and more so in the mid-twentieth. The proposition of national sovereignty was as much a threat to the premise of the republic in the 1950s as it had been a challenge to the rationale of the colony in the 1890s. Purpose was contained in the convergence of past and present, with a politics in the form of sentiments, which, if discerned at all, were mostly in the realm of feelings and passions, where cognitive certainties yielded to intuitive impulses. Hugh Thomas was correct to observe that had the ideals of Martí been implemented in 1959, "the changes in Cuba's condition would be radical" and might have resulted "in perhaps not a Communist revolution, but one certainly more 'revolutionary' than in Mexico under [Lázaro] Cárdenas."[187]

Whether by political opportunism or heartfelt persuasion or some combination of both—perhaps never to be known—Fidel Castro understood well the power of the past to drive the purpose of politics. The past was legacy to make good on, to be sure. But it existed also in the form of accumulated grievances as a wrong to right. "The grievances we carry within us are old," reflected Fidel Castro in early January 1959.[188] The sentiment had fixed itself within national sensibilities as a disposition of unsuspected depth: in part angst, in part umbrage, a condition that contained within its very properties the vision of its own transformation. It had given form to a national constituency disposed to act in realization of the promise of the past. Fidel Castro could deploy the narratives of the past as effective discourse for revolution precisely because the claim to nation evoked ideals to which Cubans were eminently susceptible: as source of program, as standard of conduct, and as scope of purpose. It was from history that Castro propounded the mandate for revolution, a self-conscious representation of the revolution as fulfillment of unmet aspirations of the past. Not since José Martí had anyone so explicitly appealed to the normative determinants of nationality as the basis of a mandate for change.

■ ■ ■

Cubans experienced the triumph of the revolution with soaring self-confidence, rising expectations, and a heightened anticipation of national fulfillment, but most of all with a powerful sense of empowerment, of a people imbued with the prerogative of Cuban in Cuba: characterized at the time— and thereafter—as a release of nationalist exaltation. But a closer examination suggests a far more complex process. This was about a people reintegrating themselves into their history, celebrating their achievement in the 1950s as fulfillment of the achievements of the 1890s, something of an act of completion and thereupon affirming the decorum of protagonists in history, what playwright Senel Paz characterized as a "people wishing to celebrate their entering into History [un pueblo que quiere festejar su entrada en la Historia]."[189]

The revolution drew vast numbers of men and women into the logic of the very history from which it claimed its origins. Cubans in 1959 were a people fully persuaded that they had recovered their history and reclaimed historical agency. "History is now," proclaimed the daily Revolución.[190] The triumph of the revolution provided Cubans with the opportunity to enter their history, to act out history, to feel their history, to become one with their history. For the men and women formed within the normative systems from which the meaning of Cuban had developed, the triumph of the revolution seemed to have signified mastery over the forces that governed their lives. Cubans believed themselves to have seized their history, on their terms, as agents and actors, fully imbued with the moral authority of their past. This had to do with the idea that in overthrowing the Batista dictatorship, unaided and unassisted, Cubans had cleared the way back to their past, back to the point from which they had been dislodged from their history, and from that point to begin anew.

The triumphant revolution produced almost immediately a new history as source of legend and lore, new founding myths in the making, a celebration of heroes and commemoration of heroic deeds, of the combats and battles large and small, all elevated to the level of decisive military victories: La Plata, El Uvero, Jigüe, El Hombrito, Palma Mocha, Arroyo del Infierno, Bueycito, Guisa, and Santa Clara, among others. And a pantheon of new martyrs of liberation. The *barbudos* became legends in their own time. "Legends surrounding the *revolucionarios* spread quickly across the island," Guillermo Vincente Vidal recalled in the early months of 1959; "they became folk heroes and celebrities, and in the popular imagination, Fidel grew larger than life."[191]

Cubans drew the inference of their accomplishments without hesitation. "The victorious revolution won on January 1, 1959," Raúl Roa affirmed, "put an end to an ominous state of affairs, and today for the first time in our history, Cuba is truly free, independent, and sovereign."[192] Journalist Andrés Valdespino celebrated the triumph of the revolution as a victory of all Cubans, and with thinly veiled allusions to the past:

> A people has given to the world a glorious example of an indomitable will. . . . A *pueblo*, above all, that has arisen . . . with faith in its own destiny. This has been, perhaps, among the greatest of all the achievements of the Revolution: of having restored faith to Cubans. . . . For the first time a Revolution has triumphed without compromise and mediation, . . . a revolution that overthrew a regime supported by great capitalist interests and the American embassy. A revolution that achieves power without foreign intervention that divests it of its nationalist sentiments and without a military coup that threatens its democratic inclination.[193]

The revolution had "radically changed the character of our circumstances," Luis Aguilar León observed: "National dignity firm and filled with pride, fully secure in our destiny, free at last of the humiliating inferiority under the northern shadow, Cubans today can return without embarrassment to the objective pursuit of all the threads that make up the fabric of our history."[194] The narrator in Daura Olema's novel *Maestra voluntaria* (1962) contemplates the panorama of the Cuban countryside from a moving train soon after the triumph of the revolution, reflecting: "It is the same Cuba of always, but in truth for the first time in history it belongs to us."[195]

The occasion of the triumphant revolution in 1959 was a time to look back, purposely, for redress and remedy, a way to connect one historic moment with another as a matter of consummation as an act of continuity. Writer Armando J. Flórez Ibarra drew the connections succinctly: "Analyzing the historical reach of the triumphant revolutionary movement, it appears to us as if the revolutionary armies of 1895 . . . have reached power, finally, free of all mediating influences. We are witness to the vindication of the triumph that the United States, through its armed intervention in 1898, cheated us of. . . . We have finally liberated ourselves from the complex of a protectorate."[196] The newspaper *Revolución* alluded often to 1898. "Independence," *Revolución* affirmed on January 15, "was frustrated by the foreign intervention." One day later, *Revolución* provided its readers a history lesson: "We are going to talk about a little history. Once upon a time, some of our grandfathers, after nearly a century of conspiracy and war, at the point of obtaining their victory as a result of the exhaustion of Spain, and its impending financial collapse, due to the futility of its arms and the fever of its sons, suddenly received the intervention of their neighbors, who until then had remained indifferent to their years of suffering. The war ended but . . . the liberators all but starved to death."[197]

Cubans received the triumph of the revolution in 1959 with a newfound sense of collective self-esteem and self-confidence, what novelist Miguel Cossío Woodward described as an "incomprehensible notion derived from a profound sense of history."[198] The debilitating sense of inferiority that had sapped Cuban morale through much of the early republic seemed to have dissipated. "It is now a pleasure to be Cuban; before it was embarrassing," proclaims the protagonist in José Soler Puig's novel *En el año de enero* (1963).[199] "Of all the 'incredible' things that your tenacity and energy have achieved," novelist José Lezama Lima wrote to Fidel Castro in early 1959, "none is perhaps greater than that of having 'resuscitated' the Cuban spirit of confidence, a spirit that appeared understandably dead and without any possible means of revival after the governments between 1944 and the present, whose fraudulence in so many ways destroyed even the possibility of optimism among the Cuban people."[200] Writer Luis Amado Blanco dedicated his novel *Ciudad rebelde* (1967) to Fidel Castro, "who one day resurrected us with the Spring of an old hope."[201] Poet Roberto Fernández Retamar published a collection of poems under the title *Vuelta de la antigua esperanza* (The Return of Old Hope).[202] Wrote Jorge Martí in early 1959: "With the triumph of the revolution, the Cuban people feel, for the first time, as fully developed protagonists in their history, as masters of their destiny. They realized their hopes without foreign assistance, without foreign limitations. There was an euphoric outburst of sentiments of independence . . . and as a consequence there developed among the Cuban people a fervent desire to suppress the old vices possessed of colonial origins and practice the ideals of the *mambises*. Such is the moment in which we live."[203] Novelist Juan Arcocha was succinct: "We can finally believe in Cuba."[204]

National fulfillment had become personal fulfillment. Vast numbers of men and women became one with their past, learning anew the meaning of Cuban. "[The revolution] makes us know who we are," Esteban Montejo explained to Andrew Salkey. "To ourselves, I mean. That's good. We didn't know that for a long time in Cuba. We are beginning to know what Cuba is, and who all the people are, living in Cuba and calling themselves Cubans."[205] Pablo Armando Fernández explained this phenomenon in slightly different terms: "The Revolution gave us a face and a voice, two things that Cuba had lacked."[206]

History seemed to advance inexorably: a people overtaken by a history set in motion almost one hundred years earlier, displacing almost everything that lay beyond the logic of the purpose from which the idea of the past had developed. There was no escape. Years later, Andrei Codrescu learned that during the 1960s the Hotel Capri in Havana had been "a favorite meeting place for dissidents," noting: "They came here to drink coffee and plot some improbable exit from Cuban history. . . . The best some of them did was to plot an exit from the island, but history was harder to shake; it followed them like a rabid dog."[207]

The past had become ends and means: the past to reclaim and redeem, to make good on, of course, but also the past as a usable framework in which to summon a people already disposed—indeed, determined—to reclaim the purpose for which the nation had been conceived in the first place. Cubans carried knowledge of the past in the form of a persuasion, the way a people know something with such certainty and with such conviction that they lose awareness that it is external to them; it assumed fully the form of faith, which in part explains the power of the past to convey moral purpose as a politics. This was historical knowledge as a compelling frame of reference to make sense of in 1959. To inscribe the triumph of the revolution within the logic of the past was to advance the claim to power as a matter of prophetic purport, of a future foretold and informed with purpose derived from the very value system from which the meaning of Cuban originated.

The promise of national sovereignty offered Cubans the possibility of agency as protagonists in historical narratives of their own making and a destiny of their own choosing. Aspirations to the sovereign nation were sentiments to which almost all Cubans—usually in principle and certainly in public—could subscribe; and as an ideal advanced by the revolutionary government these must be seen as a factor in how Cubans were early drawn into the logic of revolution. These were not sentiments invented by the leadership. They were intrinsic to the very moral order to which Cuban leaders were themselves heir and by which they had been formed. They understood intuitively the power of the ideal of national sovereignty as means of political mobilization and source of national consensus, that the claim to defend the normative systems in which Cubans were formed provided an all-encompassing discursive strategy of national purpose.

Men and women across the island gave themselves unreservedly to their history, fully persuaded that a historically foretold destiny had been realized. The triumph of the revolution implied more than a victory over the present: it was vindication of the past. Belief in a common destiny had early inscribed itself into the historical narrative of the nation: thwarted, of course, but sustained by way of a faith in the past as purpose. "Cuba has recovered confidence in its destiny," proclaimed historian Emilio Roig de Leuchsenring, "and Cubans have regained confidence in themselves."[208] This was not a matter of chance, Cubans were certain. They had determined their own destiny and in so doing had seized control of history on their terms. "What have we done?" Fidel Castro asked rhetorically, answering: "Continued the effort. What have we done? Continued the struggle, fulfilled the program of the *patria*, realized the destiny of the nation."[209]

■ ■ ■

The triumph of the revolution was a drama dense with history. The Rebel Army acting in behalf of the *mambises* marching into Santiago de Cuba, or perhaps it was the other way around, that the *mambises* had returned in 1959. In fact, it really did not matter. The ambiguity was useful, for either way the larger meaning was the same and could be inferred intuitively. "Today," *Revolución* blurred past and present in early 1959, "when we saw the troops of Calixto García led by Fidel Castro enter Santiago on January 1, we have to think that we live in different times. And if Santiago de Cuba of yesterday was the tomb of the Spanish empire in the New World, Cuba of today . . . could well be the . . . site where the now obsolete imperialism is shattered."[210] It is entirely possible to contemplate, of course, that there were many Cubans who did not fully appreciate the implications of what the premise of liberation—carried to its logical conclusion—portended.

There was perhaps no more powerful corroboration to the claim of continuity than the presence of the surviving *mambises* at public events organized by the new government and who by their attendance lent moral credibility to the claim of authority. *Mambises* were a ubiquitous presence in the early years

One-year anniversary commemorative issue of the newspaper *Hoy*, emphasizing the revolution as historical continuity. The January 1, 1960, issue—"One year of *mambises'* dreams realized"—juxtaposes, right to left, Carlos Manuel de Céspedes, Antonio Maceo, José Martí, and Fidel Castro. The picture on the bottom superimposes a representation of a *barbudo* of 1959 on an image of a *mambí* of 1895. From *Hoy*, January 1, 1960.

of the revolution, celebrated in their own right, of course, but also called upon to bear witness and validate the process made in their name with the claims of having fulfilled their aspirations. When Fidel Castro addressed the nation from Camp Columbia upon arriving in Havana on January 8, seated behind the speakers' platform, sharing the stage with the victorious *barbudos*, were surviving *mambises* of 1895.[211] At a mass rally later that January, seated on the speakers' platform, reported *Revolución*, "was a very large group of *mambises*, who drew powerful applause, and whose presence was palpable testimony of the support of those who gave us our first liberty for the brave young men who re-conquered it."[212] From time to time, interviews with aging *mambises* were published, almost all of whom ratified the claim of the revolution as the realization of the *independentista* project. "Naturally I like Fidel," proclaimed one-hundred-year-old veteran José Chamizo, "for he has the same ideals of General Antonio Maceo."[213] Eighty-seven-year-old Antonio Díaz affirmed outright: "The Revolution is doing today what the *mambises* initiated in the field of combat [*en la manigua*]."[214] "It is now," eighty-eight-year-old José Virgilio Carabaloso exulted in 1968, "one hundred years after October 10 [that is, the Ten Years War], that we can say that we are truly free." Dulce María Aguilera—105 years old—affirmed: "Fidel is doing everything that those who died in the war for independence wanted done."[215]

The moral was never difficult to divine. The remembered past mattered as a politics, to be sure, but also as a means of reckoning, which implied a politics of another kind. The meaning of the past insinuated itself into those popular domains where politics and passions converged in realms as a shared moral order, as indeed inevitably it had to, for these were issues that reached deep into national sensibilities and implicated the very value system from which nationality originated. The men and women who presumed to act on behalf of the revolution did so as self-conscious protagonists in the very history from which they emerged, as self-assured proponents of the historical purpose by which they were formed. There is no evidence of self-doubt.

■■■

The proposition of the revolution as continuity and consummation of the nineteenth-century *independentista* project—that is, the revolution as fulfillment of legacy and realization of nation—expanded into the master narrative of the new order of things. The claim was entirely plausible, of course. But plausibility was only part of its appeal. This was the history for which successive generations of Cubans had lived in anticipation. Its power was registered in those realms of memory, of a people who knew what their history was to

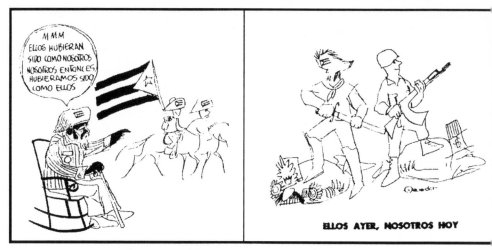

Representation of continuity of the Cuban revolution with the *mambises* of the nineteenth century. From *Verde Olivo* 9 (October 1968).

be and sensed too that the realization of their history was at hand. The most powerful memories were not always remembered as deeds and dates, but as hopes and expectations, as sentiments borne over time, to take hold in the interior narratives of a people as an article of faith. "Our Revolution," proclaimed Blas Roca, "as continuation of the history of our nation, is the legitimate offspring of all the revolutionary traditions of the past; it is the extension of a noble past given to the holy cause of liberation for which countless numbers of Cubans struggled and died in fulfillment of the task and duty that history constantly has imposed upon us."[216] Novelist José Rodríguez Feo was certain that Cubans had at last "completed the revolution initiated by our *mambises* in 1868 and Martí in 1895, truncated by the *yanqui* intervention in our republican era," adding: "We need not get into the historical details, but no Cuban doubts the fact that the struggle that resumed when the Cuban people realized that the revolution of Martí had been frustrated with establishment of the Republic under the auspices of imperialism culminated with the overthrow of the Batista tyranny in 1959."[217] On the commemoration of the date of February 24, in 1963, *Revolución* was categorical: "The struggle of the *mambises* culminates in the process of our revolution with the conquest of our national independence. The nation of Martí and Maceo can now celebrate the historic date of February 24."[218]

Few disputed the premise. Men and women who subsequently broke with the Castro government, principally over the issue of communism during the early years, remained persuaded that the triumph of the revolution represented consummation of nation. Few indeed were the numbers who repudiated the history that had made their initial support of the revolution so compelling. "To me, the Castro movement was essentially a reinvigorated manifestation of the old longing for independence, democracy, and progress which somehow had time and again been frustrated," Mario Llerena recalled years later: "I used to dwell on the idea that the antecedents of this movement could be traced back to similar ones in the recent past and even to the founders and heroes of the country from the early stages of its historical and political formation."[219] Journalist Raúl Lorenzo, who emigrated from Cuba in 1960, continued to believe that the revolution signified fulfillment of the past. "Fidel embodies the ideological inheritance of the Veterans and Patriots Movement, the Grupo Minorista, [Antonio] Guiteras, and above all the founders of the *patria*, starting with José Martí," Lorenzo affirmed. "He represents the recovery of the national spirit and the necessity of reforms in all aspects of Cuban life."[220] Fifteen years after the triumph of the revolution, Ramón Bonachea and Marta San Martín would write in exile that "the Sierra Maestra leader represented a continuation of the *mambises* of the wars of independence."[221] Former *comandante* Huber Matos, more than two decades after having completed a twenty-year prison term on charges of counterrevolutionary activity, reflected on the history that culminated on January 1, 1959:

> The historical circumstances were propitious. Ever since the War for Independence, frustrated by the intervention of the United States, the Cubans have struggled in anticipation of redemption. In that war, outstanding leaders—Martí and Maceo among them—perished. Generation after generation, the people have attempted to fill that vacuum, witnessing time and again their aspirations frustrated. . . . The Cuban people aspired to the Cuba envisioned by José Martí, a nation genuinely independent, "for all and the good of all." Fidel Castro, wrapped in the mystique of the guerrilla struggle, was the beneficiary of more than sixty years of thwarted aspirations.[222]

■■■

These were heady times, a people exhilarated by new possibilities and new promises, but most of all by the promise of a better future within their reach. Impatience overtook prudence. Cubans acted with the conviction that they had lost fifty years of their history between 1898 and 1958: so much to be done, so much to make up for. Anticipation filled the air, as if it were necessary to recover lost time, to get on with the task at hand and to return to the point of displacement to begin anew. "We have lost more than fifty years," Fidel Castro insisted, "but we are going to recover them rapidly. We are going to recover them. They made us lose fifty years since the beginning of the Republic. We will recover them."[223] Signs in government offices captured the tenor of the times: "*Hemos perdido 50 años — hay que recobrarlos — sea breve.*"

Events moved quickly: affairs of state were in continuous flux as developments with portentous implications seemed to gather momentum from one day to the next in vertiginous succession. History had speeded up. "The Revolution forces one to reorient oneself at every moment," reflects the narrator in the Hilda Perera novel *El sitio de nadie* (1972). "The process advances with such velocity that a position adopted yesterday is tomorrow untenable."[224] Change seems to beget more change as the normal course of events.

The triumph of the revolution implied the realization of a Cuba for Cubans: Cuban well-being as the principal purpose of public policy. Early reforms more than adequately fulfilled popular expectations. Electricity rates were drastically reduced. So were telephone rates. The Urban Reform Law in March 1959 reduced rents by as much as 50 percent. Labor contracts were renegotiated and wages raised. New minimum wages were established in virtually every sector. Health and educational reforms were enacted in rapid succession. The revolutionary government addressed long-standing practices of racism and racial discrimination, opening hotels, resorts, beaches, and nightclubs to all Cubans.[225] In May 1959, the Agrarian Reform Law nationalized landholdings in excess of 3,333 acres and redistributed land to small farmers in allotments of sixty-seven acres and into state cooperatives. More than 1,500 laws, decrees, and edicts were enacted in the first nine months of 1959. All in all, promising auguries — certainly for vast numbers of Cubans. Living standards improved. Wages and salaries increased. The cost of living decreased.

The revolution did indeed appear to have fulfilled historic expectations of what could be accomplished through the exercise of national sovereignty and the enactment of self-determination: a Cuba for Cubans — "with all, and for the good of all." The Cuban purpose was explicit. "It is necessary," Fidel Castro proclaimed on the occasion of the Agrarian Reform Act in May 1959, "to write once and for all on our pure solitary star the formula of the Apostle [Martí] that the *patria* belongs to all and for the good of all." And two years later: "What *patria* did they refer to before?" Castro asked rhetorically, and continued:

The *patria* where a few possessed all the opportunities and lived off the work of everyone else? The *patria* of men who did not even have work? The *patria* of the family that lived in conditions of indigence? The *patria* of hungry and barefoot children asking for alms on the streets? To what *patria* and to what concept of *patria* were they referring? The *patria* that belonged to a minority to the exclusion of opportunity and benefit of the majority? Or to the *patria* of today, where we have won the right to direct our own destiny, where we have won the right to construct the future that will necessarily be better than the present? . . . The *patria* will be from this time forward and forever what Martí wanted when he said: "For all, and the good of all." Not the *patria* for a few and the good of a few.[226]

■ ■ ■

The fulfillment of Cuban aspirations was not without a cost. Few indeed were the reforms that did not adversely affect the property and privilege of Cubans and foreigners alike, and especially the Americans. The commitment to the remedy of the historic sources of discontent, with its attending emphasis on the exercise of self-determination as a means of Cuban well-being, portended a far-reaching realignment of power relationships and redistribution of wealth. Cubans could not resolve the structural anomalies of the national system without challenging the very premise upon which the republic was founded.

The demand for the primacy of Cuban interests as the principal purpose of power implied more than a simple adjustment of policy priorities. That Cubans would assert claim to their destiny in function of their own interests, that they would affirm their interests as distinct and different from the United States and presume the priority of Cuban interests as proper to pursue, was to challenge a status quo with antecedents in the nineteenth century. So profoundly institutional, so intrinsically structural, were the sources of North American power that the determination to advance Cuban interests over foreign ones could not fail to produce a confrontation with the United States. Cuban pretensions to national sovereignty and self-determination directly challenged the presumption of North American privilege in Cuba, which was, after all, the premise upon which the republic was founded. What had mattered most to Cubans—national sovereignty and self-determination—had been precisely what one hundred years of U.S. policy had been given to preventing.

It is not difficult to understand how utterly implausible if not incomprehensible the claim of Cuba for the Cubans—and not for the United States—would have appeared to the Americans. The propriety of North American privilege in Cuba had assumed such utter commonplace normality as to acquire the appearance of the natural order of things, hardly noticed at all except as confirmation that all was right in the world. That Cubans called attention to this condition as an anomaly in their lives, as wrong and improper, drew responses of blank incredulity from the Americans: how to comprehend Cuban dissatisfaction with a relationship that most Americans—if they thought about it at all—were certain had been entirely ideal and had presumed always to be in the best interest of Cubans. The very proposition of Cuba for Cubans, that is, Cubans no longer disposed to accommodate the primacy of North American interests, was preposterous. The sheer effrontery of the Cuban challenge was breathtaking—the impertinence of it all. How utterly implausible.

Tensions between Cuba and the United States increased all through 1959 and 1960. It was not simply that Washington and Havana appeared to be talking past each other. They were in fact not even using the same vocabulary. "I think we fail to realize that Castro does not speak our language and does not want to listen to it," concluded Henry Ramsey of the State Department Policy Planning Staff in early 1960. "They do not speak our language and do not aspire to speak it. As a result, we are not likely to influence them by continuing to insist on addressing them in the language of private enterprise, the sanctity of private property, the equities of just compensation, etc."[227] Without historical depth perception, the Americans were unable to comprehend that the Cubans were in actuality addressing the past. In fact, in the early weeks and months, it was all about history. Policy disputes came later. The Americans pretended the past did not exist, or worse: they were unaware of its existence. Without knowledge of that history, the Americans mistook their ignorance for innocence: surely they had done nothing to provoke Cuban ire, they persuaded themselves. "US policy toward Cuba," the Central Intelligence Agency insisted in 1961, "had been marked by caution and restraint," further claiming that the turn of events on the island had not been "a function of US policy and action."[228] In fact, to a certain degree, this was not incorrect. But the politics was in the history. All at once the past and present conflated, and without knowledge of the former an understanding of the latter was impossible.

The defense of national sovereignty, all through the early years, in the face of unrelenting American determination to force Cubans to yield to the will of the United States, provided the government of the revolution with an enormous fund of political support and enduring moral sustenance. That the Americans opposed the revolution was received in Cuba as continuing U.S. opposition to Cuban aspirations of national sovereignty. The Cuban leadership could have no more compelling proof of the virtue of its purpose than to confront the United States in defense of national sovereignty. In a lengthy diplomatic note by Foreign Minister Raúl Roa in November 1959, published in English as "In Defense of National Sovereignty," the Cuban government reiterated a familiar theme:

> The Cuban people conquered the right to govern themselves at the cost of enormous sacrifice and innumerable courageous deeds. It is to this stubborn determination and fighting spirit that, despite the well-known constraints and subordination to which we have been subject, we owe the level of political, economic, social, and cultural developments which we have managed to achieve in our 56 years of the pseudo-republic. The triumphant Revolution of January 1, 1959, put an end to this ominous state of things, and today Cuba is, for the first time in our history, truly free, independent, and sovereign.[229]

The past was put to a purpose. This was about forging a consensus on the matter of Cuba being wronged as the basis from which the leadership claimed moral mandate to make things right. Another form of the past as a politics, of course, except in this instance it served to summon Cubans to act in defense of their history as a matter of legacy. These were extraordinary times: a triumphant revolution, a people imbued with a newfound sense of agency and achievement but also smarting, bearing grievances decades in the making, and all at once given the opportunity to act out and act on the fulfillment of their history.

These were sentiments of unsuspected depths. Few were the number of adult Cubans who did not—as a matter of a historical knowledge—bear varying degrees of resentment toward the United States. Virtually all Cubans who had completed elementary school education could offer a disquisition on the Platt Amendment. For much of the early twentieth century, a Cuban sense of inferiority was expressed in public and private, with a mixture of frustration and impotence in the face of powerlessness to control the terms of the meaning of Cuban. These circumstances served to infuse into norms of nationality a deepening tenor of defensiveness, the obverse side of which would find expression easily enough as defiance. This was a sentiment that when summoned and channeled into a politics could be relied upon to mobilize powerful popular support. Novelist Manuel Cofiño speaks through his protagonist, in *Cuando la sangre se parece al fuego* (1979): "I came to hate the North Americans who would not allow us to do what we wanted to do. They believed that because we were a small country they could bring us to our knees and do to us whatever they wanted to do."[230]

Confrontation with the United States in defense of national sovereignty served to enhance the moral credibility of the new government and indeed contributed to a national unanimity of purpose previously unimaginable and perhaps unattainable by any other means. It was all about history. "[The Americans] deprived the Cuban people of the prerogative to govern themselves," Castro recounted in early 1959; "they deprived the Cuban people of their sovereignty; they treated the Cuban people like little children to whom they said: 'We give you permission to do just this, and if you do more we will punish you.' The Platt Amendment was imposed [and] we either behaved ourselves—behaved ourselves in the manner convenient to the foreign country—or we would lose our sovereignty." And to the larger point: "It was inconceivable that after so many years of struggle, in the end the *mambises* were denied the fruit of their labor. . . . We are doing today in our *patria* what Maceo, Máximo Gómez, and José Martí, and all those who struggled for our independence, would be doing."[231] Explained Fidel Castro one year later:

> We have had to confront an old mentality. . . . We have had to confront the spirit of submission that was instilled in our people, for however sad and difficult it may be to acknowledge, our people thought little of themselves. Our people were never told the truth. . . . They were taught to look toward another nation, to look with an inferiority complex and with a spirit of impotence, to await for their needs from others. They were taught to depend on others from which was created a spirit of inferiority and cowardice. It was as if our people were like one of those children who could not take one step forward without asking someone for permission. That is what our people were taught. That is the spirit that we have had to confront. Not only the past but old ideas of the past, the vices of the past.[232]

The Americans challenged the revolution on the grounds that the leadership was best prepared to defend: a commitment to the historic ideal of *patria*, as a matter of national sovereignty and self-determination so central to the legacy upon which the men and women of the revolution validated their claim to power. Within the context of Cuban historic sensibilities, U.S. policy not only contributed to Cuban intransigence but, more important, it also lent credibility to that intransigence—not simply as a principle of foreign policy but as a means of internal governance. American policy served to bring out some of the most intransigent tendencies of the Cuban leadership in the defense of some of the most exalted notions of Cuban nationality. If, in the end, the invocation of national sovereignty and self-determination had been the last and only rationale through which to exhort defense of the revolution, the leadership would still have retained a powerful claim on the allegiance of vast numbers of Cubans. It was a sentiment of enormous vitality and resonance, one that could be defended without compromise or concession, no matter what its defense may have cost. This was the moral of the Cuban past.

Early political discontent with the Castro government notwithstanding, the patriotic consensus was preserved—as it would be for decades to come—around the defense of the sovereign nation. In a public opinion survey completed in Cuba in 1960—*Attitudes of the Cuban People toward the Castro Regime*—Lloyd Free of the Princeton Institute for International Social Research was slightly perplexed by what appeared as an anomaly in Cuban public sentiment. Free described the need to comment on "one other aspect" about growing opposition to the government: "Not only the groups less enthusiastic about the regime . . . but also the outright oppositionists, in listing the *best* aspects of the present situation, mentioned with above-average frequency . . . an item with distinct nationalist overtones: 'Cuba free and independent; the struggle for or defense of national sovereignty; etc.'" Free understood the implications with prophetic accuracy: "Since in Cuban eyes national independence tends to mean independence from the U.S., the higher degree of nationalistic sentiment apparent among the very group where oppositionist and critical sentiment tend to be the most frequent suggests that *criticisms from American sources of the regime's anti-U.S. policies are apt to fall on relatively deaf ears.*"[233]

6 HISTORY WITH A PURPOSE

In few countries are the links between history and the present as evident on the surface as in Cuba, where the struggles and passions of the last 150 years still play out in national psychology and perspectives today.
— *Diplomats Handbook* (2010)

The constant reference that Cuban revolutionaries make to our history is not an artificial construction but rather the only way to make one understand what is happening.
— Roberto Fernández Retamar, "The Enormity of Cuba" (1996)

In both the pre-Revolutionary and post-Revolutionary periods, the historian in Cuba enjoyed a special place, seen as fulfilling a special role within the national psyche and the national evolution.
— Antoni Kapcia, *Cuba, Island of Dreams* (2000)

Cuban patriotism experienced the end of its frustration and realized its hopes with the triumph of 1959, with the attainment of national liberation and full sovereignty, and the establishment of a State placed at the service of society. The Cuban socialist revolution adopted that patriotism and appropriated all its symbols and attributes. This is one of the fundamental facts necessary to understand the legitimacy of the Revolution.

— Fernando Martínez Heredia, "Pensamiento social y
    política de la Revolución" (2007)

Many believe that rhetoric and ceremony should be reformed in order to distance official comportment from a historicism that has reached a saturation point.

— Lisandro Otero, *La utopía cubana desde adentro:
    ¿A dónde va Cuba hoy?* (1993)

That the revolution addressed the historical sources of Cuban discontent, and indeed offered a plausible remedy to long-standing grievances, mattered as an achievement in its own right, of course. But it mattered more as a demonstration of what was possible in a Cuba for Cubans, a vindication of sorts, a source of empowerment: confirmation of the long-held conviction that the realization of national sovereignty and the exercise of self-determination could enable Cubans to shape the forces that governed their lives.

The evocative power of the revolution resided in its capacity to fashion a politics around the claim to sovereign nationhood as a historically warranted entitlement, that is, to realize the promise of the past, a purpose that from its origins had always implied an outcome of radical reach. At the core of the revolution's mystique was the claim to national fulfillment, of having realized the historic project of nation from which the meaning of nationality had formed. The affirmation of national sovereignty, of Cuba for Cubans, drew upon aspirations with antecedents in the nineteenth century, possessed of a moral authority intrinsic to the calculus of Cuban.

For the vast number of Cubans who had lived with the disquiet of an unfinished history, the triumph of the revolution was received with a sense of completion, a people reintegrated into their history and made one with their past. Cuban historical sensibilities had more than adequately disposed a people to embrace the proposition of the triumph of the revolution as vindication of the nation, the past as destiny fulfilled, and indeed that had set in place a near-unassailable logic with which the leadership validated its claim to power. That Cubans were susceptible to the promise of the past as a means of collective fulfillment contributed mightily to the comparative ease with which the plausibility of the revolution insinuated itself into the popular imagination. The process transformed the normative imperative of nationality into the prescriptive purpose of the revolution, understood as legacy to uphold and duty to discharge as a matter of Cuban. The revolution seemed, after all, so fully consistent with and conceived within the dominant paradigm of nationality.

Much of the joy with which Cubans initially welcomed the triumph of the revolution had to do with a powerful sense of achievement, a people who by virtue of sheer will believed themselves to have fulfilled the promise of their past. Cubans had consummated the ideal of the sovereign nation, almost everyone agreed. It was perhaps impossible to resist the appeal of the heroic men and women who emerged from the urban underground and descended from the eastern mountains: they were young, attractive, earnest, and articulate; they exuded political integrity and were filled with exuberant confidence in the promise of their achievement. They claimed power in the form of a moral mandate derived from the nineteenth-century liberation project, totally persuaded that they had indeed fulfilled the legacy that history had conferred upon successive generations of Cubans, and who in the act of completing the historic project of liberation had consummated the ideal of nation.

Cubans had challenged a government based on force and violence on its own terms and prevailed. They had consciously inserted themselves into their history, and more: they had discharged their duty to the past by inscribing the purpose of their achievement within the meaning of their history. Certainly that was the sentiment that informed the significance attributed to the triumph of the revolution. January 1, 1959, was what should have been realized on January 1, 1899, the fulfillment of the aspirations of nation, what historian Ramón de Armas would later characterize as realization of "the postponed revolution" (la revolución pospuesta).[1] The premise of the past was essential to the very rationale of the revolution, from which the men and women who governed in its name claimed moral authority and historical authenticity— legitimacy, in a word. Historian Oscar Zanetti was indeed correct to note that the revolution derived "its principal source of legitimacy from the history of Cuba."[2]

But the triumph of the revolution signified more than a seizure of power: it implied too an appropriation of history. To inscribe the moral logic of the triumph of the revolution into the rationale of history was to render the revolution as vindication of the past and the past as validation of the revolution. The evocation of the past served to corroborate the proposition of the revolution as continuity: history as an unseen force, "at work"—inexorably—toward the triumphant revolution as its climax. The revolution, Fidel Castro insisted, was "the continuity of the history of our nation at its highest stage."[3]

Central to claims of historical authenticity was the proposition of the triumphant revolution as culmination of a process whose antecedents reached deep into the nineteenth century, that is, to the very sources of nationality. These were not new claims, of course. They had been advanced all through the 1950s and had served as the principal explanatory framework through which to arrange the meaning of the revolution into coherent narrative form. There was a teleology at work here, of course, not always apparent, but always acting to join the present with the past, the latter making the former plausible. It was not so much that the revolution was of the past, but rather that the revolution was fulfillment of the past: the Ten Years War, the Little War, the 1895 war for independence, and the revolution of 1933—all rendered as historical phases of a single revolutionary process, culminating in the triumphant revolution on January 1, 1959. "[The events of] 1933 contemplated 1868 and 1895," Raúl Roa affirmed, "and 1933 is found in 1959 in the sense that its frustrated objectives were fully revived in the process inaugurated after the triumph of the armed insurrection. These revolutions are in reality one, with multiple stages."[4] The triumph of the revolution, proclaimed Rebel Army *comandante* Ramiro Valdés, "fulfilled the patriotic project of our *mambises*. It brought to fruition José Martí's aspiration of a country truly independent, free from Spain, free from the United States. It vindicated the work of the liberators, thwarted in 1898 as a result of the intervention of imperialism. It gave life to the dreams of revolution of all the men and women of this century who struggled and died for the emancipation of the poor and exploited."[5] The victorious Cubans of the 1950s, Fidel Castro insisted, "were able to derive inspiration from the heroic struggles for our independence, a wealth of combat traditions and love of liberty . . . , and nurture themselves on the political thought that guided the revolution of 1895," adding: "The ideology [of the revolution] was intertwined with the aspirations of the heroic *mambises* who spilled so much of their blood for the independence of Cuba, equality, and the dignity of their people."[6]

■ ■ ■

The claim of the revolution as continuity and consummation gained discursive ascendancy in an all-encompassing historical construct of *cien años de lucha*: one hundred years of struggle. The narrative of the revolution as culmination of *cien años de lucha* did indeed purport to fashion a new founding narrative, with 1959 consecrated as the realization of the historic project of nation. "The call for independence was made in 1868," explained Minister of Education Armando Hart, adding:

This was not a rash act, but one that had deep roots in our history. . . . Thus by 1968 we could say that this Revolution had been fought in the countryside and cities for an entire century and that it had been developing in our hearts for a century and a half. Several generations of patriots struggled and sacrificed their lives for the "Cuban Revolution," as it has been called since 1868. So when that Revolution finally triumphed in 1959, the entire

Cuban people felt, as did Martí when he landed in Cuba [in 1895], that they had come into fulfillment. That is to say, they felt their full strength that had accumulated over the course of nearly a century of struggle.[7]

The relationship of 1868 to 1959 as a matter of legacy and source of legitimacy was invoked with unambiguous purpose. Speaking at La Demajagua, physically at the place where the past happened, Fidel Castro reflected on the start of the Ten Years War and the consolidation of consciousness of Cuban: "As of that moment [1868], for the first time, the concept and awareness of nationality began to take form and for the first time the term of 'Cuban' was used to designate those who rose up with arms to fight against the Spanish colonial power." And to the point:

> The study of the history of our country will not only enlighten our consciousness and our thinking, but it will also help us find an inexhaustible supply of heroism, of the spirit of sacrifice, of the will to struggle and fight. What those combatants did, almost unarmed, should always be an inspiration for the revolutionaries of today, always a reason to have confidence in our people, in their strength, their capacity to struggle, their destiny. It should give our country the assurance that nothing or nobody in this world can defeat us. . . . And that this revolution cannot be defeated by anything, because this people, who have fought for 100 years for its destiny, is capable of fighting for another 100 years for the same destiny. This people that was capable of sacrificing its life [inmolarse] more than once, would be capable to die as many times as it were necessary.[8]

Poet Nicolás Guillén provided a slightly more evocative corroboration of cien años: "Martí promised it to you / and Fidel fulfilled it for you [Te lo prometió Martí y Fidel te lo cumplió]."[9] And Guillén again: "Martí wanted Free Cuba / And Fidel said: 'It is!' [Martí quiso a Cuba libre / y Fidel dijo: ¡Ya está!]"[10]

The revolution had emerged from the very history it claimed to have realized—a compelling narrative indeed—an explanation transacted within a well-established historical vernacular, filled with allusions to and allegories from the past as a destiny fulfilled: that is, a people conscious of and conditioned by their past, a history that vast numbers of Cubans had lived to fulfill and make good on. The men and women who assumed power in 1959 acted within the very historical constructs by which a people had arrived at an understanding of what the enactment of their history required of them.

But it was more complex still. While the revolution was of history, and profoundly so—"the Revolution is the result of a historical necessity," pronounced Fidel Castro[11]—it presumed also to have transcended history. Inscribed in the claim of the revolution as consummation of nation was a politics by which to propound the end of history. Cubans conferred on la Revolución something of an omniscient embodiment: the revolution seemingly possessed of metaphysical properties transcending the reach of human agency, greater than the collective volition of the men and women who made it, possessed of the force of natural law and let loose upon the land, acting with self-directed purpose of historical if not always discernible design, and always with the presumption of infallibility and invincibility—"a force more powerful than Nature itself," Fidel Castro proclaimed in 1963.[12] The revolution was history fulfilled, accountable only to the logic of its origins, and as such was the instrument of history, "eternal, and indestructible," pronounced the Cuban Communist Party.[13] Cubans spoke of the revolution as something to which they were obligated to deliver themselves—entregarse was the reflexive verb of choice—unconditionally and unquestioningly. "Before you do anything," the protagonist of Aida Bahr's novel Las voces y los ecos (2004) is counseled, "think always if it will benefit the Revolution or not; if you have any doubts that it may cause it harm, don't do it."[14]

The process was as pervasive as it was prepossessing, and at times it seemed as if nothing else mattered. Fidel Castro said as much. "The revolutionary," he enjoined, "places the Revolution above everything else."[15] This was Inocencia Acosta Felipe's complaint to Oscar Lewis in 1969. "The Revolution just doesn't leave time to see family," she explained, "except by chance at mass rallies, or here and there."[16] Playwright Nicolás Dorr gave voice to the same sentiment through the complaint of Graciela in Mediodía candente: "This Revolution doesn't even allow time to keep up a household."[17]

The claim of the revolution as continuity and consummation implied an epistemology of far-reaching implications, a way to organize historical knowledge in function of power, to speak as the agent of history to proclaim the end of history. This was history as a means to validate the revolution as a process of such transcendental reach as to collapse entirely the distinction between the past and the present. The act of consummation of the past had consumed history itself and signified the past at once fulfilled and transcended: history as an inexorable process toward realization of nation, to have propelled Cubans to act and into action as a way to continue to make history in fulfillment of their history. The very teleological structure of the historical narrative, inexorably and inevitably—redemption—implied the end of history. The revolution was not outside history but within history, and in bringing history to a climax it had brought the historic nation into being. There had long been a hint of the prophetic in Cuban historical narratives, a past awaiting fulfillment according to the way it should have been, almost everyone agreed, and it surely should be. "This generation has not only brought about the culmination of an era," pronounced Fidel Castro, "it has achieved definitive objectives, it has fulfilled specific goals and realized a historic task: a *patria* free, truly free."[18]

History had come to an end precisely because the promise of the past had been fulfilled. It was implied in the Nicolas Guillén refrain "*se acabó*"—it was ended: "Fidel arrived and fulfilled what Martí had promised [*Vino Fidel y cumplió / lo que prometió Martí*]."[19] Carlos Rafael Rodríguez drew the larger moral from Guillén's poetic dictum "*se acabó*" explicitly, asserting, "We have realized the Revolution of Martí," and added: " '*Se acabó*,' Nicolás Gullén said. And we can proclaim historically: ¡*Se acabó*!"[20] Historian Fernando Portuondo y del Prado was categorical: "By virtue of familiarity with history, we are certain that we live at the climax of an epoch of our country."[21] "The history of Cuba culminated in the Revolution," pronounced Sergio Benvenuto, director of the Department of History at the University of Havana.[22] It was thus possible, historian Rafael Rojas suggested, "to imagine the conclusion of the Revolution as the end of Cuban history."[23]

* * *

To claim power in the name of national fulfillment was to propound an intimidating discursive construct, one that could not be readily refuted without challenging the very normative content of Cuban. Far-reaching implications indeed, for those who presumed to govern in the name of the revolution also determined to act on behalf of the nation fulfilled, and to oppose the former was to threaten the latter. Certainly this was the purport of a politics in which power was discharged as a function of historic continuity and consummation. The proposition of the revolution as redemption contained within its premise a larger meaning, for it served to confer on the revolution—or, to be more precise, conferred on the men and women who governed in the name of the revolution—the moral claim to power, not as a party, not even as a government, but as disinterested defenders of the legacy by which the realization of nation had been fulfilled.

Authority of power implied moral mandate in the defense of the historical ideal of nation. This was not a matter solely—or even principally—of defending the policies and programs of the revolution, but rather of defending the proposition of Cuba for Cubans, to articulate and advance the interests of the nation in discharge of national sovereignty and self-determination. Vaunted claims and lofty purpose, to be sure, but very much central to the narrative of triumph with which the idea of the revolution passed into domains of near-unassailable legitimacy. Cubans loyal to their history and true to the purpose to which their history was given—*verdaderos cubanos*—could not but receive the revolution unconditionally and unquestioningly as means of fulfillment of ideals from which the moral order of nationality had originated. Anything less was suspect.

Certainly the confrontation with the United States set these issues in sharp relief. That the United States pursued policies designed to topple a government given to the defense of national sovereignty rendered the subversive purport of opposition plausible; that after 1960 the principal source of opposition to the government of Fidel Castro originated from the United States, first in the form of moral support and material assistance to disaffected Cubans at home and abroad and subsequently through successive policies of sabotage, subversion, and sanctions provided credibility to the charge of counterrevolutionary activity as a threat to national sovereignty. Once the principal source of opposition originated from abroad, the matter of defense of national sovereignty acquired a logic of its own. "All the hopes associated with the success of the counterrevolution," Castro warned, "are expectations derived from soliciting the support of a foreign power":

> Therefore, the defense of the Revolution is the defense of national sovereignty. Those who are flirting with counterrevolution in concert with foreign interests are betraying miserably their *patria* . . . and the historic aspiration for independence and national liberation. To seek foreign intervention is an act of aggression against the *patria*, because today to betray the Revolution is to betray the *patria*. We are at the point at which we are defending the sovereignty of the country, at which we must decide that we are either a free country or not. And since we decided some time ago to be a free country, we will defend our national sovereignty with the last drop of blood.[24]

There was coercive purport embedded in a paradigm of power propounded as discharge of legacy, of course, for to advance the claim of consummation of nation as source of political legitimacy was to deny the very plausibility of opposition. The premise of nation was joined with the purpose of revolution, a combination that implied an incontestable moral entitlement to power in defense of the sovereign nation. Defense of the nation required defense of the revolution—and faith in the men and women who governed in the name of the revolution. "What does it mean that we are of *Patria o Muerte*?" asks Nicolasa in Luis Ricardo Alonso's novel *Territorio libre* (1967). "It means that we would rather die, that we would rather lose everything we own than offend the *patria*. And the *patria*, *compañeras* and *compañeros*, is the Revolution. And the Revolution is the wise guidance given to us by the leader and the party, by way of the mass organizations and their representatives."[25]

The logic of the revolution in its most exalted claim—revolution as national redemption—expanded into something of a discursive totality, all-inconclusive and all-encompassing, and those who demurred, by definition, were *malos cubanos*. Not since the nineteenth century was the characterization of *verdadero cubano* as embodiment of nationality so explicitly inscribed into a particular ideological version of Cuban. The revolution revealed that the meaning of Cubanness had changed—again—and henceforth implied defense of the revolution as the measure of Cuban.

Not since the nineteenth century—and not for dissimilar reasons—was the failure to endorse that version of Cuban equated with disloyalty, a matter of exhortations to live up to expectations. It was in the spirit of the revolution, Fidel Castro insisted, "the one to which we must all commit, where all we true Cubans are found [*en ese espíritu estamos todos los verdaderos cubanos*]."[26] Opponents of the revolution were designated "enemies of the *patria*," and the *patria* would be defended, Castro affirmed, "by all true Cubans . . . together with all men of honor and men of dignity worthy of the *patria* [*todos los verdaderos cubanos . . . juntos todos los hombres honrados, juntos todos los hombres dignos de la patria*]."[27] The revolution would obtain support, Castro insisted, among "the true patriots [*los verdaderos patriotas*]"; and "the true man [*el verdadero hombre*]"; and "the true people [*el verdadero pueblo*]"; and "the true sons and daughters of the nation [*los verdaderos hijos de la nación*]"; and "the true and honorable citizens of this country [*los verdaderos y dignos ciudadanos de este país*]."[28]

Opponents of the revolution were denounced as disloyal, and indeed their very claim to being Cuban was questioned. Those Cubans who abandoned the *patria*, decried Raúl Castro—and the verb of choice was usually *abandonar*—"were born here by mistake."[29] Fidel Castro disputed outright the claim to Cuban to all who emigrated. "We cannot call those who abandon the *patria* 'Cubans,'" Castro insisted. "We cannot call and we will never call 'Cubans' those who implore criminal aggression against the *patria*, the deserters and the cowards who are among a minority. We will call 'Cubans' only those who at this time act accordingly, the very first time that one can be a true Cuban [*ser cubano de verdad*], and not those who called themselves 'Cuban' when Cuba was not Cuba and was not truly Cuban."[30]

A challenge to the revolution dedicated to the defense of the sovereign nation could not be construed in any form other than a challenge to the sov-

DIARIO DE LA MAÑANA
TERCERA EPOCA

NOTICIAS DE

UN DIARIO AL SERVICIO DEL PUEBLO

ANIBAL ESCALANTE
esta noche a las 8 y 30
"Doctrina y Acción"
espacio radial del PSP
Cadena Oriental de Radio

Año XXII No. 15   LA HABANA, MARTES 19 DE ENERO DE 1960   Precio: 5 centavos

"Defender la Revolución es defender la independencia nacional" - dijo Fidel Castro

"Los que dedican aplausos a ciertos embajadores, demuestran su falta de patriotismo", subrayó el líder

Headline from the newspaper *Hoy*, January 19, 1960, affirming Fidel Castro's pronouncement, "To defend the Revolution is to defend national independence." From *Hoy*, January 19, 1960.

ereign nation itself. Opposition to the revolution implied opposition to the nation, specifically, subversion: it implied, by definition, treason. The weekly *Bohemia* drew the parallels explicitly as early as 1960: "Once again, as in all momentous epochs of our past — remember what occurred in 1895 — Cubans are divided: between the loyal and the traitors, between the patriots and the renegades, between the free and the sell-outs. Annexationists, autonomists, reprobates, and mercenaries have reappeared. . . . The anti-Cuba, with its roots in the muck of the past, stubbornly refuses to die."[31] The survival of the sovereign nation was linked to the defense of the revolution. Proclaimed Fidel Castro:

> The counterrevolutionaries, that is to say, the enemies of the Revolution, have no rights against the Revolution, because the Revolution has a fun-

damental right: the right to exist, the right to develop, the right to prevail. Who can doubt the right of a people who have proclaimed "*Patria o Muerte*," that is to say, "*la Revolución o la muerte*," the existence of the Revolution or nothing. . . . Against the rights of an entire nation, the rights of the enemies of that nation count for nothing. . . . Against the right of the Revolution to be and to exist, no one. Given that the Revolution consists of the interests of the people, given that the Revolution signifies the interests of the entire nation, no one can reasonably dispute a single right against it. I trust this is very clear.[32]

Concluded Castro: "Within the Revolution, everything; against the Revolution, nothing."

There was something of an inexorable momentum in the history by which Cubans were overtaken, a trajectory that seemed driven by a convergence of circumstances set in motion by the sheer logic of one hundred years of history. A people formed by the promise of the sovereign nation readily received the revolution as the realization of nation. The latter was henceforth deemed dependent on the former. To dissent from the revolution was tantamount to disloyalty to the nation. To oppose the revolution, the newspaper *Revolución* warned, was "the way of treason, of the fifth column. . . . Today one is with Cuba or against Cuba."[33] The logic of the past as a politics was brought to a wholly plausible conclusion. "Those who campaign against the Revolution," Fidel Castro pronounced, "are enemies of our *patria*," and explicitly: "To commit treason against the Revolution is to commit treason against the *patria*."[34] The Association of Technicians and Professionals took a "Historic Oath" in 1960 and vowed "to remain loyal to the *patria*" in a simple refrain: "With the *patria* and against treason."[35] Luis García remembered preparing to leave the island with the knowledge that "if you leave Cuba, you are a traitor."[36]

During the Mariel boat lift in April 1980, Cubans preparing to emigrate to the United States were denounced as traitors to the nation. "In general," insisted *Granma* editorially, "they are persons who lack national sentiment and are without attachment to their *patria*."[37] The signboards, placards, and banners displayed during the demonstrations organized to repudiate Cubans departing at Mariel were filled with denunciation of treason: "Cuba yes! Traitors no!" "Here there is no room for cowards and traitors." "Traitors! Remember Girón!" "Down with traitors! Long live the *patria*!" "Revolution yes! Lumpen and traitors no!" "We are a united nation and do not accept traitors."[38]

Failure to participate in the process in which the nation had found redemption implied a dereliction of duty of Cuban—and was always suspect. "In these moments," Camilo Cienfuegos warned in June 1959, "there are only two sides in this land of ours [en estas tierras nuestras]; there are only two positions, only two paths: we are either with the Revolution or we are against the Revolution."[39] Fidel Castro was explicit in his explanation to Lee Lockwood: "In a revolutionary process, there are no neutrals; there are only partisans of the revolution or enemies."[40] In Yolanda Ortal-Miranda's play *Balada sonámbula de los desterrados del sueño*, Gabriela articulates the truth of the moment: "Whoever is not with the Revolution is against it."[41] The newspaper *Revolución* drew the distinction in stark terms: "In Cuba today there are only two ways: the way of the Revolution and the way of the counterrevolution. The two ways are irreconcilable. In the former there are 6 million Cubans, the best of our people. The way of national sovereignty, of the Agrarian Reform, of economic freedom, of culture, of social justice. The way to greatness, of dignity and of the salvation of the present and future of the *Patria*. With the way of the counterrevolution are the imperialist circles."[42] The protagonist in Alvaro de Villa's novel *El olor de la muerte que viene* (1968) is succinct: "The Revolution is Cuba."[43] For Pablo Armando Fernández, it was the other way around: "Cuba is the revolution."[44]

■ ■ ■

The premise of the revolution as consummation of sovereign nationhood could not contemplate challenge in any form other than as a threat to national sovereignty, a proposition wholly consistent with the discursive framework from which the triumphalist narratives of the revolution acquired the status of received truths. That early opposition to the revolution originated from interests long identified as hostile to aspirations of national sovereignty contributed credibility to the characterization of counterrevolution as treason. The proof was in the past. It remained only to historicize opposition to the revolution as a structural condition, one with antecedents in the previous century: the same interests that had opposed aspirations to national sovereignty also opposed the achievements of the revolution. The logic of the syllogism was inexorable.

Such was the case of the newspaper *Diario de la Marina*. Founded in 1832 and long recognized as the bulwark of conservative sentiment in Cuba, *Diario de la Marina* was fearless in its criticism of the revolution. But *Diario de la Marina* had a long history—an ignominious history, its critics charged—of arraying itself against aspirations of national sovereignty, and it was by "exposing" this history that the government sought to discredit *Diario de la Marina*: all and all, not a difficult task if it could be shown that *Diario de la Marina* had been on the wrong side of every issue of importance in Cuban history. What possible credibility could be accorded to a newspaper that had condemned the *Grito de Yara*, denounced José Martí, and celebrated the death of Antonio Maceo? That had defended Spanish colonial rule, supported the Platt Amendment, and welcomed the return of Fulgencio Batista in 1952?

By virtue of its history, critics charged, *Diario de la Marina* lacked moral standing to presume to speak as if in the best interests of the nation. On the contrary, it represented a threat to the sovereign nation. "Ever since the time of Narciso López," Fidel Castro charged, "*Diario de la Marina* has been waging a campaign against the interests of the nation. Is it not well known that it applauded the execution by firing squad of Narciso López, that it characterized our *mambises* as bandits, applauded the death of Maceo and of Céspedes, the death of Martí, and has always opposed the best ideas and hopes for the *Patria*?"

Castro staged a public reading of select nineteenth-century editorials of *Diario de la Marina*, including those commenting on the execution of Narciso López, the death of Ignacio Agramonte, and the execution of medical students in 1871. He quoted *Diario de la Marina* editorials regarding the *Grito de Yara*: "We have presented a truthful summary of the events that have occurred in the jurisdiction of Manzanillo and Las Tunas and today we have to condemn the action of the bandits—from this day forward this is the name—bandits—we are obliged to use—who have reduced a sugar mill to ashes. We have been unable to ascertain the purpose of the *insurrectos* of Yara, but their activities are sufficient to characterize them among the most dangerous criminals." On the death of Carlos Manuel de Céspedes, *Diario de la Marina* affirmed: "[He] is responsible before God and all of humanity for the blood and all the tears shed on this island since that lamentable date of October 10, 1868." On the start of the war for independence in 1895: "These are people without standing or status, despicable social elements that exist in every society, adventurers in search of glory, groups disposed to all types of madness and without scruples." On the death of Martí: "Martí has fallen forever, the delirious civilian leader of the separatist movement. . . . His death represents a great setback for the enemies of the *Madre Patria* [that is, Spain] and a glorious achievement for our forces. May God forgive him for all the evil he has brought upon his country and the numerous innocent lives lost because of him, the mourning he has brought to innumerable families and the ruin and misery he has caused as a result of his insane beliefs." And on the death of Maceo: "For such a noteworthy achievement, the *Diario de la Marina* is pleased to extend its warmest congratulations to [Spanish] Major [Francisco] Cirujeda and the valiant officers and men under his command who have rendered such valuable service to the *patria*."[45]

Noticias de Hoy accused *Diario de la Marina* outright of having committed "direct treason."[46] *Diario de la Marina* "is at the service of all the interests that are aligned against the nation," the newspaper *Revolución* proclaimed.[47] Cubans knew well that it was "the traditional enemy of our independence," adding: "The revolution and the truth are inseparable. For that reason, even if it distresses the anti-Cuban *Diario de la Marina*, we must probe the depths of our history to expose the truth." Affirmed *Revolución*: "If in the past *La Marina* attacked the *mambises*, today it directs its venom against the Revolution. Always against the interests of the Cuban people."[48] *Revolución* recalled "that infamous December 1896, when in the offices of *Diario de la Marina* they toasted with champagne the death of the Cuban hero [Antonio Maceo]": "Many years ago in 1896, one December 7, a fateful day for defenders of liberty and dignity, *Diario de la Marina* — then the official organ of Spanish colonialism as it was in these days serving as representative of the interests of the worst type of counterrevolutionary — offered a banquet in honor of the Spanish Volunteers. The banquet served as the occasion to honor the gallantry of Major [Francisco] Cirujeda, whose troops had killed Lieutenant General Antonio Maceo."[49] *Diario de la Marina* "attacked José Martí and celebrated his death," *Revolución* reminded its readers. "It characterized Antonio Maceo as an outlaw. It insulted Máximo Gómez and . . . supported the dictatorships of Gerardo Machado and Fulgencio Batista."[50]

Its editorial history had more than adequately demonstrated patterns of sinister intent, critics charged. "It is not our fault," insisted essayist Gregorio Ortega, "that *Diario de la Marina* always and on every occasion has been against national interests. It is not our fault that *Diario de la Marina* is today against national sovereignty, progress, and the well-being of the nation," and asked: "What does *Diario de la Marina* have to do with our people? It mocked the medical students executed in 1871, it disparaged the *mambises*, it defamed Martí, Maceo, and Guiteras. . . . If today it attacks the Revolutionary Government, it can only mean that the Government headed by Fidel Castro is the expression of the most profound national interests."[51]

The larger meaning was unmistakable: a newspaper given to the defense of interests historically hostile to the sovereign nation could not be permitted to malign a revolution dedicated to the defense of the sovereign nation. The net effect was to separate the opposition from the history that had given form to the nation. To rephrase the dictum: within the history, everything; outside the history, nothing. In May 1960, with the apparent approval of the government, workers of *Diario de la Marina* seized control of the editorial offices and thereupon suspended publication of the newspaper. "For 128 years," the workers' manifesto explained in the last published issue of May 12, "the people of Cuba have had to endure an insidious campaign against the interests of Cuba," and continued:

> It was the *Diario de la Marina* that defended Weyler; it was the *Diario de la Marina* that maligned the liberators struggling for independence as thieves and outlaws; it was *Diario de la Marina* that suggested that the "head of Maceo should be used as an inkwell" and that celebrated the fall of the Bronze Titan and the death of the Apostle Martí. . . . Determined as we are to defend the Revolution, which is to defend Cuba, and in consideration of the dismal history of this publication, we deem that it should cease publication and its presses should be converted to the publication of reading material for our humble peasants and the permanent eradication of illiteracy in our nation.[52]

The *Diario de la Marina* was thus demonized, and in a highly charged political environment, few indeed were the voices sufficiently intrepid to defend the freedom of the press. Those who defended *Diario de la Marina* drew the wrath of *Revolución*:

> Whoever defends *Diario de la Marina* offends the memory of the [student] martyrs of 1871.
> Whoever defends *Diario de la Marina* offends the memory of Martí.
> Whoever defends *Diario de la Marina* participates in the banquete that celebrated the death of Antonio Maceo.
> Whoever defends *Diario de la Marina* defends Valeriano Weyler.
> Whoever defends *Diario de la Marina* defends the reconcentration.
> Whoever defends *Diario de la Marina* defends foreign intervention and the Platt Amendment.
> Whoever defends *Diario de la Marina* defends the counterrevolution.[53]

"*Diario de la Marina* died because it was condemned by history," *Revolución* pronounced tersely.[54]

Opposition from the Catholic church also provided the occasion to set an equally dubious history in relief, one also noteworthy for its hostility to aspirations of sovereign nationhood. That the Catholic religious personnel in Cuba were overwhelmingly foreign, and mostly Spanish—almost 75 percent of the total number of priests and religious (1,871 out of 2,552) were

Spaniards[55]—added another level of tension to church-state confrontation in which redemption of the nation served as one of the principal legitimizing claims of the revolutionary government.

The attack against the church did not respond directly to its criticism but rather to its history, something akin to guilt by association with a disreputable past, and specifically its support of Spanish colonial rule during the 1890s. The attack on the church invoked the past, to remind Cubans of a history noteworthy for its hostility to the nation. *Revolución* republished daily the anticlerical writings of José Martí.[56] Historian Emilio Roig de Leuchsenring published a small treatise entitled *La iglesia católica contra la independencia de Cuba* (1960). "I have written this book," Roig de Leuchsenring explained, "in which I present the nefarious work of one of the mortal enemies of the Republic of Martí, of the ideal of the Republic, to which the supreme Apostle of our liberties consecrated and offered his precious life, and to which we should all aspire, for which we should all struggle, all of us who would feel as good Cubans [*buenos cubanos*]." The Catholic church lacked the moral authority to criticize the revolution, Roig de Leuchsenring emphasized, due to its "irrefutable historical realities as an organization of a militant politics in the service of the Spanish colonial regime and as an openly impudent and obstinate enemy of the independence of this land and its sons."[57] No credibility could be given to criticism by clerics who in the nineteenth century "blessed the troops who were preparing to do battle against the Cuban revolutionaries, who offered church property to serve as forts, barracks, and watch-towers to observe and assist in the war against the patriotic *mambises*, who raised funds and collected provisions and medicine for Spanish troops, and who supported the persecution of Cuban conspirators and sympathizers of the independence cause."[58] Affirmed Roig de Leuchsenring:

> The Catholic church remained allied always with the autocratic and reactionary Spanish State against Cuba and the Cubans whose only desire was liberty and justice for their *patria*. . . . Cubans can never forget that when Martí and Maceo died, Bishop of Havana [Manuel] Santander offered *Te Deums* as an act of thanksgiving to God for the special blessing. And when Maceo perished in battle at Punta Brava [on December 6] . . . [Santander] proclaimed from the pulpit that "with the death of Maceo and [Pancho] Gómez God had wanted to celebrate the Immaculate Conception."[59]

An essay published in the journal *Cuba Socialista* in 1962, entitled "El clero reaccionario y la revolución cubana," similarly attacked the church for its history, and by implication denounced the church for its attack against the

1. Llegaron con los conquistadores.

2. Lo quemaron en nombre de la Fe

3. Cuando empezaron las luchas libertarias dijeron que el ejército español era enviado del cielo.

4. Y hasta hubo curas chivato

5. Junto con Pepinillo celebraron la muerte de Maceo.

6. AMERICAN EMBASSY

Ya en la República estuvieron siempre al lado de las peores causas.

7. Y con el tirano se bañaron

8. Cuando llegó la Revolución se acabaron sus privilegios

9. Y ahora están en su lugar, junto a los asesinos y los traidores de nuestro pueblo

10. HAY QUE SACUDIR LA SOTANA

Pero no hay problema los buenos católicos y nuestro pueblo están claros

PEQUEÑA HISTORIA DEL CLERO REACCIONARIO EN CUBA

Caricature: "History of the reactionary clergy in Cuba." From *Revolución*, March 3, 1961.

revolution. "The key question has been, and continues to be," *Cuba Socialista* insisted, "the defense of the *patria* and accomplishments achieved by the Cuban people." The essay reprinted the pastoral communication prepared by Bishop Manuel Santander in 1896 to condemn the *mambises*: " 'An evil spirit appears to have taken possession of those who commit terrible acts without defined objectives, for no one knows what they seek except the ruin of this rich portion of Spanish territory and the extermination of its inhabitants,' " adding:

> Based on much of our past, there is the incontrovertible historical circumstance that the Cuban nation, ever since it began to integrate itself into a national community and inaugurated its struggle for independence, has had to go up against the tenacious resistance of the ranking Catholic hierarchy and the majority of the clergy. One or the other was the beneficiary of slavery and of colonial oppression and hence supported the feudal Spanish metropolis. . . . Sermons, pastoral letters, spiritual counsel, masses, and parish publications served to set in relief the opposition of the Church to every action directed toward the independence of Cuba.[60]

By the mid-1960s, the influence of the Catholic church had been all but totally eliminated.

■ ■ ■

Eventually all opposition was proscribed. If in fact the survival of the sovereign nation was at stake, what mattered most was unanimity of purpose and an unyielding course of action, neither of which allowed political opposition and internal division. Dissent was perceived as divisive at a time when the threat from abroad demanded unity. The terms of loyalty were set early. "Everything that tends to divide the Cuban people to make them vulnerable to imperialism is counterrevolutionary," Fidel Castro thundered.[61] Benigno Nieto's protagonist in Los paraísos artificiales (1999) phrases it in slightly different terms but with the same meaning: "Every counterrevolutionary is, objectively, an agent of imperialism."[62]

The leadership acted early to fix its claim to power, one that defended the presumption of legitimacy on the basis of the past—that is, authority exercised in defense of the sovereign nation and according to which opposition was equated with treason and a threat to the nation. The process by which power was centralized and opposition banished, including the curtailment of civil liberties and restrictions on freedom of assembly, freedom of speech, and freedom of the press, was transacted within historically determined practices whose meanings had long assumed the form of received truths. Policies invested with the moral authority of the past as a matter of "lineage" could hardly be disputed, not at least without challenging the very meanings with which Cubans had come to an understanding of their history.

The consolidation of all political groupings into a single party—"within the revolution"—first as the Organizaciones Revolucionarias Integradas (ORI) and subsequently into the Partido Comunista de Cuba (PCC), claimed historical precedent and political rationale in the founding of the Partido Revolucionario Cubano (PRC) in 1892 by José Martí. History offered a cautionary tale of the consequences attending disarray and disunity within patriotic ranks, warned the leadership. The singular achievement of the PRC had been to impose unity within a single revolutionary party, forging the multiple constituencies of Cuba Libre into a unified political movement. "The existence of a single party in Cuba," explained Georgina Suárez Hernández of the Escuela Superior del Partido Comunista de Cuba, "had juridical and political justification, and it is based on the particular historical trajectory of its struggle for independence. . . . The existence of a single party is the result of history itself."[63] The one-party system, Rafael Hernández explained, was "an unquestionable strategic necessity in the face of the constant threat that the United States poses to the sovereignty of the country."[64] The model—and moral—of the PRC was as self-evident as it was self-explanatory, the antecedents from which the PCC claimed direct lineage. "Many were the sacrifices our people made in the course of a process during which we experienced many bitter defeats," Ricardo Alarcón insisted. "From those defeats we learned that unity was the indispensable strategy. Division led to the failures of 1868, 1898, and 1933, and prolonged slavery, and perpetuated the misery and discrimination of millions of Cubans. To avoid continued division, Martí created the party of the revolution [el Partido de la Revolución], which could only be one party. To guarantee unity is the purpose given to its successor, the Communist Party."[65] The Central Committee reaffirmed the one-party system as historical continuity: "As the legitimate continuation of the Partido Revolucionario Cuba of José Martí, our party today represents the idea of an all-encompassing front of national unity against a powerful adversary. 'Our enemy follows a plan:' said Martí, 'to wreak havoc, to disperse us, to divide us, to drown us. That is why we obey another plan: to join together, to unite, to mock the enemy, and finally to make our patria free. Plan against plan.'"[66] The need for national unity, proclaimed Fidel Castro, was indispensable: "That is the most consistent lesson of our history. In 1868 we were unable to defeat the enemy after ten years of struggle . . . due principally to internal divisions within the ranks of the mambises. Later history taught us another lesson: the need to be united at all costs."[67]

The logic of a single revolutionary party as a matter of historical continuity was corroborated by the rationale that had inspired Martí to organize the PRC. "The organization of a single party," reflected former vice minister for foreign affairs José Viera Linares years later, "made perfect sense at the time. It was a way to bring internal unity, the way Martí had done."[68] Juan Antonio Blanco insisted that Cubans "did not copy our one-party system from the Soviet Union. It was really a legacy of José Martí's attempt to create one party out of several parties that existed at the end of the last century. All of them were independent clubs in conflict with one another . . . and Martí wanted to bring all of those little parties into one huge party in which they could co-exist with their points of view and vision but be united in their efforts to achieve independence."[69] As late as 2012, the PCC web page proclaimed that "the Communist Party of Cuba embodies the heroic revolutionary traditions of the Cuban people . . . and constitutes a faithful continuation with the

Partido Revolucionario Cubano (PRC) founded by José Martí in the struggle for national independence."[70]

■ ■ ■

Historical knowledge passed explicitly into realms of political socialization and ideological formation, one of the principal means designed to integrate Cubans into the premises of the revolution. "For us," explained Fidel Castro, "history, more than a meticulous and detailed chronicle of the life of a people, is the base and sustenance of their moral and cultural values with which to develop their ideology and consciousness; it is the instrument and vehicle of the revolution."[71] Historical knowledge came in many distinct genres and expanded into public spaces: from preschool to university, in mass media and popular culture, in cinema, literature, and music. History was news. Weekly magazines and daily newspapers gave past events almost as much attention as they did current events. Many established permanent feature sections devoted to serial installments of national history. *Verde Olivo* published two weekly sections: "Marchando con la historia" and "Páginas de nuestra historia." *Cuba Azúcar* for many years published a weekly feature, "Haciendo historia." *Bohemia* devoted several pages every week to "Esto es la historia." *Trabajadores* published a biweekly section titled "Recordando." *Granma* established a permanent column under the title "¿Que fué la república?" which was dedicated to chronicling the history of wrongdoings in the republic.

History occupied a position of prominence in broadcast media. Radio broadcasters and television producers routinely incorporated historical themes into daily programming. Historians attached to the Departamento de Asesoramiento Historico del Instituto Cubano de Radio y Televisión assisted in the development of the format and content of full-length historical programs and special features dealing with commemorative productions. Serialized radio melodramas were often set within specific historical contexts and gave a performative form to the lives of ordinary men and women during times of extraordinary circumstances. The resources of the Instituto Cubano de Arte e Industria Cinematográficos (ICAIC) were similarly allocated to the production of full-length feature films and documentaries addressing historical themes, including *Lucía, La primera carga al machete, Hombres del Mal Tiempo, El otro Francisco, Cecilia, La última cena,* and *Viva la República,* among others. "We are very much involved in reevaluating our past," explained film director Tomás Gutiérrez Alea in 1977. "All of us feel the need to clarify a whole series of historical problems because that is a way also of reaffirming our present reality.

It is a genuine necessity."[72] Indeed, ICAIC director Alfredo Guevara identified the role of historian as "one of the film industry's most important roles."[73]

Historical education implied a special epistemology, a way to heighten consciousness of Cuban as a means to form consciousness of a revolutionary. "Our epoch and society," insisted Manuel Romero Ramudo of the Ministry of Education, "require a man with serious historical preparation, for the formation of a political consciousness rests on a firm historical consciousness."[74] Knowledge of the past implied—as it always had implied—an intrinsically instrumental purpose, imbued with larger didactic intent, at once a repository of national values and model of exemplary conduct. This was not a new practice, of course. *Verdadero cubano* had always signified defense of sovereign nationhood.

The Ministry of Education assigned special importance to the teaching of history in primary schools, as a model and measure of Cuban. The periodization of Cuban history divided the survey course between pre-Columbian cultures through the end of the wars for independence in the fifth grade and the twentieth century in the sixth grade. "You will study the lives of many men and women who contributed to the development of the *patria*," as the fifth-grade textbook explained the purpose of history, "and you will learn to love and admire them. You will surely feel the need to follow the example of honesty, abnegation, valor, and integrity they bequeathed to us." And further:

> Knowledge of the history of the *patria* will permit you to appreciate that the audacity, the revolutionary intransigence, the patriotism, and the internationalism that has characterized our people have deep roots that have strengthened over time. These constitute a treasure that we should preserve and enrich with each passing day. The more you know and the more you study our history, the more you will love the *patria* and the better your condition to defend and struggle for it. Upon studying our history you will understand perfectly the need to fulfill your duty as a student, as a *pionero*, in sum, as a revolutionary. This will be your best contribution to the development of the socialist society to which we are committed. . . . Among you, those who today began to study the history of the *patria*, are the heroes of tomorrow, heroes—if it were to become necessary—needed to defend the *patria* and socialism . . . because you will be in your time like the heroes of past times.[75]

Historical knowledge was structured within a self-explanatory teleological framework, given to an understanding of the past as a process culminating on January 1, 1959. The study of *cien años de lucha* was "fundamental to an understanding of the Cuban historical process and offers multiple possibilities to educate students in communist morality and the duty of the revolutionary. . . . [This theme] will serve as the basis for the students to assimilate the transformations that have been registered in the lives of the Cuban people . . . that are the result of years of struggle to achieve independence, liberty, and happiness and for which many men gave their lives." The teacher's manual for fourth-grade historical education emphasized the need for students to learn "that the transformations that have been produced in the lives of the Cuban people . . . are the results of many years of struggle to achieve independence, liberty, and happiness, for which many people gave their lives." The approach to the Ten Years War—"a war of great sacrifices in which the Cuban people gave repeated examples of patriotism and valor"—emphasized the importance of the "great efforts and exemplary sacrifices" as a means to "contribute to the patriotic and moral education of the students." The lesson plan dedicated to José Martí emphasized "how even a young Martí sacrificed for his oppressed patria."[76] The nineteenth-century wars of independence, the Ministry of Education insisted, served as an example of "patriotism, altruism, valor, heroism, and revolutionary intransigence," adding: "Therein lay the paths of glory, an infinite number of deeds and attitudes that are transformed into examples of the highest order that exist in our patriotic origins and that at all times and in all places should be imitated."[77] The teaching of the armed struggle of the 1950s and the triumph of the revolution in 1959 emphasized that "the people began the construction of a new patria. On January 1, 1959, we finally achieved the ideal of the mambises."[78]

History in the sixth grade focused on the twentieth century, beginning with the U.S. intervention in 1898 and ending with the early years of the revolution. "The first half of the twentieth century of our history," the sixth-grade text explained, "was characterized by the exploitation of Yankee imperialism of Cuba and the permanent struggle of our people to realize their true independence. In 1959, with the triumph of the Revolution, and notwithstanding the hostile policy of imperialism, our people have continued forward and have achieved changes that guarantee total sovereignty, economic independence, and social justice." The text continued:

All this knowledge will contribute to your better understanding of why we permanently prepare ourselves to defend the Revolution and to what we owe the pride of being part of this heroic people which over the course of 100 years struggled to win its true independence. . . . Today you are the heirs of and constitute part of the heroic attitude of our people to safeguard its achievements. . . . If you take advantage of this [history] course, you will complete your primary school education possessing better knowledge of your *patria* and, most importantly, loving it more.[79]

The sixth-grade history text concluded with one final exhortation to students: "Now that you have completed the study of our history, you are in a better condition to understand the larger meaning of the words of our *Comandante en Jefe* [Fidel Castro], when he recently said: 'If imperialism were to seize Cuba again, it would be to exploit Cuba to the marrow of its bones—not give it petroleum, not to reduce infant mortality, not to provide a classroom for each child, not to give employment to each citizen, but to bring back illiteracy, unemployment, misery, gambling, drugs, prostitution.'"[80]

During the 1970s and early 1980s—years of expanding Soviet influence—the Ministry of Education reconfigured the principal explanatory framework of Cuban history around Marxist-Leninist understanding of the "laws of history," inscribed explicitly into materialist paradigms, what Eduardo Torres-Cuevas would later identify with understated artfulness as "a moment of dogmatism during which everything that had to do with the social sciences endured the impact of an external project."[81] Difficult times indeed, remembered writer Eduardo Heras León, "when the Revolution lost part of its fresh originality and copied or sought to copy certain cultural traditions that were foreign to our identity."[82] Years during which, observed historian Jorge Ibarra, historians "suffered the blows of a politics designed to introduce the Soviet model on the cultural and scientific endeavors," with the intent of "imposing a complete censorship on all historiographical production that was not subordinated to the needs of the political moment." The history of Cuba appeared "to have developed into an appendix to the history of the Soviet Union," Ibarra recalled.[83]

During these years, the Ministry of Education selected the fourth grade to introduce a new survey history of Cuba into the curriculum as a separate and stand-alone subject, assigned with a specific purpose. The methodological approach, pronounced the Ministry of Education, was defined explicitly— "Historical materialism will serve as the philosophical basis by which to teach scientific Marxist-Leninist history"—and the desired outcome was stated clearly: "The objective of the teaching of history is to contribute to the formation of men possessed of multifaceted development, loyal to the socialist *patria*, prepared to carry out the intense activity necessary to achieve the definitive victory of communism." History was designed to allow students "to appreciate fully the achievements of our Socialist Revolution, which will allow us to develop in them sentiments and convictions of love, admiration, respect for the historic achievements of the Cuban people." The principal approach emphasized a cause-and-effect sequence: "This is very important, for without fully assimilating the cause-effect relationship the students will be unable to develop the materialist concept of the historical process."[84]

The Cuban past was put to a new purpose: to validate the larger materialist orthodoxy of Soviet historiography.[85] "A Revolution such as ours," insisted Sergio Aguirre in 1973, "in which the ideology of national liberation of José Martí is fused with the Marxist-Leninist concept of class struggle, defies facile explanation." He added: "There exists a fundamental duty: the continuous study of Marxism and the correct interpretation of its connection to our history and to Martí's ideal of independence [independentismo martiano]. Without this it is impossible to advance." The duty of the historian, Aguirre pronounced, was "to apply the fundamental principles of Marxism-Leninism."[86] José Antonio Portuondo insisted that "one of the necessities that the triumph of our socialist revolution has imposed upon us inexorably is to study the Cuban historical process from the Marxist-Leninist perspective," for a "Marxist-Leninist history of Cuba would constitute a specific contribution by Cuban historians to the construction of socialism in our country."[87] The teachers' manual for "methodological orientation" for eighth-grade history was designed "to assist teachers in their daily work and contribute to an adequate preparation for developing a focus in the teaching of our socialist school, based on Marxist-Leninist principles," and to form "historical concepts closely associated with preparing students for a Marxist-Leninist comprehension of history."[88] The Ministry of Education ninth-grade history teacher's manual emphasized the need "to instill pride in each student . . . and to set in relief the changes in favor of the forces against imperialism to the effect that the socialist world system was emerging as a factor of decisive importance in the development of humanity."[89]

Historians occupied a special place in the new order of things. This was an intellectual environment very much of their making and indeed must be understood to have contributed mightily to shaping the historical sensibilities with which the men and women of the revolution had themselves been formed: a generation of Cubans coming to power informed by the history with which they made history. The promise of the past had been fulfilled, proclaimed the Thirteenth National Congress of History in 1960:

> The defense and exaltation of the virtues of our people . . . and the absolute right of Cuba to the fullness of national sovereignty have been themes

repeatedly emphasized in all the National Congresses of History. Today we witness with indescribable joy that these are the principles that inform national life. The heroic men of the Revolution have made the exalted concepts of *cubanía*, which we, scholars of the past, have studied and propounded through our intellectual activity, the very essence of their redemptive deed. We are a group of historians, sincerely devoted to the *patria*, for whom History has provided decisive vindication.[90]

The motif of *cien años de lucha* developed as the dominant interpretative framework of the scholarship of a generation. It had served as the master narrative of the triumphant revolution, subsequently celebrated through posters, on billboards, and on commemorative postage stamps. The mural *Alboradas de la Revolución*, painted by Orlando Suárez at the Inter-Provincial Bus Terminal in Havana, depicted the one-hundred-year struggle beginning with Carlos Manuel de Céspedes and the Ten Years War in 1868 and culminating in the triumph of January 1, 1959.

The theme of *cien años* passed easily enough into the new historiography after 1959. "This revolution began at Yara," pronounced historians Manuel Moreno Fraginals and Zoila Lapique Becali.[91] José Antonio Portuondo argued that the revolution had "realized the dreams of Martí and Maceo," insisting that "what is occurring in Cuba [is] not the result of the will of one man or a group of men but the dialectical culmination of a historical process that was initiated at the end of the eighteenth century." Portuondo was categorical: "The Revolution is on course toward the complete realization of the *patria* which the founders dreamed of [*la patria que soñaron los fundadores*], because this Revolution can inscribe onto the national flag the precept that Martí had propounded: 'With all, and for the good of all.'" The significance of 1868 was "well defined by Fidel," insisted Portuondo, "when he indicated that in Cuba there has been only one Revolution, the one that commenced in 1868 and culminated on January 1, 1959."[92]

The new history had less to do with the notions of "official history" than it did with the "truths" that gained discursive ascendancy after 1959, truths to which vast numbers of Cubans subscribed as a matter of faith. "Fidel Castro could proclaim that the Cuban revolution was none other than the continuation of the work of the *mambises*," filmmaker Alfredo Guevara remembered, "and that we revolutionaries who today founded the modern nation are none other than the *mambises* of our times."[93] This was a history in which vast numbers of men and women participated, fully persuaded that their participation had contributed to the realization of long-pending and historic aspirations.

All in all, very seductive stuff. The rationale of the revolution had become inseparable from the moral of the past, for this was a process so very much conceived within the historical logic of national formation. The claim of the revolution as a triumph of history was received as an article of faith, and indeed—certainly initially—it served as the premise with which Cubans arrived at an understanding of their times.

The importance of historical knowledge as a form of political discourse had long been central to the structure of Cuban historical narratives. The practice had its antecedents in the nineteenth century and was the context in which historians continued to practice their craft after 1959. "Historians are our best allies," proclaimed Antonio Núñez Jiménez in 1960, "because they are the ones who preserved in their written work the suffering of our people, from the Siboney Indians to the present. . . . Historians must teach Cubans with a political consciousness which course to take in order to achieve true national independence of the patria."[94]

New times required a new history. "We cannot live in a new society with old concepts of history," Manuel Moreno Fraginals insisted, and he thereupon proposed the use of "history as a weapon" (historia como arma). The revolution had created "a general demand for a new history, for a different way to see the past." Moreno called for "the creation of the true history" (la creación de la verdadera historia), insisting that it was "necessary to confront the problem of the thirst for a new written history that the Revolution needs," concluding that whoever did "not feel the moral duty to offer everything to the Revolution . . . could never be a historian."[95] Fernando Martínez Heredia similarly insisted that "history is at the center of the present ideological struggle. . . . History is today a theater of cultural struggle," and more: "It is necessary to know the past to help us understand the present, and convert historical knowledge into our weapon."[96] The duty of the historian, explained Fernando Portuondo y del Prado, was "to contribute to the Revolution by analyzing the circumstances that preceded it and justified its triumph."[97] Aleida Plasencia described the new role of the historian succinctly: "For the first time in our national existence the need is for the historian to act, not as an intellectual, but as an effective instrument in the construction of socialism."[98] José Antonio Portuondo agreed, insisting that "we historians are not simple observers of a historic Cuban process, we are also actors. We are also soldiers of our Revolution."[99] Raúl Izquierdo Canosa, president of the Institute of History, made the point succinctly: "Cuban historians are called upon to use their intelligence to analyze and counteract those who, whether from within or from without, use their books to distort our history and malign our founders."[100]

■ ■ ■

Meanings of the past change as circumstances change, and in the early 1990s everything changed. The collapse of the Soviet Union and the end of Soviet subsidies exposed the structural weaknesses of thirty years of economic planning, with calamitous consequences. Cuban problems in the 1990s were in part also the result of decades of ill-conceived projects and poorly executed programs—wholly from within, often a matter of whim and impulse, made worse as a result of miscalculation and mismanagement. Oftentimes the result of inefficiency and incompetence, sometime errors of enthusiasm, other times errors of judgment—differences without distinction, perhaps, for the outcomes were often the same. Vital resources were squandered; scarce assets were wasted. A new round of U.S. punitive sanctions in 1992 and again in 1996 made everything worse, as they were designed to do.

Cubans experienced the crisis of the post-Soviet years—the "Special Period in a Time of Peace"—as calamitous circumstances. The onset of the Special Period portended previously unimaginable hardship that demanded previously unthinkable sacrifice. Hundreds of thousands of households sank into crisis in the face of mounting shortages, increased rationing, deteriorating services, and growing scarcities. Petroleum shortages paralyzed production. Factories closed. Public transportation collapsed. Power outages plunged cities into darkness, hours and hours at a time, day after day, for weeks and months—endlessly it seemed. Food supplies dwindled. Households across the island experienced daily conditions of hunger. Fertility rates plummeted. Emigration soared, and in the summer of 1994 the deepening economic crisis erupted into a massive flight of Cubans. "The crisis was severe," ruminates the narrator in Pedro Juan Gutiérrez's *Triología sucia de La Habana* (2000), "and it reached into the deepest corner of each person's soul. Hunger and poverty are like an iceberg: the biggest parts cannot be seen at first view."[101]

Life across the island settled into conditions of grim and unremitting want and privation, in which shortage begot shortages, where the needs of everyday life in their most ordinary form were resolved only by extraordinary efforts. The Special Period assumed its place among those epochal divides, the way a people arrange memory of their lives as "before" and "after" the experience of a collective trauma, a time that seared itself deeply into Cuban sensibilities. They were a people bewildered and overtaken by history, seeming to tumble backward into time—where bicycles replaced automobiles, oxen replaced tractors, candles replaced electric bulbs—losing ready access to many of the elements that made for modernity.

Something profound had changed, certainly in the material basis of daily life, but also in the moral assumptions with which a people engaged in everyday life: a time, mused writer Lisandro Otero, in which Cubans "confront[ed] the necessity to undertake an introspection and a reordering of priorities."[102] New fault lines appeared on the moral topography of daily life and acted to reconfigure the normative boundaries with which Cubans entered the twenty-first century. Not perhaps since the early 1960s were value systems subject to as much pressure as they were during the 1990s. The "circumstances [of the Special Period] obviously shook the ideological foundations of the country," recalled writer Arturo Arango. "While the official discourse repeated the slogan 'Socialism or Death' mainly in the hopes of convincing the external enemies of the Revolution and socialism—but also ourselves—that our system was different and would not fall as part of the domino effect, the great majority of Cubans subjected its tenets to an interrogation that was almost always relentless and agonizing."[103]

Cubans found themselves increasingly isolated and adrift, battered from within and beleaguered from without, faced with dwindling aid, decreasing foreign exchange reserves, and diminishing resources, and they were confronted with the necessity of rationing goods that were already insufficient and reducing services that were already inadequate. The Special Period was a time of structural dislocation and institutional disarray, as many of the assumptions upon which Cubans had based their economic organization, developmental strategies, and social programs were no longer sustainable. Some of the most noteworthy moral and material achievements of the previous thirty years, including nutrition, health-care systems, and educational programs, faltered as a consequence of the crisis. Not a few outside critics predicted confidently that these were indeed the "final hours" of the Cuban government.

The Marxist-Leninist paradigms with which Cubans had integrated themselves into the socialist bloc during the early 1960s, and to which many continued to profess faith, had been found wanting. In fact, Marxism-Leninism may have provided Cubans with a usable "scientific" explanation of their history and a pragmatic means with which to accommodate Cuban methods to prevailing practices in the socialist bloc, but as a moral system it had offered Cubans little that they did not already possess. Cubans came to socialism previously formed within a historically determined value system of sovereign nationhood in which the proposition of the nation dedicated to collective well-being—"with all, and for the good of all"—was central to the meaning of Cuban. "We are living a revolution," reflected Raúl Roa as early as 1959, "uniquely possessed of its own roots, its own course, and its own projects. It does not come from Rousseau, or from Washington, or from Marx: it comes from within the very people of Cuba, who brought it forth, who sustain, and who defend it."[104] Rafael Hernández was correct to note that "the drive for social justice, solidarity, independence, and freedom . . . is integral to the revolutionary ideas of Cuba and is nothing more than the natural product of the island's history."[105] The moral void and political lacuna that ensued with the collapse of socialism in much of Eastern Europe did not occur in Cuba. "Our alliance with the Soviet socialism," Cintio Vitier properly observed, "was never more than just that—an alliance. Where the Soviets hoped to find an ideological voice, the community of Céspedes, Maceo, and Martí was waiting for them. It was more than an ideology; it was a true vocation for justice and freedom."[106]

A readily accessible stock of historical knowledge was summoned as a usable moral fund to sustain Cuban resolve through the post-Soviet years. The production of historical knowledge during the 1990s adapted to new circumstances and emphasized anew the national experience, with particular attention to selfless sacrifice and heroic struggle as attributes of Cuban: all very much having to do with the exaltation of heroic conduct during the 1890s as the standard of conduct for the 1990s. "It is undeniable," the final resolution of the Third Congress of the Unión Nacional de Historiadores de Cuba (UNHIC) acknowledged in 1995, "that in the aftermath of the collapse of socialism in Eastern Europe and the disappearance of the Soviet Union . . . the Cuban Revolution and the very existence of the Cuban nation are facing one of the most difficult situations in Cuban history." The role of the historian under these circumstances, the UNHIC exhorted, was "to defend our history against the skeptics, against the pessimists, and above all against all who would detract or deny that history," adding:

> The work of history should contribute to the reaffirmation of national consciousness, of a well-understood national pride. . . . Historians are obliged through their work to promote knowledge . . . of a past filled with magnificent and heroic struggles, and to extract from this past lessons that will assist us to confront present problems. One of these lessons, perhaps the most important, is that which demonstrates how the achievements and the preservation of the great popular victories all through our history have been possible only through revolutionary struggle. . . . In the end, that history is the representative reflection of the life of a society. The work of the historian is to extract from that history the experiences and lessons that help to orient us toward a solution of many of the present problems.[107]

The leadership articulated moral strategies of survival based principally on the invocation of the past, appealing to the history of the sacrifice and struggle of previous generations, in part as a source of inspiration, to be sure, but also as a summons to confront the calamity of the Special Period: the past populated with a dramatis personae that had confronted equally daunting and seemingly insurmountable adversities—and prevailed. The defense of the revolution as a means to defend national sovereignty at a time of ideological disarray relied principally on the history from which Cubans had fashioned the norms of nationality, and indeed it must be understood as central to the means by which the government of the revolution survived the withering conditions of the post-Soviet years. "We know who our teachers were and we know who pointed the way. And none of those who showed us the way abandoned their position," Castro proclaimed in 1991:

> [Carlos Manuel de] Céspedes never abandoned his position. [Ignacio] Agramonte never abandoned his post. Neither did Máximo Gómez, nor [Antonio] Maceo nor [José] Martí. Almost all of them died in that struggle for independence. . . . We do not proclaim "Patria o Muerte" without the firmest conviction that together with our people, if it is necessary to die, we will all die. Imperialism will not find slaves among our revolutionary people. . . . Any sacrifice will be preferable to losing the country's independence, losing the revolution, losing socialism, which gave us complete dignity for the first time and gave us complete freedom for the first time.[108]

There was meaning in Cuba's "noble history," one history teacher explained to journalist Christopher Hunt in the late 1990s: "Because so many things are changing Cuba, it's vital for us to stay in touch with the essence of our society."[109] All through the crisis of the 1990s, the past loomed large as the means through which to sustain the patriotic consensus so vital for national morale in the face of economic collapse: a people bound together by a history whose overriding logic was inscribed in the commitment to national sovereignty.

It was to history that Fidel Castro repeatedly appealed during the dark and desperate years of the Special Period. "The history of Cuba," Castro explained to school teachers in 1992, "is an inexhaustible source of values that should be transmitted," adding:

> Few countries have as magnificent a history as ours in the wars for independence, sustained under extraordinarily difficult circumstances, when the small population of this country confronted hundreds of thousands

of Spanish soldiers in the wars of 1868 and 1895. Our Revolution exemplifies the values of that era: patriotic values, the values of nation, the values of struggle for independence, the values contained in heroism and self-sacrifice. . . . Without knowledge of the history of Cuba, it is impossible to feel the inspiration offered by the extraordinary examples of the patriots of 1868 and 1895. They are fabulous personalities. To study our history is a form in which to acquire values, a form of finding inspiration in those men who were truly exemplary. . . . One is troubled that in moments such as these this history is not known. The great historical mission that our people today fulfill in this special period, and the values they are defending, are those that Cubans of other times defended to claim their *patria* and their independence. . . . Thus, to study history is perhaps the most extraordinary means we have available to transmit values, patriotic sentiments, revolutionary sentiments, heroic sentiments. . . . We need examples, we need paradigms, and we have within our history an inexhaustible wealth of values.[110]

To remember and reaffirm the past had larger political implications, of course, for the deployment of the founding narratives of nation as a discursive strategy of survival implied a dictum to duty, propounded as conduct intrinsically Cuban, binding and obligatory, as legacy to discharge in the form of a historical imperative. At the core of Cuban was the proposition of obligation imposed by the past. The appeal to the past had always implied pride in antecedents, of course, but it also suggested duty to precedents. The past also possessed the moral force to exact political compliance, for to break ranks with the past implied surrender and submission, that is, a breach of faith with legacy and betrayal of trust: a dereliction of duty certainly censurable, perhaps worse. Cubans of the late twentieth century were exhorted to be as worthy defenders of the ideal of nation as Cubans of the late nineteenth century, to equal the sacrifice that earlier generations had made in confronting the adversity of their times. "What are we?" asked one Havana billboard, answering: "We are one history" (¿Que somos? Somos una sola historia). And another: "Commitment to our history" (Compromiso con nuestra historia). All through the 1990s and into the early 2000s, billboards and sidewalk murals across the island invoked history as duty: "Faithful to our history" (Fieles a nuestra historia); "Reason and History Are on Our Side" (La razón y la historia están con nosotros); "We Believe in History" (Creemos en la historia).

Political discourse all through the post-Soviet decades was dominated by allusions to the past, looking back as a way forward: the past as precedent and

Wall mural: "Faithful to Our History." Photograph courtesy of Fidel J. Requeijo.

purpose, explicitly as experience, of course, but more as example, to sustain Cuban resolve to confront the adversity of the Special Period. The defense of the sovereign nation required the defense of the revolution, for the principal raison d'être of the revolution lay in its commitment to the defense of national sovereignty. It was the recurring—indeed, the incessant—theme of the principal speeches of the leadership, often with ominous allusions to the consequences of faltering resolve. "Without the Revolution," Fidel Castro asked portentously, "what meaning would our lives have? What future would our people have? We are defending the Cuban nation. We are defending national independence."[111] The logic of *patria o muerte* was carried to its logical conclusion. "Each of us [is] willing to fight to the death," Castro exhorted in 1991. "What is life for us without the *patria*?" The past as patrimony implied a duty contracted as a matter of legacy:

We will always have present with us those who died in the fight against tyranny . . . and the many who died during our wars for independence. . . . The people of 1868 . . . and the people of 1895 and the Sierra Maestra never feared being put to a test, never feared making sacrifices. . . . The example of each will be multiplied, the heroism of each will be multiplied. No worthy example, no just ideal has ever been defeated. Maceo, you were not defeated in 1868, nor in 1878. Maceo, you were not defeated the day you fell in Punta Brava. Martí, you were not defeated the day you fell in Dos Ríos. Because of you, your example and your death, today there are millions of Cubans willing to follow your example, willing to defend the ideals, and willing to die as you did to save freedom, to save justice, to save the honor and dignity of men. . . . Without honor and dignity, life has no meaning, nor do we want life, not only ours, but even the life of those we love. Without honor, decorum, independence, and dignity, a country is nothing. The life of a country has no importance.[112]

Defense of *patria* was not, in fact, rendered as a matter of choice: it was duty of legacy that all Cubans were obliged to discharge. One hundred years of sacrifice could not be permitted to have been in vain. *Verdaderos cubanos* were obliged to honor past sacrifice with more sacrifice, an exhortation based on the proposition that the *mambises* and martyrs who had sacrificed for the *patria* had the moral authority to make political demands on their descendants, that their lives did indeed provide a model of conduct that legacy obligated Cubans to emulate. This was not a new proposition, of course. It had been the purpose of nearly a century of historical narratives, and especially the twentieth-century biography genre. What was different after 1990 was the degree to which the leadership endowed the *próceres* with a voice as a means of moral suasion and political inducement. The generations of the post-Soviet decades were heir to a history from which the standard of conduct of Cuban was fixed, something akin to the past as predestination. Raúl Castro understood well the magnitude of the crisis that Cubans faced in the early 1990s:

> No previous generation has confronted tasks of such great magnitude as those that Cubans of today face. Certainly the *mambises* endured greater hardship over longer periods of time, but today Cuba assumes greater responsibilities. The liberators struggled to secure the independence of a nation that they themselves forged by virtue of their *machetes*. Today we have to defend that nation, which since January 1, 1959, has been independent and sovereign; we have to defend the accomplishments of the revolution that in three decades has transformed the nation, to defend the lives, the present, and the future of nearly 11 million Cubans.[113]

The dominant political discourses of the 1990s were not dissimilar to the exhortations of the 1890s: pronouncements of a determination to perish rather than yield on the claim to the sovereign nation. The commitment to national sovereignty had always implied disposition to self-abnegation. This was a sentiment filled with apocalyptic purport, with discernible origins in the *independentista* narratives of the nineteenth century, and it served as the dominant mode of exhortation in defense of the revolution. "They threatened us with an economic blockade?" Fidel Castro asked rhetorically as early as 1980, and he answered almost prophetically:

Let them maintain it for one hundred years if they wish! We are disposed to resist for one hundred years, if that is how long imperialism lasts. That they threaten us with a naval blockade? Let them impose a blockade of that type and they will see the capacity of the Cuban people to resist. If we have to disperse across the entire country . . . to cultivate the land with oxen and plows and with hoes and picks in order to live, we will but we would continue to resist. If they believe that we will surrender because we lack electricity, or bus service, or oil, or whatever, they will see that they can never bring us to our knees and that we are capable of resisting for one year, for ten years, for as many years as necessary, even if we have to live like the Indians that Columbus found when he arrived in Cuba 500 years ago.[114]

The degree of equanimity with which the Cuban people contemplated the prospects of living in caves is difficult to ascertain, of course. But this is really not the point. In fact, sacrifice and struggle persisted as idealized attributes of Cuban, to be invoked as the model of conduct as circumstances warranted. Carlos Manuel de Céspedes, Antonio Maceo, and José Martí, among others, were no less apocalyptic in the political pronouncements of their time as Castro was in his. How similar was the vow Nicolás Pérez made to Antonio Maceo in 1878: "To die before humiliating our cause and, if necessary, to establish the Republic of Cuba atop our dead bodies. War is a cruel undertaking, but if the despots want extermination, blood, and fire, then let us give it to them. If it is necessary for the people of Cuba to perish among the flames, they will perish with pleasure. If it necessary for the people of Cuba to burn, they will burn."[115]

Allusions to duty increased in frequency and often assumed an ominous tenor: a new generation of Cubans exhorted to confront the necessity of self-immolation in defense of self-determination. Ambrosio Fornet was surely correct to note in 1997 that while Castro's "rhetoric is often authoritarian and apocalyptic, it is integral to the nation's memory and deepest aspirations, which were formed during the arduous struggle for independence and sovereignty that began in the last century."[116]

Cubans were overtaken by the inexorable logic of their past, enjoined to discharge a legacy of duty imposed by all the history that preceded them. The past provided a time-honored paradigm, loaded with meaning from which to infer duty appropriate to being Cuban. The proposition of national sovereignty as determinant of Cuban was an ideal that could not readily be let go of. It had been the purpose for which successive generations of Cubans had been formed and to which many had dedicated their adult lives. Writer Lisandro Otero correctly noted that the "devotion to the founders of the *patria*, to the memory of martyrs of the past and present, to the thought of Martí, had served as a fundamental base of the Cuban doctrine. The collapse of the Soviet Union and the Eastern European bloc, however, tended to underscore further the base of the autochthonous traditions and reinforce the patriotic and nationalist credos of the nation."[117] Duty to nation was a matter of historical legacy, which all Cubans were enjoined to uphold. "I was born to honor a transcendental debt," broods the protagonist in Zoé Valdés's novel *La nada cotidiana* (1995). "I was to honor my ancestors. I was to honor my *patria*. I was to honor my school. I was to honor the mass organizations, and others. I was to honor the national symbols."[118]

History taught by example and offered the standard by which *verdaderos cubanos* were to discharge the duty intrinsic to nationality. All through the post-Soviet years, historical narratives turned increasingly inward and backward, drawing upon the past as a matter of moral mandate. The Ministry of Education revised the history curriculum to emphasize the lessons of the national past. "We do not aspire solely to develop the student's mind," it affirmed, "but also to form a personality that feels and experiences emotion, that loves the *patria* and its most important historical figures, as well as its national traditions and symbols." And to the point: "We can stimulate patriotic sentiments in our children only if, in studying history, we reveal to them the historic dispositions of our people and their heroes and martyrs, which will permit them to understand the identity of a nation and themselves through the course of time."[119]

The necessity to defend the *patria* as a matter of historical necessity developed as the salient political message of the Special Period. Billboards across the island all through the 1990s proclaimed the moral: "To live forever for the *patria*" (*Vivir siempre para la patria*); "Above all: *patria*" (*Por encima de todo: patria*); "Everything for the *patria*" (*Todo por la patria*); "Before everything, we have *patria*" (*Ante todo, tenemos patria*). In 1992, the National Assembly revised Article V of the Constitution of 1976, modifying the "guiding-force" function of the Cuban Communist Party, from representing "the organized Marxist-Leninist vanguard of the working class" (*la vanguardia organizada marxista-leninista de la clase obrera*) to representing the party of "Martí and Marxist-Leninist, organized [as the] vanguard of the Cuban nation" (*martiano y marxista-leninista, vanguardia organizada de la nación cubana*).[120] "In our class for the history of Cuba," explained the Ministry of Education, "the struggle for national sovereignty, self-determination, and international solidarity will be emphasized. Evidence of these sentiments abound, and include the legacy of the Liberation Army and the Rebel Army, the valor of Cuban youth in the struggle against the repressive regimes of Machado and Batista, and the defeat of the mercenary aggression of 1961. . . . These are the pages that express the purest Cuban values in behalf of the *patria*," adding: "Our great objective is to reinforce pride in the national past by way of knowledge of deeds, events, and processes at the source of national identity."[121]

There was perhaps no more usable historical metaphor for the Special Period than the Protest of Baraguá, in which Antonio Maceo repudiated the peace settlement with Spain in 1878 and vowed to continue the struggle for independence. The symbolism was unambiguous: a people undefeated and unbowed, determined to persist and prevail. The convocation of the Fourth Party Congress in 1990, on March 15—the anniversary date of the Protest of Baraguá—was filled with allusions to Baraguá. The Protest of Baraguá was declared variously to be "one of the most glorious events of our history," "the symbol of national rebellion for all times," and "Cuban revolutionary intransigence of the highest order." The Central Committee celebrated Baraguá as a timeless example of heroic intransigence: "[The deed] entered into our history and took root in our political life. The spirit of Baraguá, which has not ceased since then to serve as an expression of revolutionary intransigence, loyalty to principles, and to confront and prevail over the most difficult adversities. . . . With the example of Baraguá the spirit that has permitted us to resist and prevail for more than 30 years of aggression by *yanqui* imperialism is renewed constantly." The linkages were linked directly to the past: "This is the moment to rise up, like the Bronze Titan [Maceo] in Baraguá, to proclaim: NO! We will not renounce the Revolution. We will not repudiate our achievements. . . . We will never betray our glorious dead, from La Demajagua [1868] to the present."[122] Fidel Castro alluded repeatedly to Baraguá all through the 1990s. The moral of the example was proclaimed as duty binding on all *verdaderos cubanos*. "[Maceo] once said that there would be no peace with Spain without independence," Castro exhorted, "and that your weapons would never be laid down. Today we said there will never be peace with the empire without total sovereignty and independence of the *patria*. . . . The way you never surrendered your weapons, we will never surrender ours. The same way you know how to die in combat, we will know how to die in combat." The rhetorical practice of speaking to the dead was noteworthy during the Special Period:

Thank you, Maceo, for the example. The way you prevailed, we will prevail. The way your just cause triumphed, our just cause will inexorably triumph. . . . Thank you, thank you for your example. Thank you for the people that you and those like you forged. . . . Thanks to you and those who followed your example. Thank you Maceo for this opportunity. . . . We never had pretensions for such honors. We never had grandiose illusions. But history and life has imposed them upon us and we will fulfill our duty. . . . We are the people of 1868, and the people of Baraguá, and the people of 1895 . . . that feared no challenge, that feared no sacrifice. . . . If we must relive the years of 1868, we will relive the years of 1868. If we must relive the years of Baraguá, we will relive the years of Baraguá. If we have to return to the years of 1895, we will return. . . . We are invincible.[123]

In the years that followed, in the capital and across the island, on streets and highways, in schools and all state offices, billboards and posters proclaimed Cuba to be "*un eterno Baraguá.*" The Fourth Party Congress concluded with a categorical injunction: "The future of our *patria* will be an eternal Baraguá."[124]

■■■

From the very origins of the idea of nation in the nineteenth century, when the possibility of sovereign nationhood had seized hold of the creole imagination, sacrifice and struggle on behalf of independence had been made without flinching, always with the expectation of the nation as means of security and self-sufficiency, of Cuba as a better place to live. This had been central to the promise of the triumphant revolution in 1959: a commitment to the realization of the historical ideal of nation. The very claim to power as mandate of history obtained plausibility precisely because it pledged fulfillment of the nineteenth-century promise of sovereign nationhood, one possessed of incontrovertible moral authority and political credibility.

The defense of national sovereignty, so very much the signal achievement of the revolution, had cost Cubans dearly: decade after decade of sacrifice and struggle, relentlessly, often on a heroic scale, against insuperable odds, in the face of chronic scarcities, persistent shortages, and endless rationing, against internal mismanagement and external malice. "Patriotism, you say?" asks the protagonist in Noel Navarro's novel *Techo y sepultura* (1984). "Tradition and history, you say? Sure, but at what cost?"[125] Edmundo Desnoes brooded through his protagonist in *Memorias de subdesarrollo* as early as 1962: "The revolution is tragic—tragic because we are too small to survive. Too small and too poor. It is a very costly dignity."[126]

Hard times seemed to have no end. The early years of hard times were sustained—often joyfully—by high hopes for a better future, years that men and

Poster commemorating the anniversary of the July 26 attack on the Moncada barracks and the invocation of the Protest of Baraguá. From author's private collection.

women would later look back on with some nostalgia and occasional fondness. "We cast backward glances," historian Francisco Pérez Guzmán reminisced wistfully in 2001 about the early years of the revolution, "when we first began, when we first imagined the possibility of a better world, to the euphoria that these hopes gave to our spirits; a coming of age for a reason, a belief shared in common with so many others who also shared these hopes, that our commitment would make a difference and that difference signified a better world. It was sublime."[127] Ambrosio Fornet agreed. "For the members of my generation," he wrote years later, "it is difficult to discuss the 1960s without succumbing to the temptation of nostalgia."[128] Isabel Monal recalled the 1960s in 1999 as a time "that even today we recall with near mythical fervor [casi con fervor mítico]."[129]

So much had been promised, so much had been expected. The summons to sacrifice and struggle during the early years of the revolution—a call for selflessness, on behalf of a better future for all, had lifted the hopes of vast numbers of Cubans. Everything was ahead of them: ideals, aspirations, a new and better people, a new and better society: be gone with the old—and good riddance. Everything seemed worth the sacrifice and the struggle for the new Cuba, the more perfect social system. An exuberant confidence had lifted Cuban spirits in anticipation of a better future through the 1960s, a future countless hundreds of thousands of Cubans dedicated themselves to fulfilling: a people aroused to greater exertions, Ernesto Cardenal remarked at the time, among whom "sacrifice has been idealized."[130] Vast numbers of Cubans had very much lived for the prospects of a future implied by the promise of their past. "Things are better than before because now we're free," Eulalia Fontanés explained confidently to Oscar Lewis in 1969. "I'm telling you, Cuba has a bright future. You can see it in the way we're progressing with each day that passes. . . . We Cubans will live well in the future. I'll be rather old by then but my children will enjoy all the advantages."[131] In a survey conducted by Hadley Cantril in the mid-1960s, 74 percent of Cubans polled anticipated an auspicious future, a percentage that Cantril described as "dramatic indeed," adding: "[Cubans] felt that both they and especially the nation had made enormous strides . . . as a result of the revolutionary take-over, and they foresaw an extremely bright future both for themselves as individuals and for the nation as a whole."[132]

The men and women who celebrated the revolution as redemption of nation had committed themselves to the realization of hopes deeply inscribed in the promise of national sovereignty and self-determination: a better life, if not in the short run for themselves then certainly in the long run for their children. "Our struggle is not for today, nor even for tomorrow," Raúl Castro explained in 1960. "It is for the future, for our children." The "glorious sacrifices of today will benefit our children, our grandchildren, our future generations." He added:

> The mothers of today could say that if the *mambises* had been able to complete their goals, or had been allowed to complete their goals, their children would not have died and they would not today be in mourning and would not be in tears. . . . If the project that we are today undertaking would have been completed fifty years ago, neither we nor our parents would have to suffer this adversity. And in the same manner, we can say that our children, our grandchildren, and all our descendants, in whose behalf we work, will not have to endure what we today are suffering.[133]

That was the promise of the revolution — "so that the Cuban people could live better," affirms the protagonist in Manuel Cofiño's novel *La última mujer y el próximo combate* (1984).[134] "The Nation will help everyone," Fidel Castro promised in 1963; "the Nation will protect everyone, the Nation will provide security for everyone. For the Nation is no longer a conglomerate of individuals left to their own devices. It has developed as a vast family in which the means and the resources of the Nation will reach everyone."[135] Minister of Economy Regino Boti promised even more. "If we contemplate the future of Cuba," Boti predicted in 1961, "through the work and effort of the people, Cuba will overcome the current difficulties of transition, and we will achieve within nine or ten years the highest standard of living in all of Latin America, by a huge margin, and reach a standard of living almost as high as all the countries of Europe."[136]

The antecedents of Cuban aspirations reached deep into the nineteenth century and were central to the moral calculus that had sustained Cuban resolve through fifty years of intermittent warfare in the nineteenth century and fifty years of the revolution in the twentieth century. Successive generations of Cubans had been formed within the promise of a paradigm of sovereign nationhood as means of collective fulfillment, a condition intrinsic to the narrative structure of nationality.

But the use of the past as the discursive logic of the revolution was not without risks. Faith in the promise of the past had very much to do with the expectation of well-being in the future. The premise of the sovereign nation contained within its formulation the presumption of a better life — Cubans would assert control of their own destiny with the expectation of a better future. The invocation of history as means of moral exhortation to sacrifice —

and more sacrifice—in the classroom and at the workplace, posted on billboards and proclaimed at mass rallies and demonstrations, in the speeches at all levels of the leadership, endlessly, in the face of deepening impoverishment, combined to contribute to an ineluctable diminution of popular faith in the past as a usable moral fund. In fact, the appeal to the past was increasingly revealing itself to be without the means to realize its inherent claim.

The historically conditioned logic of sacrifice and struggle as a collective effort seemed to lack purpose in the early twenty-first century, other than to make do and get by in meeting one's own immediate and often urgent needs. "A people can withstand adversities of all types and resist tirelessly if they are under the influence of an idea," Lisandro Otero was persuaded. But Otero understood too the danger of an idea realized but unable to meet expectations with which it entered the popular imagination. "Revolutions are doomed to repeat laws they seem unable to escape," he observed. "All situate collective interests over personal ones; the *patria* is more important than the citizen. . . . An intransigent puritanism emerges that approaches intolerance. The cult of the past, to history, to the memory of martyrs, assumes such extreme adoration as to produce a new pantheon of gods."[137] Rafael Hernández did not disagree and wrote in the late 1990s that it was "the government's continued identification with the interests of the population that [justified] its popular support." But the convergence of interests was not without limits. Hernández also cautioned that "the people do not tolerate the harsh difficulties of their lives during peacetime as well as they do during wartime, nor can the politicians use the same political recourses or mechanisms of power under those different conditions."[138]

The consequences were not unpredictable. Novelist Ena Lucía Portela voiced the angst of a generation in a 2007 interview when she offered that "in truth I do not have the slightest idea of what it means to be Cuban today, assuming that it means anything at all. For me, with apologies to the patriots, these trappings of nationality [*parafernalia de la nacionalidad*] are nothing more than a bureaucratic formality, and are very fucked-up at times."[139] Alienation from the very past that had served to inform the normative sources of nationality had far-reaching implications. "An exaggerated positive message," warned playwright Senel Paz in 1993, "instead of setting an example and acting as a stimulus, acquires a demoralizing, conservative character—not to mention what happens when it is so out of line with reality that it begins to lose credibility. In that case it has no effect on the social dynamic and can even be dismissed as ridiculous."[140] The past had been tried and found wanting. Now what?

The past as moral fund was not inexhaustible. Generations of Cubans had come of age formed by a historically determined moral system inscribed in the promise of the sovereign nation. By the early twentieth-first century, the defense of the sovereign nation had been unable to sustain the promise of nation as the means to a better future. Indeed, the prospects of a better future never seemed more remote. Not a few gave up on the future. "The future," one Cuban explained to Ben Corbett. "The future. That's all everybody talks about is the future. Fuck the future. I want a now. I want my life to be more than just struggling."[141]

Decades of sacrifice and struggle on behalf of national sovereignty was accompanied with deepening impoverishment and increasing hardship and placed in jeopardy the very moral system from which nationality had obtained meaning. This was sacrifice under circumstances not simply of hardship but conditions of hardship without prospects of relief. Adversity had assumed something of a permanent condition of daily life. The effect on morale was often withering, portrayed poignantly as early as 1971 in Carlos Torres Pita's prize-winning play, La definición. "I am fed up with the promises of abundance every year that come to nothing," despairs María. "Fed up with eating the same thing day after day, or not eating at all. Fed up with the ration card, fed up with the lines even to use the public rest rooms. Fed up with the lack of bus service, of the CDR [Committee for the Defense of the Revolution], of the speeches, of the meetings, of the news of the sugar harvest. . . . There is nothing."[142] Cuban political scientist Pedro Campos Santos eloquently expressed common frustrations in 2007:

> We Cubans for the most part support the revolution and socialism, but we are weary with attributing everything that goes wrong to the embargo. We can no longer put up with the ration book, the low salaries, the high prices of basic necessities, the lack of public transportation, . . . the over-crowding of families of three and even four generations in poorly main-tained housing, the double currency that conceals exploitation and does not reach everyone, . . . the disaster of our agriculture . . . the lack of sani-tation in Havana neighborhoods, the exploitation of our professionals and workers by foreign enterprises, the prostitution that has attracted hun-dreds of thousands of youth of both sexes so that they can bring food home and dress with decorum, . . . the triumphalist and self-satisfied discourse of the officialdom in the press and on television.[143]

It would have been inconceivable in the early 1960s to have imagined that the decades to come would be given to unrelieved sacrifice and unrelenting struggle, only to end up in the 2010s—still—in circumstances of unrelieved sacrifice and unrelenting struggle. More than fifty years of extraordinary circumstances, more than adequate time—not dissimilar to the fifty years of the second half of the nineteenth century—for a people to experience profound cultural shifts, although it is impossible to divine historical outcomes inside a history in the making. Cubans had redeemed their history, and they lived with the consequences of redemption.

Cubans had long been in the thrall of their past, a commitment that was itself possessed of a proper history and from which the character of Cuban had formed. It was this devotion to the past, the faith in its promise and the hopes for its fulfillment, that had transported Cubans deeply into the realms of a revolution of breathtaking scope, fully persuaded that they acted in discharge of the moral imperatives of the past by which they were formed. This was a past that contributed powerfully to an unswerving commitment to the promise of the revolution, a commitment that could be plausibly sustained under circumstances of withering adversity and unrelieved hardship.

What remained in the decades following the collapse of the Soviet Union was defense of national sovereignty as the principal moral claim with which to defend the revolution. Not an insignificant claim, to be sure, but over the long run, perhaps an insufficient one if—in the end—national sovereignty failed to sustain the promise central to the idea of self-determination. More than fifty years after the triumphant revolution, Cubans continued to sacrifice and struggle and to be mostly, it seemed to many, worse off. Sacrifice and struggle were principally about survival, people seeking to meet the most basic needs of daily life, almost every day. What had sustained social solidarity was devotion to the idea of nation and history, which could not be let go of—that was what remained: *patria* and the past. After that, no one really knew. What was previously understood as a means had become an end unto itself—national sovereignty for the sake of national sovereignty—and inevitably with diminished expectations and decreased moral resonance with which to preserve collective resolve. The defense of national sovereignty—heroic intransigence indeed—seemed unable to keep the promise associated with its realization.

The example of heroic comportment in the past had provided the model of conduct which Cubans were exhorted to emulate. Attention was directed to parallels and patterns, to the adversities and adversaries that earlier generations of Cubans had faced. "We cannot forget that this is the people of 1868 and 1895," Fidel Castro reminded Cubans in 1992, "that we are the descendants of those who struggled for ten years, those who endured the reconcentration program of [Valeriano] Weyler, who tried to do what the United States seeks to achieve today: to force us into submission through hunger."[144] All Cubans had been called upon to suffer, Castro insisted. "We are not the first to suffer the consequences of international developments," he addressed University of Havana students in 1995. "You know well how much our forefathers suffered, from Céspedes to Martí, and for more than fifty years, in the false republic, in the neo-colony, they had to have suffered a great deal."[145] If Cubans in the nineteenth century had sacrificed and struggled in defense of the sovereign nation, how could Cubans in the twentieth do less? Circumstances provided Cubans with the opportunity to keep faith with the past, to demonstrate that they were indeed worthy of their history. "In the Cuban history classes," Tania Bruguera recalled years later, "repeated year after year with little variation, they spoke to us—some with more, some with less passion—about the privilege of living and participating in a historical moment. They made us conscious of the benefits we enjoyed thanks to the heroism of others."[146]

For fifty years, the government of Fidel Castro drew upon the moral of the past as the basis with which to sustain the patriotic consensus, and at no time with greater urgency than during the years of post-Soviet adversity. Raúl Castro continued the practice. He assumed the presidency in 2008, on February 24, on the anniversary of the inauguration of the 1895 war for independence. He made use of the occasion by drawing parallels with the past: "On a day like this, in 1895, responding to a call from Martí, the old and the new generations [los Pinos Viejos y Nuevos] resumed the struggle for the independence thwarted by the United States military intervention. Half a century later, we again managed to unite and to fight against the same enemy. . . . On this the 113th anniversary of the Necessary War, the challenges we face are in fact many and difficult."[147]

Into the early decades of the twenty-first century, the commemoration rituals of the revolution were very much given to celebration of the resilience with which the Cuban people after 1959 had sacrificed and struggled in pursuit of a noble purpose. For the men and women who had endured hard times without prospects of good times, comfort and consolation were to be found in the past, something of solidarity with previous generations, who also had endured hard times without prospects of good times. The proposition of a heroic past provided the leadership a malleable discursive template with which to continue to sustain the logic of the revolution in the face of relentless adversity. But it was also true that this was a logic that increasingly was turned upside down. New inferences were deduced from old knowledge signaling a change in emphasis of meaning. The past served as a morality tale of a different sort, used by the leadership to acknowledge—tacitly, to be sure—the failures of the revolution. History was used to mitigate the experience of chronic reversals and setbacks—that is, to historicize failure as a facet of the Cuban condition. "We live and maintain this Revolution for more than fifty years," Raúl Castro proclaimed on July 26, 2012, "with the same determination exhibited by the initiators of independence." He dedicated much of his address to the assembled public in the city of Guantánamo—a speech characterized by one official Cuban web page explicitly as "homage to history"[148]—to a recitation of a well-known history. The men and women who inaugurated the wars for independence in 1868, Raúl Castro reminded his audience, "experienced failure after failure. . . . Everything failed. But failures notwithstanding, Cubans persevered in their struggle for independence," acknowledging "all those themes that you know perfectly well." But he continued nevertheless: "The Americans intervened with the pretext of helping the Cubans, and within days of the fall of Santiago de Cuba, the first proof was revealed of what that history would be, and which came to an end on January 1, 1959. They did not allow the *mambises* to enter Santiago de Cuba." And again he acknowledged to his audience: "The rest you all know." But he continued: "Sixty years of absolute domination until January 1, 1959, sixty years later, when the *barbudos* of Fidel arrived to end this state of affairs. . . . That is the history."[149]

There was pathos to Raúl's recounting of this history. As he himself acknowledged, this was all a very familiar chronicle. The larger moral was not difficult to divine, however: a means with which to lower expectations and reconcile a people to the prospects of continuing adversity. The Cuban people had faced failure before, but they had persevered undaunted and undeterred. They had sacrificed and struggled during the last fifty years of the nineteenth century; they had sacrificed and struggled again during the first fifty years of the twentieth century; they continued to sacrifice and struggle through fifty years of the revolution. Struggle for the foreseeable future, raising the specter of another one hundred years of struggle.

Cubans in the early 2000s were exhorted to continue to sacrifice and struggle on behalf of the revolution, per the dictum of their history. History was recounted in an effort to raise flagging national spirits. A history so often recited was recited again, but no longer as triumphalist flourishes but as defeatist forebodings. It was possible that this was a history running out on itself.

The relevance of the past as source of moral sustenance settled uneasily upon a weary people. It is not that Cubans had turned against their past, of course, for this was a past by which Cubans had defined themselves. It was more complicated, for a history that had failed to fulfill the promise of its premise risked being discarded as irrelevant: pronouncements in the form of clichés and slogans, commemoration of patriots and memorialization of patriotic events, invoked in defense of conditions that revealed themselves as unable to meet Cuban needs. But perhaps even more problematical, a history that the political leadership continued to invoke as a means to exhort—and exact—popular compliance was losing its cohesive power. It is thus possible to contemplate the circumstance of a people threatened by their own history.

■■■

From its inception in the nineteenth century, the transcendental category of nationality had preempted competing claims of identity. The proposition of Cuban bore distinctive traces of the circumstances of its origins, a time when unanimity of purpose and unity of interests were deemed essential to the success of the *independentista* purpose. That the project of nation persisted deep into the twentieth century meant too that the imperative of transcendental nationality developed into something of a permanent condition.

The proposition of *patria* had always implied an all-encompassing paradigm, something to surrender to unconditionally and to which to subordinate competing identities as a way to foreclose the peril of internal disunity in the face of external adversaries. Because other categories of identity were perceived to be a subset of and—potentially—subversive to nation, and hence a possible source of distraction and division, they were consigned to the margins of national discourses, unaddressed and unattended. That nationality had been subsumed into revolution, and vice versa, meant too that Cuban and revolutionary had become one and the same. "For us," affirmed Ambrosio Fornet in 1989, "society is basically not divided between men and women, blacks and whites, old and young, heterosexual and homosexual. For us society is divided between revolutionary and counterrevolutionary: between, on one hand, those who struggle for the future and, on the other, those determined to return to the past."[150]

But it is also true that the patriotic consensus frayed under the relentless pressure of deepening impoverishment. The need for new moral arrangements increased, which meant inevitably that new claims of identity and a new character of Cuban assumed increasing prominence in the post-Soviet environment, indications of a diminishing popular confidence in the capacity of nation to provide relief and remedy of conditions of Cuban discontent. The success of the proposition of an all-encompassing nation, possessed of the means for the equitable distribution of adequate resources and services— "with all, and for the good of all"—might have sustained faith in the promise

made by the revolution in the name of the nation. This was increasingly difficult after the 1990s as the social justice project unraveled under the withering
pressure of the Special Period, and beyond. It was necessary, La Gaceta de Cuba
editor Arturo Arango observed, "to come to terms with the futility of demand-
ing that the State meet our needs, since the State was not going to give us anything else."[151] The policies set in place in the early twenty-first century served
to acknowledge that the nation was unable to sustain the expectations long
associated with the history of its formation. The promise of patria gave way
gradually to new dispositions in the face of economic adversity, something of
a turning inward, each individual for himself or herself and each family for
itself. The reforms announced at the Sixth Party Congress in 2011 suggested
that the revolution lacked the capacity to fulfill the promise of nation. It had
become a regimen of propio cuentismo.

The very promise of nationality—of being Cuban in Cuba—was subject to
unrelieved pressure. For much of the 1990s, being Cuban appeared to be a lia-
bility: Cubans of the island were denied access to expanding tourist facilities
and denied access to stores of hard currency, most of which were given over to
foreign visitors and Cuban/Cuban-Americans who had previously emigrated.
"Accustomed to hearing that in spite of economic hardships brought on by the
economic embargo," broods the disillusioned narrator in Teresa Bevin's novel
Havana Split (1998), "they had advantages far more valuable, which were sovereignty, dignity, and pride. . . . What about sovereignty? Unable to feed themselves properly from a fertile bountiful soil . . . sovereignty was an incomprehensible concept. . . . The Revolution had triumphed and prevailed under the
promise of equality. Cuba was for Cubans then, but now foreigners [tourists]
were enjoying the fruit of back-breaking Cuban labor."[152]

Reforms in the early 2000s ended some of the more onerous discriminatory facets of the new economy of the 1990s, to be sure. But it is also true
that something of a cynicism coursed its way into popular—if private—
discourses, perhaps best suggested by the popular joke during the Special
Period: parents ask their son what he wishes to be when he grows up, and the
boy responds: "A foreigner." The post-Soviet circumstances released forces
that contributed to an inexorable degradation of nationality, of Cubans being
pariahs in their own country—echoes of sentiments first heard during the
1920s and 1930s. Artist María Antonia Carrillo spoke for a generation. "I hate
our policy of tourism," she protested in 1992, "just as a lot of Cubans hate it.
I don't think it's fair that everything in Cuba is for the tourists and nothing is
for us, the Cubans."[153]

The Cuban problematic took a curious turn in 2007, when Spain enacted the

"Law of Historical Memory" and thereby extended citizenship to the children and grandchildren of Spaniards who had previously emigrated from Spain. Many tens of thousands of Cubans—descendants of Spaniards—seized the opportunity of Spanish citizenship as a strategy through which to seek to ameliorate the adversities of everyday life. It was not without irony that many tens of thousands of Cubans in the early twenty-first century reclaimed the very citizenship that hundreds of thousands of Cubans in the nineteenth century had fought so fiercely to repudiate.

* * *

Cubans remained very much a people of their history, committed to their past as a function of their formation, able to contemplate with equanimity the consequences of their commitment as a fate of becoming Cuban. The Cuban people had in fact arrived at the point to which the logic of their history had brought them: in the thrall of a past that raised the sovereign nation as the overriding purpose of being Cuban, with alternatives starkly proclaimed to be *patria o muerte*. Aspirations of national sovereignty had profoundly shaped Cuban sensibilities and had acted to commit Cubans to a course of action that had been inscribed as the character of Cuban: a people situated between the promise of the past, increasingly seeming to be unrealizable, and a United States determined to make it unrealizable. But the revolution had left multiple legacies, and certainly few would dispute the esprit of purpose of the early years. But it remains to be seen what Cubans in the future will do with the history of the second half of the twentieth century. It is not difficult to imagine a generation yet to be born arriving at an understanding of the Cuban revolution in the form of counterfactual history, with a host of what-ifs—especially, What if the United States had not subverted the noble gesture of 1959?

For the premise of national sovereignty to be proven unfounded and the promise of nationality to be revealed as unrealizable bode ill for a people whose faith in nation had provided the normative core of Cuban. The flight from nation—both literally and figuratively—was one consequence. By the early 2000s, more than 1 million Cubans had emigrated from the island, many of whom included the sons and grandsons and daughters and granddaughters of the very men and women who had made the revolution. An entire generation of Cubans endured the painful experience of seeing its children and grandchildren leave the country to seek their destiny elsewhere. Few indeed were the number of families in Cuba who did not have friends and relatives abroad. Not for the first time, of course, but it was not supposed to have been this way.

All through the early years of the twenty-first century, the transcendental identity of Cuban showed signs of adjustment to new realities, a process of adaptation to accommodate parallel identities, including race, gender, sexuality, and religion—what Rafael Hernández has characterized as a political system that "has displayed increasing decentralization, flexibility, and pluralism."[154] Tolerance—indeed, on occasion, encouragement—of parallel identities was acknowledgment of the limits of nation to meet Cuban needs, and more: that the politics of identity implied the need for the nation to accommodate constitutive identities. More concrete—less abstract, more individual—less collective. A more secure nationality, perhaps, persuaded that circumstances had obliged the development of diversity without fear of divisiveness. It was possible to contemplate the emergence of a far more responsive notion of nationality, one less invested in the nation as source of Cuban, one too that requires a rethinking of the meaning of the Cuban past.

These developments have also offered new opportunities to expand the reach of Cuban historiography in new directions. The emphasis of more than a century of Cuban historical writing—before and after 1959—given principally to the problematic of the nation has yielded its dominance to accommodate research on race, gender, sexuality, and religion, that is, projects untethered from the nation and an alternate means through which to enact the character of Cuba.

But no less certain was the tension that insinuated itself in the ethos of Cuban in the early twenty-first century. Cuba was governed by a succession of leaderships profoundly shaped by the proposition of national sovereignty and self-determination, in defense of which no price was too high to pay and with which there would be no compromise. It was indeed the character of generations formed by a set of ideals intrinsic to the very meaning of Cuban. In his 2009 memoir of the Civic Resistance during the 1950s, Nicolás Rodríguez Astiazaraín imagines time travel. He contemplates transport into the future, curious about how things turned out. A man very much of the past in which he was formed, Astiazaraín desires to know "if future generations had the capacity to discharge the historical commitment bequeathed to them by those who dedicated their lives to independence and national sovereignty, from La Demajagua [the Ten Years War] to our times. To provide continuity to the work of the Revolution. To stand up to Goliath, and prevail. These are the challenges that confront the coming generations of Cubans, above all, when they cannot count on the presence of David."[155] What Rodríguez Astiazaraín could not have anticipated in his planned time travel was that new generations had to travel through a different past and were formed by a different history.

NOTES

Abbreviations

ANC
   Archivo Nacional de Cuba, Havana, Cuba
Discursos e intervenciones
   Discursos e intervenciones del Comandante en Jefe Fidel Castro Ruz, Presidente
   del Consejo de Estado de la República de Cuba, http://www.cuba.cu/gobierno
   /discursos/
LC
   Library of Congress, Washington, D.C.
NA
   National Archives, Washington, D.C.
OAH/CE
   Oficina de Asuntos Históricos del Consejo de Estado, Havana, Cuba
RG
   Record Group

Introduction

1. Sociedad Cubana de Estudios Históricos e Internacionales, *Historia y cubanidad* (Havana, 1943), p. 48.

2. *Constitución del Gobierno Provisional de la República de Cuba, proclamada solemnemente en Jimaguayú el 16 de septiembre de 1895* (New York, 1896), p. 1.

3. Antoni Kapcia, *Cuba, Island of Dreams* (Oxford, 2000), p. 22.

4. Salvador Massip, *Factores geográficos de la cubanidad* (Havana, 1941); Fernando Ortiz, "Los factores humanos de la cubanidad," *Revista Bimestre Cuba* 45 (March–April 1940): 161–86; Fernando Ortiz, *El pueblo cubano* (2nd ed., Havana, 1997), pp. 35–36.

5. Elías Entralgo, *Síntesis histórica de la cubanidad en los siglos XVI and XVII* (Havana, 1944), p. 14; Elías Entralgo, *Apuntes caracterológicos sobre el léxico cubano* (Havana, 1941), p. 11; Elías Entralgo, *Períoca sociográfica de la cubanidad* (1947; Havana, 1996), p. 23; Elías Entralgo, "El carácter cubano," *Social* 17 (October 1932): 9.

6. Mario Guiral Moreno, "Aspectos censurables del carácter cubano," *Cuba Contemporánea* 4 (February 1914): 121–33; Ramiro Guerra y Sánchez, *Historia de Cuba*, 2 vols. (Havana, 1921), 1:70.

7. Jorge Mañach, *Indagación del choteo* (Havana, 1940), p. 34; María de la Cinta Ramblado Minero, "La isla revolucionaria: El dilema de la identidad cubana en *Fresa y chocolate* y *La nada cotidiana*," http://letrashispanas.unlv.edu/vol3iss2/Identidadcubana.htm; Salvador Bueno, "El carácter cubano: ¿Que es el embullo criollo?" *Carteles* 35 (September 5, 1954): 21.

8. Calixto Masó y Vázquez, *El carácter cubano: Apuntes para un ensayo de psicología social* (1941; Miami, 1996), p. 114.

9. Manuel Márquez Sterling, *Alrededor de nuestra psicología* (Havana, 1906), pp. 221–22; Raimundo Menocal y Cueto, *Origin y desarrollo del pensamiento cubano*, 2 vols. (Havana,

1945–47), 1:95; Mariano Aramburo y Machado, *Impresiones y juicios* (Havana, 1901), pp. 184–250.

10. Fe Iglesias García, "Historiography of Cuba," in B. W. Higman, *General History of the Caribbean*, 6 vols. (London, 1997–99), 6:343; Ricardo Pau-Llosa, "The Wages of Exile," in *ReMembering Cuba: Legacy of Diaspora*, ed. Andrea O'Reilly Herrera (Austin, 2001), p. 218; Mercedes Cros Sandoval, *Mariel and Cuban National Identity* (Miami, 1986), p. 43.

11. Florinda Alzaga, *Raíces del alma cubana* (Miami, 1976), p. 39; Ana María Alvarado, *En torno a la cubanía: Aproximaciones a la idiosincracia cubana* (Miami, 1998).

12. José Antonio Ramos, *Manual del perfecto fulanista: Apuntes para el estudio de nuestra dinámica político-social* (1916; Havana, 2004), p. 173.

13. Cintio Vitier, *Lo cubano en la poesía cubana* (Havana, 1958), pp. 12–13.

14. Leví Marrero, *Cuba: Economía y sociedad*, 15 vols. (Madrid, 1972–92), 15:vi–vii.

15. Juan J. Remos, *Colonia y protesta (Vetas del proceso cubano en sus luchas por independencia)* (Havana, 1956), pp. 34, 36.

16. Ramiro Guerra y Sánchez, "La historia y los factores históricos: Introducción al estudio de la historia de Cuba," *Cuba Contemporánea* 26 (August 1921): 326, 330.

17. Ortiz, "Los factores humanos de la cubanidad," p. 165.

18. John Quincy Adams to Hugh Nelson, April 28, 1823, in U.S. Congress, House of Representatives, *Island of Cuba*, 32nd Congress, 1st sess., Executive Document 121 (Washington, D.C., 1852), p. 7.

19. Roger Q. Mills, "Spanish Despotism in Cuba Supported by the United States," in *Story of Spain and Cuba*, ed. Nathan C. Green (Baltimore, 1896), pp. 431–32.

20. José Sixto de Sola, "El pesimismo cubano," *Cuba Contemporánea* 3 (December 1913): 276–77.

21. Angel E. Rosende y de Zayas, *De nuestras memorias de la Guerra, 1895–1898: Conspirador y de soldado a capitán* (Havana, 1928), p. 19.

22. Fernando Méndez Miranda, *Historia de los servicios prestados en la Guerra de Independencia* (Havana, 1928), pp. 33–34.

23. Robert Freeman Smith, "Twentieth-Century Cuban Historiography," *Hispanic American Historical Review* 44 (February 1964): 58.

24. Lorenzo García Vega, *Rostros del reverso* (Caracas, 1977), p. 21.

25. Ramón Vasconcelos, "Discurso," in Cuba, Congreso Nacional de Historia, *Primer Congreso Nacional de Historia*, 2 vols. (Havana, 1943), 1:91.

26. Iglesias García, "Historiography of Cuba," 6:344, 387.

27. Fernando Martínez Heredia, "Guiteras y el socialismo cubano," in *Antonio Guiteras: 100 años*, ed. Ana Cairo (Santiago de Cuba, 2007), p. 198.

28. Enrique Gay-Calbó, "Síntesis republicana de Cuba," *Humanismo* 53–54 (January–April 1959): 110.

29. Lynn Geldof, *Cubans* (London, 1991), p. 90.

30. Herminio Portell Vilá, *Historia de Cuba en sus relaciones con los Estados Unidos y España*, 4 vols. (Havana, 1938–41), 1:13.

31. Oscar Loyala Vega, "Reflexiones sobre la escritura de la historia en la Cuba actual," *Temas* 6 (April–June 1996): 94.

32. Enrique Gay-Calbó, "El sentido de nuestra historia," 1934, republished in *Ensayistas contemporáneos, 1900–1920*, ed. Félix Lizaso (Havana, 1938), p. 129.

33. Ramiro Guerra y Sánchez, "La historia patria y la formación de los sentimientos morales y patrióticos," April 1911, republished in Ramiro Guerra y Sánchez, *La defense nacional y la escuela* (Havana, 1923), pp. 20–21.

34. Teresita Aguilera Vargas, Ofelia Ledo Acosta, José de la Tejera Dubrocq, and Bárbara Rafael Vázquez, *Orientaciones metodológicos: Relatos de la historia de Cuba, cuarto grado* (Havana, 1978), pp. 38, 46.

35. Alma Guillermoprieto, *Dancing with Cuba: A Memoir of the Revolution*, trans. Esther Allen (New York, 2004), p. 185.

36. Eduardo Torres-Cuevas, *En busca de la cubanidad*, 2 vols. (Havana, 2006), 2:304.

Chapter 1

1. Luis Felipe Rodríguez, "El despojo," in *Antología del cuento en Cuba (1902–1952)*, ed. Salvador Bueno (Havana, 1953), p. 77.

2. For accounts of postwar conditions, see José Miguel Gómez to Francisco Carrillo, August 31, 1898, Fondo de Donativos y Remisiones, Legajo 180, Número 196, ANC; Manuel Piedra Martel, *Mis primeros treinta años: Memorias* (Havana, 1944); Enrique J. Conill, *Enrique J. Conill: Soldado de la patria* (Havana, 1956); and Rodolfo Bergés Tabares, *Cuba y Santo Domingo: Apuntes de la guerra de Cuba de mi diario de campaña, 1895-96-97-98* (Havana, 1905).

3. Pulaski Hyatt to William W. Rockhill, May 12, 1897, Despatches from U.S. Consuls in Santiago de Cuba, 1799-1906, General Records of the Department of State, RG59, NA.

4. Horacio Ferrer, *Con el rifle al hombro* (Havana, 1950), p. 143.

5. Avelino Sanjenís, *Memorias de la revolución de 1895 por la independencia de Cuba* (Havana, 1913), p. 144.

6. Captain Carlos Muecke to G. Creighton Webb, September 3, 1898, G. Creighton Webb Papers, Manuscript Department, New-York Historical Society, New York, N.Y.

7. José Isabel Herrera, *Impresiones de la Guerra de Independencia: Narrado por el soldado del Ejército Libertador* (Havana, 2005), p. 234.

8. Raimundo Cabrera, *Sombras eternas* (Havana, 1919), p. 95.

9. Santiago C. Rey, *Recuerdos de la guerra, 1895-1898* (Havana, 1931), p. 53.

10. Pedro Pablo Martín, *Adelina, o huérfana de La Habana: Novela histórica basada en hechos ocurridos durante la guerra civil de Cuba del año 1895 al 1898* (Havana, 1901), pp. 151–52.

11. *Washington Evening Star*, September 24, 1898, p. 21; *The State*, November 5, 1898, p. 5.

12. William J. Calhoun, "Report on Cuba," June 22, 1897, Special Agent, File 48, General Records of the Department of State, RG59, NA.

13. Fitzhugh Lee, "Special Report of Brigadier General Fitzhugh Lee, U.S.V., Commanding Department of Province of Havana and Pinar del Río," September 19, 1899, in John R. Brooke, *Civil Report of Major-General John R. Brooke, U.S. Army, Military Governor, Island of Cuba* (Washington, D.C., 1900), p. 342.

14. Major James H. McLeary, "Report of Tourism Inspection," December 19, 1898, File 1487, Records of the United States Overseas Operations and Commands, 1898–1942, RG395, NA.

15. Fermín Valdés-Domínguez, *Diario de soldado*, ed. Hiram Dupotey Fideaux, 4 vols. (Havana, 1973), 2:49.

16. Ramiro Guerra y Sánchez, "Difusión y afirmación del sentimiento nacional," *Social* 9 (November 1924): 22; Ramiro Guerra y Sánchez, *Un cuarto de siglo de evolución cubana* (Havana, 1924), p. 16.

17. Robert P. Porter, *Report on the Commercial and Industrial Condition of Cuba* (Washington, D.C., 1899), p. 5.

18. Mrs. W. A. Candler to Warren A. Candler, December 1, 1898, Warren A. Candler Papers, Special Collections Department, Robert W. Woodruff Library, Emory University, Atlanta, Ga.

19. Julián Sánchez, *Julián Sánchez cuenta su vida*, ed. Erasmo Dumpierre (Havana, 1970), p. 66.

20. Clara Barton, "Our Works and Observations in Cuba," *North American Review* 166 (May 1898): 554.

21. Joaquín Jovellar, "Habitantes de la Isla de Cuba," *Gaceta de La Habana*, June 14, 1878, p. 1; U.S. War Department, *Informe sobre el censo de Cuba, 1899* (Washington, D.C., 1900).

22. Arsenio Martínez Campos to Antonio Cánovas del Castillo, July 25, 1895, in Juan Ortega Rubio, *Historia de la regencia de María Cristina Habsbourg-Lorena*, 5 vols. (Madrid, 1905–6), 2:473.

23. Antonio Maceo to María Cabrales, March 25, 1895, in Antonio Maceo, *Antonio Maceo: Ideología política; Cartas y otros documentos*, 2 vols. (1952; Havana, 1998), 2:12.

24. Valdés-Domínguez, *Diario de soldado*, 1:34, 65.

25. Agustín Ruiz to Tomás Estrada Palma, January 16, 1870, *Boletín del Archivo Nacional* 53–54 (1956): 181.

26. *El Cubano Libre*, April 15, 1897, p. 2.

27. Manuel Sanguily, "Los exterminadores," April 1, 1875, reprinted in Manuel Sanguily, *Frente a la dominación española* (Havana, 1979), p. 39; Manuel Sanguily, "Discurso del Señor Manuel Sanguily," November 5, 1897, in *Por la independencia* (New York, 1897), p. 45.

28. Valdés-Domínguez, *Diario de soldado*, 1:221.

Chapter 2

1. Antonio Duarte y Ramos, *Apuntes para la historia de la guerra de Cuba* (Mexico, 1896), pp. 3–4 (emphasis in original).

2. Fe Iglesias García, "Historiography of Cuba," in B. W. Higman, *General History of the Caribbean*, 6 vols. (London, 1997–99), 6:343.

3. Jorge Mañach, "El estilo en Cuba y su sentido histórico," in Jorge Mañach, *Ensayos*, ed. Jorge Luis Arcos (Havana, 1999), p. 169.

4. Pedro Santacilia, *Lecciones orales sobre la historia de Cuba, pronunciadas en el Ateneo Democrático Cubano de Nueva York* (New Orleans, 1859), p. vii.

5. Ignacio José de Urrutia y Montoya, *Teatro histórico, jurídico y político militar de la Isla Fernandina de Cuba y principalmente de su capital, La Habana* (1789, 1876; Havana, 1963), pp. vii, 7, 17, 29.

6. Antonio José Valdés, *Historia de la Isla de Cuba y en especial de la Habana* (1813; Havana, 1964), pp. 15, 17.

7. Pedro José Guiteras, *Historia de la Isla de Cuba*, 3 vols. (1865–66; Havana, 1927), 1:1, 5.

8. José Martín Félix de Arrate, *Llave del Nuevo Mundo, antemural de las Indias Occidentales: La Habana descripta; Noticias de su fundación, aumentos y estado* (1830; Havana, 1964), pp. 3, 6.

In the preface to the 1949 edition of *Llave del Nuevo Mundo*, historian Julio LeRiverend Brusone praised Arrate's history for having contributed to "the love of *patria*—which is the love of self," and thereby "forming part of the chorus of creole voices in the defense to what is properly theirs." See Julio LeRiverend Brusone, "Prólogo," in José Martín Félix de Arrate, *Llave del Nuevo Mundo, antemural de las Indias Occidentales* (Mexico, 1949), p. xvi.

9. Vidal Morales y Morales, "Tres historiadores," *Revista de Cuba* 1 (1877): 16.

10. Jacobo de la Pezuela, *Historia de la Isla de Cuba*, 4 vols. (Madrid, 1868–78), 1:15.

11. José Antonio Echeverría, "Historiadores de Cuba," *Revista de Cuba* 7 (1880): 380; José Antonio Echeverría to Domingo del Monte, January 18, 1839, Academia de la Historia de Cuba, *Centón epistolario de Domingo del Monte*, ed. Domingo Figarola-Caneda, Joaquín Llaverías y Martínez, and Manuel Mesa Rodríguez, 6 vols. (Havana, 1923–53), 4:9.

12. Echeverría, "Historiadores de Cuba," p. 381.

13. Eduardo Torres-Cuevas, *En busca de la cubanidad*, 2 vols. (Havana, 2006), 1:85.

14. José Martí to Director, *La Opinión Pública* (Montevideo), August 19, 1889, in José Martí, *Obras completas*, 27 vols. (Havana, 1963–66), 12:302.

15. Antonio Maceo to General Camilo G. Polavieja, June 14, 1881, in Antonio Maceo, *Antonio Maceo: Ideología política; Cartas y otros documentos*, 2 vols. (1952; Havana, 1998), 1:160–61.

16. See "Proyecto de la Ley Orgánica de la Isla de Cuba," November 12, 1860, in *Cuba desde 1850 á 1873: Colección de informes, memorias, proyectos y antecedentes sobre el gobierno de la isla de Cuba, relativos al citado período*, ed. Cárlos de Sedano y Cruzat (Madrid, 1873), p. 243.

17. Eduardo Abril Amores, "Tierra!" in *Evolución de la cultura cubana (1608–1927)*, ed. Jose Manuel Carbonell y Rivero, 18 vols. (Havana, 1928), 12:437.

18. Dolores María de Ximeno y Cruz, *Memorias de Lola María* (2nd ed., Havana, 1983), p. 142.

19. Rosario Sigarroa, "El mártir de San Lorenzo y el de Dos Ríos," in *Florilegio de escritoras cubanas*, ed. Antonio González Curquejo, 3 vols. (Havana, 1910–19), 3:422.

20. Mariano Aramburo y Machado, *Impresiones y juicios* (Havana, 1901), p. 115.

21. See José Antonio Saco, "Réplica de Don José Antonio Saco a los anexiónistas que han impugnado sus ideas sobre la incorporación de Cuba en los Estados-Unidos," 1850, in José Antonio Saco, *Colección de papeles científicos, históricos, políticos y de otros ramos sobre la isla de Cuba*, 3 vols. (Paris, 1858–59), 3:415.

22. José Jacinto Milanés to Domingo del Monte, September 20, 1836, in Academia de la Historia, *Centón epistolario del Domingo del Monte*, 3:52 (emphasis in original).

23. Juan J. Remos y Rubio, *Tendencias de la narración en Cuba* (Havana, 1935), p. 57.

24. For an excellent anthology of the *costumbrista* literature, see Salvador Bueno, ed., *Costumbristas cubanos del siglo XIX* (Caracas, 1983).

25. *Los cubanos pintados por si mismos: Colección de tipos cubanos* (Havana, 1852), pp. 4–5. See also I. de Estrada y Zenéa, "Los cubanos pintados por si mismos," *El Almendares: Periódico Semanal Literario y de Modas* 1 (May 9, 1852): 267–70.

26. José María de la Torre, *Lo que fuimos y lo somos, o La Habana antigua y moderna* (Havana, 1857), pp. 113–14 (emphasis in original).

27. Walter Goodman, *The Pearl of the Antilles; or, An Artist in Cuba* (London, 1873), p. 121.

28. Fernando Ortiz, "La solidaridad patriótica," 1910, in Fernando Ortiz, *Entre cubanos: Psicología tropical* (2nd ed., Havana, 1987).

29. Ramón J. de Palacio, "La música popular," *Revista Matancera* 1 (September 16, 1883): 13.

30. Lewis Leonidas Allen, *The Island of Cuba; or, Queen of the Antilles* (Cleveland, 1852), p. 22.

31. Antonio de las Barras y Prado, *La Habana a mediados del siglo XIX: Memorias de Antonio de las Barras y Prado*, ed. Francisco de las Barras de Aragón (Madrid, 1925), p. 89.

32. Fredrika Bremer, *The Homes of the New World*, trans. Mary Howitt, 2 vols. (New York, 1853), 2:268, 299.

33. W. M. L. Jay [Louisa Mathilde Woodruff], *My Winter in Cuba* (New York, 1871), p. 123.

34. Zoila Lapique Becali, *Música colonial cubana* (Havana, 1979), pp. 11–75.

35. Jorge Ibarra, Manuel Moreno Fraginals, and Oscar Pino Santos, "Mesa Redonda: Historiografía y revolución," *Casa de las Américas* 9 (November 1968–February 1969): 103.

36. Jorge Ibarra, "La música cubana: De lo folclórico y lo criollo a lo nacional popular," in Radamés Giro, *Panorama de la música popular cubana* (Santiago de Cali, 1996), p. 21.

37. Alejo Carpentier, *La música en Cuba* (Mexico, 1946), p. 175.

38. Elena Pérez Sanjurjo, *Historia de la música cubana* (Miami, 1986), p. 136.

39. Luis Ruiz e Irure, *Juicio imparcial de la nación: Colección de décimas nacionales* (Matanzas, 1877).

40. Liliana Casanellas Cué, "Tradición oral de la décima cantada en punto cubano," http://www.lacult.org/docc/oralidad_10_67–75-tradicion-oral-de-la-decima.pdf; Antonio Iraizoz, *Lecturas cubanas* (Havana, 1939), p. 25.

41. Virgilio López Lemis, *Décima e identidad: Siglos XVIII y XIX* (Havana, 1997), pp. 66, 73.

42. Aramburo y Machado, *Impresiones y juicios*, p 119.

43. Carlos Felipe, "Tambores," in Carlos Felipe, *Teatro*, ed. José A. Escarpanter and José A Madrigal (Boulder, 1988), p. 131.

44. Narciso G. Menocal, "An Overriding Passion—The Quest for National Identity in Painting," *Journal of Decorative and Propaganda Arts* 22 (1996): 187, 194.

45. Miguel Barnet, *La fuente viva* (Havana, 1983), p. 120.

46. Max Herníquez Ureña, *Panorama histórico de la literatura cubana*, 2 vols. (1963; Havana, 1978), 1:16–17.

47. Roberta Day Corbitt, "A Survey of Cuban Costumbrismo," *Hispania* 33 (February 1950): 42.

48. Henríquez Ureña, *Panorama histórico de la literatura cubana*, 1:273.

49. Luisa Campuzano, *Las muchachas de La Habana no tienen temor de Dios . . . . Escritoras cubanas (s. XVIII–XXI)* (Havana, 2004), p. 39.

50. Diego Vicente Tejera, "Una novela cubana," 1886, in Diego Vicente Tejera, *Textos escogidos*, ed. Carlos del Toro (Havana, 1981), p. 36.

51. José Lezama Lima et al., *Antologia de la poesía cubana*, 3 vols. (Havana, 1965), 1:3.

52. George Lowell Austin, "Cuban Literature," *Appleton's Journal* 14 (August 14, 1875): 204.

53. Ignacio M. de Acosta, "A Cuba," *El Album: Revista Quicenal de Literatura, Ciencia, Bellas Artes e Intereses Generales* 1 (August 15, 1882): 45–46.

54. Raimundo Lazo, "Contribución de la poesía al proceso histórico de Cuba en el

siglo XIX: Conferencia pronuncia en noviembre de 1952," in *Universidad del Aire (conferencias y cursos)*, ed. Norma Díaz Acosta (Havana, 2001), p. 146.

55. Juan J. Remos, *Historia de la literatura cubana*, 3 vols. (Havana, 1945): 2:439; Juan J. Remos, *Colonia y protesta (vetas del proceso cubano en sus luchas por independencia)* (Havana, 1956), p. 42.

56. Diego Vicente Tejera, *Enseñanzas y profecías* (Havana, 1916), p. 54.

57. Eduardo F. Lores y Llorens, *Relatos históricos de la guerra del 95* (Havana, 1955), pp. 14–15.

58. Horacio Ferrer, *Con el rifle al hombro* (Havana, 1950), p. 11.

59. Ramiro Guerra y Sánchez, "La poesía popular cubana en la escuela primera," February 1911, in Ramiro Guerra y Sánchez, *La defensa nacional y la escuela* (Havana, 1923), p. 8.

60. Cintio Vitier, *Lo cubano en la poesía* (Havana, 1970), p. 88.

61. Salvador de la Fe, "Recuerdos de la patria," *Minerva* 2 (April 15, 1889): 1.

62. Belén de Miranda, "La flora cubana," 1886, in *Florilegio de escritoras cubanas*, ed. González Curquejo, 3:30.

63. Pedro Santacilia, "El desterrado," in *Cantos a la naturaleza cubana del siglo XIX*, ed. Samuel Feijóo (Havana 1964), p. 88.

64. Robert Baird, *Impressions and Experiences in the West Indies and North America in 1849*, 2 vols. (Edinburgh, 1850), 1:189.

65. Joaquin Llaverias, *Contribucion a la historia de la prensa periodica*, 2 vols. (Havana, 1957–59); *La Ilustración de Cuba* 3 (March 1, 1895): 266; Tesifonte Gallego y García, *Cuba por fuera: Apuntes del natural* (Havana, 1890), pp. 49–83.

66. John G. Wurdemann, *Notes on Cuba* (Boston, 1844), p. 216.

67. Julián del Casal, "La prensa," May 13, 1888, republished in Julián del Casal, *Poesía completa y prosa selecta*, ed. Alvaro Salvador (Madrid, 2001), p. 290.

68. Dionisio A. Galiano, *Cuba en 1858* (Madrid, 1859), p. 81. See also Ambrosio Fornet, *El libro en Cuba* (Havana, 1994).

69. Rafael María Merchán, *Cuba: Justificación de sus guerras de independencia* (1896; Havana, 1961), pp. 38–39.

70. Federico Milanés to Rita de Fuentes de Milanés, June 20, 1848, in Comisión Nacional Cubana de la UNESCO, *Homenaje de José Jacinto Milanes* (Havana, 1964), pp. 106–7.

71. Domingo Malpica La Barca, *En el cafetal: novela cubana* (Havana, 1890), pp. 43–44.

72. Manuel S. Pichardo, *La ciudad blanca: Crónicas de la exposición colombina de Chicago* (Havana, 1894), pp. 22–23.

73. Enrique Hernández Miyares, "New York primeras impresiones," *La Habana Elegante* 10 (June 24, 1894): 7.

74. Raimundo Cabrera, *Cartas a Govín sobre la exposición de Chicago: Impresiones de viaje* (Havana, 1893), p. 52.

75. Manuel J. de Granda, *Memoria revolucionaria* (Santiago de Cuba, 1926), pp. 183–84.

76. Eduardo Machado Gómez, *Autobiografía* (Havana, 1969), p. 2.

77. Enrique José Varona, "El fracaso colonial de España," December 3, 1896, in Enrique José Varona, *De la colonia a la república: Selección de trabajos políticos, ordenada por su autor* (Havana, 1919), p. 129; Enrique José Varona, "Cuba contra España: Manifiesto del Partido Revolucionario de Cuba a los pueblos hispanoamericanos," in ibid., pp. 64–65.

78. Richard Henry Dana, *To Cuba and Back* (1860; Carbondale, 1966), p. 79.

79. Antonio Carlo Napoleone Gallenga, *The Pearl of the Antilles* (London, 1873), p. 39.

80. Richard J. Levis, *Diary of a Spring Holiday in Cuba* (Philadelphia, 1872), p. 113.

81. José Mayner y Ros, *Cuba y sus partidos políticos* (Kingston, Jamaica, 1890), p. 179.

82. Dionisio A. Galiano, *Cuba en 1858*, pp. 74, 150. The words "go-ahead" appeared in English.

83. De las Barras y Prado, *La Habana a mediados del siglo XIX: Memorias de Antonio de las Barras y Prado*, p. 71. Again, the words "Go-Ahead" appeared in English.

84. Manuel Linares, "La voz de Cuba," January 15, 1882, in Manuel Linares, *Un libro mas: Fragmentos* (Havana, 1906), p. 29.

85. Fidel G. Pierra, "El fin se acerca," *Revista de Cuba* 1 (March 5, 1898): 1–2; Fidel G. Pierra, *Cuba* (New York, 1896), pp. 35–36.

86. Juan Gualberto Gómez, "Por que somos separatistas," in Juan Gualberto Gómez, *Por Cuba Libre*, ed. Emilio Roig de Leuchsenring (Havana, 1974), p. 279.

87. Antonio Gonzalo Pérez, "Cuba for Cubans," *Contemporary Review* 74 (November 1898): 694.

88. Fermín Valdés-Domínguez, *Diario de soldado*, ed. Hiram Dupotey Fideaux, 4 vols. (Havana, 1972–74), 1:272.

89. Tomás Justiz y del Valle, *El suicida* (Havana, 1912), p. 198.

90. Enrique José Varona, "Cuba y sus jueces," *Revista Cubana* 6 (September 1887): 276.

91. Gaspar Betancourt Cisneros to José Antonio Saco, October 19, 1848, in Gaspar Betancourt Cisneros, *Cartas del Lugareño*, ed. Federico de Córdova (Havana, 1957), p. 308.

92. Justo González, *Cubagua: Historia de un pueblo* (Havana, 1941), p. 67.

93. Rafael M. Merchán, "Tercer aniversario (24 de febrero)," February 1898, in Rafael M. Merchán, *Patria y cultura*, ed. Félix Lizaso (Havana, 1948), p. 145.

94. María de las Mercedes de Santa Cruz y Montalvo (Condesa de Merlin), *La Habana*, trans. Amalia E. Bacardi (1844; Madrid, 1981), 271.

95. *New York Times*, August 18, 1867, p. 1.

96. Serafín Ramírez, *La Habana artística: Apuntes históricos* (Havana, 1891), pp. 125–46.

97. See Pánfilo D. Camacho, *Marta Abreu, una mujer comprendida* (Havana, 1947), pp. 149–50.

98. De las Barras y Prado, *La Habana a mediados del siglo XIX: Memorias de Antonio de las Barras y Prado*, p. 95.

99. Mireya Cabrera Galán, *El Ateneo de Matanzas: Su historia y trascendencia (1874–1968)* (Havana, 2000), p. 7.

100. Pérez Sanjurjo, *Historia de la música cubana*, pp. 137, 153, 194.

101. Hernando Serbelló, Pilar Ferreiro, and Carlos Venegas, *El teatro 'La Caridad' en la expresión sociocultural de Santa Clara* (Havana, 1983), p. 6.

102. Dana, *To Cuba and Back*, p. 28; Samuel Hazard, *Cuba with Pen and Pencil* (London, 1871), p. 186.

103. Charles Rosenberg, *Jenny Lind in America* (New York, 1851), p. 107.

104. Edward Robert Sullivan, *Rambles and Scrambles in North and South America* (London, 1852), p. 240.

105. De las Barras y Prado, *La Habana a mediados del siglo XIX: Memorias de Antonio de las Barras y Prado*, p. 72.

106. J. Milton Mackie, *From Cape Cod to Dixie and the Tropics* (New York, 1864), pp. 255–56.

107. María Elena Orozco Melgar and Lidia Sánchez Fujishiro, "Teatro, modernización y sociedad urbana: De Coliseo a Reina Isabel II en Santiago de Cuba (1800–1868)," *Anales del Museo de América* 13 (2005): 298.

108. *New York Times*, August 18, 1867, p. 1.

Chapter 3

1. Antonio Maceo, "Exposición a los delegados a la Asamblea Constituyente," September 30, 1895, in Antonio Maceo, *El pensamiento vivo de Maceo*, ed. José A. Portuondo (3rd ed., Havana, 1971), p. 112.

2. Antonio Maceo, "Proclama: Españoles y cubanos," April 25, 1895, in Antonio Maceo, *Antonio Maceo: Ideología política; Cartas y otros documentos*, 2 vols. (1952; Havana, 1998), 1:20.

3. Bartolomé Masó to William McKinley, September 1, 1898, in *Archivo de Gonzalo de Quesada: Documentos históricos*, ed. Gonzalo de Quesada y Miranda (Havana, 1965), pp. 488–89.

4. Antonio Maceo to Anselmo Valdés, June 6, 1884, in Maceo, *El pensamiento vivo de Maceo*, p. 76; Antonio Maceo to Camilo G. Polavieja, May 16, 1881, in Maceo, *Antonio Maceo: Ideología política; Cartas y otros documentos*, 1:154–55; Antonio Maceo to José A. Rodríguez, November 1, 1886, in ibid., 1:292.

5. José Martí, "Discurso en el Liceo Cubano, Tampa," November 26, 1891, in José Martí, *Obras completas*, 27 vols. (Havana, 1963–66), 4:279.

6. Luis Victoriano Betancourt, *Artículos de costumbres* (Havana, 1929), p. xlv.

7. Manuel Sanguily, "El general Máximo Gómez y la historia de la Revolución," December 31, 1893, in Manuel Sanguily, *Obras de Manuel Sanguily*, ed. Manuel Sanguily y Arizti, 8 vols. (Havana, 1925), 6:76.

8. José Martí, "La república española ante la revolución cubana," February 15, 1873, in Martí, *Obras completas*, 1:93.

9. José Martí, "El Partido Revolucionario Cubano," April 3, 1892, in ibid., 1:366; José Martí, "La proclamación del Partido Revolucionario Cubano," April 10, 1892, in ibid., 1:389.

10. Carlos García Velez, "Cuaderno manuscrito contenido diarios del General Carlos García Velez, 1950–1960," entry date: May 31, 1951, Fondo de Donativos y Remisiones, Número 123 (fuera de caja), ANC.

11. Fermín Valdés-Domínguez, *Diario de soldado*, ed. Hiram Dupotey Fideaux, 4 vols. (Havana, 1973), 3:44.

12. José Martí, "La primera conferencia," June 18, 1892, in Martí, *Obras completas*, 1:635; José Martí, "La confirmación," April 23, 1892, in ibid., 1:311; José Martí, "¿Con que consejos, y promesas de autonomía?" April 10, 1893, in ibid., 1:403; José Martí, "La independencia de Cuba y la prensa de los Estados Unidos," August 27, 1892, in ibid., 1:663; José Martí, "Discurso," October 10, 1887, in ibid., 1:361; José Martí to Presidents, Revolutionary Clubs, Key West, June 9, 1892, in *Documentos inéditos de José Martí a José D. Poyo*, ed. Luis Alpízar Leal (Havana, 1994), pp. 28–31.

13. Antonio Maceo to Camilo G. Polavieja, June 14, 1881, in Maceo, *El pensamiento vivo de Maceo*, p. 56.

14. Lillian Guerra, *The Myth of José Martí: Conflicting Nationalisms in Early Twentieth-Century Cuba* (Chapel Hill, 2005), p. 49.

15. José Martí to Rafael Serra, March 1889, in Martí, *Obras completas*, 20:345.

16. Carlos García Velez, "Cuaderno manuscrito contenido diarios del General Carlos García Velez, 1950–1960," entry date: July 25, 1951, Fondo de Donativos y Remisiones, Número 123 (fuera de caja), ANC.

17. Raimundo Cabrera to José Ignacio Rodríguez, September 18, 1896, José Ignacio Rodríguez Papers, Manuscript Division, LC.

18. Diego Vicente Tejera, "La indolencia cubana," *Cuba Contemporánea* 28 (March 1922): 171. This article is the publication of a speech Tejera delivered in Key West in December 1897.

19. See Valdés-Domínguez, *Diario de soldado*, 2:25; and Fermín Valdés-Domínguez to Gonzalo de Quesada, March 31, 1897, in Gonzalo de Quesada, *Archivo de Gonzalo de Quesada: Epistolario*, ed. Gonzalo de Quesada y Miranda, 2 vols. (Havana, 1948–51), 2:301.

20. José Martí, "Con todos y para el bien de todos: Discurso en el 'Liceo Cubano,'" November 26, 1891, in Martí, *Obras completas*, 4:278; José Martí, "Nuestras ideas," March 14, 1892, in ibid., 1:319.

21. Diego Vicente Tejera, "La sociedad cubana," October 10, 1897, in Diego Vicente Tejera, *Enseñanzas y profecías* (Havana, 1916), p. 38.

22. Antonio Maceo, "A los cubanos de la raza negra," n.d., Fondo de Donativos y Remisiones, Legajo 525, Número 13, ANC.

23. "Protesta de los cubanos de color de Key-West," January 5, 1881, Documentos relativos a los confinados y los emigrados políticos cubanos durante las luchas por la Independencia, Fondo Adquisiciones, Caja 71, Expediente 4253, ANC. The signatories included Carlos Borrego, Manuel Gutiérrez, José Herrera, Guillermo Sorondo, Leocadio Torregrosa, Vicente León, José Villavicencio, José de J. Perdomo, and José Margarito Gutiérrez.

24. Ada Ferrer, *Insurgent Cuba: Race, Nation, and Revolution, 1868–1898* (Chapel Hill, 1999), p. 7.

25. Eusebio Hernández, "Resumen del discurso pronunciado por el doctor Eusebio Hernández," October 10, 1895, in Eusebio Hernández, *Ciencia y patria*, ed. Rafael Cepeda (Havana, 1991), p. 98.

26. José Martí, "Mi raza," April 16, 1893, in Martí, *Obras completas*, 2:298–300.

27. Juan Gualberto Gómez, "Reflexiones políticas," January 28, 1893, in Juan Gualberto Gómez, *Preparando la revolución*, ed. Lino Dou (Havana, 1936), p. 31.

28. Tomás Fernández Robaina, "El negro espacio del negro: Raza y nación en Cuba; Entrevista con Tomás Fernández Robaina," in *La imaginación contra la norma: Ocho enfoques sobre la república de 1902*, ed. Julio César Guanche (Havana, 2004), p. 119.

29. In ibid., pp. 109–10.

30. Calixto García, "Manifiesto del Comité Revolucionario Cubano," October 1878, in *Documentos para servir a la historia de la Guerra Chiquita*, 3 vols. (Havana, 1949–50), 1:43, ANC.

31. *Actas de las Asambleas de Representantes y del Consejo de Gobierno durante la Guerra de Independencia*, ed. Joaquín Llaverías y Martínez, 5 vols. (Havana, 1928–33), 3:198–99.

32. See García, "Manifiesto del Comité Revolucionario Cubano"; Carlos Manuel de Céspedes to Ana de Quesada, February 10, 1874, in Carlos Manuel de Céspedes, *Cartas de Carlos M. de Céspedes a su esposa Ana de Quesada* (Havana, 1964), p. 205; Luis Quintero, "Unión—Patriotismo," *El Pueblo*, October 13, 1875, p. 2; José A. López, "Nuestro deber," *La Nueva República* 1 (July 3, 1897): 10; Valdés-Domínguez, *Diario de soldado*, 1:470; "A la memoria de los mártires cubanos," *El Republicano*, October 17, 1874, p. 3; "Discurso pronunciado por José Martí en el Steck Hall de la Ciudad de New York," January 24, 1880, in *Documentos para servir a la historia de la Guerra Chiquita*, 3:96, ANC; and Antonio Maceo to Camilo Polavieja, May 16, 1891, in Maceo, *Antonio Maceo: Ideología política; Cartas y otros documentos*, 1:155.

33. Avelino Sanjenís, *Memorias de la revolución de 1895 por la independencia de Cuba* (Havana, 1913), p. 16.

34. Gustavo Pérez Abreu, *En la guerra con Máximo Gómez* (Havana, 1952), pp. 40, 95; Ramón M. Roa, *A pie y descalzo de Trinidad a Cuba (Recuerdos de campaña)* (Havana, 1890), p. 28.

35. Raimundo Cabrera, *Ideales* (1918; Havana, 1984), p. 183.

36. Martina Pierra de Poo, "El Ateneo," in *Florilegio de escritoras cubanas*, ed. Antonio González Curquejo, 3 vols. (Havana, 1910–19), 2:14.

37. Emilia Casanova de Villaverde to Carlos Manuel de Céspedes, October 4, 1870, in Un Contemporáneo [Cirilo Villaverde], *Apuntes biográficos de Emilia Casanova de Villaverde* (New York, 1874), p. 97.

38. José Martí, "El Partido," June 25, 1892, in Martí, *Obras completas*, 2:36; José Martí, "Fragmento: Hardman Hall, New York," April 17, 1892, in ibid., 4:330.

39. Manuel Arbelo, *Recuerdos de la última guerra por la independencia de Cuba: 1896 a 1898* (Havana, 1918), p. 24.

40. Antonio Maceo to Francisco Sánchez Hechavarría, February 18, 1895, in Maceo, *Antonio Maceo: Ideología política; Cartas y otros documentos*, 2:8.

41. Diego Vicente Tejera, "Anexionistas y autonomistas," November 14, 1897, in Diego Vicente Tejera, *Textos escogidos*, ed. Carlos del Toro (Havana, 1981), pp. 150, 154, 157.

42. José Martí to Máximo Gómez, May 6, 1893, in Martí, *Obras completas*, 2:321; José Martí to Serafín Sánchez, November 3, 1894, in ibid., 3:336.

43. República de Cuba, Secretaria de Relaciones Exteriores, "Manifiesto," *La Verdad*, September 23, 1876, p. 1.

44. José Martí and Máximo Gómez, "A los jefes y oficiales de Jiguaní," in Martí, *Obras completas*, 4:164; Máximo Gómez, "Circular del General en Jefe del Ejército Libertador dirigido a los hacendados y ganaderos," July 1, 1895, in Máximo Gómez, *Algunos documentos políticos de Máximo Gómez*, ed. Amalia Rodríguez (Havana, 1962), p. 16.

45. Cabrera, *Ideales*, p. 345.

46. *El Vigía* 1 (September 25, 1897): 1; *El Vigía* 1 (December 4, 1897): 1; *Revista de Cuba Libre* 1 (February 19, 1898): 5.

47. Valdés-Domínguez, *Diario de soldado*, 1:233, 330, 434.

48. "El pueblo cubano," *El Cubano Libre*, September 10, 1896, p. 1.

49. Raimundo Cabrera, "Prólogo a la primera edición," July 1899, in Luis Estévez Romero, *Desde el Zanjón hasta Baire*, 2 vols. (1899; Havana, 1974), 1:16.

50. *La República*, August 19, 1871, p. 1.

51. Tomás Estrada Palma to José de Armas y Céspedes, September 3, 1895, in *La revolución del 95 según la correspondencia de la delegación cubana en Nueva York*, ed. León Primelles, 5 vols. (Havana, 1932–37), 1:281.

52. Antonio Maceo to Joaquín Crespo, October 30, 1895, *Boletín del Archivo Nacional* 21 (1922): 182.

53. Valdés-Domínguez, *Diario de soldado*, 3:201.

54. Luis Rodríguez-Embil, *La insurrección* (Paris, 1911), pp. 168–69.

55. Ramón Céspedes Fornaris, "A los cubanos," *La República*, August 26, 1871, p. 2.

56. José Calero to Leandro Rodríguez, October 18, 1879, in *Documentos para servir a la historia de la Guerra Chiquita*, 2:276, ANC.

57. "Diez de octubre," *La Revolución de Cuba*, December 27, 1878, p. 2.

58. Domingo Goicuría to Amalia Goicuría, January 9, 1870, in *Un héroe pintado por sí mismo*, ed. Miguel Angel Carbonell (Matanzas, 1929), p. 29; "Cartas del mártir cubano Domingo Goicuría," *Islas* (July–December 1963): 54.

59. Valdés-Domínguez, *Diario de soldado*, 1:50.

60. Carlos Loveira, *Generales y doctores* (Havana, 1920), p. 210.

61. Calixto García to Gonzalo de Quesada, May 29, 1897, in Quesada, *Archivo de Gonzalo de Quesada: Epistolario*, 1:174.

62. Valdés-Domínguez, *Diario de soldado*, 3:112.

63. Tejera, "La sociedad cubana," October 10, 1897, in Tejera, *Enseñanzas y profecias*, p. 25.

64. Rafael E. Tarragó, "'Rights Are Taken, Not Pleaded': José Martí and the Cult of the Recourse to Violence in Cuba," in *The Cuban Republic and José Martí: Reception and Use of a National Symbol*, ed. Mauricio A. Font and Alfonso W. Quiroz (Lanham, Md., 2006), p. 70.

65. Enrique Collazo, *Cuba heroica* (1912; Santiago de Cuba, 1980), p. 442.

66. Ramiro Guerra y Sánchez, *Historia de Cuba*, 2 vols. (Havana, 1921), 1:70.

67. Sergio Aguirre, "Nacionalidad, nación y centenario," *Cuba Socialista* 7 (February 1967): 85.

68. José Martí, "Manifiesto de Montecristi: El Partido Revolucionario Cubano a Cuba," March 25, 1895, in Martí, *Obras completas*, 4:95; José Martí to Ricardo Rodríguez Otero, May 16, 1886, in ibid., 1:196; José Martí, "Fermín Valdés-Domínguez," November 28, 1893, in ibid., 4:357–58.

69. Rodríguez-Embil, *La insurrección*, p. 153.

70. Carlos García Velez, "Cuaderno manuscrito contenido diarios del General Carlos García Velez, 1950–1960," entry dates: May 31, 1951, and June 1, 1951, Fondo de Donativos y Remisiones, Número 123 (fuera de caja), ANC.

71. Raimundo Cabrera, *Desde mi sitio* (Havana, 1911), p. 77.

72. Segundo Corvisón, *En la guerra y en la paz: Episodios de la revolución por la independencia y consideraciones acerca de la República cordial* (Havana, 1939), p. 10; Ricardo Batrell Oviedo, *Para la historia: Apuntes autobiográficos* (Havana, 1912), p. 80.

73. Sanjenís, *Memorias de la revolución de 1895 por la independencia de Cuba*, p. 209.

74. Eduardo Rosell y Malpica, *Diario del teniente coronel Eduardo Rosell y Malpica (1895–1897)*, 2 vols. (Havana, 1949), 1:51.

75. Camilo G. Polavieja to Ramón Blanco, June 4, 1879, in Camilo G. Polavieja, *Rela-*

ción documentada de mi política en Cuba: Lo que ví, lo que hice, lo que anuncié (Madrid, 1898), pp. 32–34.

76. Juan J. Remos, Colonia y protesta (Vetas del proceso cubano en sus luchas por la independencia) (Havana, 1956), p. 114.

77. René Darbois León, Un episodio de la guerra de Cuba: Drama bufo en dos actos en prosa y verso, con siete cuadros (Matanzas, 1899), p. 58.

78. Emilia Casanova de Villaverde to Carlos Manuel de Céspedes, May 13, 1871, in Un Contemporáneo [Cirilo Villaverde], Apuntes biográficos de Emilia Casanova de Villaverde, p. 147.

79. Rita Suárez de Villar, Mis memorias (Cienfuegos, 1957), p. 13.

80. Ignacio Agramonte to Amalia Simoni, November 19, 1872, in Para no separarnos nunca más: Cartas de Ignacio Agramonte a Amalia Simoni, ed. Elda Cento Gómez et al. (Havana, 2009), pp. 290–91.

81. Matías Duque, Nuestra patria (Lectura para niños) (2nd ed., Havana, 1925), p. 7.

82. Aurelia Castillo de González, Ignacio Agramonte en la vida privada (Havana, 1912), pp. 38–39.

83. José Martí, "Carácter," July 30, 1892, in Martí, Obras completas, 1:661; José Martí, "Hora suprema," March 14, 1893, in ibid., 1:437–38.

84. Africa Fernández Iruela, "La mujer cubana," Florilegio de escritoras cubanas, 3:240.

85. Dolores Larrúa de Quintana, "¿Cual debe ser el ideal o aspiración de la mujer cubana?" Revista de la Asociación Femenina de Camagüey 3 (February 1923): 5.

86. Consuelo Alvarez, "¡Madre mía!" El Cubano Libre, September 10, 1896, p. 3.

87. Remos, Colonia y protesta (Vetas del proceso cubano en sus luchas por la independencia), p. 117.

88. "La madre cubana ante la Revolución," El Expedicionario, January 2, 1897, p. 5.

89. Concepción Boloña, La mujer en Cuba (2nd ed., Havana, 1899), p. 21.

90. Luis Quintero, "Unión—Patriotismo," El Pueblo, October 13, 1875, p. 2.

91. José María Izaguirre, Recuerdos de la guerra (Havana, 1936), p. 57.

92. Francisco Gómez Toro, "Discurso pronunciado en 1894 dedicado a la mujer," in Papeles de Panchito, ed. Bladimir Zamora (2nd ed., Havana, 1988), p. 151.

93. See "Nuestras mujeres," Patria, August 27, 1892, p. 2.

94. Carlos Manuel de Céspedes to Ana de Quesada, October 18, 1871, in Céspedes, Cartas de Carlos M. de Céspedes a su esposa Ana de Quesada, p. 58.

95. Valdés-Domínguez, Diario de soldado, 1:242, 1:378, 1:402, 2:69–70.

96. Carlos Manuel de Céspedes, "Al pueblo cubano," February 7, 1870, in Boletín del Archivo Nacional 53–54 (1954–55): 179–80.

97. José Abreu Cardet, Los senderos de la passion: Otra mirada al 68 (Holguín, 2010), p. 89.

98. Victoria de Caturla Brú, La mujer en la independencia de América (Havana, 1945), p. 154.

99. Dolores María de Ximeno y Cruz, Memorias de Lola María (2nd ed., Havana, 1983), pp. 144–54.

100. Mariano Benítez Veguillas, Cuba ante la historia y el sentido común (Havana, 1897), p. 60.

101. Grover Flint, Marching with Gomez: A War Correspondent's Field Note-Book Kept during Four Months with the Cuban Army (Boston, 1898), p. 57.

102. Camilo G. Polavieja to Antonio Maura, December 22, 1892, in Polavieja, *Relación documentada de mi política en Cuba*, p. 175; Camilo G. Polavieja, *Mando en Cuba del Teniente General Camilo Polavieja* (Madrid, 1896), p. 6.

103. George Clarke Musgrave, *Under Three Flags in Cuba: A Personal Account of the Cuban Insurrection and Spanish-American War* (Boston, 1899), p. 76.

104. Valdés-Domínguez, *Diario de soldado*, 4:96.

105. José Miró Argenter, *Cuba: Crónicas de la guerra*, 3 vols. (Havana, 1945), 1:101.

106. Demoticus Philalethes, *Yankee Travels through the Island of Cuba; or, The Men and Government, the Laws and Customs of Cuba, as Seen by American Eyes* (New York, 1856), p. 379.

107. Antonio Pirala, *Anales de la guerra de Cuba*, 3 vols. (Madrid, 1895–95), 1:355.

108. Rodolfo Bergés, *Cuba y Santo Domingo: Apuntes de la guerra de Cuba de mi diario en campaña, 1895–96–97–98* (Havana, 1905), p. 188.

109. "La muger cubana y la insurrección," *Diario Cubano*, June 24, 1870, p. 1; Eusebio Sáenz y Sáenz, *La siboneya, o episodios de la guerra de Cuba* (3rd ed., Madrid, 1891), p. 141.

110. Federico Cavada to Fernando Escobar, July 22, 1870, in Mary Ruiz Zarate, *El General Candela: Biografía de una guerrilla* (Havana, 1974), pp. 220–21.

111. Juan Maspon Franco, *Maldona, novela cubana* (Havana, 1927), p. 260.

112. Manuel J. de Granda, *Memoria revolucionaria* (Santiago de Cuba, 1926), p. 181.

113. Ramón Céspedes Fornaris, "Pensamientos: Palabras de una insurrecta," *La República*, September 30, 1871, p. 5.

114. Antonio Maceo to José Martí, January 12, 1894, in Maceo, *El pensamiento vivo de Maceo*, pp. 97–98.

115. Enrique Loynaz del Castillo, *Memorias de la guerra* (2nd ed., Havana, 1989), p. 18.

116. Carlos García Velez, "Cuaderno manuscrito contenido diarios del General Carlos García Velez, 1950–1960," entry date: July 26, 1951, Fondo de Donativos y Remisiones, Número 123 (fuera de caja), ANC; José Miguel Abreu Cardet, *Las fronteras de la guerra: Mujeres, soldados y regionalismo en el 68* (Santiago de Cuba, 2007), p. 134.

117. Horacio Ferrer, *Con el rifle al hombro* (Havana, 1950), pp. 10, 15.

118. Junta de Güinía de Miranda, "A las ciudadanas de Las Villas," 1869, in Pirala, *Anales de la guerra de Cuba*, 1:653.

119. Mercedes García Tudurí de Goya, "La familia cubana: Su tipo y medio de vida," *Revista Bimestre Cubana* 42 (1938): 286; see also Rosario Rexach, "Las mujeres del 68," *Revista Cubana* 1 (January–June 1968): 123–42.

120. Flora Basulto de Montoya, *Una niña bajo tres banderas (Memorias)* (Havana, 1954), p. 8.

121. "Cuba and the Cubans," *North American Review* 79 (July 1854): 115.

122. Benito Aranguren y Martínez, *Recuerdos* (Havana, 1934), pp. 23, 83, 87.

123. Alberto de la Cruz Muñoz, *Compendio de mi vida revolucionaria* (Matanzas, 1903), pp. 5–6.

124. Corvisón, *El la guerra y en la paz*, pp. 103, 193.

125. Manuel Sanguily, "Un insurrecto cubano en la corte," November 1888, in Manuel Sanguily, *Frente a la dominación española*, ed. Violeta Serrano (Havana, 1978), pp. 110–11; see also Manuel Sanguily, "Diario de Manuel Sanguily, desde agost 19 de 1896 al 29 de diciembre de 1897," Fondo de Donativos y Remisiones, Caja 86, Número 152, ANC.

126. Carlos García Velez, "Cuaderno manuscrito contenido diarios del General Carlos García Velez, 1950–1960," entry dates: May 31, 1951, and June 1, 1951, Fondo de Donativos y Remisiones, Número 123 (fuera de caja), ANC.

127. Blancamar León Rosabal, La voz del mambí: Imagen y mito (Havana, 1997), p. 17.

128. Valdés-Domínguez, Diario de soldado, 1:468–69.

129. Suárez de Villar, Mis memorias, p. 13.

130. Serafín Espinosa y Ramos, Al trote y sin estribos (Recuerdos de la Guerra de Independencia) (Havana, 1946), p. 21.

131. Manuel Piedra Martel, Mis primeros treinta años: Memorias; Infancia y adolescencia—la Guerra de Independencia (2nd ed., Havana, 1944), p. 30.

132. Angel E. Rosende y de Zayas, De nuestras memorias de la Guerra, 1895–1898: Conspirador y de soldado a capitán (Havana, 1928), pp. 19–20.

133. Benítez Veguillas, Cuba ante la historia y el sentido común, p. 60.

134. Flint, Marching with Gomez, p. 85; see also José Miguel Trujillo, "La independencia y los niños," Bohemia 9 (November 24, 1918): 4.

135. Mariano Torrente, "Memoria presentado al Gobierno," September 28, 1852, in Cuba desde 1850 á 1873: Colección de informes, memorias, proyectos y antecedentes sobre el gobierno de la isla de Cuba, relativos al citado period, ed. Cárlos de Sedano y Cruzat (Madrid, 1873), p. 174.

136. Dionisio A. Galiano, Cuba en 1858 (Madrid, 1859), p. 28.

137. Camilo G. Polavieja to Antonio Maura, December 22, 1892, in Polavieja, Relación documentada de mi política en Cuba, p. 176; Camilo G. Polavieja to Antonio María Fabié, December 10, 1890, in ibid., p. 115.

138. Conde de Valmaseda, "Proclama," April 4, 1869, in Melchor Loret de Mola y León, El 6 de enero de 1871: Episodios de la guerra de Cuba (Puerto Príncipe, 1893), p. 104.

139. Musgrave, Under Three Flags in Cuba, pp. 80–81.

140. Horatio S. Rubens, Liberty: The Story of Cuba (New York, 1932), p. 248.

141. Sanjenís, Memorias de la revolución de 1895 por la independencia de Cuba, p. 118.

142. María Josefa Granados, La otra María, o la niña de Artemisa, ed. Ana Núñez Machín (Havana, 1975), p. 73.

143. Juan Jorge Sobrado, Recuerdos de la guerra (Remedios, 1898), p. 11.

144. "Desposition of Enrique Ubieta," Claim 196, Case No. 293, Hormiguero Central Company v. the United States, Records of Boundary and Claims Commissions and Arbitrations, RG76, NA.

145. Gustavo Robreño, La acera del Louvre: Novela histórica (Havana, 1925), p. 15.

146. Rodríguez-Embil, La insurrección, pp. 13–14.

147. Santiago C. Rey, Recuerdos de la guerra, 1895–1898 (Havana, 1931), pp. 42–43.

148. Gonzalo de Quesada, "10 de octubre de 1891," in Gonzalo de Quesada, Páginas escogidas (Havana, 1968), pp. 77, 79.

149. José Martí to Gonzalo de Quesada, May 9, 1892, in Martí, Obras completas, 1:440.

150. José Martí and Máximo Gómez, "Manifiesto de Montecristi," March 25, 1895, in ibid., 4:93.

151. Manuel de la Cruz, Episodios de la revolución cubana (Havana, 1890), p. xi.

152. El Criollo, Album de 'El criollo' (Havana, 1888), pp. 3–4.

153. Cabrera, Ideales, p. 237.

154. Manuel Sanguily, "Negros y blancos," January 31, 1894, in Sanguily, *Frente a la dominación española*, p. 268.

155. Ramiro Guerra y Sánchez, *Guerra de los Diez Años*, 2 vols. (1950–52; Havana, 1986), 2:341–42.

156. Eliseo Giberga, "Apuntes sobre la cuestión de Cuba por un autonomista," 1897, in Eliseo Giberga, *Obras de Eliseo Giberga*, 4 vols. (Havana, 1931), 3:318–19.

157. Leví Marrero, *Cuba: La forja de un pueblo; Estudios y conferencias* (Barcelona, 1971), p. 11.

158. Sanguily, "El general Máximo Gómez y la historia de la Revolución," December 31, 1893, in Sanguily, *Obras de Manuel Sanguily*, 6:79.

159. Camilo G. Polavieja to Antonio María Fabié, November 30, 1890, in Polavieja, *Relación documentada de mi política en Cuba*, p. 96.

160. Valdés-Domínguez, *Diario de soldado*, 3:112.

161. Jorge Ibarra, *Ideología mambisa* (Havana, 1972), p. 71.

162. Camilo G. Polavieja to Ramón Blanco, April 19, 1881, in Polavieja, *Relación documentada de mi política en Cuba*, pp. 62–63; Camilo G. Polavieja to Antonio Maura, December 22, 1892, in ibid., p. 116.

163. Arsenio Martínez Campos to Antonio Cánovas de Castillo, July 25, 1895, in Carlos O'Donnell y Abreu, *Apuntes del ex-Ministro de Estado Duque de Tetuán para la defense de la política internacional y gestión diplomática del gobierno Liberal-Conservador*, 2 vols. (Madrid, 1902): 2:115–17.

164. Rey, *Recuerdos de la guerra, 1895–1898*, p. 42.

165. Giberga, "Apuntes sobre la cuestión de Cuba por un autonomista," 3:230–31, 249–50.

166. "Deposition of General Jose Lachambre," entry 352, *Central Teresa v. the United States*, Claim No. 97, entry 352, RG76, NA.

167. Joel James Figarola, *Fundamentos sociológicos de la revolución cubana (siglo XIX)* (Santiago de Cuba, 2005), p. 154.

168. Frantz Fanon, *The Wretched of the Earth*, trans. Constance Farrington (New York, 1963), p. 233.

Chapter 4

1. *La Lucha*, May 21, 1902, p. 1.

2. Federico Villoch, *Viejas postales descoloridas: La guerra de independencia* (Havana, 1946), p. 225.

3. Máximo Gómez to Sotero Figueroa, May 8, 1901, in *Papeles dominicanos de Máximo Gómez*, ed. Emilio Rodríguez Demorizi (Santo Domingo, 1954), pp. 396–97.

4. "Salvar un legado de memoria colectiva (Entrevista con Graziella Pogolotti)," in *En el borde de todo: El hoy y el mañana de la revolución en Cuba*, ed. Julio César Guanche (Mexico, 2007), p. 243.

5. William L. Marcy to Pierre Soulé, November 13, 1854, in *Diplomatic Correspondence of the United States: Inter-American Affairs*, ed. William R. Manning, 12 vols. (Washington, D.C, 1932–39), 11:197; William L. Marcy to Augustus C. Dodge, May 1, 1855, in ibid., 11:210.

6. Serafín Espinosa y Ramos, *Al trote y sin estribos (Recuerdos de la Guerra de Independencia)* (Havana, 1946), p. 279.

7. Máximo Gómez, *Diario de campaña del Mayor General Máximo Gómez* (Havana, 1940), pp. 424–25.

8. Gustavo Robreño, *La acera del Louvre: Novela histórica* (Havana, 1925), p. 300.

9. José Puig Soler, *Un mundo de cosas* (Xalapa, 1989), p. 151.

10. Philip Jessup, "Interview with Mr. Root," November 19, 1929, Philip Jessup Papers, Manuscript Division, LC.

11. Elihu Root to Leonard Wood, February 9, 1901, Elihu Root Papers, Manuscript Division, LC.

12. Rafael Fernández de Castro, "Realidades," in Rafael Fernández de Castro, *Para la historia de Cuba* (Havana, 1899), p. 496.

13. Agustín Cebreco to Editor, *El Fígaro* 16 (October 28, 1900): 482.

14. *The Statutes at Large of the United States of America*, 32 vols. (Washington, D.C., 1875–1936), 31:897.

15. File 568 of the records of the Bureau of Insular Affairs (RG350) and Files 1400, 3051, and 4000 of the Military Government of Cuba records (RG140) of the U.S. National Archives contain hundreds of cables, letters, and petitions protesting the Platt Amendment.

16. Juan Gualberto Gómez, "Ponencia del Sr. Juan Gualberto Gómez, miembro de la Comisión designada para proponer la respuesta a la comunicacón del Gobernador Militar de Cuba," March 26, 1901, in Juan Gualberto Gómez, *Por Cuba Libre*, ed. Emilio Roig de Leuchsenring (Havana, 1974), pp. 494–95.

17. Leonard Wood to Theodore Roosevelt, October 28, 1901, Leonard Wood Papers, Manuscript Division, LC.

18. Elihu Root to Andrew Carnegie, March 20, 1920, Philip Jessup Papers, Manuscript Division, LC.

19. Enrique Gay-Calbó, "El sentido de nuestra historia," *Revista Bimestre Cubana* 34 (1934): 51.

20. Ofelia Rodríguez Acosta, *Sonata interrumpida* (Mexico, 1943), p. 117.

21. Manuel Piedra Martel, *Mis primeros treinta años: Memorias; Infancia y adolescencia—la Guerra de Independencia* (2nd ed., Havana, 1944), pp. 487–90.

22. Manuel Arbelo, *Recuerdos de la última guerra por la independencia de Cuba, 1896–1898* (Havana, 1918), p. 304.

23. Marcelo Salinas y López, *Un aprendiz de revolucionario* (Havana, 1937), pp. 55–56.

24. Enrique Collazo, *Los americanos en Cuba*, 2 vols. (Havana, 1905), 1:8.

25. See *La Lucha*, April 11, 1899, p. 2; *La Discusión*, September 23, 1900, p. 1; and "Confidential Report: Province of Santiago de Cuba," n.d., Records of the Post Office Department, RG28, NA.

26. Salvador Quesada Torres, "El silencio," in Salvador Quesada Torres, *El silencio* (Havana, 1923), pp. 18–19.

27. Alejandro Rodríguez to Gonzalo de Quesada, June 13, 1899, in Gonzalo de Quesada, *Archivo de Gonzalo de Quesada: Espitolario*, ed. Gonzalo de Quesada y Miranda, 2 vols. (Havana, 1948–51), 2:179–80.

28. Ramón Roa, *Con la pluma y el machete*, 3 vols. (Havana, 1950), 1:222.

29. Esteban Montejo, "Todavía mi machete me basta," *Cuba* (Número Especial) (October 1968): 51.

30. Santiago C. Rey, *Recuerdos de la guerra, 1895–1898* (Havana, 1931), p. 122.

31. Regino Martín, "Día del Veterano: Una bandera cubana en cada pecho," *Carteles* 35 (October 10, 1954): 36.

32. Speech is summarized in Avelino Sanjenís, *Memorias de la revolución de 1895 por la independencia de Cuba* (Havana, 1913), p. 348.

33. Alejandro de la Fuente, *A Nation for All: Race, Inequality, and Politics in Twentieth-Century Cuba* (Chapel Hill, 2001), p. 35.

34. Ricardo Batrell Oviedo, *Para la historia: Apuntes autobiográficos de la vida de Ricardo Batrell Oviedo* (Havana, 1912), p. 170.

35. Rafael Serra to Juan Sardiñas y Villa, January 26, 1901, in *Para blancos y negros: Ensayos políticos, sociales y económicos* (Havana, 1907), pp. 92–93.

36. *La Lucha*, June 9, 1902, p. 1.

37. Miguel Balanzó, "El 20 de mayo de 1902," *Minerva* 3 (May 1911): 17.

38. In *Historia y americanidad: Cuarto Congreso Nacional de Historia; Discursos y acuerdos* (Havana, 1946), p. 46.

39. José González Lanuza to John R. Brooke, 1899, John R. Brooke Papers, Historical Society of Pennsylvania, Philadelphia.

40. Ramón M. Alfonso, *Viviendas del campesino pobre en Cuba* (Havana, 1904), p. 8.

41. Arturo Montori, *El tormento de vivir* (Havana, 1923), pp. 20–21.

42. Antonio Iraizoz, *Lecturas cubanas* (Havana, 1939), pp. 187–89.

43. Carlos de Velasco, "La obra de la revolución cubana," *Social* 9 (February 24, 1924): 13–14.

44. Ramiro Guerra y Sánchez, "La patria y el patriotismo," October 21, 1921, in Ramiro Guerra y Sánchez, *La defensa nacional y la escuela* (Havana, 1923), p. 2.

45. José Martí, "El Partido Revolucionario a Cuba," May 27, 1893, in José Martí, *Obras completas*, 27 vols. (Havana, 1963–66), 1:336.

46. Anselmo Suárez y Romero to Domingo del Monte, October 21, 1839, in Academia de la Historia de Cuba, *Centón epistolario de Domingo del Monte*, ed. Domingo Figarola-Caneda, Joaquín Llaverías y Martínez, and Manuel Mesa Rodríguez, 6 vols. (Havana, 1923–53), 4:100.

47. Carlos Manuel de Céspedes, "Al pueblo cubano," February 7, 1870, *Boletín del Archivo Nacional* 53–54 (1954–55): 179.

48. Emilia Casanova de Villaverde to Federico Cavada, October 4, 1870, in Un Contemporáneo [Cirilo Villaverde], *Apuntes biográficos de Emilia Casanova de Villaverde* (New York, 1874), p. 99.

49. Salvador Cisneros Betancourt, "Manifiesto," July 13, 1896, in Cuba, Secretaria de Gobernación, *Documentos históricos* (Havana, 1912), p. 158.

50. Antonio Maceo to Francisco Sánchez Hechavarría, February 18, 1895, in Antonio Maceo, *Antonio Maceo: Ideología política; Cartas y otros documentos*, 2 vols. (1952; Havana, 1998), 2:4.

51. Manuel Piedra Martel, *Campañas de Maceo en la última Guerra de Independencia* (Havana, 1946), p. 93.

52. Antonio Penichet, *¡Alma rebelde!* (Havana, 1921), p. 64.

53. Julio Antonio Mella, "Los cazadores de negros resucitan en Santa Clara," March

1925, in Julio Antonio Mella, J. A. Mella: Documentos y artículos, ed. Eduardo Castañeda et al. (Havana, 1975), p. 165.

54. Loló de la Torriente, Mi casa en la tierra (1956; Havana, 1985), p. 18.

55. José Soler Puig, Bertillón 166 (2nd ed., Havana, 1975), p. 164.

56. Stephen Leech, "Annual Report on the Island of Cuba, 1910," March 11, 1911, Foreign Office Records, Embassy and Consular Archives, Cuba, 1870 onwards, Record Class 277, No. 174, National Archives, Kew, Surrey, England.

57. Gerardo Machado, Memorias: Ocho anos de lucha (Miami, 1982), p. 15.

58. U.S. Congress, Senate Committee on Judiciary, Communist Threat to the U.S. through the Caribbean, August 30, 1960, 86th Congress, 1st sess. (Washington, D.C., 1960), Part 9, p. 700.

59. Manuel Rionda to Czarnikow, MacDougall, and Co., March 17, 1909, Series 1, Record Group 2, Braga Brothers Collection, University of Florida Library, Gainesville.

60. In Elías Entralgo, "La república: El proceso político interno," in Elías Entralgo, Lecturas y estudios (Havana, 1962), p. 10.

61. Agustín Acosta to Juan Marinello, July 22, 1924, in Cada tiempo trae una faena . . . Selección de correspondencia de Juan Marinello Vidaurreta, 1923–1940, ed. Ana Suárez Díaz, 2 vols. (Havana, 2004), 1:61.

62. Francisco José Moreno, Before Fidel: The Cuba I Remember (Austin, 2007), p. 98.

63. Spruille Braden, "Memorandum for Policy Committee on Conditions in Cuba and Our Policies in Respect Thereto," August 1, 1944, Spruille Braden Papers, box 15, Rare Book and Manuscript Library, Columbia University, New York, N.Y.

64. Fernando Ortiz, "What Cuba Desires of the United States: An Address at the Afternoon Session of the First Institute of Cuban-American Affairs," Washington, D.C., December 10, 1932, mimeograph copy, Frank McCoy Papers, Manuscript Division, LC.

65. Jorge Mañach, "Revolution in Cuba," Foreign Affairs 12 (October 1933): 49, 51.

66. Luis Aguilar León, "La fe en Cuba y la interpretacion positiva de su historia," Carteles 40 (March 8, 1959): 58.

67. José Manuel Poveda, "Elegía del retorno," January 20, 1918, in José Manuel Poveda, Prosa, ed. Alberto Rocasolano (Havana, 1981), p. 32.

68. Carlos García Velez, "Cuaderno manuscrito contenido diarios del General Carlos García Velez, 1950–1960," entry dates: April 19, 1951, and August 17, 1951, Fondo de Donativos y Remisiones, Número 123 (fuera de caja), ANC; Martín, "Día del Veterano: Una bandera cubana en cada pecho," p. 34.

69. Manuel Bisbé, "Homenaje de Martí: Discurso," in Cuba, Congreso Nacional de Historia, Primer Congreso Nacional de Historia, 2 vols. (Havana, 1943), 1:48.

70. Heberto Padilla, Self-Portrait of the Other, trans. Alexander Coleman (New York, 1990), p. 17.

71. "Manifiesto-Programa del Movimiento 26 de Julio," November 1956, Humanismo 7 (November–December 1958): 15.

72. Cristina García, Dreaming in Cuban (New York, 1992), p. 164.

73. José Antonio Ramos, "Páginas salvadas: Fragmento de las memorias," Nueva Revista Cubana 1 (October, November, December 1959): 137, 149.

74. Jorge Mañach, *Pasado vigente* (Havana, 1939), pp. 222–23; Juan Marinello, "Sobre la inquietud cubana," *Avance* 3 (December 15, 1929): 357.

75. Gustavo Pittaluga, *Diálogos sobre el destino* (Havana, 1954), p. 193.

76. Raúl Roa, *En pie, 1953–1958* (Havana, 1959), p. 21.

77. Office of Middle American Affairs, "Cuba—A Summary of Situations, Interests, and Policies Affecting the United States," February 20, 1953, 737.0012-2453, Confidential State Department Central Files, Cuba, Internal Affairs, 1950–54, General Records of the Department of State, RG59, NA.

78. René Vázquez Díaz, *La isla del Cundeamor* (Madrid, 1995), p. 95.

79. José Angel Bustamante, *Raíces psicológicas del cubano* (Havana, 1959), p. 93.

80. "Acta Final: Declaración de Principios," November 17, 1952, in Cuba, Décimo Congreso Nacional de Historia, *En el cincuentario de la República* (Havana, 1953), pp. 140–41.

81. José Antonio Ramos, *Las impurezas de la realidad* (1929; Havana, 1979), p. 170.

82. Raimundo Cabrera, "La Sociedad de Amigos del País se dirige a los elementos que representan la conciencia nacional," March 17, 1923, http://www.amigospais -guaracabuya.org/g_intro.php.

83. Ramiro Guerra, "Difusión y afirmación del sentimiento nacional," *Social* 9 (November 1924): 22.

84. Fernando Ortiz, *El pueblo cubano* (2nd ed., Havana, 1997), p. 1.

85. Waldo Medina, "El tesoro de un pueblo," 1953, and "Recuento necesario," 1954, in Waldo Medina, *Cosas de ayer que sirven para hoy* (Havana, 1978), pp. 68, 112–13; Medina, "Eustaquio y Liborio," 1955, in ibid., pp. 44–45.

86. José Enrique Varona, *Desde mi belvedere* (Barcelona, 1917), p. 7.

87. Luis Rodríguez-Embil, "Las impurezas de la realidad: Carta respuesta," *Social* 17 (July 1932): 7–8 (emphases in original).

88. Ramiro Guerra y Sánchez, *Historia elemental de Cuba: Para uso de las escuelas primarias* (Havana, 1922), p. 5; quoted in Yoel Cordoví Núñez, "Las enseñanzas de la historia nacional y local en las escuelas públicas de Cuba, 1899–1930," in *Perfiles de la nación II*, ed. María del Pilar Díaz Castañón (Havana, 2006), p. 38.

89. Miguel Varona Guerrero, *La guerra de independencia de Cuba, 1895–1898*, 3 vols. (Havana, 1946), 3:1792.

90. El Curioso Parlanchín, "La representacion en piedra de nuestra nacionalidad," *Carteles* 10 (January 30, 1927): 12.

91. Frederick A. Ober, *Our West Indian Neighbors* (New York, 1904), p. 27.

92. Joseph Hergesheimer, *San Cristóbal de La Habana* (London, 1921), p. 30.

93. This vast literature includes Luis de Radillo y Rodríguez, *Autobiografía del cubano Luis de Radillo y Rodríguez, o, Episodios de su vida histórico-político-revolucionaria de el 24 de febrero hasta el 1° de enero de 1899* (Havana, 1899); Luis Lagomasino Alvarez, *Reminiscencias patria* (Manzanillo, 1902); Oviedo, *Para la historia: Apuntes autobiográficos*; Sanjenís, *Memorias de la revolución de 1895 por la independencia de Cuba*; Arbelo, *Recuerdos de la última guerra por la independencia de Cuba, 1896–1898*; Angel E. Rosende y de Zayas, *1895–1898: Conspirador y de soldado a capitán* (Havana, 1928); Fernando Méndez Miranda, *Historia de los servicios prestados en la guerra de independencia* (Havana, 1928); Rey, *Recuerdos de la guerra, 1895–1898*; José Hernández Guzmán, *Memorias tristes: Apuntes históricos* (Havana, 1934); José María Izaguirre,

Recuerdos de la guerra (Havana, 1936); Luis Rodolfo Miranda, Con Martí y con Calixto García (Recuerdos de un mambí del 95) (Havana, 1943); Eduardo Rosell y Malpica, Diario del teniente coronel Eduardo Rosell y Malpica, 2 vols. (Havana, 1950); Gustavo Pérez Abreu, En la guerra con Máximo Gómez (Havana, 1952); and Eduardo F. Lores y Llorens, Relatos históricos de la guerra del 95 (Havana, 1955).

94. Diana Iznaga, Presencia del testimonio en la literatura sobre las guerras por la independencia nacional (1868–1898) (Havana, 1989), pp. 320–21.

95. See Roscoe R. Hill, "Captain Joaquín Llaverías and the Boletín del Archivo Nacional," American Archivist 10 (October 1947): 323–27.

96. Luis Rodolfo Miranda, "La Agrupación Pro Enseñanza de Hechos Históricos y los Congresos Nacionales de Historia," in Cuba, Quinto Congreso Nacional de Historia, Un lustro de revaloración histórica (Havana, 1947), p. 86.

97. Miguel A. Cano, La enseñanza de la historia en la escuela primaria (Havana, 1930), p. 49.

98. Luis Báez, ed., Secretos de los generales (Havana, 1996), p. 466.

99. Carlos Martí, ed., La Jura de la Bandera: Crónicas, artículos, discursos, etc. (Havana, 1910), p. 53.

100. Eduardo Abril Amores, Bajo la garra (Havana, 1922), pp. 185–87.

101. José Juan Arrom, De donde crecen las palmas (Havana, 2005), p. 402.

102. Secretaría de Instrucción Pública y Bellas Artes, "Decreto/Reglas," July 28, 1910, in Martí, La Jura de la Bandera: Crónicas, artículos, discursos, etc., pp. 11–12.

103. Tania Quintero, "Penúltimos días: De mis recuerdos," July 10, 2008, http://www.penultimosdias.com/2008/07/10/de-mis-recuerdos.

104. Emeterio Santovenia et al., La enseñanza de la historia en Cuba (Mexico, 1951), p. 10.

105. In William Gálvez, ed., El joven Camilo (Havana, 1998), pp. 18–19.

106. Ibid., p. 19.

107. Janisset Rivero and Dagoberto Valdés, "Entrevista al Sr. Huber Matos," Convivencia/Sociedad Civil, October 3, 2009, http://www.convivenciacuba.es/.

108. Carlos Franqui, Diario de la revolución cubana (Madrid, 1975), p. 41.

109. Luisa Campuzano, "Cuarenta años enseñando, cuarenta años aprendiendo," in Casa de las Américas, Cultura y revolución: A cuarenta años de 1959 (Havana, 1999), p. 135.

110. República de Cuba, Gaceta Oficial de la República de Cuba 20, no. 99 (April 27, 1922): 8673; Antoni Kapcia, "Cuban Populism and the Birth of the Myth of Martí," in José Martí: Revolutionary Democrat, ed. Christopher Abel and Nissa Torrents (Durham, 1986), pp. 32–64; João Felipe Gonçalves, "The 'Apostle' in Stone: Nationalism and Monuments in Honor of José Martí," in The Cuban Republic and José Martí: Reception and Use of a National Symbol, ed. Mauricio A. Font and Alfonso W. Quiroz (Lanham, Md., 2006), pp. 18–33.

111. José Antonio Portuondo, Proceso de la cultura cubana (Esquema para un ensayo de interpretación) (Havana, 1938), p. 53.

112. For Carlos Loveira: Los inmorales (Havana, 1919) and Generales y doctores (Havana, 1920); for José Antonio Ramos: Coaybay (Havana, 1926) and Las impurezas de la realidad (Barcelona, 1929); for Miguel de Carrión: Las honradas (Havana, 1917) and Las impuras (Havana, 1919); for Luis Felipe Rodríguez: Como opinaba Damián Paredes (Valencia, 1916) and La conjura de la ciénaga (Madrid, 1923); for Jesús Castellanos: La manigua sentimental (Madrid, 1910).

113. José Antonio Grillo Longoria, "Escribimos para un pueblo que no sólo es inteligente, sino además instruido," in *Quiénes escriben en Cuba*, ed. Jorge L. Bernard and Juan A. Pola (Havana, 1985), p. 350.

114. Conrado Massaguer, *Massaguer: Su vida y su obra; Autobiografía, historia gráfica anecdotario* (Havana, 1957), n.p.

115. See Graciella Pogolotti, "Art, Bubbles, and Utopia," *South Atlantic Quarterly* 96 (Winter 1997): 171.

116. Juan A. Martínez, *Cuban Art and National Identity: The Vanguardia Painters, 1927–1950* (Gainesville: University Press of Florida, 1994), pp. 48–49, 95.

117. Enrique Serpa, *La trampa* (1956; Havana, 1980), p. 217.

118. Gay-Calbó, "El sentido de nuestra historia," pp. 50–51.

119. Pedro E. Sotolongo, "La utilidad histórica," *Minerva* 3 (April 1911): 12.

120. Roberto Pérez de Acevedo, "Sobre la historia de Cuba: Enseñanza de la historia," in Cuba, Congreso Nacional de Historia, *Primer Congreso Nacional de Historia*, 1:160.

121. José Antonio Ramos, "Seamos cubanos," *Cuba Contempóranea* 15 (December 1917): 269–70.

122. Emilio Roig de Leuchsenring, "Función social del historiador," in *Historia y americanidad: Cuarto Congreso Nacional de Historia; Discursos y acuerdos* (Havana, 1946), pp. 42–45.

123. Ibid., pp. 45, 48.

124. Emilio Roig de Leuchsenring, "Superemos la agudísima crisis de patriotismo que padece nuestra República," in Cuba, Congreso Nacional de Historia, *La lucha por la independencia de Cuba: Duodécimo Congreso Nacional de History* (Havana, 1957), p. 124.

125. Elio Leiva, "Bienvenido a los congresistas," in Cuba, Décimo Congreso Nacional de Historia, *En el cincuentario de la República* (Havana, 1953), pp. 57–58.

126. Juan M. Leiseca, *Historia de Cuba: Escrita de acuerdo con el plan de estudios vigentes en las escuelas públicas* (Havana, 1925), pp. 1, 7, 9.

127. Elio Leiva and Edilberto Marbán, *Historia de Cuba: De acuerdo con el programa vigente para el bachillerato elemental* (3rd ed., Havana, 1944), p. 1.

128. Fernando Portuondo del Prado, *Historia de Cuba* (5th ed., Havana, 1953), p. 3.

129. Ramiro Guerra y Sánchez, "La historia patria y la formación de los sentimientos morales y patrióticos," April 1911, in Guerra y Sánchez, *La defensa nacional y la escuela*, p. 22.

130. Herminio Portell Vilá, *Historia de la guerra de Cuba y los Estados Unidos contra España* (Havana, 1949), p. ii.

131. Matías Duque, *Nuestra patria (Lectura para niños)* (2nd ed., Havana, 1925), p. 20.

132. Ciro Espinos, "Ideario y república a través de la adolescencia," *Revista Cubana* 21 (January–December 1940): 103–4.

133. Luis Ricardo Alonso, *El palacio y la furia* (Barcelona, 1976), p. 9.

134. Pedro García Valdés, *Enseñanza de la historia* (2nd ed., Havana, 1940), pp. xi, 370–72, 378.

135. Ramiro Guerra y Sánchez, "La Patria en la escuela," November 1913, in Guerra y Sánchez, *La defensa nacional y la escuela*, pp. 28–29.

136. María del Carmen Boza, *Scattering the Ashes* (Tempe, 1998), p. 31.

137. Santovenia et al., *La enseñanza de la historia en Cuba*, pp. 6, 9–10, 141–74.

138. Cano, *La enseñanza de la historia en la escuela primaria*, pp. 7, 31.

139. Carlos A. Valdés Codina, *Lecciones de historia de Cuba: Lecciones preparadas para que sirvan de guía a los maestros en los primeros grados de la enseñanza* (Havana, 1905), p. 4.

140. Isabel Carrasco, "La patria," *Revista de la Asociación Femenina de Camagüey* 5 (May 1925): 7.

141. Néstor Carbonell y Rivero, *Resumen de una vida heroica* (Havana, 1945), pp. 40–41.

142. Luis Rolando Cabrera, *El centenario de Antonio Maceo* (Havana, 1945), p. 32.

143. José Mesa Vidal, *Hombres de la revolución cubana: Guillermo Moncada ("Guillermón")* (Santiago de Cuba, 1914), pp. 20–21.

144. Francisco de Arredondo y Mirando, "Prólogo," in Eugenio Betancourt Agramonte, *Ignacio Agramonte y la revolución cubana* (Havana, 1928), pp. 7–9.

145. Matías Duque, *El comandante Antonio Duque* (Havana, 1928), p. 11.

146. Benigno Vázquez Rodríguez, *Precursores y fundadores* (Havana, 1958), p. 7; see also Mario García Kohly, *Grandes hombres de Cuba* (Madrid, 1919); and Néstor Carbonell, *Próceres: Ensayo biograficos* (Havana, 1919).

147. Ofelia Rodríguez Acosta, *En la noche del mundo* (Havana, 1940), p. 136.

148. Cintio Vitier, *Lo cubano en la poesía* (Havana, 1970), p. 488.

149. José Manuel Poveda, "Bronce de libertad: La campana de La Demajagua," October 13, 1918, in Poveda, *Prosa*, pp. 129–31 (emphasis in original).

150. Eduardo Torres-Cuevas, *En busca de la cubanidad*, 2 vols. (Havana, 2006), 2:336.

151. Nicolás Rodríguez Astiazaraín, *Episodios de la lucha clandestina en La Habana (1955–1958)* (Havana, 2009), pp. 7, 9.

152. Edmundo Desnoes, *No hay problema* (Havana, 1961), pp. 86–87.

153. Vitier, *Lo cubano en la poesía*, p. 486.

154. Julio Antonio Mella, "Glosas al pensamiento de José Martí," 1926, in Mella, *J. A. Mella: Documentos y artículos*, p. 268.

155. Cintio Vitier, "Algunas reflexiones en torno a José Martí," in Cintio Vitier, *Resistencia y libertad* (Havana, 1999), p. 81.

156. Julio César Gandarilla, *Contra el yanqui* (1913; Havana, 1973), pp. 154–55, 184.

157. Pedro José Cohucelo, *Apostado de amor: Por la mujer, por la patria, por la raza* (Havana, 1925), pp. 233–35, 300.

158. Duque, *Nuestra patria* (Lectura para niños), p. 24.

159. Luis Araquistain, "La Cuba de hoy y de mañana," *Social* 13 (May 1928): 40.

160. Roa, *En pie, 1953–1958*, p. 21.

161. Enrique José Varona, "Entrevista con el director del diario *El País*," in *Documentos para la historia de Cuba*, ed. Hortensia Pichardo Viñals, 5 vols. (2nd ed., Havana, 2000–2002), 3:452.

162. Rubén Martínez Villena et al., "Falange de Acción Cubana: Exposición," April 11, 1923, in Ana Núñez Machín, *Rubén Martínez Villena* (Havana, 1971), p. 337.

163. Rubén Martínez Villena, "Baire: 24 de febrero 1895–1923," in Rubén Martínez Villena, *Un nombre: Prosa literaria* (Havana, 1940), pp. 148–49.

164. Junta Cubana de Renovación Nacional, "Manifiesto a los cubanos," April 2, 1923, in *Documentos para la historia de Cuba*, 3:137–38.

165. A. Betancourt and R. Montero to A. Calvo, December 13, 1925, *Boletín del Archivo Nacional* 58 (1959): 120.

166. "Directorio Estudiantil Universitario al pueblo de Cuba," July 1933, republished in *Manifiestos de Cuba*, ed. Roberto Padrón Larrazabal (Seville, 1975), p. 154.

167. Directorio Estudiantil Universitario, "El DEU contra la prórroga de poderes: Texto de la exposición que el Directorio Estudiantil dirige al pueblo de Cuba explicando su actitud y los motivos en que fundan los estudiantes su protesta," July 1927, in *Las luchas estudiantiles universitarias, 1923–1934*, ed. Olga Cabrera and Carmen Almodóvar (Havana, 1975), pp. 223–35.

168. Justo Carrillo, *Cuba 1933: Estudiantes, yanquis y soldados* (Miami, 1985), p. 57.

169. Julio Antonio Mella, "El porqué de nuestro nombre," May 1928, in Mella, J. A. *Mella: Documentos y artículos*, p. 415.

170. ABC, "El ABC al pueblo de Cuba: Manifiesto-Programa," November 1932, in *Documentos para la historia de Cuba*, 3:502–30.

171. Francisco Ichaso, "Sentido histórico del ABC," December 11, 1938, in *Cuba y el ABC* (Miami, 1977), pp. 209–11.

172. Mañach, "Revolution in Cuba," p. 56.

173. Enrique Lumen, *La revolución cubana, 1902–1934: Crónica de nuestro tiempo* (Mexico, 1934), pp. 149–54.

174. "Estatutos para el Gobierno Provisional de Cuba," *Gaceta Oficial de la República de Cuba*, Edición Extraordinaria 30 (September 14, 1933): 2.

175. Directorio Estudiantil Universitario, "Al pueblo de Cuba: Declaraciones del Directorio Estudiantil Universitario sobre el Decreto Presidencial No. 1298," 1933, in Cabrera and Almodóvar, *Las luchas estudiantiles universitarias, 1923–1934*, p. 312; Directorio Estudiantil Universitario, "Al pueblo de Cuba: Acuerdos del Directorio Estudiantil Universitario," 1933, in ibid., p. 325.

176. Sumner Welles to Cordell Hull, September 25, 1933, 837.00/4007, and Sumner Welles to Cordell Hull, October 13, 1933, 837.00/4193, General Records of the Department of State, RG59, NA.

177. "Discurso de contestación al inaugural de la Conferencia, pronunciado el 4 de diciembre de 1933 por el Dr. Angel A. Giraudy, jefe de la delegación cubana," in Herminio Portell Vilá, *Cuba y la Conferencia de Montevideo* (Havana, 1934), p. 60.

178. "Portell Vilá, en la II Comisión, a nombre de Cuba, condena la intervención y la Enmienda Platt: Sesión de diciembre 19, 1933," in ibid., pp. 76–79; Herminio Portell Vilá, "Portell Vilá, a nombre de Cuba, condena la intervención y la Enmienda Platt," *Bohemia* 26 (April 22, 1934): 12, 56.

179. "Programa de Joven Cuba," 1934, in Antonio Guiteras, *Antonio Guiteras: Su pensamiento revolucionario*, ed. Olga Cabrera (Havana, 1974), pp. 183–84 (emphasis in original).

180. José Antonio Ramos, FU-3001, in José Antonio Ramos, *Teatro*, ed. Francisco Garzón Céspedes (Havana, 1989), p. 339.

181. Pablo de la Torriente, "La voz de Martí," January 28, 1936, in Pablo de la Torriente, *Algebra y política y otros textos de Nueva York*, ed. Ana Cairo (Havana, 2001), p. 112.

182. Raúl Roa, *La revolución del 30 se fue a bolina* (2nd ed., Havana, 1969), pp. 182–83, 237–38; Raúl Roa, "Rescate y proyección de Martí," May 19, 1937, in *Letras: Cultura en Cuba*, ed. Ana Cairo, 10 vols. (Havana, 1989–92), 1:82.

Chapter 5

1. María de los Angeles Torres, "*Donde los Fantasmas Bailan Guaguancó*: Where Ghosts Dance el Guaguancó," in *By Heart/De Memoria: Cuban Women's Journey In and Out of Exile*, ed. María de los Angeles Torres (Philadelphia, 2003), p. 30.

2. Interview with Gladys Marel García-Pérez, January 21, 2011, Havana.

3. José F. Fernández, ed., *Los abuelos: Historia oral cubana* (Miami, 1987), p. 121.

4. Alicia Hernández de la Luz, "Una dama en los predios de la política," in *Luz y sombra de mujer*, ed. Yamilé Ferrán and Maithée Rodríguez (Havana, 1998), p. 66.

5. Marta Harnecker, ed., *Pinceladas de la historia de Cuba (Testimonios de 19 abuelos)* (Havana, 2003), p. 99.

6. Giraldo Mazola Collazo, *Encuentros con la memoria* (Havana, 2010), p. 39.

7. Carlos Franqui, *Diario de la revolución cubana* (Madrid, 1975), p. 41.

8. Dora Alonso, "Yo vi besar las metralletas," in *Quiénes escriben en Cuba*, ed. Jorge L. Bernard and Juan A. Pola (Havana, 1985), p. 16.

9. Alvaro de Villa, *El olor de la muerte que viene* (Barcelona, 1968), p. 398.

10. Lourdes Gil, "Against the Grain," in *ReMembering Cuba: Legacy of Diaspora*, ed. Andrea O'Reilly Herrera (Austin, 2001), pp. 178–79.

11. Flor Fernández Barrios, *Blessed by Thunder: Memoir of a Cuban Girlhood* (Seattle, 1999), pp. 79–81.

12. Aida Bahr, "Ausencias," in Aida Bahr, *Espejismos* (Havana, 1998), p. 79.

13. Francisco José Moreno, *Before Fidel: The Cuba I Remember* (Austin, 2007), p. 10.

14. Guillermo García Frías, *Encuentro con la verdad* (Havana, 2010), pp. 24–29.

15. Neill Macaulay, *A Rebel in Cuba: An American's Memoir* (1970; Micanopy, Fla., 1999), pp. 82–83.

16. Luis Báez, ed., *Memoria inédita: Conversaciones con Juan Marinello* (Havana, 1995), p. 15.

17. Mazola Collazo, *Encuentros con la memoria*, p. 21.

18. Enzo Infante Uribazo, *La complejidad de la rebeldía*, ed. Reinaldo Suárez Suárez and Oscar Puig Corral (Havana, 2010), p. 27.

19. Rita Suárez del Villar, *Mis memorias* (Cienfuegos, 1957), p. 28.

20. José Juan Arrom, *De donde crecen las palmas* (Havana, 2005), p. 393.

21. Consejo Nacional de la Asociación de Veteranos de la Independencia, "Los Veteranos de la Independencia al pueblo de Cuba," January 29, 1910, in *La justicia en Cuba: Patriotas y traidores*, ed. Manuel Secades and Horacio Díaz Pardo, 2 vols. (Havana, 1912), l:49.

22. Jorge Mañach, "Respuesta a los veteranos," *Bohemia* 44 (April 6, 1952): 51.

23. Tania Quintero, "Penúltimos días: De mis recuerdos," July 10, 2008, http://www.penultimosdias.com/2008/07/10/de-mis-recuerdos.

24. Juan Padrón, "Fue una última e inútil guapería," in *Como el primer día*, ed. Pedro de la Hoz (Havana, 2008), p. 193.

25. Julio A. Carreras, "La institucionalidad republican: Estado, nación y democracia; Entrevista con Julio A. Carreras," in *La imaginación contra la norma: Ocho enfoques sobre la república de 1902*, ed. Julio César Guanche (Havana, 2004), p. 88.

26. Lorenzo García Vega, *Rostros del reverso* (Caracas, 1977), p. 24.

27. Noel Navarro, *El nivel de las aguas* (Havana, 1980), p. 74.

28. Fernando Martínez Heredia, "El problemático nacionalismo de la primera república," in Centro de Investigación y Desarrollo de la Cultura Cubana 'Juan Marinello,' *Historia y memoria: Sociedad, cultura y vida cotidiana en Cuba, 1878–1917* (Havana, 2003), p. 282.

29. "Acta Final: Declaración de Principios," November 17, 1952, in Cuba, Décimo Congreso Nacional de Historia, *En el cincuentario de la República* (Havana, 1953), pp. 119–41.

30. Raúl Roa, "Rescate y proyección de José Martí," May 19, 1937, in Raúl Roa, *15 años después* (Havana, 1950), p. 497.

31. *El Mundo*, March 11, 1952, p. 5.

32. See Guillermo Alonso and Enrique Vignier, *La corrupción política administrativa en Cuba, 1944–1952* (Havana, 1973).

33. "La ciudad cuesta pero vale" (interview with Mario Coyula), October 2000, in *El hombre en la cornisa*, ed. Hilario Rosete Silva and Julio César Guanche (Havana, 2006), p. 41.

34. Rubén Darío Rumbaut, "Esta es la hora de la generación del cincuentenario," *Bohemia* 44 (April 13, 1952): 35.

35. Raúl González de Cascorro, *El mejor fruto*, 1958, in Raúl González de Cascorro, *Arboles sin raíces* (Havana, 1960), pp. 216–17.

36. Ernesto Ardura, "Raíces de la crisis cubana," *El Mundo*, January 11, 1953, p. A-6.

37. Lisandro Otero, *Llover sobre mojado: Memorias de un intelectual cubano (1957–1997)* (Mexico, 1999), p. 28.

38. Jorge Mañach, "Palabras preliminares," in Gustavo Pittaluga, *Diálogos sobre el destino* (Havana, 1954), p. 8.

39. Carlos Hevia to Jack M. Cabot, July 31, 1953, 737.00/7-3153, Confidential State Department Central Files, Cuba, Internal Affairs, 1950–54, General Records of the Department of State, RG59, NA; Arthur Gardner to Department of State, February 21, 1955, 837.2351/2-2155, 1955–58, ibid.

40. John Dorschner and Roberto Fabricio, *The Winds of December* (New York, 1980), p. 132.

41. Andrés Felipe Labrador, "Soberanía del espíritu," *Revolución*, September 12, 1959, p. 2.

42. Hernández Travieso, "La lección del martes," *El Mundo*, November 10, 1956, p. A-8.

43. *El Mundo*, March 29, 1952, p. 6.

44. Herminio Portell Vilá, "Futilidad de la ley," *El Mundo*, June 20, 1952, p. A-6.

45. José Lezama Lima, *Diarios*, ed. Ciro Bianchi Ross (Mexico, 1994), pp. 107–8.

46. Cintio Vitier, *Lo cubano en la poesía* (Havana, 1958), p. 484.

47. Joaquín Martínez Sáenz, "Cuba libre e independiente," *Bohemia* 49 (May 19, 1957): 40–41.

48. Navarro, *El nivel de las aguas*, p. 139.

49. Moreno, *Before Fidel: The Cuba I Remember*, p. 150.

50. Rufo López-Fresquet, *My 14 Months with Castro* (Cleveland, 1966), p. 10.

51. Carmen Castro Porta et al., *La lección del maestro* (Havana, 1990), pp. 56–57.

52. Gloria Cuadras de la Cruz, *El rostro descubierto de la clandestinidad: Memorias de Gloria Cuadras de la Cruz*, ed. Marta Cabrales (Santiago de Cuba, 2006), p. 62.

53. *Barricada*, December 7, 1954, p. 1, Colección Prensa Clandestina, 1952–58, OAH/CE.

54. "Proclama mecanografiada de las mujeres cubanas contra la dictadura de Fulgencio Batista," December 1957, No. 63, Inventario 1 (Antiguo 188, Legajo 10), Fondo Especial, ANC.

55. Belarmino Castilla Mas, *La razón de las armas o las armas de la razón* (Havana, 2004), p. 18.

56. "Daremos el grito de Libertad: Nuestra sangre guiará el pueblo," *Alma Mater*, January 1956, p. 3, Colección Prensa Clandestina, 1952–58, OAH/CE.

57. Consejo Revolución Cubana, "Proclama revolucionaria de Santiago de Cuba y la Sierra Maestra," November 30, 1956, p. 1, ibid.

58. Luis Ricardo Alonso, *Los dioses ajenos* (Barcelona, 1971), p. 51.

59. Conrado del Puerto, "Incorporación al Movimiento 26 de Julio: Testimonio de Conrado del Puerto sobre actividades en la clandestinidad en Matanzas," in Unión Nacional de Historiadores de Cuba: Filial Matanzas, *La clandestinidad en Matanas: Selección de testimonios* (Matanzas, n.d.), p. 135.

60. Julio Travieso, *Para matar el lobo* (Havana, 1981), p. 22.

61. Interview with Guillermo Jiménez, January 20, 2011, Havana.

62. "'Somos un ejército político, con plena conciencia de lo que defendemos': Entrevista al general de brigada Harry Villegas," in *Haciendo historia: Entrevistas con cuatro generales de las Fuerzas Armadas Revolucionarias de Cuba*, ed. Mary-Alice Waters (Havana, 2006), p. 102.

63. Mazola Collazo, *Encuentros con la memoria*, p. 11.

64. Roberto Hernández Zayas, *Memorias de un combatiente por la libertad* (Havana, 2009), pp. 3–4.

65. Interview with Gladys Marel García-Pérez, January 21, 2011, Havana.

66. Infante Uribazo, *La complejidad de la rebeldía*, p. 33.

67. Castro Porta et al., *La lección del maestro*, p. 236.

68. Vilma Espín, "Deborah," in Mirta Aguirre et al., *Dice la palma: Testimonio* (Havana, 1980), p. 92; Vilam Espín, "Deborah," *Santiago* 18–19 (1975): 59–60.

69. "La ciudad cuesta pero vale" (interview with Mario Coyula), p. 41.

70. Julio García Oliveras, *Contra Batista* (Havana, 2006), p. 204.

71. Interview with Guillermo Jiménez, January 20, 2011, Havana.

72. Arnaldo Rivero, "La disciplina revolucionaria en la Sierra Maestra," *Humanismo* 53–54 (January–April 1959): 371, 377.

73. Jules Dubois, *Fidel Castro: Rebel-Liberator or Dictator?* (Indianapolis, 1959), p. 276.

74. Belarmino Castilla Mas, *Recuerdos imborrables: Memorias* (Havana, 1997), p. 15.

75. Luis R. Saíz Montes de Oca, "¿Por que luchamos?" May 1957, *Pensamiento Crítico* 22 (1968): 243–58.

76. Camilo Cienfuegos to José Antonio Pérez, May 1, 1956, in *Hablar de Camilo*, ed. Guillermo Cabrera Alvarez (Havana, 1970), pp. 33–34.

77. Pedro Miret, "Un grupo verdaderamente heroico," *Verde Olivo* 3 (July 29, 1962): 7.

78. Faustino Pérez, "Yo vine en el 'Gramma [sic],'" *Bohemia* 51 (January 11, 1959): 36.

79. Mario Lazo Pérez, *Recuerdos del Moncada* (Havana, 1987), p. 28.

80. Infante Uribazo, *La complejidad de la rebeldía*, p. 229.

81. José Soler Puig, *En el año de enero* (Havana, 1963), p. 13.

82. Bernardo Viera Trejo, *Militantes del odio y otros relatos de la revolución cubana* (Miami, 1964), p. 91.

83. Juan Almeida Bosque, *La única ciudadana* (Havana, 1985), p. 137.

84. Camilo Cienfuegos, "Discuro pronunciado el 21 de octubre de 1959 en el teatro Agramonte, provincia de Camagüey," in William Gálvez, *Camilo, señor de la vanguardia* (Havana, 1979), p. 558.

85. Janisset Rivero and Dagoberto Valdés, "Entrevista al Sr. Huber Matos," Convivencia/Sociedad Civil, October 3, 2009, http://www.convivenciacuba.es/; Huber Matos, *Cómo llegó la noche* (Barcelona, 2002), p. 37.

86. García Oliveras, *Contra Batista*, pp. 13–14.

87. Benigno Nieto, *Los paraísos artificiales* (Madrid, 1999), p. 171.

88. "Pacto de Caracas," July 20, 1958, Centro de Documentación de los Movimientos Armados, http://cedema.org. Among the signatories to the Pact of Caracas were the following: Movimiento Revolucionario 26 de Julio, Directorio Revolucionario, Organización Auténtica, and Movimiento Resistencia Cívica.

89. Agustín Tamargo, "¿Por que lucha actualmente el pueblo de Cuba?" *Bohemia* 49 (July 28, 1957): 64–65.

90. "¿Merecemos el gobierno propio?" *Carteles* 34 (March 15, 1953): 27.

91. René L. Díaz, "Adelante, cubanos," *Batalla* 2 (June 9, 1957): 4, Colección Prensa Clandestina, 1952–58, OAH/CE.

92. Alfredo Guevara, *Revolución es lucidez* (Havana, 1998), pp. 34, 102.

93. Rafael Rojas, *Isla sin fin: Contribución a la crítica del nacionalismo cubano* (Miami, 1998), p. 85.

94. Federación Estudiantil Universitaria, "Declaraciones de principios de la Federación Estudiantil Universitaria," *Bohemia* 44 (March 23, 1952): 54.

95. "Declaración de principios," *Alma Mater* 1 (April 8, 1952): 4.

96. See José Antonio Echeverría, "Declaraciones en la prensa," February 24, 1955, in José Antonio Echeverría, *Papeles del presidente: Documentos y discursos de José Antonio Echeverría Bianchi*, ed. Hilda Natalia Berdayes García (Havana, 2006), pp. 26–27.

97. José Antonio Echeverría, "Constitución del Directorio Revolucionario," February 26, 1956, in Organización Nacional de Bibliotecas Ambulantes y Populares, *13 documentos de la insurrección* (Havana, 1959), p. 34; Directorio Revolucionario, "Alocución al Pueblo de Cuba," March 13, 1957, in ibid., p. 43.

98. Directorio Revolucionario, "Proclama del Escambray," February 25, 1958, in Enrique Rodríguez-Loeches, *Bajando del Escambray* (Havana, 1982), pp. 186–87; "Proclama del Escambray (D.R.)," February 25, 1958, in Organización Nacional de Bibliotecas Ambulantes y Populares, *13 documentos de la insurrección*, pp. 53–58.

99. "El Movimiento Revolucionario Nacionalista [sic] (MNR): Historia, doctrina, estrategia, principios," April 1953, in Organización Nacional de Bibliotecas Ambulantes y Populares, *13 documentos de la insurrección*, pp. 13–14; Movimiento Revolucionario Nacional, "Propósito inmediato y bases del Movimiento Nacional Revolucionario," in Luis Alberto Pérez Llody, *Rafael García Bárcena: El sueño de la Gran Nación* (Havana, 2007), p. 164.

100. Rafael García Bárcena, "Una nueva generación y un nuevo Movimiento Nacional Revolucionario," *Bohemia* 44 (May 25, 1952): 56, 96.

101. Biographer Luis Conte Agüero noted that Castro won a prize at Belén for having distinguished himself in Cuban history. See Luis Conte Agüero, *Fidel Castro, vida y obra* (Havana, 1959), p. 13.

102. Heberto Padilla, *Self-Portrait of the Other*, trans. Alexander Coleman (New York, 1990), p. 12.

103. In Conte Agüero, *Fidel Castro, vida y obra*, p 25.

104. Movimiento Revolucionario 26-7, "Manifiesto de los revolucionarios del Moncada a la nación," July 23, 1953, in Organización Nacional de Bibliotecas Ambulantes y Populares, *13 documentos de la insurrección*, pp. 19–21.

105. Marta Rojas, *La generación del centenario en el juicio del Moncada* (3rd ed., Havana, 1973), p. 264.

106. Fidel Castro, *La historia me absolverá*, ed. Pedro Alvarez Tabio and Guillermo Alonso Fiel (Havana, 1993), pp. 33, 107–8.

107. Mario Llerena, *The Unsuspected Revolution* (Ithaca, 1976), p. 84.

108. Teresa Casuso, *Castro and Cuba*, trans. Elmer Grossberg (New York, 1961), p. 103.

109. Haydée Santamaría, *Haydée habla del Moncada* (Havana, 1978), pp. 77–81; Haydée Santamaría, "A los once años del Moncada," in *Mártires del Moncada* (Havana, 1965), p. 19.

110. Franqui, *Diario de la revolución cubana*, p. 112.

111. Ibid., p. 89.

112. Fidel Castro to Luis Conte Agüero, March 1955, in Fidel Castro, *Cartas del presidio*, ed. Luis Conte Agüero (Havana, 1959), p. 85.

113. Fidel Castro, "Mensaje al congreso de militantes ortodoxos," August 15, 1955, in Conte Agüero, *Fidel Castro, vida y obra*, p. 303.

114. Fidel Castro to Luis Conte Agüero, December 12, 1953, in Castro, *Cartas del presidio*, pp. 21–22.

115. Luis Ricardo Alonso, *El palacio y la furia* (Barcelona, 1976), pp. 235–36.

116. "Revolución: Única salida," *Aldabonazo*, May 15, 1956, in Armando Hart, *Aldabonazo: Inside the Cuban Revolutionary Underground, 1952–1958; A Participant's Account* (New York, 2004), pp. 124–26.

117. *El Morillo* 1 (December 15, 1958): 3, Colección Prensa Clandestina, 1952–58, OAH/CE.

118. Fidel Castro, "Manifiesto No. 1 del 26 de Julio al pueblo de Cuba," August 8, 1955, *Pensamiento Crítico* 21 (1968): 207, 217, 221.

119. Movimiento 26 de Julio, "Manifiesto—Programa del Movimiento 26 de Julio," November 1956, *Humanismo* 7 (November–December 1958): 9–25.

120. "Necesidad de revolución," in *Revolución*, February 15, 1957, p. 3, Colección Prensa Clandestina, 1952–58, OAH/CE (emphasis in original).

121. "El sentido de nuestra lucha," *Patria: Organo Oficial del Ejército Rebelde '26 de Julio'* 1 (December 7, 1958): 1, 11–12, ibid.

122. *Batalla* 2 (July 21, 1957): 2, ibid.

123. *Sierra Maestra: Boletín Oficial del Movimiento Revolucionario '26 de Julio'* 1 (April 26, 1957): 1, ibid.

124. Infante Uribazo, *La complejidad de la rebeldía*, pp. 22–23.

125. Armando Villa, "La Sierra señala el camino," *Batalla* 2 (April 7, 1957): 3, Colec-

ción Prensa Clandestina, 1952–58, OAH/CE; Armando Villa, "De Oriente viene la luz," *Batalla* 2 (February 24, 1957): 2.

126. Gladys Marel García-Perez, *Insurrection and Revolution: Armed Struggle in Cuba, 1952–1959* (Boulder, 1998), pp. 61–98.

127. *Candela: Organo Oficial de la Sección Obrera del Movimiento Revolucionario 26 de Julio de Tintorerías y Lavandarías de Cuba* 1 (November 1958): 1, Colección Prensa Clandestina, 1952–58, OAH/CE.

128. See Mariano Rodríguez Herrera, "¿Nuestro jefe? ¡José Martí!" *Trabajo* 5 (July 1964): 4–7; Georgina Jiménez, "Martí: Presencia subversiva en el Moncada," *Granma*, July 26, 1973, p. 2; Guillermina Ares, "Martí en el Moncada, Martí en revolución," *ANAP*, January 1973, pp. 4–5; Rolando López del Amo, "José Martí y el Moncada," *Granma*, January 23, 1973, p. 5; Ramón Roa, "José Martí: El autor intelectual," *Bohemia* 65 (August 3, 1973): 32–37; and José Antonio Alonso M., "Martí, autor intelectual," *Verde Olivo* 16 (July 28, 1974): 30–33.

129. Movimiento Revolucionario 26-7, "Manifiesto de los revolucionarios del Moncada a la nación," July 23, 1953, in Organización Nacional de Bibliotecas Ambulantes y Populares, *13 documentos de la insurrección*, p. 20.

130. Castro, *La historia me absolverá*, p. 108.

131. Fidel Castro to Luis Conte Agüero, August 14, 1954, in Castro, *Cartas del presidio*, pp. 59–60.

132. Cubillas, "Mitin oposicionista en Nueva York," p. 82.

133. See *El Cubano Libre*, November 1957, p. 1, Colección Prensa Clandestina, 1952–58, OAH/CE; and *El Cubano Libre*, February 1958, p. 10, ibid.

134. Dariel Alarcón Ramírez, *Memorias de un soldado cubano: Vida y muerte de la Revolución* (Barcelona, 1997), pp. 51–52.

135. Máximo Gómez to Tomás Estrada Palma, September 26, 1896, in Partido Revolucionario Cubano, *La revolución del 95 según la correspondencia de la delegación cubana en Nueva York*, 5 vols. (Havana, 1932–37), 5:267; see also "Sabotaje: Arma revolucionaria," *Vanguardia Obrera*, February 28, 1958, p. 7, Colección Prensa Clandestina, 1952–58, OAH/CE.

136. *Revolución*, January 1958, p. 2, Colección Prensa Clandestina, 1952–58, OAH/CE.

137. *Avanzada: Organo Oficial del Movimiento Revolucionario '26 de Julio' en la Provincia de Matanzas*, October 5, 1957, p. 3, ibid.

138. *Sierra Maestra* 1 (December 16, 1957): 1, ibid.

139. See Enrique Collazo, *Cuba independiente* (Havana, 1900), p. 162.

140. Broadcast transcripts of Radio Rebelde, July 1957–December 1958, Carlos Franqui Collection, Princeton University Library, Princeton, N.J.

141. Herbert Matthews, *The Cuban Story* (New York, 1961), p. 54.

142. María de los Reyes Castillo, *Reyita, sencillamente (Testimonio de una negra cubana nonagenaria)*, ed. Daisy Rubiera Castillo (Havana, 1997), p. 126.

143. Soler Puig, *En el año de enero*, p. 137.

144. Freddy Artiles, *Adriana en dos tiempos* (Havana, 1972), p. 150.

145. Otero, *Llover sobre mojado: Memorias de un intelectual cubano (1957–1997)*, p. 13.

146. Julio García Espinosa, "Mi aniversario cuarenta," in Casa de las Américas, *Cultura y revolución: A cuarenta años de 1959* (Havana, 1999), p. 138.

147. *Revolución*, January 23, 1959, p. 14.

148. Fidel Castro, "Declaraciones del Comandante en Jefe Fidel Castro, dirigidas al pueblo de Santiago de Cuba, a través de Radio Rebelde, el 1ro. de enero de 1959," in *Documentos de la revolución cubana*, ed. José Bell, Delia Luisa López, and Tania Caram (Havana, 2006), p. 12.

149. José María Cuesta Braniella, *Treinta y dos días antes y después de la victoria en Cuba* (Havana, 2010), p. 146.

150. Fidel Castro, "Declaraciones del Comandante en Jefe Fidel Castro, dirigidas al pueblo de Santiago de Cuba, a través de Radio Rebelde," pp. 12–13.

151. *Revolución*, January 5, 1959, p. 4.

152. Fidel Castro, "Discurso pronunciado por el Doctor Fidel Castro Ruz, en el Parque Céspedes, de Santiago de Cuba," January 1, 1959, Discursos e intervenciones; *Revolución*, January 3, 1959, p. 4.

153. César Leante, "El día inicial," in *Aquí once cubanos cuentan*, ed. José Rodríguez Feo (Montevideo, 1967), p. 90.

154. Fidel Castro, "Discurso pronunciado por el Comandante Fidel Castro Ruz, en la Plaza de la ciudad de Camagüey," January 4, 1959, Discursos e intervenciones.

155. Fidel Castro, "Discurso pronunciado por el Comandante Fidel Castro Ruz, en la ciudad de Santa Clara," January 6, 1959, ibid.

156. Fidel Castro, "Discurso pronunciado desde el Balcón de la Sociedad 'El Progreso,' de Sancti-Spíritus, Las Villas," January 6, 1959, ibid.

157. Fidel Castro, "Discurso pronunciado en el Parque 'La Libertad' de la Ciudad de Matanzas, en su recorrido hacia La Habana," January 7, 1959, ibid.

158. Fidel Castro, "Discurso pronunciado por el Comandante Fidel Castro Ruz, en la ciudad de Santa Clara," January 6, 1959, ibid.; Fidel Castro, "Discurso pronunciado en el Parque 'La Libertad' de la Ciudad de Matanzas, en su recorrido hacia La Habana," January 7, 1959, ibid.

159. Guillermo Vincente Vidal, *Boxing for Cuba: An Immigrant's Story of Despair, Endurance and Redemption* (Denver, 2007), pp. 40–41.

160. Marcia del Mar, *A Cuban Story* (Winston-Salem, 1979), p. 19.

161. Hiram González, "The Escape Artist," in *Cuba: The Unfinished Revolution*, ed. Enrique G. Encinosa (Austin, 1988), p. 26.

162. A. S. Fordham to Selwyn Lloyd, January 10, 1959, File FO 371/139398, Foreign Office Files for Cuba, Public Records Office, Kew, London, UK.

163. Ruby Hart Phillips, *Cuba, Island of Paradox* (New York, 1959), p. 404.

164. Dubois, *Fidel Castro: Rebel-Liberator or Dictator*, p. 363.

165. Dorschner and Fabricio, *Winds of December*, p. 453.

166. López-Fresquet, *My 14 Months with Castro*, p. 13.

167. Jorge Mañach, "La revitalización de la fe en Cuba," *Bohemia* 51 (March 15, 1959): 26–27.

168. Francisco Brentano, "Entrevista '13 de Marzo': Tres comandantes en un tiro," *13 de Marzo: Organo Oficial del Directorio Revolucionario*, January 1959, p. 10, Colección Prensa Clandestina, 1952–58, OAH/CE.

169. Waldo Medina, "Basta ya," *El Mundo*, January 17, 1959, p. A-6.

170. Roberto Fernández Retamar, *Entrevisto* (Havana, 1982), p. 112.

171. Cintio Vitier, "Revolución, historia y poesía," in Casa de las Américas, *Cultura y revolución: A cuarenta años de 1959*, p. 124.

172. "De las tinieblas a la luz," *Bohemia* 51 (January 11, 1959): 29.

173. *El Mundo*, January 6, 1959, p. B-1; *Diario de la Marina*, January 7, 1959, p. A-11.

174. *El Mundo*, January 6, 1959, p. A-7; ibid., January 11, 1959, p. A-3.

175. *Revolución*, January 17, 1959, p. 11.

176. Ibid., January 10, 1959, p. 2; ibid., February 23, 1959, p. 12.

177. Ibid., February 23, 1960, p. 19. For an excellent examination of the use of historic imagery in the early years of the revolution, see Yamile Regalado Someillán, "The Cartooned Revolution: Images and the Revolutionary Citizens in Cuba, 1959–1963" (Ph.D. diss., University of Maryland, 2009).

178. See Mayra Aladro Cardoso, Servando Valdés Sánchez, and Luis Rosado Eiró, *La Guerra de Liberación Nacional en Cuba, 1956–1959* (Havana, 1957).

179. Bernardo Viera Trjo, "7 preguntas fundamentales al comandante Camilo Cienfuegos: '¡Aquí no hace falta más arma que la Constitución,'" *Bohemia* 51 (February 22, 1959): 54.

180. *Revolución*, February 25, 1959, p. 4.

181. Fidel Castro, "Discurso pronunciado en el acto de apertura de la Primera Plenaria Revolucionaria de la Federación Nacional de Trabajadores Azucareros, en el Palacio de los Trabajadores," December 15, 1959, *Discursos e intervenciones*.

182. *Revolución*, April 8, 1959, p. 8.

183. Leví Marrero, "Presencia de la otra Cuba," *El Mundo*, January 6, 1959, p. A-4.

184. Carlos Todd, "Let's Look at Today," *Times of Havana*, January 8, 1959, p. 9.

185. Jorge Mañach, "El drama de Cuba," *Cuadernos* 30 (May–June 1958): 76.

186. Sherman Kent, Office of National Estimates, Central Intelligence Agency, "Memorandum for the Director: Why the Cuban Revolution of 1958 Led to Cuba's Alignment with the USSR," February 21, 1961, http://www.foia.cia.gov/docs/DOC_0000132656/pdf.

187. Hugh Thomas, *Cuba, the Pursuit of Freedom* (New York, 1971), p. 829.

188. Fidel Castro, "Discurso pronunciado desde el balcón de la Sociedad 'El Progreso,' de Sancti Spíritus, Las Villas," January 6, 1959, *Discursos e intervenciones*.

189. Senel Paz, "Cuarenta años después," in Casa de las Américas, *Cultura y revolución: A cuarenta años de 1959*, p. 146.

190. *Revolución*, February 23, 1959, p. 2.

191. Vidal, *Boxing for Cuba: An Immigrant's Story of Despair, Endurance and Redemption*, p. 42.

192. *Revolución*, November 14, 1959, p. 18.

193. Andrés Valdespino, "La batalla que aún falta," *Bohemia* 51 (January 18–25, 1959): 13.

194. Luis Aguilar León, "Hacia la superación del esquema histórico de Cuba," *Nueva Revista Cubana* 1 (July–August–September 1959): 23.

195. Daura Olema, *Maestra voluntaria* (Havana, 1962), p. 16.

196. Armando J. Flórez Ibarra, "La hora del deber americano," *Revolución*, February 2, 1959, p. 2.

197. "Contra el perdón," ibid., January 15, 1959, p. 4; "Esta tarde la cita es en Palacio," ibid., January 16, 1959, p. 1.

198. Miguel Cossío Woodward, *Sacchario* (Havana, 1970), p. 166.

199. Soler Puig, *En el año de enero*, p. 137.

200. José Lezama Lima to Fidel Castro, February 1959, in José Lezama Lima, *Como las cartas no llegan*, ed. Ciro Bianchi (Havana, 2000), p. 155.

201. Luis Amado Blanco, *Ciudad rebelde* (Barcelona, 1967), front matter.

202. Roberto Fernández Retamar, *Vuelta de la antigua esperanza* (Havana, 1959).

203. Jorge L. Martí, *Cuba: Consciencia y existencia* (Havana, 1959), p. 31.

204. Juan Arcocha, "¿Qué es la revolución?" *Revolución*, August 26, 1959, p. 2.

205. Andrew Salkey, *Havana Journal* (Harmondsworth, UK, 1971), p. 170.

206. "[Entrevista con] Pablo Armando Fernández," in *Escribir en Cuba: Entrevistas con escritores cubanos, 1979–1989*, ed. Emilio Bejel (Río Piedras, P.R., 1991), p. 86.

207. Andrei Codrescu, *Ay, Cuba! A Socio-Erotic Journey* (New York, 1999), p. 55.

208. Emilio Roig de Leuchsenring, *Males y vicios de Cuba republicana: Sus causas y sus remedios* (2nd ed., Havana, 1961), p. 350.

209. Fidel Castro, "Discurso del Comandante Fidel Castro en el onceno aniversario del 26 de julio," *Obra Revolucionaria* 18 (1964): 29.

210. "24 de febrero," *Revolución*, February 23, 1959, p. 24.

211. Ramón L. Bonachea and Marta San Martín, *The Cuban Insurrection, 1952–1959* (New Brunswick, 1974), p. 329.

212. *Revolución*, January 22, 1959, p. 13.

213. Félix Contreras, ed., "Con el centenario a cuestas," *Cuba* (Número Especial) (October 1968): 51.

214. Ubaldo R. Paz Camejo, "Ninguno de sus hermanos regresóo de la manigua," *Granma*, October 10, 1968, p. 22.

215. Arbesún Estevez, "'Como ayer, sabré cumplir mi palabra y mi deber como cubano'—cuenta Virgilio Carabaloso," *Granma*, October 10, 1968, p. 24; Milagros Oliva, "Una centenaria," ibid., p. 6.

216. Blas Roca, "Discurso de Blas Roca en la velada solemne," *Obra Revolucionaria* 35 (December 26, 1963): 16.

217. José Rodríguez Feo, "Prólogo," in *Aquí once cubanos cuentan*, ed. José Rodríguez Feo (Montevideo, 1967)p. 8.

218. "24 de febrero," *Revolución*, February 23, 1963, p. 2.

219. Llerena, *Unsuspected Revolution*, p. 170.

220. Raúl Lorenzo, "La revolución rompió todos los esquemas," in *Los que se fueron*, ed. Luis Báez (2nd ed., Havana, 2008), pp. 172–73.

221. Bonachea and San Martín, *Cuban Insurrection, 1952–1959*, p. 382.

222. Matos, *Cómo llegó la noche*, p. 337.

223. *Revolución*, July 7, 1959, p. 20.

224. Hilda Perera, *El sitio de nadie* (Barcelona, 1972), p. 99.

225. See Devyn Marie Spence Benson, "Not Blacks, but Citizens! Racial Politics in Revolutionary Cuba, 1959–1961," Ph.D. diss., University of North Carolina, 2009.

226. Fidel Castro, "Discurso pronunciado resumiendo los actos del Día Internacional del Trabajo," May 1, 1961, Discursos e intervenciones.

227. Henry C. Ramsey to Gerard C. Smith, February 18, 1960, in Department of State, *Foreign Relations of the United States: Cuba, 1958–1960* (Washington, D.C., 1991), p. 795.

228. Kent, "Memorandum for the Director: Why the Cuban Revolution of 1958 Led to Cuba's Alignment with the USSR."

229. The full text of the Cuban note appeared in *Revolución*, November 14, 1959, pp. 18–19; it was published in English as Republic of Cuba, Ministry of State, *In Defense of National Sovereignty* (Havana, 1959).

230. Manuel Cofiño, *Cuando la sangre se parece al fuego* (Havana, 1979), p. 212.

231. Fidel Castro, "Discurso pronunciado en el Club Rotario de La Habana," January 15, 1959, Discursos e intervenciones.

232. Fidel Castro, "Discurso pronunciado por el Comandante Fidel Castro Ruz, Primer Ministro del Gobierno Revolucionario, en el acto de entrega de la quinta estacion de policia al Ministerio de Educacion para convertirla en centro escolar," January 11, 1960, ibid.

233. Lloyd A. Free, *Attitudes of the Cuban People toward the Castro Regime in the Late Spring of 1960* (Princeton, 1960), pp. 18–19 (emphasis in original).

Chapter 6

1. Ramón de Armas, *La revolución pospuesta: Contenido y alcance de la revolución martiana por la independencia* (Havana, 1975).

2. Oscar Zanetti Lecuona, "Trayectoria de la historiografía cubana en el siglo XX," *Debates Americanos* 10 (July–December 2000): 16.

3. Fidel Castro, "Discurso pronunciado en el acto solemne en conmemoración del XXX aniversario del triunfo de la Revolución, en Santiago de Cuba," January 1, 1989, Discursos e intervenciones.

4. Raúl Roa, *La revolución del 30 se fue a bolina* (2nd ed., Havana, 1969), p. 313.

5. *Granma*, December 2, 1976, p. 1.

6. Fidel Castro, *Análisis histórico de la revolución cubana* (Havana, 1982), pp. 36, 79.

7. Armando Hart Dávalos, *Cambiar las reglas del juego* (Havana, 1983), pp. 122–23.

8. Fidel Castro, "Si las raíces y la historia de este país no se conocen, la cultura política de nuestras masas no estará suficiente desarrollada," *Granma*, October 11, 1968, pp. 4, 6.

9. Nicolás Guillén, "Se acabó," in Nicolás Guillén, *Obra poética, 1958–1977*, ed. Angel I. Augier, 2 vols. (Havana, 1985), 2:140.

10. Nicolás Guillén, "Son del bloqueo," in ibid., 2:146.

11. Fidel Castro, "Discurso pronunciado por el Comandante Fidel Castro, Primer Secretario del Comité Central del Partido Comunista de Cuba y Primer Ministro del Gobierno Revolucionario, en la velada conmemorativa de la derrota del imperialismo yanki en Playa Girón, efectuado en el teatro 'Chaplin,'" April 19, 1967, Discursos e intervenciones.

12. *Obra Revolucionaria* 27 (October 22, 1963): 30.

13. "Declaración del Buró Político del Partido Comunista de Cuba: En relación con el día de Navidad," November 30, 1998, http://www.cuba.cu/gobierno/documentos/index .html#mo30200.

14. Aida Bahr, *Las voces y los ecos* (San Juan, 2004), pp. 145–46.

15. Fidel Castro, "Discurso pronunciado como conclusión de las reuniones con los intelectuales cubanos, efectuadas en la Biblioteca Nacional," June 16, 23, and 30, 1961, Discursos e intervenciones.

16. Oscar Lewis, Ruth M. Lewis, and Susan M. Rigdon, *Four Women, Living the Revolution: An Oral History of Contemporary Cuba* (Urbana, 1977), p. 413.

17. Nicolás Dorr, "Mediodía candente," in Nicolás Dorr, *Dramas de imaginación y urgencia* (Havana, 1987), p. 331.

18. Fidel Castro, "Discurso pronunciado en el resumen de la velada conmemorativa de los cien años de lucha, efectuada en la Demajagua, Monumento Nacional, Manzanillo, Oriente," October 10, 1968, *Discursos e intervenciones*.

19. Nicolás Guillén, "Se acabó," in Guillén, *Obra poética, 1958–1977*, 2:140–41.

20. Carlos Rafael Rodríguez, "En el aniversario del nacimiento de José Martí," *Obra Revolucionaria* 3 (February 20, 1963): 30.

21. Fernando Portuondo y del Prado, "Discurso del Dr. Fernando Portuondo y del Prado al tomar posesión de la presidencia del XIII Congreso Nacional de Historia," in Oficina del Historiador de la Ciudad, *Historia de Cuba republicana y sus antecedentes favorables y adversos a la independencia: XIII Congreso Nacional de Historia* (Havana, 1960), p. 46.

22. Sergio Benvenuto, "Investigación histórica y acción práctica," *Cuba Socialista* 4 (March 1964): 77.

23. Rafael Rojas, *Isla sin fin: Contribución a la crítica del nacionalismo cubano* (Miami, 1998), p. 86.

24. *Revolución*, January 19, 1960, p. 13.

25. Luis Ricardo Alonso, *Territorio libre* (Oviedo, 1967), p. 157.

26. Fidel Castro, "Discurso pronunciado en el acto de entrega del antiguo Cuartel Goicuría convertido en centro escolar mártires del Goicuría al Ministerio de Educación," April 29, 1960, *Discursos e intervenciones*.

27. Fidel Castro, "Discurso pronunciado a los empleados del comercio," December 20, 1959, ibid.

28. See Fidel Castro, "Discurso pronunciado en la conmemoración del Aniversario de la caída de Frank País, efectuada en el Instituto de la Segunda Enseñanza, Santiago de Cuba," July 30, 1959, ibid.; Fidel Castro, "Discurso pronunciado en la concentración celebrada en la Avenida de Michellson, en Santiago de Cuba," March 11, 1959, ibid.; Fidel Castro, "Discurso pronunciado en el acto de apertura de la Primera Plenaria Revolucionaria de la Federación Nacional de Trabajadores Azucareros, en el Palacio de los Trabajadores," December 15, 1959, ibid.; and Fidel Castro, "Discurso pronunciado en la clausura de la reunión de Coordinadores de Cooperativas Cañeras, en el Teatro de la CTC Revolucionaria," August 10, 1960, ibid.

29. Raúl Castro, "Habla Raúl Castro de una conmemoración y de un mártir," *Obra Revolucionaria* 30 (November 24, 1960): 11.

30. Fidel Castro, "Congreso de maestros y graduación de alumnos: Conclusiones de Fidel Castro," *Obra Revolucionaria* 9 (April 11, 1963): 14.

31. "A los 52 años: La posición de *Bohemia*," *Bohemia* 52 (May 22, 1960): 52.

32. Fidel Castro, "Discurso pronunciado como conclusión de las reuniones con los intelectuales cubanos, efectuadas en la Biblioteca Nacional," June 16, 23, and 30, 1961, *Discursos e intervenciones*.

33. *Revolución*, May 13, 1960, p. 6.

34. Ibid., September 30, 1959, p. 8; ibid., January 19, 1960, p. 13.

35. "Junto a la patria y frente a la traición," *Verde Olivo* 6 (November 19, 1960): 4–5.

36. Luis M. García, *Child of the Revolution: Growing up in Castro's Cuba* (Adelaide, 2006), p. 2.

37. *Granma*, April 27, 1980, p. 1.

38. "Antología de las consignas del pueblo en la marcha del pueblo combatiente," *Granma*, April 23, 1980, p. 4; see also *Respuesta del pueblo combatiente* (Havana, 1980), pp. 50–62.

39. Camilo Cienfuegos, "Discurso pronunciado el 28 de junio de 1959 en Sagua la Grande, provincia de Las Villas," in William Gálvez, *Camilo, señor de la vanguardia* (Havana, 1979), p. 523.

40. Lee Lockwood, *Castro's Cuba, Cuba's Fidel* (New York, 1969), p. 231.

41. Yolanda Ortal-Miranda, *Balada sonámbula de los desterrados del sueño/The Sleepwalkers Ballad* (New York, 1991), p. 62.

42. *Revolución*, May 13, 1960, pp. 1, 6.

43. Alvaro de Villa, *El olor de la muerte que viene* (Barcelona, 1968), p. 321.

44. Marc Cooper, "Interview with Writer Pablo Armando Fernandez: 'All We Have Are Mosquitoes, Cubans, and the Revolution,'" *Village Voice*, May 1, 1990, p. 24 (emphasis in original).

45. *Noticias de Hoy*, December 19, 1959, p. 6; ibid., May 15, 1960, pp. 8–9; Fidel Castro, *Declaraciones del Comandante Fidel Castro Ruz, Primer Ministro del Gobierno Revolucionario, en el juico contra el ex-Comandante Hubert Matos* (Havana, 1959), pp. 40–41.

46. *Noticias de Hoy*, May 4, 1960, p. 1.

47. "Sartre y la Marina," *Lunes de Revolución*, February 29, 1960, p. 23.

48. *Revolución*, April 1, 1960, pp. 1, 3; ibid., May 4, 1960, p. 1.

49. Ibid., May 13, 1960, p. 3.

50. Ibid., May 16, 1960, p. 22.

51. Gregorio Ortega, "128 años de infamia," *Lunes de Revolución* 39 (December 14, 1959): 6, 10.

52. "Al pueblo de Cuba y al Gobierno Revolucionario," *Diario de la Marina*, May 12, 1960, p. 1.

53. *Revolución*, May 13, 1960, p. 6.

54. Ibid.

55. Aurelio Alonso Tejada, *Iglesia y política en Cuba revolucionaria* (Havana, 1997), pp. 9–10; Margaret E. Crahan, "Cuba: Religion and Revolutionary Institutionalization," *Journal of Latin American Studies* 17 (November 1985): 320.

56. See *Revolución*, December 15, 1960, p. 1; December 17, 1960, p. 1; and December 22, 1960, p. 1.

57. Emilio Roig de Leuchsenring, *La iglesia católica contra la independencia de Cuba* (Havana, 1960), pp. 13–14.

58. Ibid., p. 20.

59. Ibid., pp. 35, 41.

60. Santiago Cuba Fernández, "El clero reaccionario y la revolución cubana," *Cuba Socialista* 2 (June 1962): 13–17.

61. Fidel Castro, "Firme denuncia de las tácticas divisionista," *Obra Revolucionaria* 33 (December 17, 1960): 15.

62. Benigno Nieto, *Los paraísos artificiales* (Madrid, 1999), p. 44 (emphasis in original).

63. Georgina Suárez Hernández, "Political Leadership in Cuba," in *The Cuban Revolution in the 1990s*, ed. Centro de Estudios sobre América (Boulder, 1992), pp. 54–55.

64. Rafael Hernández, *Looking at Cuba: Essays on Culture and Civil Society*, trans. Dick Cluster (Gainesville, 2003), p. 22.

65. Ricardo Alarcón de Quesada, "El regreso de los sesenta," in Casa de las Américas, *Cultura y revolución: A cuarenta años de 1959* (Havana, 1999), p. 176.

66. Comité Central del Partido Comunista de Cuba, *Llamamiento al IV Congreso del PCC, 15 de marzo de 1990: El futuro de nuestra patria será un eterno Baraguá* (Havana, 1990), p. 21.

67. Fidel Castro, "Discurso pronunciado en el Acto de Constitución de Unidades de Milicias de Tropas Territoriales de la Provincia Granma, efectuado en Guisa," January 20, 1981, *Discursos e intervenciones*.

68. Interview with José Viera, January 20, 2010, Havana.

69. Medea Benjamin, ed., *Talking about Revolution: Conversations with Juan Antonio Blanco* (Melbourne, 1994), p. 11.

70. "Historia del Partido Comunista de Cuba," July 13, 2012, http://www.pcc.cu/i_historia2.php.

71. Fidel Castro, "Carta a los trabajadores de la Oficina de Asuntos Históricos del Consejo de Estado," May 4, 1984, *Granma*, May 5, 1984, p. 1.

72. Julianne Burton, "'Individual Fulfillment and Collective Achievement': [Interview with] Tomás Gutiérrez Alea," 1977, in *The Cineaste Interviews on the Art and Politics of the Cinema*, ed. Dan Georgakas and Lenny Rubenstein (Chicago, 1983), p. 160.

73. Janet Stevenson, "Cuban Life—Cuban Film," *In These Times* 2 (August 16–22, 1978): 10.

74. Manuel Romero Ramudo, "Tendencias actuales de la didáctica de la historia," in *Enseñanza de la historia: Selección de lecturas*, ed. Horacio Díaz Pendás (Havana, 2002), p. 36.

75. Regla María Albelo Ginnart et al., *Historia de Cuba, quinto grado* (Havana, 1991), pp. 7, 9.

76. Teresita Aguilera Vargas, Ofelia Ledo Acosta, José de la Tejera Dubrocq, and Bárbara Rafael Vázquez, *Orientaciones metodológicos: Relatos de la historia de Cuba, cuarto grado* (Havana, 1978), pp. 155–57, 189, 195.

77. Regla María Albelo Ginnart et al., *Historia de Cuba, 11no grado* (Havana, 1985), pp. 30–31.

78. Aguilera Vargas et al., *Orientaciones metodológicos: Relatos de la historia de Cuba, cuarto grado*, pp. 279.

79. Marta María Valdés López et al., *Historia de Cuba, sexto grado* (Havana, 1994), pp. 2–4.

80. Valdés López et al., *Historia de Cuba, sexto grado*, p. 152.

81. Eduardo Torres-Cuevas, *En busca de la cubanidad*, 2 vols. (Havana, 2006), 2:339.

82. Eduardo Heras León, "A los cuarenta años: Diez maneras de decir la verdad sobre la Revolución Cubana," in Casa de las Américas, *Cultura y revolución: A cuarenta años de 1959*, p. 112.

83. Jorge Ibarra, "Historiografía y revolución," *Temas* 1 (January–March 1995): 8–9; interview with Jorge Ibarra, January 20, 2012, Havana.

84. Aguilera Vargas, Ledo Acosta, Tejera Dubrocq, and Vázquez, *Orientaciones metodológicas: Relatos de historia de Cuba, cuarto grado*, pp. 6, 9, 13, 72–73, 74.

85. See Félix Julio Alfonso López, "Balance, perspectivas y desafío de la historiografía cubana en cincuenta años de Revolución," *La Ventana*, October 5, 2010, p. 12, http://laventana.casa.cult.cu.

86. Sergio Aguirre, "La trampa que arde," *Revolución y Cultura* 19 (March 1974): 16–17.

87. José A. Portuondo, "Hacia una nueva historia de Cuba," *Cuba Socialista* 3 (August 1963): 24–25, 39.

88. Regla Maria Albelo Ginnart et al., *Orientaciones metodológicas: Historia de Cuba, 8vo. grado* (Havana, 1986), pp. 1, 15.

89. Regla Maria Albelo Ginnart et al., *Historia de Cuba, 9no grado* (Havana, 1986), pp. 4–5.

90. "XIII Congreso de Historia: Declaración de principios," in Oficina del Historiador de la Ciudad, *Historia de Cuba republicana y sus antecedentes favorables y adversos a la independencia: XIII Congreso Nacional de Historia*, p. 166.

91. Manuel Moreno Fraginals and Zoila Lapique Becali, "Esta revolución comenzó en Yara," *Cuba Internacional* 6 (October 1974): 20–27.

92. José Antonio Portuondo, "Cuba, nación 'para sí,'" *Cuadernos Americanos* 119 (November–December 1961): 147, 172; José Antonio Portuondo, "Resumen del acto," in Oficina del Historiador de la Ciudad, *Historia de Cuba republicana y sus antecedentes favorables y adversos a la independencia: XIII Congreso Nacional de Historia*, p. 63; José Antonio Portuondo, "¿Quién no conoce nuestros días de cuna?" in *Casados con la verdad*, ed. Mercedes Alonso Romero (Havana, 2007), p. 138.

93. Alfredo Guevara, *Revolución es lucidez* (Havana, 1998), p. 301.

94. Antonio Núñez Jiménez, "Visita a la cooperativa agrícola 'Cuba Libre,'" in Oficina del Historiador de la Ciudad, *Historia de Cuba republicana y sus antecedentes favorables y adversos a la independencia: XIII Congreso Nacional de Historia*, p. 53.

95. Manuel Moreno Fraginals, "Historia como arma," *Casa de las Américas* 40 (January–February 1967): 30–38.

96. Fernando Martínez Heredia et al., "Historia oficial," *Contracorriente* 2 (July–August–September 1996): 123–24.

97. Portuondo y del Prado, "Discurso del Dr. Fernando Portuondo y del Prado al tomar posesión de la presidencia del XIII Congreso Nacional de Historia," in Oficina del Historiador de la Ciudad, *Historia de Cuba republicana y sus antecedentes favorables y adversos a la independencia: XIII Congreso Nacional de Historia*, p. 46.

98. Aleida Plasencia, "Panorama de la historiografía cubana de 1959 a 1967," *Universidad de La Habana* 186–88 (1967): 96.

99. José Antonio Portuondo, "Discurso del Dr. José Antonio Portuondo," in Oficina del Historiador de la Ciudad, *Historia de Cuba republicana y sus antecedentes favorables y adversos a la independencia: XIII Congreso Nacional de Historia*, p. 71.

100. Raúl Izquierdo Canosa, "La crítica y los críticos de la historiografía cubana," in *La historiografía en la Revolución cubana: Reflexiones a 50 años*, ed. Rolando Julio Rensoli Medina (Havana, 2010), p. 37.

101. Pedro Juan Gutiérrez, *Triología sucia de La Habana* (Barcelona, 2000), p. 118.

102. Lisandro Otero, *La utopía cubana desde adentro: ¿A dónde va Cuba hoy?* (Mexico, 1993), p. 23.

103. Arturo Arango, "To Write in Cuba, Today," *South Atlantic Quarterly* 96 (Winter 1997): 118.

104. Raúl Roa, *En pie, 1953–1959* (Havana, 1959), p. ii.

105. Rafael Hernández, "The Paradoxes of Cubanology," *South Atlantic Quarterly* 96 (Winter 1997): 152.

106. Cintio Vitier, "Martí and the Challenge of the 1990s," *South Atlantic Quarterly* 96 (Winter 1997): 215.

107. Unión Nacional de Historiadores de Cuba, *Documentos* (Havana, 1995), pp. 52–61.

108. *Granma*, December 18, 1991, p. 6.

109. Christopher Hunt, *Waiting for Fidel* (New York, 1998), p. 91.

110. Fidel Castro, "Discurso pronunciado en la clausura del encuentro 20 años después de la creación del Destacamento Pedagógico 'Manuel Ascunce Domenech,' efectuada en el Palacio de las Convenciones," May 30, 1992, *Discursos e intervenciones*.

111. *Granma*, January 4, 1994, p. 5; ibid., October 31, 1992, p. 6.

112. Fidel Castro, "Closing Speech: Proceedings of Fourth PCC Congress," October 14, 1991, Castro Speech Data Base, Latin American Network Information Center (LANIC), University of Texas, Austin, http://lanic.utexas.edu.

113. *Granma*, November 7, 1992, p. 5.

114. Fidel Castro, "Discurso pronunciado en el acto clausura del Segundo Congreso del Partido Comunista de Cuba, efectuado en la Plaza de la Revolución," December 20, 1980, *Discursos e intervenciones*.

115. Nicolás Pérez to Antonio Maceo, December 12, 1878, in Antonio Maceo, *Papeles de Maceo*, ed. Emeterio Santovenia, 2 vols. (1947; Havana, 1998), 1:158.

116. Ambrosio Fornet, "Introduction," *South Atlantic Quarterly* 96 (Winter 1997): 10.

117. Otero, *La utopía cubana desde adentro: ¿A dónde va Cuba hoy?* p. 63.

118. Zoé Valdés, *La nada cotidiana* (Barcelona, 1995), p. 161.

119. Haydée Leal García, *Pensar, reflexionar y sentir en las clases de historia* (Havana, 2000), pp. ii–iii, 22, 30.

120. República de Cuba, Constitución de la República de Cuba, 1976, Political Database of the Americas, http://pdba.georgetown.edu/Constitutions/Cuba/cuba1976.html; "Constitución de la República de Cuba," *Gaceta Oficial de la República de Cuba* 101 (January 31, 2003): 8.

121. Nicolás Garófalo Fernández, "Introducción," in *Historia de la revolución cubana*, ed. Juan M. Castellat Falcón (Havana, 1994), pp. ix–x.

122. Comité Central del Partido Comunista de Cuba, *Llamamiento al IV Congreso del PCC, 15 de marzo de 1990: El futuro de nuestra patria será un eterno Baraguá*, pp. 2–21.

123. Fidel Castro, "Discurso pronunciado en la clausura del IV Congreso del Partido Comunista de Cuba, efectuada en la Plaza General 'Antonio Maceo,' en la Ciudad Héroe de Santiago de Cuba," October 14, 1991, *Discursos e intervenciones*.

124. Comité Central del Partido Comunista de Cuba, *Llamamiento al IV Congreso del PCC, 15 de marzo de 1990: El futuro de nuestra patria será un eterno Baraguá*, p. 21.

125. Noel Navarro, *Techo y sepultura* (Havana, 1984), p. 131.

126. Edmundo Desnoes, *Memorias del subdesarrollo* (1962; Havana, 1975), pp. 124–25.

127. Interview with Francisco Pérez Guzmán, May 28, 2001, Havana.

128. Ambrosio Fornet, *Narrar la nación* (Havana, 2009), p. 359.

129. Isabel Monal, "Imperativo de la cultura," in Casa de las Américas, *Cultura y revolución: A cuarenta años de 1959*, p. 159.

130. Ernesto Cardenal, *In Cuba*, trans. Donald D. Walsh (New York, 1974), p. 66.

131. Oscar Lewis, Ruth M. Lewis, and Susan M. Rigdon, *Neighbors: Living the Revolution; An Oral History of Contemporary Cuba* (Urbana, 1978), p. 399.

132. Hadley Cantril, *Pattern of Human Concerns* (New Brunswick, 1965), p. 127.

133. Raúl Castro, "Raúl le habla al pueblo," *Obra Revolucionaria* 2 (May 17, 1960): 6, 18–19.

134. Manuel Cofiño, *La última mujer y el próximo combate* (Havana, 1984), p. 218.

135. "Compariencia del Primer Ministro Comandante Fidel Castro," *Obra Revolucionaria* 28 (October 1963): 17.

136. Regino Boti, "Informe del Dr. Regino Boti, Ministro de Economía," *Obra Revolucionaria* 30 (August 26, 1961): 19.

137. Lisandro Otero, *Llover sobre mojado: Memorias de un intelectual cubano (1957–1997)* (Mexico, 1999), pp. 18, 266–67.

138. Rafael Hernández, "The Paradoxes of Cubanology," *South Atlantic Quarterly* 96 (Winter 1997): 153.

139. Iraida H. López, "Ena Lucía Portela: entrevista," *Hispamerica* 38 (2009): 58.

140. Magda Resik, "Writing Is a Sort of Shipwreck: An Interview with Senel Paz," *South Atlantic Quarterly* 96 (Winter 1997): 85; originally published in *La Gaceta de la Habana* in 1993.

141. Ben Corbett, *This Is Cuba: An Outlaw Culture Survives* (Cambridge, 2002), p. 266.

142. Carlos Torres Pita, *La definición* (Havana, 1971), p. 23.

143. Pedro Campos Santos, "Cuba: Dilema y esperanza II," July 13, 2007, http://www.analitica.com/va/internacionales/opinion/9142974.asp.

144. Fidel Castro, "Discurso pronunciado en el acto por el XXXIX aniversario del asalto al Cuartel Moncada y el XXXV del levantamiento de Cienfuegos, efectuado en Cienfuegos," September 5, 1992, Discursos e intervenciones.

145. Fidel Castro, "Discurso pronunciado en la clausura del V Congreso de la Federacion Estudiantil," March 25, 1995, ibid.

146. Tania Bruguera, "Postwar Memories," in *By Heart/De Memoria: Cuban Women's Journey In and Out of Exile*, ed. María de los Angeles Torres (Philadelphia, 2003), pp. 171–72.

147. Raúl Castro, "Discurso pronunciado en las conclusiones de la sesión constitutiva de la VII Legislatura de la Asamblea Nacional del Poder Popular, Palacio de las Convenciones," February 24, 2008, Discursos e intervenciones del Presidente de los Consejos de Estado y de Ministros de la República de Cuba General de Ejército Raúl Castro Ruz, http://www.cuba.cu/gobierno/rauldiscursos/.

148. Anybis Labarta García, "Homenaje a la historia en el Día de la Rebeldía Nacional," July 26, 2012, http://www.visiontunera.icrt.cu/index.php/nacionales.

149. This text was transcribed by the author directly from a video broadcast of Raúl Castro's speech in Guantánamo on July 26, 2012, found on http://www.radioflorida.icrt.cu. At the time this book went to press, the Cuban government had not published the text of the twenty-one-minute speech. A summary of the speech was provided in *Granma*, July 26, 2012, http://www.granma.cubaweb.cu/2012/07/26.

150. "[Entrevista con] Ambrosio Fornet," in *Escribir en Cuba: Entrevistas con escritores cubanos, 1979–1989*, ed. Emilio Bejel (Río Piedras, P.R., 1991), p. 157.

151. Arturo Arango, "To Write in Cuba, Today," *South Atlantic Quarterly* 96 (Winter 1997): 119.

152. Teresa Bevin, *Havana Split* (Houston, 1998), p. 194.

153. "María Antonia Carrillo: Afro-Cuban Dance Troupe Director and Artist," in *Voices of Resistance: Testimonies of Cuban and Chilean Women*, ed. Judy Maloof (Lexington, 1999), p. 67.

154. Hernández, *Looking at Cuba: Essays on Culture and Civil Society*, p. 107.

155. Nicolás Rodríguez Astiazaraín, *Episodios de la lucha clandestina en La Habana (1955–1958)* (Havana, 2009), p. 2.

INDEX

H. EUGENE AND LILLIAN YOUNGS LEHMAN SERIES

Lamar Cecil, *Wilhelm II: Prince and Emperor, 1859–1900* (1989).

Carolyn Merchant, *Ecological Revolutions: Nature, Gender, and Science in New England* (1989).

Gladys Engel Lang and Kurt Lang, *Etched in Memory: The Building and Survival of Artistic Reputation* (1990).

Howard Jones, *Union in Peril: The Crisis over British Intervention in the Civil War* (1992).

Robert L. Dorman, *Revolt of the Provinces: The Regionalist Movement in America* (1993).

Peter N. Stearns, *Meaning Over Memory: Recasting the Teaching of Culture and History* (1993).

Thomas Wolfe, *The Good Child's River*, edited with an introduction by Suzanne Stutman (1994).

Warren A. Nord, *Religion and American Education: Rethinking a National Dilemma* (1995).

David E. Whisnant, *Rascally Signs in Sacred Places: The Politics of Culture in Nicaragua* (1995).

Lamar Cecil, *Wilhelm II: Emperor and Exile, 1900–1941* (1996).

Jonathan Hartlyn, *The Struggle for Democratic Politics in the Dominican Republic* (1998).

Louis A. Pérez Jr., *On Becoming Cuban: Identity, Nationality, and Culture* (1999).

Yaakov Ariel, *Evangelizing the Chosen People: Missions to the Jews in America, 1880–2000* (2000).

Philip F. Gura, *C. F. Martin and His Guitars, 1796–1873* (2003).

Louis A. Pérez Jr., *To Die in Cuba: Suicide and Society* (2005).

Peter Filene, *The Joy of Teaching: A Practical Guide for New College Instructors* (2005).

John Charles Boger and Gary Orfield, eds., *School Resegregation: Must the South Turn Back?* (2005).

Jock Lauterer, *Community Journalism: Relentlessly Local* (2006).

Michael H. Hunt, *The American Ascendancy: How the United States Gained and Wielded Global Dominance* (2007).

Michael Lienesch, *In the Beginning: Fundamentalism, the Scopes Trial, and the Making of the Antievolution Movement* (2007).

Eric L. Muller, *American Inquisition: The Hunt for Japanese American Disloyalty in World War II* (2007).

John McGowan, *American Liberalism: An Interpretation for Our Time* (2007).

Nortin M. Hadler, M.D., *Worried Sick: A Prescription for Health in an Overtreated America* (2008).

William Ferris, *Give My Poor Heart Ease: Voices of the Mississippi Blues* (2009).

Colin A. Palmer, *Cheddi Jagan and the Politics of Power: British Guiana's Struggle for Independence* (2010).

W. Fitzhugh Brundage, *Beyond Blackface: African Americans and the Creation of American Mass Culture, 1890–1930* (2011).

Michael H. Hunt and Steven I. Levine, *Arc of Empire: America's Wars in Asia from the Philippines to Vietnam* (2012).

Nortin M. Hadler, M.D., *The Citizen Patient: Reforming Health Care for the Sake of the Patient, Not the System* (2013).

Louis A. Pérez Jr., *The Structure of Cuban History: Meanings and Purpose of the Past* (2013).

Jennifer Thigpen, *Island Queens and Mission Wives: How Gender and Empire Remade Hawai'i's Pacific World* (2014).

George W. Houston, *Inside Roman Libraries: Book Collections and Their Management in Antiquity* (2014).

Daniel M. Cobb, ed., *Say We Are Nations: Documents of Politics and Protest in Indigenous America since 1887* (2015).